A HOUSE IN BRYANSTON SQUARE

ὁ δὲ ἀνεξέταστος βίος οὐ βιωτὸς ἀνθρώπῳ.
The unexamined life is not worth a man's while to live.
(Plato, Apology 28.)

BY

ALGERNON CECIL

HARCOURT, BRACE AND COMPANY
NEW YORK

LIBRARY OF CONGRESS CATALOG CARD NUMBER: 52—6454

PRINTED IN THE UNITED STATES OF AMERICA

CONTENTS

PREFACE

IN a world so well-accustomed to be shown the way in which it should go as is now our own, no great apology seems to be needed for volunteering to act as a guide to one's own writings; and, therefore, if still a little reluctantly, I take the advice of a friend and tender my services, such as they are, to indicate the design and drift of this book. Not, of course, that, in saying so much, I am presumptuous enough to insinuate any sort of comparison between myself and those eminent men—duces, führers, comrades in marshal's clothing, or marshals in mufti, great men in occupation of high places or their imitators in low ones—who, with the approbation of their several nations, have lately directed the affairs of Europe. I am but such a 'valet-de-place' as in other days than ours one might meet, at home or more likely abroad, at the entrance to a church or museum in (shall we say, since these cities happen to stand on the horizon of this book?) Rome or Florence; and I solicit employment as a guide so much the more humbly that the sources at all events of my spiritual and intellectual livelihood are, even as I write, gravely threatened by the princes of the power of the air, vigorously engaged as they are, or at least intend to be, in saving the soul of civilisation by consigning its body to the flames. Liberty, needless to say, has to be saved; and, if this is quickest attained by delivering Europe from the Teutons and delivering it over to the Slavs, it would not become a poor devil of a valet-de-place to complain. Besides, by the time this book appears, all may be changed. Blacks and Whites may be contending once more in Rome; and Guelfs and Ghibellines, or their modern successors, in Florence. Or again, the Angles, in conflict with the Saxons, may have swept 'the whole show' away; and there may be no occasion any more for any showman. Nevertheless the monuments of Christendom, and of the Humanities they stand for, are at the moment as gravely threatened as if the Goths had poured over the Alps or the Vandals (no reflection, of course, upon the Allied Armies, urgent, as at Monte Cassino, to preserve everything they are not compelled to destroy!) had slipped across from Africa. And in the circumstances a mere spectator of events may reasonably be excused if, recalling the comparison drawn both by Landor and Swinburne between cities situated respectively on the Avon and the Arno, he should sit down beside the waters of Bath and wonder whether he will some day weep, when he remembers thee, O Florence! Such tears over things, needless to add, would be idle tears—the tears of a mere provincial guide—and would deserve no attention at all from the metropolitan magnates who, in Whitehall or Westminster, guide our counsels and shape our destinies, even to the very tips of our trousers.

It is, then, in all humility that I venture to make some attempt to classify and clarify the contents of this book for the benefit of any contemporary pilgrim through time or casual visitor to a bookstall. To suggest that it might occupy the lowest place in a list at the head of which stood such poems as Amiel's Journal or Senancour's "Obermann", or such prayers as Eugénie de Guérin's diaries or Mrs. Craven's "Récit d'une Sœur", might appear an impertinence, even though, conceivably, the influence of these masters and mistresses of intimate reminiscence and reflection and, should the reader insist, of exotic tendency, may be suspected. Rather, if, to assist in its correct classification, I had to mention any single book, should I name "The Education of Henry Adams". In that great American's autobiographical self-examination I found a resolute attempt to purge the mind of cant, to see life steadily and whole, to give as full value to the twelfth century as to the twentieth, and to do as much justice to our Lady—"the greatest force", so Adams affirmed, "the Western World ever felt"—as to the gigantic dynamo that he contemplated at the Paris Exposition of 1900 and evaluated as the express image of the energy of our own times. In such a man, cynically wise as regards the ways of men and, though more or less agnostic in mind, so preternaturally alive in spirit to the ways or works of God as to declare that in the twelfth century "man held the highest idea of himself as a unit in a unified universe",* I see, and modestly salute, one 'travelling' in truth and armed with honest thought. My own criticism of, or, as he would have preferred to say, education in life has led me to more definite conclusions than any he proclaimed; but his estimate of the high place in history of the Virgin-Mother's Court has done not a little to confirm one (who, like himself, took a first glance at history from the standpoint of the 'age of reason') in the suspicion, amounting in my own case, though not perhaps in his, to a conviction, that there is more to be learnt about life on this planet from the architecture of the Twelfth Century than from the literature of the Eighteenth. If we stand on

* "Education of Henry Adams", p. 369.

the threshold of 'an American century', I trust we may see, within the White House and without it too, many Adamses and no more Wilsons. Both Henry Adams and Woodrow Wilson were students of history, but, whereas Adams was, so far as it is given to a man to become, a spectator of all time and all existence, Wilson remained a puritan and a doctrinaire. "We are winning," he called out, as he lay dying, to a visitor with reference to the future of the League of Nations. But he was not winning at all; and the 'collective security' that he fondly imagined himself to have established produced the final collapse of European civilisation. He had failed to dig deep enough into the past to find the real foundations upon which the structure of Christendom had rested.

Like others alive at that time, I hoped, with whatever misgivings, that the Liberal idea of a League would meet with success, and, like others, did what I might (utterly trifling as this must seem) to advance its interests. Men with more experience of life and human affairs saw from the first that the plan had little promise in it. I remember in the year 1924 taking an opportunity of saying to the late Cardinal Merry del Val that I feared there was a good deal of opposition to the League in Rome. He replied that he had not come across that, but that he had found scepticism. Rome is old in knowledge of history and wise from much contact with human vanity. Where our Lady's Regency, as Adams called it, had failed to establish peace on earth, it was improbable, on the face of it, that President Wilson's suzerain-League of States at Geneva would succeed in doing so. Vain, indeed, is the help of man!

This book, however, is nothing in the nature of Adams's great work on "Mont St. Michel and Chartres". In conception it is merely the record of the latter days of a London house—of thoughts that passed through the mind of one of its last inhabitants, of Voices that were once heard there, of some 'adventures of ideas'—if I may borrow a term or two from Professor Whitehead's philosophy—that once had their 'mode of location' in that place. The argument, such as it is, rises from plane to plane of human life as the storeys rise in the house, until, upon reaching the house-top, a sudden, and by me unanticipated catastrophe leaves it poised between heaven and earth and free to wander off into wonderland. And this, so to say, extroversion of the theme should, if it has been correctly used, serve to test the truth of the previous introverted vision.

One does not easily escape from the implications of one's trade;

and I do not doubt that from time to time I become preoccupied with certain prolegomena to history which, as I judge, historians neglect at their peril. In seeking the standpoint from which one may see life most truly and, as nearly as possible, whole, one is also seeking that where one may best hope to write without improper indignation or undue partiality. This will seem even clearer to those who think with Acton that "the first of human concerns is religion" * or with Leibniz that "history is the true demonstration of religion". The bent, however, is better excused or explained as the book proceeds.

As for the House, it is enough to say here that it has fallen; that the Voices that haunted it are heard no more; and that only memory now holds open a phantom door to let this moving finger write the tale upon the dust and rubble of the ruin, and, having writ, move on. It is but a solitary scribe who writes: yet the book is, as I believe, the work of two people—of him whose name is on the title-page, but also of her whose portrait appears on the frontispiece. As such, anyhow, it is meant to be read; and the scribe must take the blame if it prove otherwise. For this is primarily and essentially a record of two souls, each coming some way to meet the other yet meeting ever more and more until, in the words of a modern poet, it became true, more or less, of one of them, that

> all at once he came to understand
> the dead through her, and joined them in their walk,
> kin to them all; he let the others talk,
> and paid no heed to them, and called that land
> the fortunately placed, the ever-sweet—
> and groped out all its pathways for her feet.†

From such seemingly casual meetings does the Human Race descend, and from their spiritual continuity and completion do all the deepest Humanities derive.

I must confess that when I began to write this book I had been so bold as to hope that it might do something, however slight, to revive that sense of providential direction which seems to be disappearing from human life in sympathy with the growing disintegration of human society. Only some sense of design in the world can preserve us from coming to be 'designing', each man for himself, each party or nation for itself, and so producing swift collision and ultimate chaos. But whether what is set down here can serve for an

* Inaugural Lecture as Regius Professor of History at Cambridge.
† Rilke, "New Poems—The Death of the Beloved".

approach to future time, no less than for a lament over time past, it is not for me to say. I fully recognise that, where a great estate has been as prodigally flung away as that which the Victorians passed on to their children, the profligate generation has little claim to be heard with patience by its successor, required as this is to shoulder a huge burden of debt, both moral and material, instead of developing a splendid inheritance. The loss of the Two-Power Standard at sea in the last war, and in this one of the Supremacy-of-the-Seas, even though that be passing to our kinsmen in America; the impending downfall, not only of the once stately homes of England and of the country-houses with them, but of the Englishman's time-honoured right to call his house his castle and to keep his children out of the clutches of a servile state—these, with other things that might be named, constitute a condemnation so crushing that a new generation whose courage in the air, on the sea and in the field has had to make good the want of prudence in the council-chamber may well scorn traditional advice from any of its elders. Nevertheless no country will be great, nor any world tranquil, where there is no partnership between the living, the dead and those about to die; and, if this book serves to the smallest extent to revive a despised or dying tradition, I shall be well satisfied.

It is through failure to think things out to their foundations that a muddle-minded age has come to grief. The greatest spiritual and political geniuses of the Nineteenth Century in Britain blazed a brilliant trail, of which their countrymen failed to perceive the relation to the perils ahead. Cosmopolitan issues were met by continental entanglements. Britain surrendered that freedom of action in foreign affairs upon which Salisbury had insisted to the end of his life and instead of continuing to hold the balance-of-power consented to place herself in one of the scales. Thus at all events I read the past in the light of the present; and thus, I believe, it will be read when men are again content to think freely and firmly. Meanwhile this book—this modest attempt to clear my own thought —may conceivably serve some minds entering upon the adventure of life as some sort of a Pisgah. The flesh-pots of Egypt lie behind us; and in all probability a good many years in the wilderness lie ahead. We may lose all hope and even fall into hopeless decline, unless we learn to think once again theocratically and to recognise upon what terms alone the Kingdom of God can be brought to earth.

Many, doubtless, will disagree with me; and some few may perhaps write to complain. To such I can only say that they have their remedy in their own hands. They can shut up the book; it is not intended either to rebuke or to annoy them. It claims no more than they claim for their own ideas in a, supposedly at least, free country.

For the rest my best thanks are due to all, both living and dead, who have taught me by word or book. I have tried, at the risk of seeming to quote too freely and refer too frequently, to acknowledge a few of my debts, but many remain obvious and unpaid and some are hidden. It cannot well be otherwise when one is looking back over the anthology of a lifetime. And, if some of the quotations seem to some of my readers trite, they will perhaps allow that the real appraisement of any accepted truth or incontestable beauty lies, for each one of us, in the correct placing of it in the pattern of life and remember that this is what I am concerned to do.

Acknowledgments of another kind are due to those who have most kindly read and advised on the proofs for me—old friends to whom I am infinitely obliged for these and many other favours—Mgr. Ronald Knox and Mr. Leslie Hartley. To the Hon. Mrs. Arthur Pollen I owe most grateful thanks for the tender grace with which she has executed a most difficult task—the drawing of Allegra's portrait from a photograph. To Mr. Douglas Jerrold also I am greatly in debt for all the interest and trouble he has taken in the production of the book itself. And to the Abbot and Community of Downside Abbey who, when after the bombing of Bath I was obliged to seek some other habitation, gave me free access to their extensive and valuable Library, I lie also under a deep obligation. The Marchesa Origo and Sir Richard Livingstone were so kind as to read some chapters; and to them too I return my warm thanks.

Some imponderable assistance—the most difficult of all to do justice to—still remains to be mentioned. Though I cannot adequately acknowledge, I can never forget the constant encouragement and discriminating counsel given me by three of "Allegra's" friends—Lady Cynthia Asquith, Mrs. Raymond Asquith and the Hon. Mrs. Aubrey Herbert. They will not themselves want me to say more; yet I fear what I have said may seem to some far from enough.

It remains only to add that those whose names I have mentioned above have no responsibility for any of the facts, hypotheses or opinions advanced in the book.

ALGERNON CECIL.

May, 1944.

A HOUSE IN BRYANSTON SQUARE

Chapter I

A HOUSE IN BRYANSTON SQUARE

A TOWN house; a London house; a house in a region where some eighty years ago or less such fashionable ladies as did not consider it becoming to visit north of Oxford Street would not have shown their faces;* a house with a view indeed, but a view extending no farther than a garden fast bound in rails of iron—what contribution to a criticism of life can a man hope to make in face of such evident limitations? In the street nowadays they know everything, for every one of us, whilst there, may surely feel himself, as the vain Frenchman is alleged to have done when he looked into his looking-glass, to be some thirty or forty millionth part of the sovereign power and entitled to assume airs in proportion. But a man in a house is a nobody, an idle spectator of the scene without, a seer of mortal things through the grime upon his windows, and so much the more darkly for that. Yet perhaps, even so, a case may be made out for listening to his opinions. Lookers-on, one might urge, proverbially see most of the game; and old houses become store-houses of experience; and walls are well known to have ears. Tell-tale books, besides, with much accumulated knowledge of the world without, are to be found standing in serried ranks or lurking in obscure recesses—tell-tale books that spring to life when flesh and blood has failed us and afford spectral companionship in a silence that may be felt.

> Back upon back the firelight licks their spines;
> Author and title flicker in the gloom,
> Until across the room
> The books parade, bright coats in even lines.
>
> .   .   .   .   .
>
> And authors growing rash
> Take form and slip, slim spirits, from the pages,
> Spirals of smoke where thought asleep had lain,
> With characters in train,
> Take form and turn to poets, priests and sages.†

---

* "A lady of good social position had been introduced to her and, having found her conversation agreeable, had asked for her address in order that the acquaintance might be continued. When, however, Lady Robert mentioned Fitzroy Square, she drew back and announced regretfully but firmly that she 'never left cards north of Oxford Street'."

(Lady Gwendolen Cecil, "Life of Robert, Marquis of Salisbury", I, p. 63.)

† D. Wellesley, "Poems of Ten Years", p. 56.

These, indeed, are spirits that all men may call up from the vasty deep of human speculation, and that will come, moreover, when we do call for them. But every house has, besides, its own familiars; and to be able to summon these we must know it well, for they are not to be conjured back just for the asking.

The house that I have in mind had seen the passage of four generations. Built on the eve of the Regency—in the very year, in fact, in which George III finally went mad—it had passed through a number of hands since Parkinson, a noted builder in his time, secured the earliest lease of it. To my knowledge it had sheltered men as various as a field marshal, a solicitor eminent for his firm's association with causes célèbres, and a man of letters, who had climbed painfully to fame; and, were every London house compelled to keep a sort of log book in which the activities of its owners and the names of its habitués were recorded, I might have been tempted to insert some portraits not altogether imaginary and some scenes not wholly unsuited for *genre* treatment in the tapestry of my design. For here and there a relic of former inhabitants—a bas relief, maybe, of amoretti with garlands in their hands, or a pair of mahogany doors of a rarer beauty and finish than even the epoch of mahogany fittings could be expected to produce, or a wall-decoration intended to complete the end of a divan—would catch the eye and cause the whisper of the walls to become more audible.

It was in the fall of a year, now somewhile joined to its forerunners, that I first had conscious sight of the house which, so to speak, circumscribes these pages; and the accordant, autumnal aspect of its interior, resulting evidently enough from the fact that it was in process of changing hands, remains with me still. In the retrospect I could fancy that even then it had conveyed to me in its elegant, urban way something of the same effect of a glory departing which the trees, as their produce fell and their foliage faded, had but lately proclaimed with ambrosial banquets of fruit and riots of colour. Autumn, as most of us learn, can be almost unbearably rich in sweetness and sadness. Even Jane Austen, who says so little about Nature, pauses, as her devotees are doubtless aware, more than once, to mark its supreme power of arousing emotion. But it was Maurice Hewlett who had contrived, as it seemed to me, to add one word more to all that the poets had said upon the subject. "The man", he remarks of Maitland of Lethington in recording an imaginary conversation between that subtle statesman and Mary Fleming, "was sensitive to climate, and, like all sensitive men, loved autumn best. 'This slope sun, which will neither scorch nor refuse his clemency, dearest lady,' he said; 'these milky skies, which never seem to lose the freshness of dawn; the very gentle death—most merciful!—which each Day suffers; the balm of Night's dipped fingers shed upon our brows: are not these things an augury (O my true love!) of even life for you and me? Even life, a peaceful ending of our days, with the angry solstice turned, the dry heat, the bared wrath of the sun far from us! Indeed, indeed, I do believe it.' . . . 'And I, sir,' she would answer, 'pray for it daily.' " *

To such a thought the House might easily have been supposed to assent with all the grace of its own personality. It fell within the definition of a period-house. It had plainly reached maturity. It told, if more diffidently than wood or orchard, of the melancholy, the mystery, the mellow fruitfulness that invade the soul as well towards the fall of life as at the fall of the leaf. Its atmosphere was tense with the wisdom that waits in all things to see the end before coming to judgment.

Facing as it did to the east and west, the building, like some sensitive soul alive to the full charm of light and shadow, might have been supposed to court the hours of dawn and sunset as best suited to its inward and spiritual grace. Doubtless Mr. Wells is right when he declares that "Being is surrounded, east, west, south and north, by wonder".† Yet, for all that, the house seemed to me to have appropriated, so to say, the symbolism of the sun at its two metaphysical extremities, and in such a manner as to excite trains of reflection denied to the dwellers in town houses that face the poles and are sunlit only upon one side and in the glare of noon-day. Within its spaces the searching play of the invading sunshine, as it shifted from point to point, was eloquent with the suggestion of mutability—of that subtle flux in human circumstance which gave to its classic Greek exponent his title of the weeping philosopher of Ephesus. It did not make an excessive demand upon fancy to imagine the tears of things welling up from the water that lay sleeping in the design of a Chinese paper upon the wall of a certain room in the house, and flowing away, as the phrase goes, beneath the bridges of time.

How often in the past have I not watched the rays of the wester-

* M. Hewlett, "The Queen's Quair", p. 329.
† "An Experiment in Autobiography", p. 226.

ing sun move across that characteristic piece which seemed, by its witness to a certain community of taste, to span in a moment of time the long century between the days of the Fourth and Fifth Georges as well as all the distance from London to Cathay? Into it, as of course still more into some old Chinese papers that may be found in English country-houses, there might be read, if we chose, the appeal of the rational soul for light from the East and for culture to a civilisation where the partnership between the living and the dead, so eloquently stressed by Burke as an essential feature of a true society, had been exceptionally apparent in the worship of ancestors. Eothen! Did not that word contain a suggestion that the natural movement of thought was ever from the east westwards, at least, that is, as things are for us in England, and did we not, if we neglected to remember it, become like men uncivilised who would pass the wine the wrong way round at dinner? Recall those "Letters of John Chinaman" which came, some thirty years ago, from Lowes Dickinson's delicate pen, and consider whether their argument has not since appreciably strengthened, and whether any criticism of life to run true must not, like the sun itself, start at the eastern end of our intellectual horizon and not too far from the first cradle of the human race and the first psychological traditions of human childhood. Orientation—there, precisely, is the spiritual gift which came to us westward-walking men at the dawn of history as the true symbolic word. We travel daily farther from the east, so that the sight of a woman with the west in her eyes can make us turn chill and chillier yet. Yet, as with John Inglesant at the sun's setting, there comes the assurance that the sun will rise again; and the east must be ever in our thoughts as our eyes strain westwards.

Symbolism, doubtless, of the simplest, yet lying near the core of poetry, as poetry itself lies near the core of truth! No argument, indeed, can force these values upon an inhospitable mind; and they can alike be scorned as fancy or dismissed as dreams. Yet the witness of the world is still strong in their favour. Securus judicat orbis terrarum. The great poets sit enthroned above the tide of change; and he who cannot confess to the appreciation of one at the least among them must be reckoned as much a defective as the deaf or the blind. Keats, who was singing still, whilst the house in Bryanston Square was building, may have overshot the mark in claiming that beauty was truth, truth beauty, and that this was all we knew on earth or needed to know. But the hyperbole, if it be one, has been too often cited to leave much doubt that it missed its mark rather from excess of strength than lack of direction. If beauty be not truth, there is at least some deep-set truth in beauty which secures to art an assured position beside physical science in any finished critique of life. Does not mere cold philosophy put all charms to flight?

Heracleitus's lament—his famous πάντα χωρεῖ καὶ οὐδὲν μένει,* possesses indeed just such an admixture of hard fact with poetic sensibility as we creatures, compounded of thought and feeling, instinctively demand of any proposition that is to secure our lasting assent. Everything—all appearance—flows away, nothing remains. Nothing, that is, except the memory! Yet of that insecure relic how immensely much can be made! "To perceive universal mutation, to feel the vanity of life," observes one of the ripest critics of our time, "has always been the beginning of seriousness. It is the condition for any beautiful, measured or tender philosophy."†

The weeping philosopher, had he taken his stand about the year 1935 in the Square that I speak of, might even then have found much material to his liking. All around, Victorian London was perishing; and the Square itself had for some while seemed a beleaguered fortress beset, like its old neighbour Montagu, by the all-conquering flat. At the foot of the garden an old urn still commemorated some deceased resident who, in his day, had seemed eminent enough, but whose place, as proprietor of a great journal, had long been filled, so that his very name was now pretty well forgotten. Of him we had, in fact, a memorial, but no memory. But about the house memories still played freely. Every room appeared to have been lately instinct with human life; and I could not but suppose that the echo of forgotten footfalls might yet be caught by the hearing ear. Out of the crowd of its former occupants, the house seemed to me to be still preternaturally sensible of the passage of two; and I came to share this sensibility. These familiars, influences, spirits—call them what you will—were, as I thought, alike in something, but unlike in more. Their common instinct, according to their different capacity, had been, as I felt, to make the most of life. Their vision had been clear, their judgment fine and delicate. Their disposition had turned to foreign lands; in each case, to be precise, towards the Latin culture of the south and the sunshine of the Mediterranean. I could imagine them conversing with great contentment.

* Everything departs and nothing remains.
† Santayana, "Three Philosophical Poets", p. 24.

Yet, for all that, I was conscious that, in regard to the things that mattered to me most, they were as the poles apart. When I caught their accents clearly I might have supposed myself to be listening to Tennyson's Two Voices. The one was strong with the irony, the disillusionment, the harsh cynicism, the bitter pathos of which Swift is the supreme master. But the other voice was gay, sweet and melodious as a May evening, and might have broken as easily out of a book, as does Bridges's 'Virgin-Mother clad in green' when he touches the strings of his lyre. There was nothing, I repeat, to show that those two voices would not have talked together as friends; even as winter, if it comes to that, might be said merely to debate with spring the passage of the snowdrop through the snow. Yet still in my heart I knew that in conjunction they raised for me in the most definite form the supreme issue that confronts us all—the question whether life has meaning or is all a cheat, the question of faith or unfaith in human destiny, the question, as Carlyle has it, of an everlasting yea or nay.

In this supreme debate the elder and earlier inhabitant of the House assumed in my eyes the spirit of negation at its boldest; and his championship was so much the more impressive that he was obviously gifted with very excellent perception. His understanding, if not his vision, had carried him far. Profoundly impressed by the genius of Spain, he had travelled further than either Cortez or Columbus. He had practised the exercises of the Jesuits. He had pursued the Spanish mystics into their strongholds. In El Greco he had recognised a mind congenial to his own and capable of interpreting according to his need that world half-realised in which all mystics move. In the tortured baroque forms, the 'melodramatic expression of a high-pitched religiosity',[*] the dream cities, the men of the world with 'the faces of dreamers in action',[†] characteristic of that master's work, he seemed to find the artistic expression of the world he knew. Whether he believed it to have any real relation to the world around him or to be merely some deceitful mirage thrown up by the human mind I could not pretend to say. All that I felt certain of was that he perceived there neither final purpose nor hidden God. To his shrewd and shrunken eye life had all the look of a Persian carpet into which a weaver might introduce what pattern he pleased.

[*] Roger Fry, "Vision and Design" (On El Greco).
[†] Arthur Symons, "A Study of Toledo" (*Monthly Review*, March 1901).

Here was a philosophy that relieved man of all responsibility and God, if any God there was, of all reproach. Subject only to a proper regard for Mrs. Grundy and the policeman up the Square, human beings were, in fact, at liberty to take their fill of pleasure and damn the consequences; for of consequences there were none except in this limited and local sense. The irony of the situation was, of course, exquisite. Men kept looking for point in a universe that was actually pointless and building themselves spiritual homes that were properly houses of bondage. To eat, to drink, to philander, to make as merry as one might and avoid as much pain as one could—this, it seemed, became the plainest wisdom, and all the rest a quixotry to be watched with the half-complacent, half-contemptuous surprise of (shall we say?) a Sancho Panza. The Voice, as its theme drew to a close, would seem to me to be accompanied by a chorus of tongues. Here and there I fancied that I could recognise accents that I already knew —the mournful numbers of Lucretius declaring that life is no free-hold, but a mere tenancy;* the bold bass of Haeckel asserting that matter, now as ever, is lord of all; the exceeding bitter cry of Macbeth seeking to reassure himself that his works and days have been but an explosion of sound and fury without any real significance; and even the child's voice of Alice, taking up her parable on the very threshold of Wonderland. ' "It might end, you know," said Alice to herself, "in my going out altogether like a candle. I wonder what I should be like then." ' She might well wonder. It had puzzled larger minds than hers in a world where the conservation of matter and energy, if these were scientifically distinguishable, had long seemed to invite the opinion that nothing was lost. Into what could personality dissolve, if it could dissolve at all?

The concordant melancholy of what I came to call the Alien Voice and its choral accompaniment reached me like the sound of singing heard at some distance, for it was carried by the medium of the printed page. But the other voice of which I have spoken—the sweeter voice—fell upon my ears much more distinctly, and would by some gentle compulsion of its own evoke a response so vibrant that I could not doubt that its appeal was as intimate as that of its rival was remote. It was something that I knew, and not merely that I knew of. I must therefore be permitted to speak of it quite simply and directly, as if it possessed the full force of personality. Only by so doing can I feel confident that I am keeping in close touch with

* "De Natura Rerum", III, 971—"Vitaque mancipio nulli datur, omnibus usu".

reality as it came to me. For, if Plato was entitled to claim that the world of ideas in which our minds are at work was an invisible world of universals, Aristotle was as much justified in teaching that universals possess significance for us only as we perceive them in and through contact with the world of sense. This appears most noticeably in reference to those values which by common consent we place, or profess to place, highest—in reference, that is, to Beauty, Truth and Love. Yet even from her lovely companions Love would seem to draw a little apart. For, whilst we recognise the beauty in a scene or the truth in a fact, love, to be apprehended, postulates personality and, in the case of perfect love, a perfect personality or—which appears to be the same thing—a divine incarnation. Even the Alien Voice in summing up its harsh impression of life would sometimes seem to me to leave room for just this possibility—for the bare chance, that is, that in pure love Humanity had chanced upon something of an absolute nature instinct with eternal meaning. And so I shall suppose that hollow Alien Voice and its echoing chorus to be silent for a time, whilst I endeavour to convey to the reader the ethos of the other Voice, with all its grace of personality, as I recall hearing it long since within the precincts of the house that I have endeavoured to describe.

Chapter II

"ALLEGRA"

IT is now ten years and more since I learnt of the death of Allegra. She had long been ill, and had endured much suffering, but she was so much beloved and cared for that I had always believed she would recover. Dis aliter visum! Of all the women I have known she was, I think, the most exquisite; and this in no common sense of the word. She loved, indeed, to have her surroundings of the finest; but she had so great a power of moulding the fashion and circumstance of life to the pattern of her nature that everything about her seemed, not so much a studied effect, as the response or homage of an environment to her own ethereal personality. I remember to have noticed at a dinner where we were both of us guests an old familiar of the great world of the past turn, after looking in her direction, to his neighbour with the enquiry whether she were not in truth refinement itself. She seemed, in fact, within the limits of our mortal vision, the perfection of grace. All of her, from the shaping of the delicate hands and feet to the lovely curve of the shoulders, appeared to contribute something to the effortless poise and stillness of her body when at rest, and, after a manner, to train the eye for a fuller appreciation of the delicate finish of the head. To look at that last enchantment was indeed to be fully satisfied rather than finally astonished. The perfect eye of her Maker had guarded the vital secret of her being too carefully to risk even the suspicion in her features of a fresh surprise. Divine wisdom, playing in the world and moulding matter to its mind, would never have wanted anything so sensational, not to say garish, as the launching of a thousand ships to have come about because of her. Her beauty of face was of a piece with her beauty of form, and ended, as it began, without ostentation.

Restrained and unchallenging, content to make sure of the spiritual harmonies of proportion and to use the secret subtleties of charm, her loveliness remained thus always that of a princess rather than of a queen, of a bud rather than of a full-blown flower. Neither she, nor any that knew her, could have easily borne that it should be otherwise. It was of the very essence of her that she loved beauty for itself and desired it in others; that she sought no pre-eminence; that she excited no rivalry; that she evoked no malice. The white neck;

the dark hair; the complexion blush-lily or, on a sudden, reddening to pale-rose; the ears that might have graced a Venus emergent from the sea; the lips that love had framed for sweetness, but that wit was always borrowing to make fun—such things not a few have possessed and not a few have celebrated. But in one feature—and that the most subtle of all—she, as I thought, excelled.

The great portrait-painters of the interior life of man, and Rembrandt most of all among them, made of that enigmatic hue which the rainbow lacks—so it has been ingeniously maintained* —the colour-symbol of the soul, and especially of a soul surveying from end to end the vista of historic time. This 'studio-brown' of theirs is not to be found in the early Florentines but, according to the theory advanced, was a product of the late Renaissance, deriving from the so-called 'infinitesimal greens' of Leonardo's backgrounds, and carried forward by the rich influence of Giorgione's tones until it reached at length full expression in the Dutch school of painting and found, as alleged, a spiritual counterpart in the temperamental ethos of Port-Royal (perhaps one might add, as rendered by Sainte-Beuve).

In the brown beauty of Allegra's eyes there moved a music beyond description, a light so lustrous that all who cared to look could have known them for the windows of a soul all glorious within. Such depth of colour as theirs would, as I thought, have made harmony with that aureate glow which played about the Blessed Damozel as she leaned out from the gold bar of Heaven—a harmony of deepest hazel gazing into golden haze. With such translucent vision might Beatrice, as I fancied, have read the soul of Dante. Out of such wells of light, as I dreamed, might Leonardo have drawn living water as he gathered whole centuries of experience into a single face, until, in the famous phrase of the critic, the Gioconda stood in the line of descent both from Leda, the mother of Helen, and of St. Anne, the mother of Mary. Was it, then, no more than an idle conceit to suppose that the subtle radiance of that 'studio-brown' was exceptionally favourable to those brown studies of which men spoke as deeper than the rest and which made the very mind-stuff of history?

It happened that more than once I saw Allegra stand in the Louvre beside that very portrait of the Gioconda to which I refer. I know not through what subtle play of feature the fancy came to me,

* Spengler, "Decline of the West" (Eng. tr.), I, p. 250.

but I saw there a likeness that I could not doubt, and that made me recall at a later date how it had been said of Monna Lisa that hers was a beauty wrought out from within upon the flesh by thought and reverie and exquisite passion to the sound of lyres and flutes. It was then, perhaps, that I began to know whence Allegra came and what spirit she was of.

I came but slowly to this knowledge. I had sought for it first in other countries and centuries; for I could see that she had come from far and was in truth a 'princesse lointaine', and that much had gone to her making as well of fine lineage as of fond thought and casual circumstance. At one time I had looked for her in the society of the English Restoration, since she numbered, not only in a spiritual sense but according to the flesh, both Margaret Godolphin and Dorothy Osborne amongst her kinswomen, and combined so perfect a courtesy of spirit with her native purity of soul that I could fancy her passing, unsullied and undimmed and in a manner also un-critically, through a corrupt Court with no greater embarrassment than her ancestress through that of Charles II. But I sought her there in vain; not in that soil was this delicate flower rooted. Nor did I meet with better success when I looked for her elsewhere within kings' houses, though I was not quite without justification for so doing. I knew that once, in a game where the interest turned upon imaginary attributions of parentage, she had been given Sir Philip Sidney for her father and Marie Antoinette for her mother; and I could see that this flight of fancy was both very brilliant and very plausible, and in a sense very true. Yet neither in the constellation of Elizabeth nor in that of the Ancien Régime could I feel her fixed; nor, though for a moment I might dream that in Cyrano's Roxane I had seen her likeness, was she quite of his date or country. Such devotion as his, indeed, she could inspire, such desolation as his provoke, but the rest of the resemblance seemed as a shadow that departed.

And then, at length, I learnt, as I thought, her secret, and per-ceived behind all the disguises of time and place to what citizenship she had been born and into what company her spirit led her. It was her love of Florence that betrayed her, and at Florence her delight in the work of Leonardo. As she gazed at his Adoration of the Magi and marvelled at the strength and pathos and beauty of the faces depicted there, just as when she had stood beside the portrait of La Joconde at the Louvre, I came to know her for what she really was.

From the cloud of mystery she had stepped forth, a woman of that world of the Catholic Renaissance which had its home in Italy, which was alive with light and line and colour, and across which the blight of puritanism had never passed. Intolerant as she was of little except controversy among Christians, her mind at its deepest and loveliest seemed to visualise the Holy Crib after the manner of the great Florentine painter who, more perhaps than any other, tends to turn every traveller through time into a pilgrim of eternity. I speak of Leonardo, yet in the very effort to express his peculiar power I am forced to think of Byron. Goethe says of the English Poet, so much underrated by Englishmen, that he approached a subject, as women do the bearing of beautiful children, without thinking of it or knowing how it came about.* And that same sort of approach to things might, perhaps, have been alleged of Allegra, who herself, in the judgment of a deeply affectionate but not the less critical eye, was clearest seen and best thought of as walking in a night of cloudless climes and starry skies. The portrait of her on the frontispiece of this book, conceived as it was years after her death with such aid as photographs could afford, offers such a likeness as I suppose the water of time, flowing away into the dim distance of the sketch, must have borne, together with faithful shadows of olive and cypress, upon its bosom. The pose and fashion of a head carrying its own assurance of thoughts 'serenely sweet'; the 'nameless grace' of an expression shifting somehow, under the magic of the artist's hand, from grave to gay as one catches it at different angles; the wistful sadness as of a soul waiting to lavish some latent, lovely smile upon a child—these things are perhaps rendered plainer by the preternatural power of Art than by the native force of Nature; and thus out of the well of tears, where the still likeness of her face had seemed to sleep, has flowed the mobile wonder of a reflection playing evermore amid the ripples of time's river and discovering new beauties as it dances on, renewing its youth, into eternity.

Never in loneliness, however, had it been Allegra's habit to take her way; and, as I turn back from the vision of art to the recollection of things as they appeared to be, the portrait of her would seem to change again into a conversation-picture so vivid as to permit one to apply that test of good company, perhaps qualitative as well as quantitative in its bearing, that to make good talk 'il faut être moins que les

---

* Conv. with Eckermann, Feb. 24th, 1825. "Zu seinen Sachen kam er wie die Weiber zu schönen Kindern; sie denken nicht daran und wissen nicht wie."

Muses et plus que les Graces'. La Gioconda, the gay one! That
significant title, which only came to Monna Lisa by right of marriage,
seemed to have come to Allegra by right of birth. Gay she was, most
exquisitely gay, mixing mirth and mockery in even measure—gay,
so that all were glad and none was wounded. As a child, they told
me, she had been always singing; and that rare legacy of joyous feeling, inherited perhaps from a grandmother who had thus played
fairy godmother to her, remained, I think, always in her heart, even
when pain had checked or silenced the flow of song. 'Leader' she
would sometimes call herself, when I came to know her, making
some play with the name and declaring herself to be no better than
a bear-leader or, alternatively, punning on the word Leda, to have
been unfortunate in an affair of the heart and to have found her
swan no other than a goose. But for my part I am content to think
that one letter in that conceit of hers had been lost and that another
had been a changeling, and that her rightful name was Laeta, the
joyful one. Yet I have called her here Allegra, both because one who
knew her well had called her so before me and because, whilst there
was so much about her to suggest the bright children of the South,
she had little use for the complementary Roman virtue of austerity,
either in its pagan or its Christian aspect. Her soul's argosy had, as
it seemed to me, been borne across the tideless sea from Athens to
Florence; and to my eye she symbolised, of course in utter uncon-
sciousness, that migration of the graces from the one city to the
other which preceded the final permeation and purification of the
Humanities by Christian culture. All that Italy meant to some of
the best English minds between the days of the Grand Tour and the
days of Italian Unity; all that half-forgotten, wholly Catholic element in civilisation which, out of the depth of their insularity and
sometimes in ignorance of its true meaning, Englishmen felt after
and found in the cities of the much-criticised Latin tradition—this
she unconsciously recovered and instinctively exemplified. Her
appearance, coupled with the facility in the Italian tongue which
she had acquired in childhood, added to her qualifications for this
mediatory, this reintegrating rôle. And so entirely did the part
become her that, when she came back to her own country, she
retained, as I thought, about her always something suggestive of a
bird of passage; and to such a degree that, had all the world been once
again required to be enrolled, one might have felt justified in preferring spiritual to secular accuracy and entering Italy as her native

land and Florence as her domicile. Certainly, if I were to be told that this world of ours had in some way reclaimed her spirit, I should seek her there and, maybe, in those very streets, did I know how to find them, where over six centuries ago a boy-poet was wont to hunt for glimpses of a divinely graceful girl, once clad in finest crimson, but later in virgin white—a girl the remembrance of whom burnt ever in his heart and seemed to work there continually with all the force of reason informed by love.*

It was of a piece with all this that Dante and the Brownings were the loved companions of Allegra's ways, and that she was to an unusual extent mistress of their secrets and saw the deep things of life in some degree through their eyes. I would even risk saying that in her attitude something too was to be discerned of the courteous mind of Virgil who, as an accomplished commentator observes, stands in the Divine Comedy for 'worldly wisdom', though in no worldly sense; whilst, for any presentation of her sensuous life against the background of her Italian environment, the longest search will, I feel sure, yield nothing more apt than the lines forthwith to be stolen from "Sordello" and adapted by the substitution of Allegra's name for his to the purpose in view:—

> . . . a soul fit to receive
> Delight at every sense; you can believe
> (Allegra) foremost in the regal class
> Nature has broadly severed from (the) mass
> . . . and framed for pleasure, as she frames
> Some happy lands that have luxurious names
> For loose fertility; a footfall there
> Suffices to upturn to the warm air
> Half-germinating spices; mere decay
> Produces richer life; and day by day
> New pollen on the lily-petal grows
> And still more labyrinthine buds the rose.

A rose indeed, and budding once in a land of roses! Yet now only the spectre of a rose, whose fragrance haunts me still, now that the brief ballet of life is over and the memories of a day that is gone return in the firelight. But, if a spectre only, surely dancing yet, as the Blessed dance in the rich imagery of Dante's visions. Of such, as the poet assures us, the angels scent the sweetness in the celestial air as they pass like bees from petal to petal of the Great Rose of Heaven.†

* "Vita Nuova", Sec. II.   † "Paradiso", XXXI, 7.

The conception of such heavenly presences as an element in human life had not in truth been wanting to the child's outlook of Allegra, but, by the time I knew her, had crystallised into a special feeling for that picture of Guercino's—that 'picture at Fano'—which Robert Browning made so famous. She carried, as I have some reason to suppose, across the threshold of another world this particular cult of the guardian-angel, whom Artist and Poet had united to depict with hands outstretched to welcome the expectant, trusting child beneath into the House of Heaven; and I traced with satisfaction the reappearance of the theme, somewhat modified and extended, in the panel which the best sculptor, perhaps, of our time was so good as to execute for her tombstone. Anyhow, there came early to her mind some power of visualising the angelic choir; and I believe she owed something of its strength to the days when the old poet and preacher, George MacDonald, struck with the child's grace both of mind and of body, had cast her in his fancy for the part of a child-madonna, and so guided her towards a rich expression of her imaginative gifts in certain Nativity plays of singular charm and purity. As at once the author and producer for a small family circle of these pieces, she must have gone some way towards recalling Dante's description of the Virgin Mother smiling with so much beauty at sports and songs as to make gladness in the eyes of the beholders.* And those who later knew the savour of her letters—their lightness of touch and delicacy of humour, so well satisfying the hopes aroused by an exquisite calligraphy—will find the sweetness, if not the salt of her personality reflected in those early masques.

Christmas, thus, with its heavenly choirs and earthly carols, was beyond all doubt her season. She counted all labour light that went to its making; and for those who came to think of her as the very genius of its festivities, Christmas comes no more. It may well be that this particular attraction to a season of pure, unclouded joy contained in it some element of reaction against the pain which came to her early and grew towards the close of her life to a great pitch of suffering. If I dwell upon that final memory, it is only that I may record a last perfection. She, who might almost have satisfied the

* Vidi quivi ai lor giochi ed ai lor canti
  Ridere una bellezza, che letizia
  Era negli occhi a tutti gli altri santi.

("Paradiso", XXXI, 133.)

traditional tests of a tenderness that shrinks from the killing of a fly and of a sensitiveness matching that of the princess robbed of her sleep by a crumpled rose-leaf beneath the mattress—she it was whom, as the long days of trial drew towards the close, I have heard maintain that from such beings as ourselves one would not wish all pain away. Along some pathway of her own, and with a full knowledge of its stones and steepness, she had come, I can but suppose, to perceive in pain what the poet* dares to call 'Love's mystery'.

.   .   .   .   .

I saw her at length when life's last fever was past and those radiant eyes of hers had closed on time forever. 'Animula, vagula, blandula . . .!'—She had long loved that address of the dying Emperor to his soul; preferring it a little, I think, in the still more playful form that Ronsard gave to it. And now 'the guest and comrade of her body'—hospes comesque corporis—had wandered out into a world whither as yet one might not hope to follow. It seemed like a consummation of what' I had seen of its passage through time that in her last hours her mind had dwelt upon the thought of another comradeship—of the comradeship of the Eternal Spirit as more fully the companion of the soul ('dulcis hospes animae', as the old Latin hymn has it) than even the soul is of the body. And thus, behind the darkened glass of our vision, Love itself seemed to be wrapping her in warmest raiment as, with a conscious peace and happiness in her heart and 'without a sigh or a resistance', she passed beyond the care of our undying, yet so impotent affection.

> Non come fiamma che per forza è spenta,
>   Ma che per se medesma si consume,
>   Se n'andò in pace l'anima contenta;
> A guisa d'un soave e chiaro lume
>   Cui nutrimento a poco a poco manca;
>   Tenendo al fin il suo usato costume.†

Her form, now turned to marble, yet still most lovely, alone remained with us; and Death's pale flag implanted there, and thus far advanced despite our utmost effort, advanced no further. So much it lay within our power to secure. Untouched by time the body passed to its last resting-place. "I caused her corpse, lovely even in death, to be embalmed",‡ wrote John Evelyn of Margaret Godolphin. And

* Coventry Patmore.
† Petrarch's "Il Trionfo della Morte", I, 160–165.
‡ Evelyn's Diary, Sept. 9th, 1678.

that precedent was followed in the death of her descendant. She, whose it was, had seemed to gather life's choicest flowers and to be gone before they faded. And now, tokens both of abiding remembrance and of returning Spring, flowers lay piled—not in figure only, but in fact—above Allegra's grave. I shall never forget their rich profusion. Florence, the city of flowers, through which, on a Holy Thursday long ago, I had wandered with her from one 'reposoir' to another, catching her infectious joy at each successive burst of radiant blossom, could scarcely have done more than her English friends to clothe the earth, where she was laid, with beauty.

"Cold in the earth", she lay; and I could have fancied that the south wind, passing up across the sunny land of France from an Italian garden, where the cypress avenue, obedient to the ancient charge to all its kind to mourn with mourners, stares ever skywards,* had brought to her graveside the music of the incomparable lament which those bleak words serve to introduce:—

> Now, when alone, do my thoughts no longer hover
> Over the mountains, on that northern shore,
> Resting their wings where heath and fern-leaves cover
> Thy noble heart, for ever, ever more.†

· · · · ·

Some years after Allegra died I came, as I thought, upon her epitaph, though in fact it had been traced by a master-hand‡ some while before she was born. The few extracts that follow must be read with the indulgence accorded in more spacious times than ours to the oraison funèbre or the mural tablet.

"There are", the passage ran, "some unworldly types of character which the world is able to estimate. . . . The saint, the artist, even the speculative thinker, out of the world's order as they are, yet work, so far as they work at all, in and by means of the main current of the world's energy. . . . It is also patient of doctrinaires of every degree of littleness. As if dimly conscious of some great sickness and weariness of heart in itself, it turns readily

---

* Ovid, "Metamorph", X, 106–142.

· · · · ·

Sidereum gracili spectare cacumine caelum,
Ingemuit tristisque deus 'lugebere nobis,
lugebisque alios, aderisque dolentibus', inquit.

† Emily Brontë, "Remembrance".
‡ "Le parfait prosateur", Paul Bourget on Walter Pater.

to those who theorise about its unsoundness. To constitute one of
these categories, or types, a breadth and generality of character is
required. There is another type of character . . . rare, precious
above all to the artist, a character which seems to have been the
supreme moral charm in the Beatrice of the Commedia. It does
not take the eye by breadth of colour; rather it is that fine edge
of light, where the elements of our moral nature refine themselves
to the burning point. . . . The world has no sense fine enough
for those evanescent shades which fill up the blanks between con-
trasted types of character—delicate provision in the organisation
of the moral world for the transmission to every part of it of the
life quickened at single points. . . .

   " 'Sibi unitus et simplificatus esse,' that is the long struggle of
the Imitatio Christi. The spirit which it forms is the very opposite of that which regards life as a game of skill and values things
and persons as marks or counters of something to be gained, or
achieved, beyond them. It seeks to value everything at its eternal
worth. . . . It is the spirit that sees external circumstances as
they are, its own powers and tendencies as they are, and realises
the given conditions of its life. . . . The character we mean to
indicate achieves this perfect life by a happy gift of nature without any struggle at all. . . .

   "Simplicity in purpose and act is a kind of determinate expression in dexterous outline of one's personality. It is a kind of moral
expressiveness; there is an intellectual triumph implied in it.
Such a simplicity is characteristic of the repose of perfect intellectual culture. . . . Like the religious life it is a paradox in the
world . . . cutting obliquely the spontaneous order of things.
But the character we have before us is a kind of prophecy of this
repose and simplicity coming as it were in the order of grace, not
of nature, by some happy gift or accident of birth or constitution,
showing that it is indeed within the limits of man's destiny. Like
all the higher forms of inward life this character is a subtle blending and interpenetration of intellectual, moral and spiritual elements. But it is as a phase of intellect, of culture, that it is most
striking and forcible. It is a mind of taste lighted up by some
spiritual ray within. Its beautiful way of handling everything that
appeals to the senses and the intellect is really directed by the laws
of the higher intellectual life, but while culture is able to trace
those laws, mere taste is unaware of them. In the character before

us taste . . . is like the reminiscence of a forgotten culture that once adorned the mind. It has the freshness without the shallowness of taste, the range and seriousness of culture without its strain and over-consciousness. . . . It is just this sort of entire transparency of nature that lets through all that is really life-giving in the established order of things; it detects without difficulty all sorts of affinities between its own elements and the nobler elements in that order. But then . . . a confidence in perfection it has makes it love the lords of change. . . . Revolution is often impious. . . . But in this nature revolutionism is softened, harmonised, subdued as by distance. It is the revolutionism of one who has slept a hundred years."

People, so the argument continued, had often tried to find a type of life that might serve as basic. But, in this, saint and sage and artist alike had failed them, no less than the pedant, the conservative and the radical. So transparent a nature as had been indicated was alone equal to the blending of old and new ideas and, as the writer concludes in a last challenging sentence, a majority of such natures "would be the regeneration of the world". *

·　　　·　　　·　　　·　　　·

Diaphaneitè, which gave its title to this exquisite, forgotten monograph, had, as I saw at last, been Allegra's second and secret name. She had always valued crystal highly for its graceful effect in a room; and now it became clear to me that, all unconsciously, she had thus indicated the proper symbol of her own transparent self in relation to the social world about her.

* Pater, "Diaphaneitè" in "Misc. Studies".

Chapter III

ORGANIC EPISTEMOLOGY

"IN his yearning for her who sped beyond the sea," runs the well-known chorus in the "Agamemnon", "a phantom will seem to be lord of the house." * Nothing less resembled the great and gracious ways of Allegra than the lewd exploits of Helen; yet the words, freed from their context, would return to mind when I used to visit the house which Allegra had once inhabited. Especially was it so in connection with that Chinese room, already mentioned, into which she had put so much of her personality. It is there that in remembrance I can still see her, dancing, as I have seen her do, from sheer joy of possession, or arranging, disarranging or re-arranging the furniture until she had brought every item of it into line with her own exacting sense of perfection. It was there, too, above all, that the phantom of her who sped so swiftly across the sea of life seemed to rise through the revealing mists of time at an enchanted distance— a wonder even more mysterious than when first I knew her and clothed, in this its consummation, with a beauty not of time nor subject to accident. Of such a dreamer's vision I have sought, however imperfectly, to throw the shine and shadow over the coming pages, since without them the house were nothing, its débris dust, and this book an idle fancy not born of the partnership between the living and the dead.

Any personality graced by a true poise between the things of time and the thoughts of eternity must always leave behind it the material for two portraits, the one objective and impressionist, the other subjective and intimate. Each is, doubtless, true within the terms of its reference. In respect, for example, of the two portraits of Socrates, admitting though they do, as Grote assured us,† of being blended into a consistent whole, there will always be some, like Sir Richard Livingstone, to whom it will seem that Xenophon approached the closer to reality, and others, like Professors Burnet and Taylor, who would give that praise to Plato; and to decide between them might require a preliminary excursus into meta-

* Aeschylus, "Agamemnon", 414, 415.

πόθῳ δ'ὑπερποντίας
φάσμα δόξει δόμων ἀνάσσειν.

† Grote, "History of Greece", Ch. LXVIII.

physics and a prior decision as to what reality is and in what manner it may be recognised by us.

There was a greater than Socrates; and in respect of the other supreme literary example of comparative portraiture, if one may make so bold as to bring it under discussion, a lack of verisimilitude has likewise been alleged. There is, however, no conflict of beauty between the content of the Gospels of St. Luke and of St. John. Renan could see in the former the most beautiful book in the world; * yet taste as critical as his would elect in favour of the latter. Where no æsthetic inequality is proved, no psychological contradiction need be suspected; nor any illicit process of idealisation be assumed to have been at work. The portrait of the Holy Child, growing with wisdom and stature into the best friend of the poor, seems to desiderate the portrait of the mystical Lover; and the divine humanity of the Third Gospel to demand the incarnate deity of the Fourth. The triptych presented by the Synoptic Gospels might, indeed, even appear incredible, if we had to study it without the inward and spiritual grace afforded by the Johannine portrait.

The principle involved in these considerations is present, though of course in a much more modest degree, in all portraiture, and to such an extent that Ranke's exacting injunction to describe events as they really happened will seem child's play beside the attempt to paint men and women as they really were. If, then, in seeking to draw the likeness of Allegra, I should seem to any to have allowed lesser dispositions to be lost in deeper lines, I shall nevertheless believe that I have shown her more truly by permitting time to do its perfect work and elicit from her personality something more of its ultimate meaning. Wordsworth, in a well-known, exquisite lyric, has depicted the gradual apprehension of a lovely woman, first as a 'phantom of delight', then as she comes to seem 'a creature not too bright and good for human nature's daily food', and at length, after a man's vision has pierced to 'the very pulse of the machine', in that full grace of being when, 'though spirit still and bright with something of angelic light', she is found to be like the rest of us 'a traveller between life and death'. It needs poetry of as high, or even higher power to render the converse phases of this metamorphosis—the recession in memory of such a wonder once again into phantom beauty, its ascension from the partly physical to the purely spiritual plane, its assumption of a new loveliness, its enhanced de-

* "C'est le plus beau livre qu'il y ait." ("Les Évangiles", c. xiii.)

mand, with all that this involves of moral and mental development, upon the interior vision of the beholder. Shakespeare is, of course, alive to this growth of knowledge, as he is to most things in life affecting the relationship of man and woman. What may, however, be found by some less obvious to expect is that he gives the fact to one of his humble, holy friars to express:—

> The idea of her life shall sweetly creep
> Into his study of imagination,
> And every lovely organ of her life
> Shall come apparelled in more precious habit,
> More moving, delicate and full of life,
> Into the eye and prospect of his soul,
> Than when she lived indeed. *

Here, then, was a truth best seen, in the playwright's judgment, from the standpoint of a priest and a celibate; and to that standpoint one might perhaps find oneself ultimately returning. But it was irresistible first to study it, still under Shakespearean guidance, in its origins. The poet had early surveyed the implications of man's love of woman as it bore upon his theory of knowledge. It was, in fact, the first large question in life that he analysed through the medium of drama. In the earliest of his plays he had been plainly preoccupied with this relationship between love and understanding. The young men—cast, as we may reasonably suppose, more or less in the mould of Essex, Southampton and Rutland †—whose reflections are caught in the mirror of "Love's Labour's Lost" are the prototype of the prigs or pedants who fancy in every age that study can complete the education of the mind without any aid from the affections. There is, of course, comedy enough to be found in the easy collapse of the sworn celibates before their self-denying ordinance. Yet the mocking young French intellectual, into whose mouth Shakespeare, we can hardly doubt, has thrust his own sentiments, finds something more striking than comedy to notice in their downfall. It is in Biron's well-known speech that the searching significance of the play appears:—

> "But Love, first learned in a lady's eyes,
> Lives not alone immured in the brain,
> But, with the motion of all elements,
> Courses as swift as thought in every power,

---

* "Much Ado About Nothing", IV. i.
† Dover Wilson, "The Essential Shakespeare", p. 66.

And gives to every power a double power,
Above their functions and their offices.
It adds a precious seeing to the eye;
A lover's eyes will gaze an eagle blind;
A lover's ear will hear the lowest sound . . .

     .   .   .   .   .

For valour, is not Love a Hercules,
Still climbing trees in the Hesperides?
Subtle as Sphinx; as sweet and musical
As bright Apollo's lute, strung with his hair;
And, when Love speaks, the voice of all the gods
Makes heaven drowsy with the harmony.

     .   .   .   .   .

From women's eyes this doctrine I derive:
They sparkle still the right Promethean fire;
They are the books, the arts, the academes,
That show, contain and nourish all the world;
Else none at all in aught proves excellent.*

It is all there—the theory of knowledge for lack of which philosophies, like virtue, are praised, yet left so generally to grow cold. Two centuries and more before the young Keats had declared that philosophy would clip an angel's wings, the young Shakespeare had, in his own fashion, produced the complementary truth that manly thought needs to be animated by the love of woman. His was, however, more than a virile protest against the inhumanity of mere systems and the comic pedantry of those who, like Faust's jackal, Wagner, look to mere learning to read the riddle of life. The thought, reinforced by all that reflection and experience had to give him, returned, more powerful still, in that dark night of sense when, if one critic is right, Shakespeare came near to madness. "I do love thee," cries Othello, "and when I love thee not, Chaos is come again."

On this showing the cosmic order of which our souls are forever in search must be assumed to suffer partial or total eclipse whenever our finest feelings fail to co-operate in affording light. Love, in brief, however blind it may sometimes appear, when it casts pearls before the eyes of Helen's daughters, indites letters to inadequate beggarmaids in the grand style of Don Adriano de Armado, and, in a word, mistakes faces for souls, has still its true songs of Apollo. If I have not yet mentioned Shakespeare's Sonnets, it may be because they best enter the argument here. So good a critic as Santayana has

* "Love's Labour's Lost", IV, 3.

observed that 'as a whole' they are 'spiritual' and that in them 'passion' is 'transmuted into discipline'.* Of Sonnet CXVI, which is the one most in point, this appears to be pre-eminently true:—

> Let me not to the marriage of true minds
> Admit impediments. Love is not love
> Which alters when it alteration finds,
> Or bends with the remover to remove:
> O no! it is an ever-fixèd mark,
> That looks on tempests, and is never shaken;
> It is the star to every wandering bark,
> Whose worth's unknown, although his height be taken.
> Love's not Time's fool, though rosy lips and cheeks
> Within his bending sickle's compass come;
> Love alters not with his brief hours and weeks,
> But bears it out even to the edge of doom.
>   If this be error, and upon me prov'd,
>   I never writ, nor no man ever lov'd.

Language strong enough in all conscience to satisfy the precepts of the Church, yet important here only in so far as it serves to protect from contamination and defend from ridicule the love that men have need of, first to clarify, then to exalt their intellectual souls.

How delicate, complex and immortal a thing the whole issue had seemed to the Poet was best seen, perhaps, in the strange, mystical threnody concerned with the mutual devotion of the Phoenix and the Turtle:—

> To this urn let those repair
> That are either true or fair;
> For these dead birds sigh a prayer.

Why on earth, the ordinary, sensuous man might be expected to enquire, should 'the true of heart and fair of face' be recommended to look to the orisons of these love-birds without progeny, yet not without power to produce? The answer, which Shakespeare puts into the mouth of Reason, is that neither truth nor beauty, rarity nor grace can come to fruition without such love as the Phoenix and the Turtle bore to one another—a love, however, which they cannot pass on as an inheritance because its supreme ecstasy consists, not in the mingling of two bodies, but in the welding of two souls.

> Reason, in itself confounded,
> Saw division grow together;
> To themselves yet either neither,
> Simple were so well compounded;

---

* Santayana, "Poetry and Religion", p. 15.

That it cry'd, How true a twain
Seemeth this concordant one!
Love hath reason, reason none,
If what parts can so remain.

It is Santayana who has remarked, in the essay already referred to, that the poetry of Shakespeare—perhaps because the Puritan influences of the time were uncongenial to so catholic an observer—had fallen short of the 'dignity, simplicity and peace' induced by that of Dante and Homer in virtue of their respective religious standpoints. Let so much be admitted for the sake of argument; and still one might protest that the supreme Poet of our English Renaissance had sung us at least as far as Heaven's Gate, if not right into Heaven. But let that be, for the Florentines had anticipated him. Before he was thought of, the organic epistemology which his writings confirm had come to rich fruition on that fertile soil of Florence where, indeed, the new Academy of the Medici bore formal witness to the renascent power of Platonic realism. Not for nothing had Virgil's upraised finger pointed Dante's vision to the sweet ray of her 'whose bright eye saw all', whose gracious lips could foreshow the journey of his life.* It was from the City, lily-crowned and fruitful as any garden ever owned by the daughters of Hesperus, that Michelangelo, moved by his master Dante, had risen to heights beyond the force of Hercules to climb. Consider for a moment the tremendous confession addressed to Vittoria Colonna:—

A man within a woman, nay, a god,
Speaks through her spoken word:
I therefore, who have heard,
Must suffer change, and shall be mine no more.
She lured me from the paths I whilom trod.
Borne from my former state by her away,
I stand aloof, and mine own self deplore.
Above all vain desire
The beauty of her face doth lift my clay;
All lesser loveliness seems charnel mire.
O lady, who through fire
And water leadest souls to joy eterne,
Let me no more unto myself return.†

Or again consider such a sonnet as John Addington Symonds

* "Inf.", X, 130–133.
† Translation by J. A. Symonds ("Life of Michelangelo", II, p. 122).

rendered into English under the title of "The Heavenly Birth of Love and Beauty":—

> Love from God's bosom when our souls did part
> Made me pure eyes to see, then light to shine,
> And I must needs, half mortal though thou art,
> In spite of sorrow know thee all divine.
> As heat in fire, so must eternity
> In beauty dwell; through thee my soul's endeavour
> Mounts to the pattern and the source of thee;
> And, having found all heaven in thine eyes,
> Beneath thy brows my burning spirit flies
> There where I loved thee first to dwell for ever.

Enough has now been said to explain both the place that Allegra has in this book and her share in the argument. Enough, that is to say, if it is clear that Christian Humanism at its finest postulates the thought of womanhood at its most sublime. The Virgin-Mother of God and the virgin figure of Beatrice dead alike satisfy the exacting purity of this demand, but, though the poets have been slow to recognise it, the idea of Christian marriage here constitutes the norm and furnishes the only symbolism adequate to the notion of the spiritual marriage or of the marriage of true minds. And, were some intellect more specifically catholic than Shakespeare's, more massive and Dantesque even than Michelangelo's, to demand a plainer warrant for this conditioning of finished thought by contact with the grace of womanhood, I should feel tempted by glimpses of man's first beginning to strengthen a theory of truth that can perhaps scarcely prove itself to demonstration except at his final end. "Marriage of itself", says St. Thomas of Aquin, reviewing man's condition before the Fall, "would have been then more honourable than virginity, since in that condition the integrity of the mind would have lost nothing." * Thus, as a profound theologian of our own time may be found arguing, had there been no Incarnation to bring God before our eyes, marriage would have been "the normal condition under which man would learn to love God".† Of that primeval condition, it can hardly be presumptuous to suppose that synteresis has preserved more than the trace in human nature; for,

---

* Lib. Sent. II: Dist. 20: Art. 3: Expos. "Sed potuerunt in paradiso eis esse nuptiae honorabiles; quia in statu illo nuptiae simpliciter virginitate honorabiliores fuissent, eo quod in nullo integritate mentis laesa fecunditas carnis in matrimonio, sterilitati virginitas praevaluisset."

† E. Mersch, S.J., "Love, Marriage and Chastity", p. 59, note.

the 'affirmative way' of the mystic who is a humanist besides seems to require no less. Substitutes there can be, but in a lay mind substitutes they remain. Montaigne, the consummate humanist, has told of a love for Étienne de la Boétie such as that of David for Jonathan—a love assuredly in his case passing all love for women, and colouring, by his own confession, the whole content of his mind. And in Pascal's diviner reflections there can be found an epistemology issuing in mystic ecstasy at its psychic climax.

I am directly concerned here, however, with Allegra. It was, I feel sure, no wayward fancy that brought the letters of the Brownings so often into her hands. In those lovers—in Robert Browning and Elizabeth Barrett—she had early discovered spirits compatriot with her own, spirits who had shared her love for Italy and her joy in song, who had known, as well in power as in word, how to make their life a poem, and who had none the less moved freely and fruitfully within the lines of married love. For, whilst it would have been unlike her, and indeed impossible for her, not to recognise all the misery that can come of an unhappy marriage, her eye for its beauty did not turn dull, so that, maybe, she would have consented to an opinion that I once heard advanced by Sir James Barrie, with her in his mind as he spoke, to the effect that marriage was too wonderful a thing ever to have been conceived by man.

If I pause for a moment at this point, it is because in no other connection can I hope to illustrate better how, without a suspicion of dogmatism, she would show me that the human, or at least the humane soul, is naturally Christian. As fully alive as Dante himself to the power of the theme of Paolo and Francesca, and perhaps even readier to recognise its compelling pathos, she moved herself to a different music. Poise rather than precept gave loyalty to her love; and she took her way here as through other problems of life, not like a theologian quoting his book, nor like a philosopher picking a middle path between precipices on either hand, but like a dancer who retains perfect balance on the very tiptoe of achievement. With her, indeed, it was 'solvitur saltando'. She could have touched the sublime with her finger or have caught a falling star in her hand, even whilst she rolled forward the ball of the ridiculous with her lovely feet. In her own way she had made herself mistress of the maxim 'semper agens, semper quieta'.

Such reflections are, however, rather in the nature of a digression designed to show a characteristic curve in the sweep of Allegra's humanism. The main argument, as the reader has doubtless perceived, takes a straighter course; and upon its ancient causeway the very stones cry out that no theory of knowledge can become truly organic which does not take full account of such feelings as the beating of heart upon heart * is able to afford. The desire of wisdom demands no pulse less quickened; the enigma of life yields to no ecstasy less strong.

Some man will doubtless protest at this juncture that I am cheating. Life, he will say, is no game, that you should be able thus to pass judgment upon it by loading dice with emotion. I answer, as the Schoolmen would say, that the so-called adventure of life has indeed much the look of a game, yet that I take it to be rather a game of skill than of chance. I answer that I have not put an illicit weight into a die, but rather a just bias upon a bowl. I answer that no bowl will run true, even upon the smoothest greensward, without its own interior incline. But, if the critic must have it that we are in a law-court, and not upon a bowling-green, and that life, with all its content of good and evil, is upon its trial, then I answer that, just as in judicial proceedings it is necessary to suppose men to be free agents and responsible for their acts, even though there are scientists and statisticians who regard necessity as a law and take liberty for an illusion, so in any criticism of life a presumption has to be made that the finest of all human emotions in its purest essence informs the eye and is accorded its proper place in the work of judgment. Love is no less essential and inevitable a presupposition in the assize of human life than free will in a court of law. If there is one thing clear, it is that such creatures as ourselves, except under the influence of the sort of ascetic scepticism which by its very failure to come to a decision condemns itself as incompletely vital, can never think without some kind of at least suppressed emotion. Not without curiosity did I notice how quavering and uncertain the Alien Voice in the House was apt to become whenever this topic was touched upon. It had loved, it would whisper, but had never been loved in return; and so would die slowly away, like an old man's muttering.

Something more, however, was needed than such pathetic confessions, significant as they might be in their way, to show that a theory of knowledge, restricted to experience, tested by repeated observation and checked by numerical computation, fell short by

* The thought here, in so far as it stretches beyond platitude, is owed to Tennyson's "Romney's Remorse".

a great deal of what was required in a comprehensive criticism
of life. This might not, indeed, be in dispute among the most
thoughtful critics; yet to the common reader it sometimes seemed
so. On the same page, for instance, on which T. H. Huxley
observed that he had 'never given the slightest ground for the
attribution to him of the ridiculous contention that there is nothing
true outside the bounds of physical science', he had declared his conviction that 'the logical methods of physical science were of universal applicability' and constituted the sole method of arriving at
intellectual truth, whether the subject-matter of investigation belonged to the world of physics or of consciousness.* It was no more,
not to say rather less, obvious that the postulates of physical science
were appropriate to the world of ethics and aesthetics than that
Euclidean postulates and axioms were applicable to the universe
as conceived by Einstein. It was less obvious still to suppose with
Huxley that "physical science may and probably will, some day,
enable our posterity to set forth the exact concomitants and conditions of the strange rapture of beauty".† Wherever the metropolis
of love and beauty lay—and, to judge from the common conversation
of mankind, all roads might be supposed to be converging on it at
least as certainly as all roads to be leading to Rome—no compasses,
to my eye at any rate, seemed to promise less assistance than the
syllogisms of logic, the propositions of Euclid or the methods of
scientific induction. The rose-red city of Eros, old as homo sapiens,
if not so old as man, lay, in the midst of the map of life, in-
accessible as a mirage; for one might as well try to locate it precisely by ratiocination as the baffled scientist with his working
hypotheses to correlate the position and velocity of a particle. But the
man of the world no less than the mystic, the mathematician no less
than the artist, had generally caught a glimpse of it, or stumbled on
it in day-dreams, or at the worst been confronted with so trustworthy a report of its existence as to render scepticism absurd.
And thus the heart of man had the power to make every theory of
knowledge which left it out of account appear pedantically foolish.
In his autobiographical record of his early years Mr. Churchill ‡ has
recalled the deep impression made upon him by the discovery among
Bartlett's Familiar Quotations of 'a French saying' to the effect
that the heart has its reasons of which the reason is unaware, and

* T. H. Huxley, "Collected Essays—Evolution and Ethics", p. 126.
† *Ibid.*, p. 123.   ‡ "My Early Life", p. 130.

has added that he found there a convenient apology for resorting to prayer in hours of peril, whilst apparently resuming those rational processes with which he had become familiar in the pages of Gibbon, Lecky and Winwood Reade during his hours of ease. Pascal might have been astonished to find so departmental (or, should we say, ministerial?) a use made of a once profound observation.* But the misuse of the phrase is useful nevertheless; for nothing better illustrates the quaint shifts to which an extremely powerful modern mind is bound to come for lack of a theory of knowledge adequate to the facts of life. This only in passing.

Looking in more scientific quarters for some further reflections on this vital point, I came across some words in the preface to Tyndall's much-abused Belfast Lecture to the British Association in 1874 that gave me pause. Here were to be read the admissions of an intellectual ascetic, requiring of the things of life just that rigid kind of proof which physical science is often seen endeavouring to impose in matters patently impatient of it.

"In connection with the charge of Atheism", Tyndall had observed, "I would make one remark. Christian men are proved by their writings to have their hours of weakness and of doubt, as well as their hours of strength and of conviction; and men like myself share in their own way these varieties of mood and tense. Were the religious views of many of my assailants the only alternative ones, I do not know how strong the claims of the doctrine of 'material atheism' upon my allegiance might be. Probably they would be very strong. But, as it is, I have noticed during years of self-observation that it is not in hours of clearness or vigour that this doctrine commends itself to my mind, that in the presence of stronger and healthier thought it ever dissolves and disappears as offering no solution of the mystery in which we dwell and of which we form a part."

"Stronger and healthier thought"! By what title except his own emotional reactions does any man lay claim to that? What is here,

* Cp. Bremond, "Hist. Litt. du Sent. Rel. en France", I, p. 521, ". . . cette géographie spirituelle . . . distingue dans l'âme trois sortes de zones: la zone des sens; celle de la raison raisonnante, celle enfin où Dieu réside et se fait 'sentir' à nous. C'est 'le coeur' des pensées de Pascal, c'est la fine pointe dont les mystiques partent constamment et où ils placent le théâtre de leurs sublimes expériences. C'est aussi le pays des muses, de toutes les muses; le lieu des inspirations; la patrie des humanistes."

then, but a man's heart-whole assurance that all, in spite of all, is yet right with the world—an assurance perhaps as truly the prize of mature life as such a favourite catch as that in Pippa's passing song ("God's in his heaven—all's right with the world!") is the prize of a pure heart in the morning of life and the spring of the year? What is here but a wind rising as it lists; an inspiration of which we can confidently declare that its breath is sweet and wholesome; a sense of spiritual sanity that comes and goes and comes again in its own time and season, according to the measure of our capacity? When it tarries we can but pray for it to return, and when it is there we can but embrace it. To it we owe those finer varieties of mood and tense that Tyndall speaks of—moods and tenses conditioning the discoveries of science and the researches of history no less than the graces of art. In some such mood, perhaps, had Archimedes cried 'Eureka'. In some such aorist indicative of heart and mind had Newton, looking back upon his life and contrasting what the world made of him with what he had made of the world, seen himself as an eternal boy playing upon the ocean-shore of truth and picking out here a pebble smoother and there a shell prettier than the rest. In some such historic present of the soul had Gibbon sat, rapt in creative wonder, upon the Capitol and, as the Franciscan Friars sang Vespers in the Church of the Ara Coeli, beheld old Rome crack to decay and crash to ruin, until his mood was changed to high inspiration and, when he set himself to write, the genius of his style echoed the tramp of legions, and the thing he wrought sprang to life like Galatea under Pygmalion's hand and took such hold upon his heart that the consummation of it seemed to him like the parting with an old and valued friend. After some such manner do men philosophise with love. In such great heart, perchance, did Virgil dream his dream of some heavenly child enthroned as lord of the world and see his vision of a golden age returning. In such an ecstasy, for sure, did Dante learn from Beatrice that he must become a citizen of that Rome of which Christ had deigned to receive the freedom.*

So, perhaps, after life's silver cord has been loosed and its golden bowl been broken, may a man, during some strong aorist imperative of the soul, aspire to find the future in the historic past, the evidence of what is yet to come in the recollection of that which once has been. So may the spirit burn with that 'gem-like flame' commended

* "Purg.", XXXII, 103.

by the critic as if it were itself success in life; so may we grow sufficient to see things, as another critic of life would have us do, both steadily and whole; so may the reason develop that so-called 'illative sense' wherein Newman perceived both the seat of certitude and the glass of form. So may the logic of life be seen to be no less of an art than of a science. So, since we can never hope to have all the facts of the universe before us (and there is little reason enough to suppose that, did we have them, such intellects as ours could do them justice), may we grow content to recognise that to wait upon full knowledge is to commit ourselves to lasting hesitation more truly than to honest thought, and indeed, if all the truth be told, to risk resembling none so much as Horace's immortal bumpkin, of whom it was said "Rusticus expectat dum defluat amnis". The Augustan urbanity of one-half Rome had known better than to gape when greatness beckoned, but it was the Augustinian urbanity of the other-half Rome which had shown the finer intuition and out of the metropolis of mankind made an Eternal City—a City of God.

It fell into line with what has just been said that, as T. H. Huxley has somewhere noted (and Professor Whitehead has more recently said something to the same purpose *), the Italian mind had deserved to be regarded as the finest intellectual instrument that the world contains. I am not thinking, of course, of that over-praised Italy of the Risorgimento which has illustrated under our eyes and to our inconvenience the pathetic fallacy of the Liberal-Nationalists, but of the earlier Italy of the Middle Age and the Renaissance, which in its spring-tide covered all the orchards of knowledge with the fairest blossom and in its autumn glory with the choicest fruit. Only a rare sensibility to what the verdict of the world, as ratified by the judgment of its finest minds, must ultimately be, could have raised and gathered such produce; and, whatever mistakes were made in the handling of the merchandise, the Italian achievement remained an unparalleled feat of intellect. Some underlying sense of values seemed to have preserved, beneath all the turbulence characteristic of the Italian States and beside all the turmoil of the Reformation, a rare tranquillity of spirit enabling thought, art and

* A. N. Whitehead, "Science and the Modern World", p. 50. Submitting a list of names to prove his contention that the seventeenth century alone "consistently and throughout the whole range of human activities, provided intellectual genius adequate for the greatness of its occasions", Prof. Whitehead adds, "There is only one Italian there, whereas Italy could have filled the list from its own ranks".

even discovery (if the exceptions of Galileo and Bruno may be allowed to prove the rule) to move without haste or rest along a path where the lilies of Florence for long showed no languor and the roses of Rome, despite scandals both ecclesiastical and secular, retained a rapture so real as to draw, even in the late nineteenth century and even from so detached a critic as Henry Adams, the remark that "Rome before 1870 was seductive beyond resistance".* No conflict of faith had disgraced a city in the last resort at one with itself. Of no country in the world, once possessed of great military power, could it be more fairly affirmed than of Italy that its swords had become tools of science and its spears been turned into instruments of music in the widest meaning. No country, therefore, appeared to have been better qualified to act as the custodian of a humane civilisation; and it was there precisely that one might expect to see developed the clear-cut thought and considered judgment so necessary to the presentation of the Christian religion to the critical intelligence of mankind. For, as Wordsworth reminds us in "Laodamia", "the gods approve the depth and not the tumult of the soul".

The peaks and vales of high Olympus lie, however, beyond the proper venture of this book. Here is but a little genre-painting or chamber-music designed, if it prove fortunate, to enable a man reminiscent by the fireside to recover, as from some sunset-touch falling upon a picture on the wall, the recollection of high altitudes, or through the striking of some chord upon harp or viol the echo of songs no longer heard.

In Plato's "Phaedrus", more obviously perhaps than in his other writings, the function of reminiscence in winging the soul to the top of the world, bringing it within sight of the divine things, and thus making it in some sort a spectator of all time and all existence, is brought into the closest connection with the ecstasy of love. It is true enough that in the allusion to παιδεραστία there may be detected a bad taste no less damaging to the admired Greek genius than is the suggestion of a community of wives which disfigures Plato's fair image of an ideal republic. Yet, for all that, the comparison of the soul, as it reaches out to embrace the science of life, to a lover's enthusiasm for his beloved remains the classical Hellenic expression of the fact that the heart must overtake, and even outstrip, the senses if a man is to come even within a pagan's prospect of that

* "Education of Henry Adams", p. 89.

lovely light—'luce intellettual piena d'amore' *—which, as Dante was presently to explain, plays about the abode of truth. A lover born, and created a pilgrim of eternity, Man, if he is not to lose the path of knowledge, had, at least as Plato saw him, but little option except to go upon his way singing hymns to intellectual beauty. For the love of beauty in the Platonic philosophy shone with so soft a brilliance that the mind, wherein wisdom and other lovely realities might have aroused too violent emotion, could suffer it and the ecstasy that it induced.†

As may be noticed in passing, a philosophy of pure sensation, from which Aristotle (everywhere, as Professor Taylor observes, 'a Platonist malgré lui' and owing to 'the Platonic element in his thought . . . its hold over man's minds') only saved himself by pointing out that induction merely fixes our attention upon principles beyond its power to demonstrate,‡ necessarily loses some degree of philosophic consideration at this crisis of thought about life. Reviewed as an enumeration of particulars, sensation could supply, and perhaps must be present to supply, a stimulus to reflection: but no real perception of universals dividing off, as in the scholastic philosophy, a 'concept' from a 'common phantasm' could be reasonably expected to arise in a soul impotent to share its sublime sense of intellectual beauty with other intellects or intelligences, and thus, not merely confirm its rational conviction of an exterior world of thought, but blend its inmost being—its joie de vivre and deathless love—with the smiling of women and the tears of things without. Something at least in the nature of such ecstatic power was needed if, as Socrates remarks in the "Phaedrus", he who came to the doors of the Muses with the assurance of his poetic gift were not to go away empty.§ It was of a piece with this that, as the sage continues, the merely clever, as opposed to the truly wise, never recognised the virtue of what he terms a divine madness nor tasted the supreme happiness that it had in its power to bestow.§

---

* "Parad.", XXX, 40.   † "Phaedrus", Sec. 31.

‡ "Aristotle is always anxious to insist on the difference between his own doctrines and those of Plato, and his bias in this direction regularly leads him to speak as though he held a thoroughgoing naturalistic and empirical theory with no 'transcendental moonshine' about it. Yet his final conclusions on all points are hardly distinguishable from those of Plato, except by the fact that, as they are so much at variance with the naturalistic side of his philosophy, they have the appearance of being sudden lapses into an alogical mysticism" (A. E. Taylor, "Aristotle", p. 27).   § "Phaedrus", Sec. 22.

If so much were admitted, it was not to be wondered at that the Platonic philosophy, with its great cry for beauty in the soul, its great bid for companionship, either human or divine, its longing for some word of life, should have been couched, unlike its Aristotelic, Cartesian or Kantian competitors, in a form of marked informality—in dialogue undefiled. It lay so far removed from solitary speculation as to appear as alien from a philosophy of pure sensation as from any that rashly claimed the name of pure reason. It seemed to flee the schools almost as eagerly as it fled the study. Intimate, persuasive, even domestic in its technique, it appeared at every turn to invite, and even to demand, the conversation of friends, the companionship of souls, or, at the last and loftiest level, a communion with God. Its dialectic was, in fact, par excellence dialogue; the wheels of its earthly chariot were poetry and parable; and when it flew heavenwards its wings were the wings of love. So, perhaps, one might find again its peculiarity of operation in the convivial discourses of Rabelais, in the abiding influence of Étienne de la Boétie upon Michel de Montaigne, even in the association of Pascal with the little community at Port-Royal, which has still, despite all extravagance and error, a fascination for every company of Christians aspiring to become, in deed and in truth, a society of the perfect. And the more discerning of educationalists have not failed to feel the force of this gracious way of pursuing reality. "Monsieur," said his examiners at the Sorbonne to Pierre Rousselot, potential Thomist though he was, "nous vous félicitons d'avoir compris qu'un examen est une conversation".†

Between the poetry and truth of Plato's dialogues and the grace and glory of the fourth Gospel there is a wide valley to be spanned. Yet still one might be pardoned at moments for underestimating the distance from the one peak to the other of that mountain-chain, so similar seem the charm of the vegetation, the intoxication of the air and the wide sublimity of the scene to the mounting soul, when, as it first battles its way through storm to sunshine, it pauses, poised aloft, to watch the solvent hues of beauty, truth and love arching the vault of heaven and then, still subtly commingled, fading as they fall to earth in rainbow-ends. St. John the Divine excepted, no other eagle had winged its way from height to height across that chasm in a straighter course than St. Augustine; and a man might well be thought to have missed the greatest sight in all the history of

* "Phaedrus", Sec. 24.
† Rousselot, "Intellectualisme de S. Thomas", p. vi.

Platonic or Patristic thought who had not watched him spread his wings for flight and marked the great metaphysical strength that lurked behind his plumage.

"Too late have I known Thee, O Ancient Truth", so runs the famous passage, "Too late have I loved Thee, O Beauty ever ancient and ever new! And behold Thou wast within and I was abroad, and there I sought Thee, and, deformed as I was, ran after those beauties which Thou hast made. . . . Thou wast with me, and I was not with Thee; those things kept me far from Thee which could have no being but in Thee. . . . Thou hast sent forth Thy fragrance and I have drawn my breath and pant after Thee. . . . O Love which always burnest and art never extinguished, true Charity, my God, set me all on fire."

It was all there—what I have been trying to speak of—the passion for Truth in its old original; the light of Beauty suffusing all the marvel of identity and change; the enkindling lambent flame of Love. Augustine had seized it and, holding it, as it were, between his talons, had torn its secrets from it and, with a piercing cri du coeur, sent the strange knowledge of his prize and prey echoing down the valley of time and over the hills of eternity.

The technique of this communion of friends—of man with man, and then of man with the Incarnate God—plainly transcended all powers of sense and made some special demand upon interior vision. In the delicate vignette of the Risen Christ and the Magdalen, to be found in an Evangel illuminated in all its margins by interlacing legends of the vine and the branches, the 'Noli me tangere' scene has long illustrated for minds with mystical dispositions the authoritative call of love, at a certain milestone on the mystic way, to exchange the vehicle of sensuous apprehension for one to which, falling somewhat short as it must do of perfect intuition, the name of 'contuition' has been applied. The final act of a mortal's mysticism, after it has (so to speak) borrowed the eyes of the Blessed Virgin to adore Christ, is, according to the French school of Bérulle,* so to lose itself in communion with the Incarnate Deity as at last, contuitionally, to see God.

This latter end of the road in a theory of knowledge which I have here dared to name organic epistemology was assuredly not plain to me, even if visible at all, on the day that I accompanied

* See Bremond, "Hist. Litt. du Sent. Relig. en France", III, c. i, ii.

Allegra into the House where that theory was to gain point and precision. If, then, I have indicated here whither the road was leading, it is rather in the hope that a glimpse of the goal may facilitate a little the pursuit, through the labyrinth of thought and time, of a thread not the more easy to pursue that it was spun of the finest silk and tinted to the colour of pale gold. For the knowledge of truth with Plato, as with One greater than Plato, is inextricably entangled with the ideas of a way and of a life. "In spite of the demand he makes for certainty and exactness and what is absolute in all real knowledge", observes Walter Pater, "Plato does think, or inclines his reader to think, that truth, precisely because it resembles some high kind of relationship of persons to persons, depends a good deal on the receiver; and must be, in that degree, elusive, provisional, contingent, a matter of various approximation. . . . 'Socrates in Plato', remarks Montaigne acutely, 'disputes, rather to the profit of the disputants, than of the dispute' ".*

In this delicately balanced judgment may perhaps be found a bridge both light and strong across all the waters of time that have flowed between the appearance of the Platonic Dialogues and the Essays of Montaigne. That last-named superb practitioner of the art of essay-writing reproduced, indeed, much of the express virtue of dialogue; the semblance of self-communion overheard by the world being, as we may suspect, in reality rather the continuance of a conversation with a dead friend whose sweet influences had so pervaded his own soul that the withdrawal of them had deprived him, as he felt, of no less than the half of his life. Montaigne has some place in what follows later; and I hope that his entry into a house of lights and shadows may in due course justify itself in the eyes of the reader. Coming as he did of that renascent humanism which enabled the Latin races to escape, to a greater or less degree, the reactions from Catholic Christianity towards the Mosaic Dispensation of the Calvinist and the Puritan, he exemplified anew in his dissertations and disquisitions the persuasive candour of Socrates, and, though men have chosen to accuse him, as the Greeks accused Socrates, of religious scepticism, his approach to the problems of life had to my judgment the half-formed virtue of a Christian no less than the engaging charm of a Humanist liberating his soul in the hearing of a friend. It is possible that this technique of Montaigne's will never be surpassed in the presentation of human life and its con-

* "Plato and Platonism", p. 187.

ditions to those sensible men who never reveal, yet sometimes betray, their religion. But, however that might be, it seemed certain that, whilst doubtless there would always be philosophers who preferred to assert "Alone I did it", a finished theory of knowledge both human and divine, must normally be procreated and presently conceived by the intercourse of two souls, and would discover its dual parentage in its face, even though it might seem to bear more resemblance to one parent than the other in its salient features. And if, as Lucretius supposed, Venus had greater influence upon the nature of things than Mars; if, as Dante declared, Love moved the sun and the other stars besides; if, as Goethe concluded, the eternal-feminine pointed the way to higher things; then only a theory of knowledge that did full justice to such overpowering realities could be rightly based.

It followed that solipsism was as implicitly excluded from a sound metaphysic as egotism from a healthy ethic; and I could easily suppose that the last tenants of the House in Bryanston Square came there with a common soul so unconsciously permeated by this quasi-sacramental truth that intellectual monism must have been no less latently repugnant to them than philosophic idealism patently appeared to be. For they were perhaps in less danger than many people of supposing that the House, with its inherited attributes, could become any mere projection of their common mind. It had evidently been there long before they came upon the scene; and it promised to remain there a good while after they were gone. It was a real thing, already formed to beauty, and so heavily weighted with tradition as even to possess something akin to a personality of its own. Of this they were as fully assured as that they brought to it thoughts aglow with desire to cast some new spell upon its 'period' grace and make of it an enchanted castle. Children of the Renaissance, both of them in different degrees, they drew from their antecedents and carried in their souls the architectural impulse of that age to transfer to the dwelling-house something of the tranquillity of architectural order, which up to that time had been almost exclusively the property of Church and Abbey. And, if they knew little or nothing of scholastic philosophy, they possessed something at least of that confident cheerfulness of the Schoolmen to which the Merrie England of Chaucer's Tales pays tribute, though in Allegra it tended to dwell upon the glad benefit of this life, and in her companion rather perhaps upon the fair prospect of another.

These, then, were the dispositions in which the newcomers met upon its threshold the prior dispositions of the House. With its wide windows, its domed skylight and lightsome graceful stair, its quiet elegance and good proportion, it might have seemed to argue forcibly for the power of form to subdue crude matter to its purpose. The idea of a modest London house had rarely, as it seemed to me, received better aesthetic expression than at the date already indicated. Design was everywhere apparent, and spoke, though without silly sentiment, of what has become celebrated under the denomination of 'England, Home and Beauty'. Others had laboured, well and wisely enough, under such influences to make the House what it was; and its new inhabitants entered into their labours. To work wildly, as reformers so commonly do, would obviously have been desecration. These transformers had the sense to see that, before they could hope to make any particular contribution themselves, they must grasp the concept of the House and understand what it stood for. Even this knowledge was not enough. Aristotle, since I have been dabbling in philosophy, it might pertinently be observed, had been called magister scientiae, but it was to Plato that the title of magister sapientiae had been reserved. Wisdom is greater than knowledge; and between knowledge and wisdom lies understanding. The change that Allegra sought to bring about in the House was thus precisely "the revolutionism of one who had slept a hundred years". There are sermons in brick and plaster as eloquent as those in stones.

Chapter IV

ON THE DOORSTEP

THE House, as I have said, looked east and west, and at sunrise, and again towards sunset, was swept by light both physical and metaphysical. But the devil who walks in the noon-day would sometimes get his foot into it at the meridian hour and beckon me towards the window and bid me consider the world without; and the same or another devil would now and again in like manner tempt me out upon the doorstep, which faced east, or even, in the cool of the day, into the Square, and would set me eavesdropping with the ears that understand, even if they do not precisely hear. At such times Allegra's voice would grow fainter and that other voice which was not hers become more insistent and challenging.

"One can make a pattern, as I told you, for oneself," it would say, "and I dare say you did so with such a woman as Allegra to help you; but now take a look down the Square and give me an honest account of what you have seen there. Just look at the medley of people, both young and old, who drift or hurry along the pavement with their dull, dismal or dissatisfied faces, some tripping along to St. James's, where things are still as fine and fair as money can make them, and others tramping off to Mile End and Whitechapel, where the funerals have long been the costliest sights to be seen. The 'two nations', you see, are always there—the rich and the poor, not to speak of the young and the old—agreed upon nothing for the most part except that life is ultimately dull and would become intolerable but for its pleasures and the money to get them. Their designs, as is natural, are a mere patchwork of cross purposes, full of swearing colours and eccentric forms. Look closer if you doubt me!

"There, for instance, goes a body, with what you are pleased to call a soul inside it, possessed of the by no means negligible significance that a vie-de-bohême can provide. I take it to be bound for Soho and the company of such substitutes for Villon and Verlaine as London produces. In its paradise of 'sharps' and 'mugs' there is good food to be found for the films, and other good food, too, of a more succulent type, and wine that can be had cheap, and women that have something in common with the wine. Out of these things

52

one can make a life, or, if you prefer to call it so, an existence that is easier written up and read about than the lives of the saints, even though its wealth of gaudy attraction and damaged goods is comparable only to the charms of a bargain basement. And, if you are so rash as to remind me that it takes all sorts to make a world, I shall observe that you merely prove my point. For the most popular shrines in Bohemia are dedicated to Autolycus and Doll Tearsheet; and, if death would only keep away, our friend over there, though bored eventually to tears, would probably continue, for lack of more congenial occupation, to frequent them to all eternity. In other words, the quota required of his part of the town in order to make our world artistically complete is an army of rogues and prostitutes; and the reputed character and general interest of the locality are incompatible with any humane conception of men or women.

"Did you ever happen to read a much-admired story of Mr. Somerset Maugham's called "Rain", which records the seduction of a pious missionary by an unprepossessing harlot! It illustrates as well as anything I have ever read the range and depth of the human enigma. It stresses, with a strength of line and fulness of colour nothing less than ruthless, the force of a particular relationship between man and woman which Art will no more willingly forgo than Nature. It depicts, in common with much recent literature, that force, not as an incident in human frailty, but as an element in human life. It brings us back, as D. H. Lawrence brings us back, to solid earth—to the soil from which we sprang. I go further. I say that all similar matter has a good title to appear, not as a blot upon man's 'scutcheon, but as a quartering upon his shield. I claim that its ready submission to artistic treatment discovers its independence of ethic. An artist is instantly aware that his work would be the poorer for its absence. Sex is central in his philosophy; and he is instinctively and wisely indifferent to all attempts at sexual restriction. He has taken all experience for his province, and he passes no judgment upon its content. What more do I need to say to show you that in any true criticism of life patterns must be of private manufacture and are impatient of public design? Doubtless the world prefers to wink at what I am stressing; but you will refuse to allow yourself to be humbugged by Mrs. Grundy. I have always admired the candour of those mediaeval prelates who, so they say, licensed brothels in the City of Winchester and in London on the Surrey side of the Thames. They looked at things as they really were; and on the Continent the police authorities at the present day are no less amenable to the force of facts. English Protestantism, after the Puritans had exhausted the efficacy of the Rod and the Scarlet Letter, has preferred to walk in blinkers. Bohemia, however, continues to be justified of all her gipsy tribe of children; and modern art would gladly lose its life to save them, if they stood in any danger of destruction. Why stick to sober pencil studies in black and white when the world is a riot of colour predominantly red from a Cardinal's scarlet shoes up to Bardolph's nose or the flaming cheeks of Moll Flanders? The nature of things is evidently 'a-moral'."

"A bastard word", I would retort, "not ill suited to introduce illegitimate thoughts! In fact, you artists appear to share and not to escape the parsons' dilemma. Aesthetically the eye must desire bodies modelled upon those of Venus and Adonis, just as morally the conscience should desiderate souls like-minded with St. Francis and St. Clare, or, if you prefer, with St. Francis de Sales and 'Sainte Chantal'. What a world of mystery, then, is here, when even a glance down the street can bring sharply into view the problem of the one and the many—of the perfect type and some highly questionable variety!"

A little vexed and not a little bewildered by this colloquy, I would let my eyes wander on to find relief, if they could, by abandoning Soho for Bloomsbury. And forthwith I would see, or think that I saw, Bloomsbury incarnate advancing from the end of the Square—Bloomsbury for all the world as if it had just been epitomised in a fashion-plate with the face of Lytton Strachey at the summit of the costume. Had rational dress, I would ask myself, ever displayed fuller freedom from old conventions or recommended more assiduously the advent of the wholly nude? Here was surely one at length who feared neither God nor man nor Mrs. Grundy. Tell it not in Chelsea, lest Carlyle should turn in his grave; whisper it not in Westminster, where they still affect to praise famous men; but our little brother has no heroes, and would valet all men of renown for the mere pleasure of seeing them naked! Nay, he would in his zeal even drag corpses from their coffins and skeletons from their cupboards and tell you what manner of men these relics of mortality had contained from the leer left upon their skulls. "Such", he would say in the manner of Aristotle, "was the magnificent man", and then add in an aside, "when you really knew him".

Thus, then, the Bloomsbury-Man; and the Alien Voice at my elbow would not allow me to forget that few districts of London had produced more eminent Georgians. "See", the Voice would whisper, "how much the thesis that life has no pattern is strengthened by contact with this kind of genius. The lance of Cervantes, the rapier of Voltaire, the stiletto of Beaumarchais have not served me so well as the pins and needles of Bloomsbury. Their pricks and prods pierce the harness of philanthropists and schoolmasters as readily as the robes of cardinals or queens, and, striking now above and now below the girdle, they have achieved by manifold incisions the results of a single mortal blow. Mischievous as Ariel, mocking as Molière, masked like the Red Death itself, the spirit of Bloomsbury has shattered the structure and spent the heritage of the Victorians with hardly more than a sneer. Why, this very embodiment of it that comes wandering down the Square is capable of a metamorphosis as striking as if the figure of Lytton Strachey were suddenly to dissolve into that of Julian Bell. The pacifist can turn warrior, the agnostic go atheist, the democrat become patrician, whilst, as they say, you wait. Every idea may be put into reverse, if one only knows the way how."

The Bloomsbury-Man would come right past my door as these random fancies crossed my troubled mind. I could hear him assuring his companion that Labour was no more than Bottom with an Ass's head on it, and that all the poetry of toil and pathos of the under-dog was no truer than Titania's fond imaginations under the compulsion of Puck's philtre. Nay, he said worse than that. "Hardly any Europeans have ever been civilised," he declared, "and the Greeks least of all." * In vain, it appeared, had the frieze of the Parthenon been transported to the precincts of Bloomsbury. The Silver Age had passed, and we were come to the age of quicksilver, when the words of Mercury sounded harsher than ever after the songs of Apollo. So at least it seemed to me as the Bloomsbury-Man sauntered on, and I might have been altogether lost in the region-cloud hanging over that district, if at this juncture a Lombard-Street-Man had not appeared to recall my mind to earth and to remind me that our times had likewise contained one who had been well named 'Lord Copper'.† "Behold", cried the Voice beside me, "our modern Magus, our worldly-wise man from the West, whose wealth nobler

---

* Julian Bell, "Essays, &c.", p. 239.
† By Evelyn Waugh in one of his novels.

souls despise, desire, and in due course despoil him of—to distribute it, no doubt, with as great a show of bounty as if they had made it themselves."

Entering the Square, as great men should, with elephantine paces, Dives was greeted with what, if a rhyme were required, might perhaps be described as fawning graces. One of those little vulgar boys who in the days of Mr. Ingoldsby were to be found at Margate in July, advanced to do him honour.

"Sir," he says, "I ain't 'ad nothin' to eat to-day."

"I wish I hadn't," remarks the man of aldermanic mind, with stentorian laughter and, with that, pulls out a sixpence. "Very reprehensible of me!" I hear him observe to Young London of the London School of Economics at his side. "Very reprehensible indeed! I don't know what the Charity Organisation Society wouldn't say. I believe they'd swear at me—so to speak, I mean. There was one of their people," he concludes for the edification of his offspring, "who was heard muttering on his deathbed, 'Thank God, I have never given a penny in the street'."

"But why shouldn't he have given it?" remarks Young London. "The other fellows probably needed it a lot more than he did himself."

"That's the mistake so many of you young men make," rejoins Dives. "I thought like that at your age, but I hadn't thought far."

"I don't get your meaning," protests Young London.

"Self-help, young man," says Dives; "that's my meaning. Your grandfather helped himself, and I've helped myself, and I trust you will help yourself. Now, all the help I've given to that youngster who's run off with my sixpence is to send him downhill quicker than he would go otherwise. And that's only an example, mind you, of what the Modern State is doing and, according to the politicians and the schoolmasters, ought to do. Boys and girls are growing up in the belief that it's the business of the State to house them, and feed them, and clothe them, and educate them, and amuse them, and find them the jobs they fancy. And you young fellows, even when you have been sent to the best schools, don't seem to know much better. You're spoiling the race in my belief, killing its pride, ruining its initiative, playing on its sentiment."

"Nineteenth-century England talked itself hoarse on those lines," rejoins Young London, "but what came of it? When our century opened, a prime minister asserted that there were a million people on the edge of starvation."

"I dare say," returns Dives rather testily, "and to-day a prime minister might tell you that for at least a decade we shall have two million unemployable living upon their fellow-citizens. What solution of the problem, I should like to know, have your friends produced? Whereas we tried to make all surplus wealth flow into wages, they want to rush it into doles. That's the basic difference between us. And, I ask you, is a man the better for living like a parasite when he might be providing the community with goods or services, however modest, and so adding something to the snowball of productivity? Don't you see that you can't raise a dole without reducing a wage and that, when you give old women pensions, as likely as not you throw young men out of work? Leave money, as Gladstone used so rightly to say, to fructify in the pockets of the people—of all the people, rich and poor—and you will get much better results than by depriving them of it. There are more parasites now, more people battening on the work and wealth of others, than ever there were when the old Liberal ideas were in vogue. Why, even 'unproductive' labour, as the classical economists used to call it, is a deal better for men's souls than no labour at all! Your solution of the problem, as I keep telling you, is no solution whatever. Besides, it's been tried and found wanting again and again. Did you ever hear of the so-called 'Speenhamland Act of Parliament'? I thought not. They don't say too much about that, I'll be bound, at the London School of Economics; nor about the ateliers nationaux of 1848. You boys persist in talking without knowledge."

The old gentleman had waxed so eloquent as he developed his discourse, and was tapping so violently upon the pavement outside my door as he concluded it, that I feared Young London might grow excited also. He never lost, however, even for a moment his supercilious smile.

"There's nothing to be learnt from the past, father," he said, "nothing at all. Stephen Blackpool in 'Hard Times' said the only thing worth saying about the old economy when he observed that it was all a muddle. We've got to change the system. That's what your generation can't understand. Capitalism must go. Everything in future must be collective, co-operative, planned. And the scheme of reconstruction has already been thought out in every detail by men like Webb and Cole and Laski, and is working already with great success in Russia. It's a new civilisation and the beginning of a new era of enlightenment."

"Very well, young man," replies the old boy, "you can have

your Marx, and I will keep my Spencer; and I'll undertake not to prove the loser in the bargain. It will save me your allowance to begin with, for I conclude that you can rely upon Marx and his friends to make up for any deficiencies on my side. Your stream of cocktails, your cartloads of tobacco, your nightly cinemas, your choice little supper-parties after the theatre, and the other requirements of yourself and your best girl whilst you are putting the world to rights—all these, I take it, Mr. Marx's emporium will be able to provide at less cost than Mr. Spencer's."

"But you don't understand, father," cries the young man, his superior smile suddenly working off, "that our new civilisation can only come by degrees. We shall have for the present to work upon capitalistic lines, even though they are the wrong lines."

"Oh! I see," says Dives. "Socialism after your time—that's what you want, is it? But I see no reason why you, at least, should not have it during your time. If you can't get it here and now, you have means enough to settle in Russia, where, from what you have just told me, the change to a better state of things is already accomplished."

I strained my ears to catch what Young Hopeful replied to that; but Dives was waddling away as he spoke, and his companion, though with a less springy step than before, departed with him. My disappointment was, however, somewhat mitigated by the sudden appearance, at the end of the Square, of Modernity in her motorcar. I could tell at a glance that the young woman knew her way, not only about our district, but about the world. If I ventured to doubt whether she had ever heard of Octavia Hill, I felt instinctively that she had read her Wells and even her Woolf, not to speak of his works who, with Shavian courtesy, had volunteered to guide intelligent women to Socialism. As I beheld her—a feminist complete—I seemed to see our man-made civilisation shrivelling into flames beneath her vestal fires. But, since no phoenix issued from the ashes, I dismissed the vision as no more than one of those mirages in which our social atmosphere abounds.

Modernity, meanwhile, was driving round the Square; and what should happen but that, as she drew near my door, one of our most venerable and venerated residents, who had been making his way by slow stages along the pavement, came level with it likewise. Upon this worthy citizen all the ends of a family refreshed by repeated infusions of Quaker blood and stabilised by generations of honesty proving the best policy might be said to have come in the shape of a peerage. Once in a way virtue had not been its own, or at least its only reward.

Very benevolent and a little blind, old Urbanity, as we called him, entertained the belief that liberty was always on the increase and that, under its beneficent influence, men grew, if possible, better and better every day and nations loved one another ever more and more. He was, in fact, the very stuff of which Liberal peers are made. Raising his hat, he waved to Modernity.

"I felt," he explained, "that I must enquire after your parents. Such dear people! I always say they are the sugar as well as the salt of the earth."

"Oh! They are all right," replies Modernity. "Pops goes on fussing about what's wrong with the world, and Moms goes on fussing about what's wrong with Pops; and that keeps them both alive. I expect they will knock up their centuries at the present rate of going and exemplify the declining death-rate."

"My dear young lady," returns the venerable Victorian, "you don't do your parents justice. But we older ones must not be impatient. Time, as the greatest of all our English statesmen once observed, is on our side—time is on our side."

"It was on your side once," she replies. "But really, Lord Parbrook, the clock does move on. You and Pops had your chance of putting the world to rights a quarter of a century ago; and you didn't make at all a good job of it. Now it's our turn. We shan't let human nature loose in the way you did. We know better than that. We're going to chain it up, and train it up, and ticket it with care. I don't think you or anyone else will in the end have cause to regret that. Freedom comes of people doing what they ought, and not what they like; and we shall see to it that they do their duty in future. Ninety-nine per cent. of people don't know what's good for them, and never will. Some of us have got to take charge and see that the others are shown the way in which to go. Our new civilisation will be birth-controlled and mate-controlled and death-controlled, and all our pleasures will be planned."

The old man muttered something that I could not catch as he raised his hat and moved off. But I could almost have sworn that I heard Modernity's unuttered comment. How right Professor Haldane * is, she seemed to say, to tell us that all persons over sixty-five

* J. B. S. Haldane, "Inequality of Man", p. 35 (Penguin ed.).

should be disfranchised. Of course they should! They are quite 'gaga' by that time."

The breeze, meanwhile, had set the foliage rustling right down the Square. Crabbed age and youth, the high plane trees seemed to whisper to one another, cannot live together. Was that, I asked myself, all that it really came to—a battle of opposites in the very heart of things where the particular issue was of no real consequence, but in which the old strove for stability and the young for change? Liberty had seemed lovely once and been seen at the end of every road; now it had become the creed of old men, and youth was everywhere swinging along to some kind or other of totalitarian music— barrack-room ballads, most like, though not à la Kipling. But here came one, who marched to time-honoured tunes. All esteemed the Colonel, a man so various that whilst he fancied himself in the descent of Colonel Esmond and Colonel Newcome, others were apt to call him Colonel Blimp, or even Colonel Blood. Simultaneously, at the other end of the Square, there entered the Rector of a neighbouring parish. Soldiers two, only lacking a converted pacifist to make them soldiers three, and fully representative of the most militant forces of the nation!

"How is it going, Padre?" says the Colonel. "Parish keeping fit in our disordered world?"

"Fairly fit," replies the clergyman, "but the young people won't come to church."

"Never would!" returns the Colonel. "But that don't much matter, so long as they get some discipline. If they'll join the Scouts and the Terriers, that's what the country needs. 'How are they recruiting?'—That's what *I* keep asking myself."

"Not too badly, I'm told," says the Padre. "But that's only half the battle. Every war has got to be won on the home front as well. We won the last war, and then went and lost the peace."

"Not a bit of it!" affirms the Colonel. "We made the mistake of not marching to Berlin. You may take the word of an old soldier for that. I said so at the time, and I say so still. Don't you be moved by all that namby-pamby stuff that these old women of both sexes are talking. Have you noticed that spinsters of a certain age have a lot more sense in their heads than mothers; in fact, that they are the only women who are really fit to have the vote?"

"Well! I've always maintained that the soldier had the finest vocation next to the priest," says the Padre, who had drawn his own conclusions about spinsters as well as the Colonel, and had no wish to pursue the subject.

"The finest, Sir, the finest of all!" returns the Colonel. "Why, Sir, this is a world all stamped with warfare! Survival of the fittest—what? Struggle for existence—eh? Not a doubt of it? Man, Sir, is a fighting animal, and at his finest when he shows it. Make that the subject of your next sermon, and I'll be proud to listen to you. The Old Testament before the New, Sir; justice before mercy! Always knock your adversary down before you shake hands with him. Well! I must be off to the War Office."

The clergyman looked a little confused, but before he could collect his thoughts for a reply, the Colonel had hurried away, and an elderly lady had sighted and seized upon him.

"You will make a mention of our jumble sale in church next Sunday, dear Dr. Fisherman, won't you?" I heard her say. "It's so very important. You will remember I told you we must make a success of it, for we are paying our organiser a lump-sum down or 25 per cent. on the profits, whichever comes to the more, as she is so poor. It's quite an original venture, with a wonderful new idea in it—a prize for the oldest article sent in. Sure to attract, isn't it? And the proceeds—that is, if there are any proceeds after the organiser has been paid—will go towards a fund for wireless-sets to be used, if war breaks out, in the trenches in the parks during an air raid. Oh! It's real national service work."

The good man gave some temporising consent by reason of her importunity and also, as I saw a moment later, because he wished to make sure of a word with an old friend—a lean-faced lawyer, to all appearance, who was advancing up the Square. The two men greeted one another, as it seemed to me, after the manner of contemporaries at college.

"Not got all the ruffians locked-up yet, I'm afraid?" observed the clergyman, feeling about for an opening.

"No, nor likely to!" replied the other. "I'm not even sure that crime's on the decrease. You've got to get ahead with your job, I fancy, before we get that better world that our optimists promise us. I've not much faith myself from that point of view in punishment, and still less in vicarious punishment—hanging or flogging or, for the matter of that, 'sanctioning', which is only another word for starving some million or more innocents to suppress a dozen or so of rascals. What I want to see is what you parsons are so fond of talking about—a change of heart both in men and nations."

"You mustn't expect too much of our ministrations," the clergyman replied. "Human nature responds quite as easily to fear as it does to love; and it might be rash to suppose that the Bench of Bishops will succeed where the Bench of Judges fails us. We have our successes and our disappointments, and I dare say they nearly balance out. Did you ever hear how Clemenceau once enquired of a missionary up the Nile how many converts he had made, and was given a figure—I forget what—with this rider appended to it: 'Mais il faut avouer qu'ils se déconvertissent de temps en temps' ?"

The lawyer laughed. "Not much deconversion needed where I work! They've most of them never been converted. Get rid of the money and the women, and you might get on with it. But I fancy avarice and adultery, like the poor, will be always with us."

The clergyman looked meditative.

"Well, well!" the lawyer continued, "you and I mustn't quarrel, at our time of life, with our bread and butter. No doubt we should begin furiously to think if prosecution or persuasion were to become so successful as permanently to turn the wicked man away from his wickedness. It would break us both, I am afraid. The liberal professions have their roots in the criminal ones."

With that he moved on, leaving the parson, as it seemed to me, somewhat thoughtful. Indeed, had it not been for the sudden appearance of the Catholic priest at the other end of the Square, I believe the good man would have fallen into a brown, or, perhaps I should rather say, a black study upon my very doorstep. But, unlike that Anglican army chaplain of whom Kipling reported that, whenever there was a problem in human nature, he would turn for aid to his Catholic colleague, the good man contented himself with a distant salute, turned on his heels, and hurried away. It may well have been that at the moment Christianity seemed to him quite complicated enough, without any reminder of a church that he could neither comfortably include in, nor yet comfortably exclude from, his ecclesiastical philosophy.

In the meanwhile the old Priest had progressed up the Square and, not far from my house, run straight into a sceptical young doctor of my acquaintance. The two had, I suppose, got to know each other at sick beds, and were at all events familiars. I could tell, in fact, from their manner that, whatever differences divided these physicians respectively of the soul and the body, temperament was not one of them; and I looked to see whether I could find in the younger man's eyes any trace of the profound compassion that gleamed in those of the elder.

"Morning, Padre," I heard the Doctor say. "Haven't provided you with any corpses to inter lately! No, nor even with a sick devil to make into a saint—a saint, that is, until I put him back on his legs, when, as like as not, he'll turn devil again!"

"Very possibly!" says the Priest. "But your utmost skill won't keep him going for ever and, when it fails you, he'll slip back into my hands. So, you see, I shall get the last word; and I think his considered criticism of life, for whatever it may be worth, is more likely to approximate to mine than to yours. But you doctors seem to be afraid of letting men look facts in the face and are for shuffling your victims out of the world without letting them know it is the hour of departure and that they must prepare for the journey."

"Departure!" said the Doctor. "Why can't you call it death? 'Earth to earth, ashes to ashes, dust to dust!'—that's just what it is; and that's the last word to be said about it. And I dare say in ten years' time, at the pace we're going now with our discoveries, we shall be able to sum up the whole significance of life with as much brevity."

"Then everything will seem odder than it did before," observed the Priest, with a twinkle in his eye, "and matter even cleverer than you make it out at present. It was hard enough to imagine oneself the descendant of a bacillus, but really, if it came to life being spontaneously generated by the prince of the power of the air—an impersonal prince, of course—you will have to fortify the forces of credulity. Otherwise human vanity might be proof against your blandishments."

The Doctor did not look entirely pleased. "It is useless," he observed sententiously, "to reject the revelations of science."

" They are more easily assimilated," remarked the Priest, "in association with those of religion. But I must not take up your time, for I can see you are wanting to be gone. Allow me only to conclude this little colloquy of ours by recalling a remark which I remember to have found in the writings of a profane author and which has a way of returning to my mind whenever we meet one another. Did you ever, during your student-days in Paris, chance upon a book by Anatole France entitled 'Les dieux ont soif', a tale of revolutionary

Paris in which a priest figures and philosophises? 'Souffrez', he observes to one, like yourself, possessed of a quiverful of those quips and, if I may say so, quibbles, with the aid of which men mostly arm themselves against the revelations of God—'Souffrez que je ne dispute pas avec vous. J'y aurais trop de raison et trop peu d'esprit'."

"Bravo! Padre," I heard the Doctor return. "Stick to your guns and die in the last ditch. I like a good soldier, though why men fight with so much zeal for their fancies, both spiritual and temporal, I can no more make out than did old Kaspar."

"We all have our limitations," the Priest replied mildly. "But for the present 'good-bye', and may God—for I think He is not very far from any one of us—bless your labours. The healing of the sick is an interest we have in common; and the sickness of the soul, I believe I am correct in saying, is not regarded by all physicians conversant with modern therapeutics as so widely removed from that of the body."

With that they went their different ways, leaving me more than ever disposed to believe that, despite outward appearance, the House stood at an ancient crossways where, from time immemorial, men had been moved to stop and talk and, perhaps as they walked home from some grim scene hard by at Tyburn, take their moral and intellectual bearings. Here, too, maybe, there had been some interred who had so far forgotten Socrates's warning that we are the chattels of the gods as to pass an adverse criticism upon life by taking leave of it with violence. Here, at all events, whether the cause lay in my own mind or in the locality, was a rendezvous of many shadows—shades of humanity; shapes of things past and to come; the shadows that we are and the shadows that we pursue. Evidence of this, indeed, seemed to be accumulating so fast that the very paving-stones had come, as it seemed to me, to look like enchanted ground. Had Dunsinane's Hill faced more bravely the advancing foliage of Birnam Forest than did one coming up, as I guessed, from Chelsea, await the impact of St. John's Wood now making towards him from the north end of the Square—the former hatless and unkempt, the latter spick and span as the proverbial new pin. The two soon sighted one another, saluted and stopped as they reached my door; and then the elder began talking. I could not catch every word that he said, but I heard enough to guess upon which theme he was discoursing. He spoke with pomp and pride of El Greco, of

Poussin, of Cézanne; and there was some mention too of 'significant form'.

As soon as he had finished, the other began to answer somewhat excitedly and exuberantly, after the manner of youth. It was obvious that he worshipped other gods. Yes! There it came—the expected, the enigmatic word, the mot de Cambronne—surrealism. Art, it appeared, had arrived at last at humanity's holy of holies, and was depicting man as the jumble-sale that he really was. Top hats, oranges, Turkish delight and old bones—such and a great deal more under the influence of that young man's eloquence did I see as the content of the human soul, or at least of the one that animated him. But in the leafy banner of St. John's Wood (if I may prolong the conceit) the foliage had begun to flap furiously, as before a coming storm. Assuredly there would have been wigs on the green; but that Jove's celestial waters intervened before the mortal's thunder broke. In a moment the hatless orator was drenched and, having everything to fear and nothing to hope from his companion's umbrella, incontinently fled; whilst St. John's Wood remained master of the field and in due course resumed his progress southwards to the Athenaeum.

"Those two were getting a bit excited. Just as well the rain came on!" I heard one well-caped policeman observe to another as they passed the window.

"Yes, I don't know what we would do without the rain," replied his companion. "Keeps the country quiet like! That was an artist that passed then, and a successful one too, I'm told. Nothing in his job to get excited about! Yet those sort o' academic gents can get every bit as violent about their ideas as if they mattered. Queer thing—human nature! Now, if that old gent 'ad done like Herbert Spencer—him that found out things was unknowable at the bottom of them—and had had a couple of pads in his pockets to pop in his ears when he got put out with the young 'un's talk, there'd 'a been no trouble at all."

Scotland Yard passed by; and the storm had no sooner followed it before Westminster appeared. It was the Minister of Misinformation himself, strolling up and down the Square in the lucid interval after the rain. At the corner he ran into Whitehall similarly occupied, and they joined forces.

"Been at the match?" I could hear the Minister enquire as they came past the door.

"Yes," says Whitehall, "I got there for a bare half-hour and had a dramatic glimpse of the Don's innings. It doesn't look well for us. Country's on the down grade, I suppose. Signs of it everywhere!"

They passed out of hearing, but presently came round again.

"You may well be right," the Minister was saying. "Democracies don't last. They disintegrate like Athens or turn into despotisms like Rome. But I couldn't say that on the platform; it would be as much as my place is worth. I have to give them 'Land of Hope and Glory' in one form or another, and tell them Democracy is a heaven-sent form of government and that it makes them a free people. That satisfies them; and for the rest they've got the dole to keep them quiet and the sporting news to make them glad."

"Panem et circenses!" muttered the old civil-servant, for they had by now come to a standstill outside my door. "One always comes back to Juvenal in the end."

"I prefer Horace to Juvenal," says Westminster.

"Doubtless!" returns Whitehall. "He is the more genial cynic of the two. But presumably you bowdlerise him for the benefit of your constituents. 'Odi profanum vulgus et arceo' was never meant for democrats to hear. To think that Raleigh—our own Georgian Walter Raleigh, not the Elizabethan one—should have as good as repeated the sentence! Let me see; what were the lines? 'I do not love the human race, I do not like its ugly face.' Something of that sort, wasn't it?"

"It is not from critics or poetasters," says Westminster in the grand manner, "that I take my politics, but from the historians."

"I wonder from which of them," says Whitehall. "Not Tacitus or Gibbon, I'll be bound!"

"No, from the Greeks," says Westminster. "From Thucydides; and from the funeral oration of Pericles, in particular. Athens, violet-crowned Athens, is my spiritual home."

"Precisely!" says Whitehall, "so was Germany Lord Haldane's! The two States had, as you have doubtless noticed, a little in common. Both bullied their weaker neighbours whenever they saw fit; and both, under the influence, in the one case of good Paganism and in the other of advanced Protestantism, committed political atrocities, the like of which it is not particularly easy to match. On the whole I am inclined to give the palm to the Athenians. The fate of Melos, not to speak of Mytilene, Skione or Thyrea, was a nasty business; we have your own chosen historian's word for it. The

Inquisition in Spain, the torture-chamber in Tudor England, St. Bartholomew's Day and the September Massacres in France can plead, I suppose, some distorted pretence of reason or some by-gone fear of treason as an excuse for the horrors they recall. But the treatment of the wretched Melians, who were the most inoffensive of neutrals, by the glorious Athenians, who had listened to Pericles's eloquence, has nothing to be said for it. The adult males, as you will remember, were slaughtered and the women and children enslaved by the very generation of Greeks who are constantly held up to us as models of citizenship. It is a detail, perhaps, that your chosen historian, who has the virtue of never blinking the truth, remarks elsewhere that Athens, though a democracy in name, had in fact fallen under the domination of its foremost citizen. So here we have democracy evolving into dictatorship under the best auspices, and power-politics concluding in crime.

"It is monstrously unfair," cries Westminster, "to judge one age by the standards of another."

"I am not doing so," remarks Whitehall. "Xenophon * will show you in the 'Hellenica' that the Athenians themselves regarded their subsequent collapse as the consequence of their crime; they were, therefore, presumably conscious of criminality. Plato, as you remember, traces in the 'Republic' the progress of national decline from the aristocratic through the timocratic man to the democrat, and so on to the despot. As Thucydides disclosed the historic, so did Plato the philosophic truth about his countrymen. It is no fault of theirs if, as Winwood Reade† alleges, the Greeks have 'swindled history and obtained a vast amount of admiration under false pretences'."

"Confound your learning!" says Westminster with emphasis. "Ministries like mine subsist on half-truths and inhabit clouds with silver linings. Old civil servants like you should be pensioned off and given rooms in deserted palaces of truth."

"Indisputably!" rejoins Whitehall, quite unperturbed. "There are, however, some gentlemen, as Dizzy observed, who retire from business, and others from whom business has retired. I ought perhaps to be placed in the latter class. The age of Disraeli and Gladstone has receded; the age of the bureaucrat and the socialist arrived. The choice before us is between the old gang and the new gangster. These new idealists of ours, if you look close enough to see them

* "Hellenica", II, ii, 3. 10.   † "The Martyrdom of Man"—"War".

aright, are merely gangsters in search of swag, though they have all the unction and some of the air of archbishops (who, maybe, might be found among them). Whoever made the stuff they are after, I am quite sure they didn't; they are much too busy distributing it to have had the time for that, and rather too stupid, I think, to have found the means. I should guess, from the way they go on, that politics has seldom produced a purer stock of parasites. They get their seats by promising plunder, and retain their salaries by calling for more. Gladstone would have scorned them as heartily as Disraeli. The old gang at least got nothing out of the business, and had some idea of letting money fructify in the pockets of the people."

"Cynical old man! Go back to your tub," replies the Minister, "and when you get there meditate on the merits of Penelope's web. There's the true secret of government. We just go on doing and undoing one another's work. We've done that, if you observe, on large lines all through English history; and it gets rid, more or less, of political boredom. The medievalists produced a coherent commonwealth much on the lines of Plato's Republic. There were three orders of men—ecclesiastics, knights and burgesses, corresponding to the guardians, the warriors and the artisans of the Greek conception. But the system became a little tedious, and the Reformers, the Whigs and the Liberals pulled it about until presently they pulled it down. Now, with the help of Labour, if not with the help of God, we are going to put the pieces together again and every man back into his place. So there's always something doing, yet never anything done. Politics is almost as good a joke, when you think about it, as the nativity of Tristram Shandy. Man is always going to be born, or rather born again; but the business, though interminably discussed, never gets finished, any more than Tristram Shandy is ever quite born within the covers of his book. But come into my house and I'll give you a cocktail; and we'll fight our battles over again with all the zest of Uncle Toby and Corporal Trim."

They passed out of view, leaving me with a suspicion that the Minister of Misinformation had betrayed the Englishman's secret. It was, then, no more at bottom than make-believe—this boasted evolution of our British institutions. I half wished that Lambeth would come past in apron and gaiters so that I might test my theory upon the Established Church as well as upon the Mother of Parliaments. For to such as wore that quaint old-time clergyman's riding-dress had been entrusted the official conclusions of the

English people concerning a world invisible. I could always fancy the angels of Lambeth best upon horseback. I could fancy them watching, like Browning's Grand-Duke in "The Statue and the Bust", the effect of mortal indecision, as the water flowed on down the river between the Lollards' Tower and the Houses of Parliament. I could fancy Cranmer leading the long procession, and in his hand his two books of Common Prayer and the tell-tale note, addressed to his all-powerful lord and master upon some point of doctrine and saying "This is mine opinion and sentence at this present, which, nevertheless, I do not temerariously define, but refer the judgment thereof wholly unto your Majesty". Always the huge figure of the Monarch, with all that he stood for, would interpose to divide the Tudor Establishment from the Primitive Church; for, if in the first century there had been no pope as supreme head of the Church on earth, there had assuredly been no king.

Cranmer had created a precedent in make-believe the effect of which could be seen in much subsequent English history. Montaigne had had something to say about it; as will presently be noticed, for it bears upon the charge of hypocrisy so unfairly brought against the English people, complacent and compromising though they may be. Cranmer's methods in fact were well calculated to afford no small liberty of invention. It must have been difficult to convert a King by the Grace of God into a King by the will of Parliament; and Bishop Ken and his fellow Non-Jurors had proved unequal to the occasion and fallen by the way. Yet the thing had been done. It must have been more difficult still, when the world began counting wisdom by heads and proclaiming that the voice of the people was the voice of God, to suppose that some four million or so of Englishmen, somewhere back in Tudor times, or some forty million or so alive in our own, could reconstruct the primitive faith of the Church, whilst some four hundred million souls to-day upon this earth were of a clean-contrary opinion. But that, too, had been achieved by Lambeth on horseback. Fine riding, indeed, which could stand such rocking, and fine tailoring, too, which could patch clothes to meet such wear and tear! Yet, over the tale of years, and as from the quadrangle of New College, where we had walked together as undergraduates, there would return to mind the caustic remark of a Scottish Presbyterian destined to rise to eminence as a historian and subsequently to become Principal of Glasgow University—the late Sir Robert Rait. "High Churchmen", he had been annoying enough to tell me in those distant days, "are all special pleaders." And the time arrived when I grew to be of his opinion. For Maitland's "Canon Law in the Church of England" had plainly unhorsed Bishop Stubbs and rent his conclusions about Anglican continuity from end to end.

Did Lambeth never reflect, as it looked at the state of Europe to-day, what the Anglican secession had done to the idea of Christendom? Was it uncharitable to credit that phantom line of departed prelates with the sentiments of the Statue and the Bust in the poem:—

> Still, I suppose, they sit and ponder
> What a gift life was, ages ago,
> Six steps out of the Chapel yonder.
>
> Only they see not God, I know,
> Nor all that chivalry of His,
> The soldier-saints who, row on row,
>
> Burn upward each to his point of bliss—
> Since, the end of life being manifest,
> He had burnt his way thro' the world to this.

I had fallen into a day-dream. Instead of Lambeth riding by with a royal air, behold instead before my doorstep, South Kensington in the guise of a hatless, tousled youth with baggy grey-flannel trousers! A student confessed in lollop and limb, he moved up the Square, whilst Bedford College, with fuzzy head, short skirt and shabby stockings, moved down it, but whether coincidently or collusively I could not tell you.

"Hallo, Jemima," the young man called out. "Been gipsying? Or has old Partington with her mop prevailed against the waves, miscalled permanent, that used to break across your pate? And where are the sanguinary streams which flowed of old into your finger-nails? Have they run dry?"

"Don't be facetious, Johnny!" the girl answered. "You're not the least amusing. Why shouldn't my hair retreat from art and my finger-nails return to nature?"

"Why, indeed," he returned, "if only we knew where nature ends and art begins, or wherein lies the difference between them?"

"Oh! for heaven's sake, don't begin that stuff, Johnny," she replied. "Everyone knows the difference between art and nature."

"Not I!" says he. "Nakedness is what we call a state of nature;

yet it seems to be thought natural to wear clothes. Did you ever hear tell of the misadventure that once overtook a learned judge—Avory by name, I believe—on the golf links at Rye? Perceiving a young woman somewhat scantily clad after a bathe, he cried out, 'Hi! hi! you can't go about like that.' Whereupon she answered, 'All right, uncle, don't get excited!' and therewith proceeded to disrobe herself still further. Upon which His Majesty's Judge, being greatly discomfited, took refuge in flight. Now, oh! daughter of Eve, tell me, had the blushing Judge or the unblushing maiden the better sense of the natural?"

"You idiot, Johnny," says the girl, laughing.

"Idiot!" says he. "Not a bit of it! Ignoramus, if you will; but not idiot! An ignoramus in search of his antecedents, and just as ready to find a clue to them in that little episode on the Rye golf-links as Hegel to find the prolegomena to a philosophy of history in somewhat similar occurrences in Eden. Do they not cause you to reflect, in company with the aforesaid philosopher, upon the fact that your, at the moment somewhat disorderly dress has a spiritual as well as a physical origin, and therefore throws a searchlight upon human nature!"

"For God's sake stop, Johnny, and talk some sense!" cries the girl.

"Not for God's sake, Jemima! Supposing He's in existence—which you assume without proof—we might just possibly get at Him not by knowing ourselves as Socrates advised, but by knowing why we keep our clothes on, as Carlyle recommended. 'Sartor resartus', you know, and all that! It seems natural enough to see you doing yourself up to the eyes and fiddling about with your lipstick: but I dare say it's only a sort of unnatural vice which that old Judge ought to have been punishing with such means as he had in his power. To be or not to be—clothes or no clothes—that is the question! Of which the answer should put us, as I think the Yankee-Noodles call it, 'in tune with the Infinite'. Answer me that, if you can, most excellent Jemima, and prove that you are, not my equal in ignorance, but rather my superior in wisdom, since, you know, Havelock Ellis is prepared to credit women with a possibly greater brain-mass than mere males can aspire to."

"Oh! what a bore you are, Johnny," she broke in. "Almost as great a bore as Socrates!"

"Doubtless!" he returned, "O daughter of Xantippe, whom for

a moment I was misguided enough to mistake for Hypatia. Doubtless, so long as I defer putting the question of questions! But, as I happen to know already what the answer to that particular enquiry is going to be, and, as I happen to hold, with Warden Brodrick of Merton, that I could marry any woman in the world that I wished to, if only I were 'to concentrate my whole attention upon the matter', there seems no particular occasion to hurry it to the front."

"Damn you, Johnny!" she tossed over her shoulder, as she made off.

"Bless you, Jemima!" he called back, and with that likewise went on his way.

These last amenities set me wondering how it would go with them when they got to Greenery Street or Yallery Street, or wherever it might be they were bound for, and then, when again they left it and turned from children into parents. "About as much religion as my William likes"—that naïve epitome of an eligible bride's convictions was calculated, according to Robert Louis Stevenson, "to make a happy couple of any William and his spouse". But as for this poor Jemima that had wandered past my door, how in the world was she to know how much religion her Johnny liked or their children were to look for? The problem sent me back into the house, for I could myself find no reply to it in the street, nor extract it from the men and women that walked there.

Chapter V

THE LOWER STUDY

THE house had two studies—a lower and an upper—and in the ordering of their bookcases I fancied I could discern a disposition to make the former the receptacle of the solid, if sometimes discarded, museum-pieces of learning, and the latter of such works as, being things of beauty and genius or, as the French would call them, belles lettres, remain perennially pleasing. Certainly the bindings of the books suggested something of the kind; for cloth prevailed in the lower study, but, in the upper, leather. Other circumstances, too, tended, I think, to enforce the notion of a certain inferiority in the contents of the ground floor. It was not that famous names were lacking behind the ugly, back-sliding glass fronts of the bookshelves. They were present in so great abundance that their very number seemed to produce a distressing sense of mental confusion, such as one might have anticipated, had one invited all the most eminent men of a modern university to a garden party in the hope of producing a great feast of reason, not to speak of a flow of soul.

The Alien Voice did not, of course, fail to point this out. "The Schools", it would whisper, "are no better than the Street. All these pundits are at issue with one another, and have no more inclination or intention to reach a common conclusion than the passers-by in the Square. Take, for instance, that wrangling group of eminent philosophers in the corner. They will never find any premises on which they can agree. Some declare that our senses alone can tell us anything; others, though not altogether denying that, remark that the information we get from our senses has become so personal by the time it reaches us as not to be in any degree objective; whilst others again profess to descry a noumenal world behind the phenomenal. Some of these wiseacres, moreover, are stoics, and discover morality in the endurance of pain; others are epicureans, and derive morality from the pursuit of pleasure, individual or collective. There are always at least two schools about everything, and generally a good many more. And, in short, so far as I can see, Universities serve no other purpose than to point this out beyond fear of contradiction.

"It certainly looks rather like that," I would feebly reply.

"Oh, but don't take my word for it," the Alien Voice would rejoin. "I am very possibly prejudiced. Listen only to such a good Humanist as Sir Richard Livingstone; and he will tell you, I think, that there is not a fundamental problem being raised now that was not in principle present to the mind of the Greeks."

"And by them disposed of," I would hazard, "as he implies."

"How 'disposed of'?" said the Voice. "Does he not himself find them all reappearing, a little changed by circumstance, upon the tongues of the Wellses, the Galsworthys, and the Shaws? Why, if Plato and Aristotle disposed of the sceptical criticism of life, has it again become so cogent?"

"Because the human mind goes round in circles," I would risk.

"Quite so," he would say. "We have no compass, and just revolve like electrons—aimlessly, uselessly, eternally."

"I didn't mean that," I would answer. "I meant only that minds of the second order do not easily accept the conclusions of minds of the first order; and that this happens again and again."

"Do you really mean to tell me," the Voice would cry, "that Plato and Aristotle were in a better position to form a judgment on these matters than a world that has some twenty centuries more of experience and knowledge behind it?"

"I should think it quite arguable," I would venture. "The Greeks at their best appear to have had the finest conceivable sense of proportion, and consequently faced the problems of life more correctly than many of our scientists. If they knew less about the exterior world than we do, they knew more about their own interior being. The wisest of them even affirmed that there is nothing of more importance than to know oneself, nor anything more worth while devoting one's time to."

"Anyhow," the Voice would return rather testily, "you can't pretend that any pattern has resulted from all this logomachy. A patchwork quilt to hide the nakedness of our slumbers—that is all, I maintain, that the philosophers have to show as the outcome of centuries of confabulation. And the legend round its border epitomises the whole debt of humanity to their labours. I hesitate to read it to you, so stale has its truth become with repetition. But here it is:—

> Myself when young did eagerly frequent
> Doctor and Saint and heard great argument
> About it and about; but ever more
> Came out by the same door wherein I went.

"That may serve for the doctors," I would say, "though I say it without prejudice. But the saints, or rather their works, live a floor or two higher up. They get levitated. It is a familiar mystical phenomenon, as I dare say you know, for which the evidence seems quite sufficient. So, if you should find any books here of saintly origin, they must be classed with the cloak of Elijah, which fell, if you remember, during his ascension."

"Let us return to our senses," the Voice would resume sarcastically, "and keep our feet upon the ground. Take a look there at Mr. Ayer, grinning in the corner, whilst the metaphysicians wrangle. He knows what nonsense they talk—these blind men in dark rooms, hunting for black hats that aren't there. Take a look at him, I say, cutting off the tall heads of metaphysics, theology, atheism, agnosticism, ethics and aesthetics like a Tarquin, and leaving us nothing but a lot of sensations and possibilities of sensation to frame hypothetical laws from. That's the man for me. No nonsense about him!"

"I have had a look at him," I would observe, "and have already passed on. But that is not to say that I may not take another glance his way presently. 'Nihil in intellectu quod non prius in sensu' is but a half truth until you have added the rider, 'Nihil in sensu quod non melius in intellectu'. We may have to climb a storey or so before we can get a good view of things in general."

"I am interested," the Voice would return, "in the facts of life, not in your ill-disguised expostulations with them. Those facts are comprised within the compass of our sense-content. All the rest is private speculation. But now leave the philosophers and see if you can derive any comfort from the historians. There they stand, a motley crowd, in that bookshelf with the 'Cambridge History' that Acton planned at the bottom of it. Will you tell me that that omnibus is moving in any certain direction? From its Catholic author to his agnostic successor in the Chair of Modern History it affords a thousand angles of vision, but it starts from nowhere and leads to nothing. The facts selected are chosen on no system; the praise and condemnation bestowed derive from no principle; the ideas of good and evil expressed rest upon no considered basis; and the whole apparatus resembles nothing so much as a transport-train ploughing its way through the sands of time."

"A composite work", I would argue, "cannot, perhaps, make its significance hit you in the eye, but the significance may be there none the less."

"It is not there, as it seems," the Voice would answer dryly, "for one of the most widely read of modern historians, Herbert Fisher, whose 'History of Europe' I see on the shelf, observes there that 'men, wiser and more learned than himself, have discerned in history a plot, a rhythm, a predetermined pattern', but that 'these harmonies are concealed from him'. That is precisely what I told you. There is in human history no agreed pattern or rhythm or plot. He and I are at one in that."

"He says that wiser and more learned men than himself have discerned one," I would say feebly.

"There have not been very many such in our time," the Voice would answer. "And, besides, I have never denied that anyone may make a pattern to suit himself. But a general survey of the tapestry of time cannot, in face of his opinion, be said to yield any generally acceptable result. And now you might take a look at the corner consecrated to biography. Perhaps biographers keep nearer to life than philosophers or historians; but I doubt whether you will find their criticism more consistent."

I looked in the direction which the Voice indicated, but with no particular confidence. My vision was rather dazzled than clarified by the infinite variety of characters exposed and celebrated in the bookshelves. There lay a record of Napoleon, as the late Lord Rosebery had conceived him in his last phase—Napoleon, that is, chained to his rock, Titanic, like Prometheus, having indeed brought fire of a kind to the earth, and, if war be indeed, as Rosebery asserted, 'the gambling of the gods', then assuredly at the least a demi-god! It was evident that this British Prime Minister had had a soft spot in his heart for that greatest of gangsters, as indeed, from one casual allusion to him in a public utterance, I suspect may be likewise the case with Mr. Churchill, though I find it hard to understand why that should seem so engaging in the Corsican which has seemed so blameworthy in the Germans. "On parlera de sa gloire, Sous le chaume bien longtemps" *—there I supposed was the explanation. Wicked wars, if one only let them be talked about for a century, would grow glorious; and the dead, who had buried their dead, could be left to do the mourning likewise. So, it appeared, statesmen argued, with their customary lucidity of thought, playing out the slain with dead marches in Saul, and playing in the slayer with Eroica symphonies. Wellington seemed to have

* Béranger.

had a better perspective if, as is said, he observed that there was nothing worse than victory except defeat.

Rosebery, it appeared, had had other as conflicting admirations as those he entertained for Napoleon Bonaparte and William Pitt. When Newman died he had telegraphed to Father Neville to ask if he might come down to Birmingham to view the body of one whom he had never seen in the flesh, but had only admired in the spirit. The reply was affirmative. Accordingly he visited the Birmingham Oratory. As he entered the room or chapel where the dead Cardinal was lying, he began to regret his request; for the features had begun to fall in. He walked round to the other side of the bier. There, by some freak of nature or providence of God, decay was invisible and the profile perfect. He stooped down and kissed the face of one greater in the sight of God—if that be of any consequence—than the French Emperor.* But, had he been given the choice of the two men's careers, it is a nice point to consider which he would have preferred, but not, perhaps, a nice point to raise.

Hard by Newman's Life lay the monumental biography in six volumes of Disraeli; and his now recumbent figure seemed to laugh at one through its cloth-coffin. What an alchemist he had been, transmuting Tories into Democrats and transposing the imponderables in the war of evangelical tradition with physical science, so as to make 'the religion of all sensible men' appear an auxiliary on the side of the angels! Close by the memorial to 'the Hebrew conjuror' lay Morley's huge reliquary with the remains of Gladstone. A glance at it was enough to awaken the echo of great rolling sentences, beating in like the toss of breakers against a cliff and then, all sound and fury spent, subsiding into a waste of waters. Had it signified anything, the Voice would whisper, that battle of giants, or were they and their like in every age only part of Humanity's 'supreme ironic procession, with laughter of gods in the background'?

"Turn, however," the Voice would pursue, "to those human, or shall I say subhuman documents lying in the shelf below, if you would appraise correctly the worth of all this agitation. Assembled by as smart a detective as ever entered the service of Clio, these 'vieux papiers', together with those 'vieilles maisons' to which they relate, may be said to reconstruct, perhaps as skilfully as has ever

* I tell the story as I recollect Wilfrid Ward, who had heard it from Rosebery himself, telling it to me; but it will be found substantially in Lord Crewe's "Lord Rosebery". There, however, Rosebery only says he kissed the ring.

been done, the history of a crime. The grossness of human nature beneath the veneer of civilisation has never been made plainer than by Lenôtre. The Terror of Revolutionary France epitomises the terror of all time. The soil of society is volcanic; and behind the jungle of human motives lurks an incalculable and savage beast. We stand, in fact, upon the crust of custom, and hide our real selves behind nothing more effective than fig-leaves. Is man more truly known when society is quiescent or when it is convulsed, when he is clothed or when he is naked? Consider, for instance, the case of Papa Pache, that amiable botanist dwelling in the mountains of Switzerland, of whom it could be said, in his pre-Revolutionary days, that 'provided he had periwinkles in his garden, black bread and milk food on his table, and romances to play, this wise man wished for nothing'. And then behold him again, recommended by the accident of a friendship to the notice of the Rolands, accepting a post in the Ministry of the Interior on the condition that it should bring him neither emolument nor honour, living laborious days at his desk like the most exemplary of confidential clerks, and returning at sundown to his lodgings, his harp and his children! Behold him rising in reputation, transferred to the Ministry of War at the Minister's request, then in due course replacing his chief, and so at length, as Minister of War himself, controlling the armies of Revolutionary France! Look again, and you will see him installed as Mayor of Paris with all the power of the Commune at his back, turning against his old friends, the Girondins, defending the September Massacres, putting his name to the document, as false as it was foul, which contained the Dauphin's disgusting deposition against his mother and thus measured the depth of Pache's own callousness. "The Terror", as Lenôtre observes, "was personified in this mild-mannered man." For still he played his harp, and still he gathered his children about him, and still he was Papa Pache to those who marked the benignant look with which botanical or similar pursuits had stamped his countenance. But, after Thermidor had closed the Terror and men had begun to breathe and think again, Papa Pache was styled the Tartuffe of the Revolution, and narrowly escaped the scaffold. Freed by the general amnesty, he hid himself in his little property in the Ardennes, resumed his botanical studies, refused some friendly advances from Napoleon, and ruminated for the remainder of his life. Mild and musical as of old, though rendered somewhat melancholy, as time went on, by the death of his daughter and the refusal of his son to have anything to say to him, he completed after this manner the tale of his days—a man seemingly capable of the purest benevolence and content with the most innocent pleasure, 'nisi imperasset'. Here was no Jekyll turning into Hyde with the aid of a wizard's draught. Here was no Dorian Gray with his true face concealed by a miracle. Here was mutation without magic; here was a man turned into a fiend for some months only of a lifetime, and then resuming his former shape without an effort, a relapse, or, so far as can be seen, a regret. Character, you see, goes for nothing. Everything lies on the knees of circumstance. There are no gods."

At this I would remain for some while silent; and in due course the Alien Voice would resume its observations.

"There is another strange story worthy of your attention," it would remark, "in Lenôtre's collection. The British Parliament, they say, can do everything but change a man into a woman or a woman into a man. But the French Revolution could do even that. During the Second Empire, in 1858 to be precise, there died, without a razor-blade among her chattels, a woman once known in Parisian society, and even still a familiar figure in Versailles; and behold, when they came to lay her out, she was a man. The story was complicated. It is enough for my purpose to remind you that at the height of the Terror a young adventurer found himself left as the protector in exile of a young girl of good family; that they became a little more than kind to one another in Holland; and that, with the rise of Bonaparte, she returned to France, and ultimately married into her own milieu. Not till the Restoration did she see her lover again. Then, disguised as a woman, he blackmailed her into asserting his identity with the deceased daughter of a certain M. Savalette de Langes, to whom the Royal Family had been indebted. The identification was accepted; and the man-woman was pensioned and admitted, on the strength of his mistress's testimony, into some of the best houses in Paris. For some forty years the hideous old hermaphrodite battened on the lie, dying still undiscovered in the odour of femininity. Even Balzac's Vautrin, as Lenôtre observes, 'was very inferior to the adventurer, Savalette de Langes'. For in his time the latter had actually carried on love affairs in the guise of a woman and contrived to break a man's heart. You will not surely affirm that such a creature as this was the creation of a God, or pretend to me that you can bring it within the four corners of any metaphysic of being. It was just a conglomeration of cells, a tissue of sense-contents, an octopus struggling for self-preservation in a wild and stormy sea."

"You might call it that or a good many other names with equal propriety," I would say. "Yet the description would fall short in strangeness of the whole truth. This Caliban was not unacquainted with Setebos. Did you notice that there was a document found amongst its effects and addressed as from God to itself? "The day", it wrote, "has at last arrived on which I am going to tear off the veil which covers your terrible iniquities. Tremble, eternal sinner . . . tremble lest I reveal to this world, which is seeking for you, the execrable monster who approaches it." That tells more on my side than on yours; for how will you account for so vivid a sense of iniquity in so gross a piece of matter? Here is no baffling problem of a dual personality, such as seems to present itself in Père Pache, but just the old dualism of purpose that we all know and confess to. The creature is human all right; but it has sunk even below the normal level of humanity, by doing the things that it would not or by not doing the things that it would. It remains, you see, on the side of the angels in its belief that there was right to be done or, which is the same thing, that life has some meaning."

"You are too serious for me," the Alien Voice would reply. "I see nothing in life but man turning into woman, and woman again into fox. Our bodies are dust, and to dust return; our minds are animal, and to animal revert. Look and see now what the novelists have to say about it all. A sorry sort of world it is that they paint. The moderns have become half-hysterical in their efforts to satisfy the public zest for tales of sex and crime; but the ancients, though their constitutions were more robust, or their technique was less developed, hardly afford you a more pleasing picture of mankind. Fielding, over there, with all his experience as a police magistrate, can, I suspect, point you to no better critic of life than his old 'Man of the Hill', who, if you remember, explained to Tom Jones how he had travelled through Europe, holding his nose with one hand and defending his pockets with the other. Vanity Fair—that's what the world works out to—and the pious Bunyan and the cynical Thackeray are well agreed upon it. It is Moll Flanders and Becky Sharp who really know their ways about it. In them you have the basic types of women—the hot and the cold."

"Base," I would interject, "not basic!"

"By no means!" the Voice would resume. "The immortal Knight-errant of La Mancha and his following excepted, men see women when they write of them far more clearly than women see themselves. Madame Bovary, please observe, and Anna Karenin are made of the same material as Moll and Becky, and make each her own pattern of life as certainly. Beside them the Jane Eyres and Anne Elliots, the Maggie Tullivers and Dorothea Brookes appear frail fancies in porcelain, modelled by women of good sense, but small sensibility and little charm."

"You must have been unfortunate in your acquaintance," I would return coldly. "As for the Knight of La Mancha," I would go on defiantly, "I have as high a regard for him as one can have for a goose. And, if the world is so mad, that, as the Melancholy Jaques would have us believe, motley is needed to cleanse it, then Don Quixote's homoeopathic treatment deserves high commendation."

"If you think the world mad," the Voice would pursue, "you are merely saying in your way what I say in mine—that it has no meaning. Quixotry is one way of expressing that, irony another. Life's little ironies are nothing to its large ones. But let that be for the present; for there are one or two other vagrant persons besides the Spaniard with whom you might travel to your advantage. There is Gulliver, for instance, who knows a thing or two. And then there is Candide, who with his sweet simplicity finds out pretty well everything that is to be known about mankind, and advises at the end, very much as I do, the cultivation of one's garden. No better tract for all times exists than the little volume that bears his name. Try it upon this period of ours, and see whether it doesn't fit there like a strait waistcoat."

"I am willing," I would say. "It is a fair enough challenge."

"But you mustn't cheat," the Voice would add suspiciously. "It is so easy to make the worse appear the better argument."

"I am a student of history," I would rejoin, "or at least have sought to be so; and I shall try my best to do justice to your case. But don't forget on your side that Voltaire was a deist, and not one of those dogmatic atheists who gathered in force round d'Holbach's table. Like Johnson, though with less positive results, he had a penchant for common sense; and that is perhaps all one can look to find on the ground floor of any house, even the House of God."

"Get on with your adaptation of Candide," the Voice would sneer, "and, when at the close you start to cultivate your garden, I shall be surprised if you find God walking there in the cool of the evening, or, for the matter of that, in the heat of the noonday. Terra firma is not, so far as I have seen, the soil that He frequents."

To this taunt I, supposing it not as yet ripe for a rejoinder, would pay no attention, but would proceed instead to take up the challenge.

"There was born then," I would say, "a few years before this century, and in one of those opulent English houses that at the time were common, a boy upon whom nature and circumstance had alike agreed to confer their fairest favours. His parentage was unexceptionable; his health proved excellent; his looks were engaging; and his fortune promised to be large. A gracious and kindly spirit made him the most docile of pupils. He accepted without question and upon authority the simple faith of his parents that the world grew better and better every day; and he would maintain an identity of meaning between happiness as conceived by a voluptuary, a savant or a saint, and then its close correspondence with the notion of pleasure entertained by the most part of men and women—and this with so vehement a conviction as to provoke the remark that the soubriquet of l'Ingénu might have suited him, if possible, even better than the name of Candide. It was the consummation of his good fortune that his studies were directed by an incomparable preceptor. Dr. Pansides, who had himself been taught at an English University to venerate in equal measure the philosophers of Germany and Greece and to mingle with surprising facility the systems of Kant and Hegel and the thoughts of Plato and Aristotle, had concluded his education for life as secretary to an eminent English statesman, who never closed a speech and rarely a conversation without some reference to the benefits of freedom. 'Let men be but free to think for themselves,' the great man would proclaim, 'and they will think wisely: let nations be but free to choose their rulers, and they will choose rightly: let the world be but free, and international amity will displace the wars of religion and the competitions of commerce: let freedom abound, and charity will yet more abound.' These sentiments had taken almost exclusive possession of the soul of Dr. Pansides, who blessed, without seeking to define, the lofty thought of liberty. Morning by morning he would require his pupil to repeat to him the poet's words, 'We must be free or die'; and the educational result was all that he could have desired. Having no disposition to die, Candide became quickly satisfied that in freedom lay the only way of living. Nor did he see any reason to regret it. It was no more disagreeable to him to find himself under a moral obligation to choose his own way than to feel that his every change of opinion demonstrated the possession of an open mind. Thus, under the tuition of the admirable Pansides, he learnt that it was better for men to be free than to be sober, and that a truly liberal spirit works after the manner of a weathercock, surveying in turn every side of circumstance and adjusting itself automatically to every breath of change. 'Convinced as I am,' he would say to himself, 'that the world grows better and better every day, what need have I of any other stable conviction?'

"The time arrived at length when the task of the excellent Pansides was completed. The desolation of Candide at parting from his preceptor was, however, tempered by the prospect of continuing his studies at the famous University of Marx-cum-Spencer, where the law of contradiction had been so far abrogated as to leave everything in doubt. About Liberty itself there existed two schools of thought: one affirming that it could only be reached through the independence of the Individual, the other as confidently associating it with the intervention of the State. The gentle Candide, as was his wont, maintained an open mind, and gave his support impartially first to one side and then to the other. He emerged consequently from the Schools with the highest academic honours, the fondest hopes and the fewest intellectual commitments of any man of his year.

"It was about this time that Candide first beheld the lovely Cunégonde, with her permanent wave and her platinum hair, and fell as rapidly in love with her as she did with him. An event, however, of less than cosmic consequence, yet of some little importance, suddenly disturbed his idyll. The world went to war. It is debateable to this day whether the Prussians assailed the Russians or the Russians the Prussians; but no one at the time doubted the guilt of his opponents, with the one exception of Candide, who, perceiving that data were not available for any judicial decision, continued to regard the matter with an open mind. His detachment, however, did not pass undisturbed. He noticed that frenzied women presented him with white feathers and that fiery sergeants beckoned him towards the recruiting-office. An appeal for counsel to the admirable Pansides afforded him no great assistance; for the good man was already hoarse with the exhortations to battle that he was delivering to excited audiences all over the country. When Candide

observed that there were two sides to every question, the good Pansides vehemently asserted that to this question there was but one.

" 'We are morally certain', he observed, 'that the Prussians
attacked the Russians.'

" 'Can we be sure,' asked Candide, 'since it has not been adjudi-
cated upon?'

" 'We have absolute certitude,' returned Pansides with thunder
in his voice.

" 'Can we have absolute certitude about anything?' inquired
Candide modestly, 'when even the Euclidean geometry is no longer
said to be of universal efficacy?'

"Pansides vouchsafed no further reply; and Candide was incorporated in the army the following week. No time was lost in teaching
him to march; and he reflected that this was also one of the mani-
festations of progress. Never did he allow himself to doubt that
men grow better and better every day; and least of all when in his
military exercises enthusiasm or discipline impelled him to drive a
spike through a dummy with a sense of growing excitement. He
soon became perfectly satisfied that warfare promoted the greatest
happiness of the greatest number. How, he would say to himself,
can I doubt it when, because a band of assassins in the Balkans,
with the connivance of their Government, murder the heir to a
neighbouring Empire, black men may be seen fighting in the fields
of France and white men in the heart of Africa, yellow men storming
citadels in far Cathay, and red men deserting their coral strands to
turn the soil of Europe crimson. Killing, he perceived, could be no
murder, but might be made the healthiest of exercises. How providential, he would reflect, that I was not born a ruler! For then I
might have been tempted hastily to hang those assassins, whereas
now I may perhaps live to see a monument erected to their memory.
Doubtless they belong, as the good Pansides assures me, to a gallant
little people who are teaching us to grow better and better in every
way and on every day.

"It would be tedious to dwell upon the valour displayed by
Candide in the light of these discoveries; for it was the admiration
of all that beheld it. Some compared him to the Cid and others to
the Knight of La Mancha. At length, after he had lost in succession a
tooth, a finger, an eye and a leg, he was compelled to give up active
service and accept an occupation more suited to his reduced cap-
acities. He was the better content to do so that, at the height of his

fighting fame, the fair Cunégonde had consented to marry him, and that he might, therefore, look forward to many years of domestic bliss. When, however, he returned to announce his intentions to his wife, Cunégonde speciously maintained that he was no longer the man that she had married; which, in view of his recently acquired disabilities, could not be easily refuted by the physical observations of scientific or medical men; and within a while she left him, in company with a certain M. Embusqué, who possessed some of the most gleaming teeth, glad eyes and becoming legs imaginable.

"It was in these circumstances that Candide turned to his old tutor for comment upon so unexpected, not to say disconcerting, an occurrence. The good Pansides instantly reassured him by reminding him that love and freedom were amongst the best things in the world, and that, when seen in combination, as in the case of Cunégonde, they were evidently still more worthy of reverence than when seen alone. He thanked Pansides for the unfailing insight which had again illuminated the obscurity of events, and subsequently thanked Parliament for the delicate consideration which enabled Cunégonde's infidelity to be swiftly endowed with all the charm and status of marriage. 'How wonderful is man,' he said to himself, 'who thus contrives to enrich with lofty beatitude every turn and twist of circumstance! Nothing, it is evident, can ever prevent so noble a creature from growing better and better every day.'

"One anxiety, it is true, still sometimes haunted the beneficent soul of Candide. The good Pansides in his eloquent speeches had said so much about the late War being one which would end war for ever, that Candide was almost afraid lest mankind, under the leadership of popularly elected assemblies and popularly acclaimed dictators, might be deprived of that ancient and royal pastime with all its inestimable benefits. His fears, however, fortunately proved groundless. After long and laboured consultation, the new statesmen of the victorious nations contrived to frame a Peace the terms of which were so nicely calculated to excite unrest as to ensure the return of hostilities at an early date. A League to keep frontiers as they had been finally fixed made the assurance doubly sure. But, as if this were not enough, the good Pansides almost wore himself out in proclaiming that he who wishes for peace should not prepare for war. Example, however, to his clear eyes had always appeared even more precious than precept; and he did his utmost to elucidate and enforce his meaning by going about with one side of his body left naked to attack and the other side defended by an antiquated shield, commonly reputed to have been bequeathed him by Don Quixote. Thus symbolically attired, he would perambulate the world to prove his points, and if by any good fortune he chanced upon an inn where a quarrel was in progress, he would, like the legendary Irishman, proceed to inquire whether it were a private quarrel or whether he might not also take part. His aid was generally accepted; and if his blows were feeble, his protests did much to extend the conflict.

"This accumulation of effort sufficed to maintain the cause of militarism. The Prussians, who had been falling behind in martial exercises, resumed their goose-step and forged ahead once more; and all their neighbours followed, but at a most respectful distance. Candide, unable any longer to take part in soldiering, resolved to cultivate his garden the more zealously. There would, he said to his friends, be much call for his produce with the return of hostilities, and he hoped in time to reap a handsome profit by his foresight. His circumstances had been rather straitened, but his good fortune did not fail him.

"A bonne-à-tout-faire had, meanwhile, presented herself in the person of a Hebrew maiden of uncertain age who had been driven during her life out of thirteen countries in turn, and was commonly known in the district as the Wandering Jewess. Her wide experience enabled her to produce delectable dishes derived from all parts of the world; and Candide both fed and crowed like a fighting-cock. His happiness was consummated by the return of Cunégonde, lately deserted, in view of impending hostilities, by M. Embusqué, who had decided to establish himself in a South Sea Island among a tribe of those peaceful survivors from the Golden Age of the world, known as savages. It was, however, the decision of the excellent Pansides to reside with him that filled up the cup of Candide's contentment. His excellent preceptor was now showing signs of age, and in truth at moments appeared a little confused by the vicissitudes of thought that he had passed through. He declared as fervently that the piling up of armaments was the best security for peace as he had formerly declared that it was the cause of war. 'How right you are, my beloved Candide,' he would say, 'to cultivate your garden. For the time must certainly come when your ploughshare will be needed for a sword and your pruning-hook for a spear. And this, if my memory serves me, is the sure and certain intimation of the approach of the earthly paradise.'

" 'I have always, my dear tutor,' Candide would gently reply, 'kept intact my early faith that we grow better and better every day, though I have learnt to perceive that this is quickest and best achieved by promoting the greatest unhappiness of the greatest number. But I am free to confess to you that the ways of men have come to seem to me no less inscrutable than those of Nature and that the peace of the politician, even more certainly than the peace of God, passes all understanding.'

" 'Liberty is the greatest of gifts and warfare the foundation of freedom,' Pansides would answer him. 'Let us go out and build our barracks.' "

.   .   .   .   .

"That is not so bad, for a first attempt," the Alien Voice would cry as I finished. "Most schemes of political improvement are, as Dr. Johnson remarked, very laughable things, and the credulity of modern reformers, so far as I have observed, outstrips even the credulity of old-time Christians." And at that some words of an old friend, now somewhile dead, who had seen much of the great world and reigned long over a small one, would return to mind with poignant effect. "When I was young", she had said, as I re-collect her words, "I knew Grey and Asquith and Haldane, and I used to think if only they got into power, all would go well. And they got into power—and now this!" If the secrets of all hearts were uttered, how often should we not hear "And now this!" repeated in many different tones of disappointment, exasperation or despair? Dr. Johnson had not missed the mark by much. However, I kept up my end, or at least the end of some I had loved, and said what I might in their favour. So I would cry angrily:—

"I won't have Liberals abused. I have found some of them my best friends in life; and I owe a great deal to their understanding sympathy."

"But you will allow that the course of events has made them look a little foolish."

"I will allow nothing," I said. "Even if they have made a grand muddle of the world, they tried to make it kinder. Some of them certainly have hearts of gold."

"And some," said the Alien Voice tartly, "the brains of rabbits. It's no worse than a 'tu quoque' to say so; for Mill, if I rightly recollect, called the Conservatives the stupid party. But, as the event has shown, one party is pretty nearly as stupid as the other. Neither has a pattern that fits the facts of life. What has happened to Mill's 'Logic', or to his 'Liberty', or to his 'Political Economy'? Time and circumstance have to all appearance fatally damaged those empirical, libertarian and laissez-faire theories even in the eyes of his own disciples; and the Liberals are looking again for a pattern of life, which they can't, of course, find because it isn't here, there, or anywhere."

"It was John Morley", I would observe rather inconsequently, "who called Mill the saint of rationalism; and Herbert Fisher used to exhort me to read Mill carefully on the ground that his was the only first-class mind one came across in the Oxford History School at the opening of this century."

"And you liked that advice, I suppose," sneered the Alien Voice, "because Mill made an idol of his wife, to the despair of his friends, who placed her intellectual powers far below his transcendental valuation of them."

"Organic epistemology, as I see it," I would rejoin, "postulates an eye for transparent beauty of being. One can't prove positively that Mill hadn't got that, any more than one can prove positively that a man who delights in the noise of a tom-tom hasn't got any ear for melody. One can only say that very few agreed with his taste or judgment. And if Mrs. Mill—Mrs. Taylor that was—really influenced Mill's work even to half the extent that he supposed, it might account for the lucidity which does not give light that one feels in his writings. In any case the place which this utilitarian individualist gave to love, and eventually to married love, in the making of his mind is from my standpoint rather significant." And I said no more.

Chapter VI

TO THE DINING-ROOM

IT was characteristic of Allegra, as I recall her, that, in her own exquisite way, she showed a proper regard for the pleasures of the table. Her approach to them was, indeed, no advent of an epicure to a feast of Lucullus, but rather the descent of some winged goddess upon a minute provision of nectar and ambrosia. But nectar and ambrosia it needed to be, or the goddess would abstain with all the rigour of an ascetic. Her cuisine, ethereal for herself, was, however, Continental in respect of her friends. Not for nothing had she lived in countries into which Puritanism, with its joyless gastronomy, had never penetrated. Every 'petit dîner' with her required to be 'bien servi'. The ox must become truly beef, and the sheep truly mutton— à la Normande, as we might say, since historians assure us that we owe our initial refinement to the entry of French names for cattle-flesh through the Norman gate of our history.

Subject, however, to such reservations, the consumption of meat did not seem to offend her, or produce any recoil towards the vegetarianism apparently congenial to our first parents. But, then, with her infinitesimal meals, she had no cause to fear any such appalling experience as Froude * has imagined happening to himself after falling asleep in a railway carriage. He had suddenly, as it appeared, woken up to find that the train had been run into a siding and that all the passengers were required to get out to have their moral baggage examined. On reaching the customs-house, where the Recording Angel was apparently in charge, he had flattered himself, indeed, that he was getting through with the business not too badly, when, of a sudden, a shutter was drawn aside in the wall, an endless multitude of animals displayed to view, and an accusing voice heard proclaiming that all these had died to keep the human cormorant, now upon his trial, alive.

Allegra's demands upon the animal world were in fact so modest that I cannot persuade myself they would not have been as willingly met by the creatures concerned, as if St. Francis had asked the Wolf for a haunch or the Birds for a wing. It was clear at a glance that here at least the law of sacrifice, which all in some measure

* "A Siding at a Railway Station", in "Short Studies".

obeyed, either as priests or victims or possibly as both, was not mocked. No pig could have felt that it was feeding a human hog, no lamb that it was nourishing a two-legged lion. The carnivorous demands of Humanity upon a groaning and travailing world fell in her instance so plainly within the conception of the lower sustaining the higher life as to invest that operation with a grace of devotion faintly foreshadowing the friendship which calls upon one being to lay down his life for another.

Allegra would not, however, have troubled her head with such hypersensitive considerations. It was part of her wisdom to take things as she found them; and degree and function went unquestioned in her philosophy as part of the settled order of a universe, where God was still to be found in His Heaven even when all was not right with the world. There was little or no challenge in her mind to those hierarchical and sacrificial mysteries of Nature which come so near the core of things in the meditations of the contemplative, and may have found unconscious apologists and accomplices, from 'meek' Walton to jovial Jorrocks. Connected as she was with great lovers of hunting-field and covert, race-course and river, there was latent in her, if I do not deceive myself, something of that sane understanding of and sympathy with wild creatures (not excepting those confined in the bear-garden at Mappin Terrace) which is more often to be met with among old sportsmen than professed humanitarians, and might lead us far towards a true cosmogony, did we but know how to develop and deepen it. Had this, for some of us tormenting, problem been carried to any extended discussion, I fancy that she might have briefed Blake as her advocate. His lyrics, together with Swinburne's study of him, were to be found amongst her best-bound books; and his "Songs of Innocence and Experience" afforded as good an idea as I can give of the mystical quality in her approach to life. To that eternal rhythm of ideas which, as St. Augustine * argues, must first be sought, if the significance of form in the exterior world is to be rightly apprehended, Blake's familiar excursus on the Tiger might, as I suppose, have seemed to her the proper prelude. On the one hand, the fearful power and symmetry of the beast left no room for questioning its transcendental artistry. It was plainly conceived beyond the flaming ramparts of our world; and the majesty of its eyes and limbs postulated, nay proclaimed, the hand of a designer as forcibly as does the power of Leviathan in the poetry of Job. But of the stupendous genius of the artist what

* "De Lib. Arb.", II, xvi, 41–42.

was to be said? Interrogate the shining monster as it ranges through the palpable darkness of the forest?

> Did he smile his work to see?
> Did he who made the Lamb make thee?

The shock comes, it need hardly be said, not from any lack of wonder at the make of the creature, in itself a marvel so perfect and coherent after its manner as to cause any suggestion of chance in its formation to appear the latest-born of old wives' fables, but from the perception of its hostile relationship to other objects, obviously designed by the same hand and belonging to the same universe. Nor was this some unaccountable exception to a contrary rule of kindness. It was as much present in principle in the teeth of the lamb as it crops the tender grass, or in the leaves of the daisy as it asserts itself against adjacent plants and deprives them of light and air. The tiger had merely presented the problem in terms of burning thought and fierce lucidity.

Into the maze of this enigma there seems to enter for Blake precisely at this point the figure of a child with all its connotations. Immediately after "The Tiger" * there follow those "Songs of Experience" which he has denominated "The Little Girl Lost" and "The Little Girl Found"; and I venture to think it more than probable that if, like George Macdonald, he had known Allegra as a child, her name would have been substituted for that of Lyca in the poem.

> In futurity
> I prophetic see
> That the earth from sleep
> (Grave the sentence deep)
>
> Shall arise and seek
> For her Maker meek;
> And the desert wild
> Become a garden mild.
>
> In the southern clime,
> Where the summer's prime
> Never fades away
> Lovely Lyca lay.

. . . . . .

* See Sampson's Oxford edition of Blake's Poems, p. xxv. "The sequence here observed is taken from a MS. index in Blake's autograph, headed 'The Order in which the Songs of Innocence and of Experience ought to be paged and placed', which coincides with that of the Monckton Milnes copy (printed not earlier than 1818) sold at the Crewe sale in 1903."

> Sleeping Lyca lay
> While the beasts of prey,
> Come from caverns deep,
> View'd the maid asleep.
>
> . . . .
>
> Leopards, tigers, play
> Round her as she lay,
> While the lion old
> Bow'd his mane of gold. . . .

This vision of the beasts adoring, as the reader may possibly remember, gives way in due course to that of the distracted parents in pursuit; and these latter presently stumble upon the Lion.

> 'Follow me,' he said;
> 'Weep not for the maid;
> In my palace deep
> Lyca lies asleep.'
>
> Then they followèd
> Where the vision led,
> And saw their sleeping child
> Among tigers wild.
>
> To this day they dwell
> In a lonely dell;
> Nor fear the wolvish howl
> Nor the lions' growl.

A dream! Perhaps no more than the shadow of a dream! At best a prophet's dream, needing 'God's holy mountain' for its fulfilment! Yet, for all that, not so wild with fancy as the visions politicians appear to entertain about the approaching pacification of their own species! For every kind of beast and bird, fish and reptile is said to have been tamed of mankind; so that the travel-diary of one of our contemporary philosophers (Count Keyserling) even contains some account of a visit to one who for preference dwelt alone with a horde of poisonous serpents. But who is going to tame mankind, with its insatiable desire to add field to field, province to province, kingdom to kingdom, dollar to dollar, and tax to tax? Who will stay the competition of men and nations for material advantages far beyond the requirements of animal sustenance? Who will bring their contending purposes into a common pattern? Who will build the heavenly Jerusalem in England's green and pleasant land or any other land known to us?

I might, perhaps, fancy myself listening after this manner to some such echo of Blake's philosophy, and then at this point find myself compelled to recognise that the Alien Voice had suddenly broken in upon my meditations and begun mocking me again in its most trenchant style. "You see," it would say, "that it is ever the same. You are always trying to find harmony where it does not exist and meaning where it is absent. All this visionary stuff—what is it worth as an answer to the hard hostilities of human evolution? You are merely getting your head into the clouds and losing yourself on the mountain-tops of imagination."

"Better men than myself", I would reply, "have got their heads there before me. Yet Socrates has left a deeper impression on the world of thought than Aristophanes; and so, after all, I may be making no mistake in star-gazing. In any case, I never expected to get the better of you upon the plane of the senses, for my ideas are a little impatient of the ground-floor. Imagination will keep breaking in upon my sensible perceptions and grouping them anew, in the manner of dreams. And that is what happens with the poets; and, if you take poetry for nonsense, God help you."

"I should prefer illumination from some other quarter," the Voice would instantly return.

"You shall have it in a moment, but listen still a little longer to Blake," I would answer. "For he gets in a smart right and left directed at the blind guides of his century—and indeed of all centuries. Listen:—

> Mock on, mock on, Voltaire, Rousseau;
>   Mock on, mock on; 'tis all in vain!
> You throw the sand against the wind,
>   And the wind blows it back again.
>
> And every sand becomes a gem
>   Reflected in the beams divine;
> Blown back they blind the mocking eye,
>   But still in Israel's paths they shine."

"I'm not blinded yet," the Voice would observe, with its usual suggestion of sang-froid.

"Then we may as well continue the conversation in the dining-room, with the human body as the leading topic of discussion," I would rejoin. "It merits some attention, even if it is not—so to say—ultimately all we are. And, nowadays, with the Democrat predominant at Dinner and replacing the old Autocrat of the Breakfast-table, we may reasonably hope to talk the matter out, untroubled by the elegant reserves of a past century. Meanwhile the subject of our inquiries should be properly warmed and filled, lest it turn corpse-like before its time. You remember Tranio's recipe for debate—to do, forsooth,

> . . . as adversaries do in law,
> Strive mightily, but eat and drink as friends."

"A voice cannot drink," the Voice would murmur drily.

"Surely", I would urge, "every organ of the kind must be able to wet its whistle. Or can it be that you, who but a little time ago insinuated that I was confusing counsel with imperceptibilities, have now yourself slipped into metaphysics? Is a voice no evidence of a mouth and throat behind it? Is a sound located only in my ear and not on the tongue whence it comes? Will you tell me that it is just such a phantom will-o'-the-wisp as a ray of light which, emanating from some solar system that has had its day and ceased to be, makes me, no less than the drunkard, see stars that are not there?"

The Alien Voice would make no response to this, thereby arousing a strong suspicion in my mind that it had lost its way in the cloudy borderland between the physical and the metaphysical world. And, upon seeing it thus caught up into the clouds—whether in the body or out of the body, it were hard to tell—I would smile inwardly, but grow outwardly more pressing and attentive still. For I cherished a vivid recollection of a passage in Chesterton's little monograph on Blake in which he discovers a correspondence between men's taste in drink and their views about religion, and I wanted to see whether this haunting Echo, if it were no more, had not at least some inform-ing memory of old preferences in liquor.* For the affinity, so Chesterton declares, of the Catholic disposition is with wine, of the Protestant with ale, and of the agnostic with water, clear and cool. To the moralist pur sang, he assigns soda-water as being particularly congenial to that effervescent ado about nothing in which the idealistic mind delights; whilst in the café noir that keeps one awake, yet leaves one still insufficiently nourished, he perceives the appointed beverage of a socialist, or at least of a Shavian one. And finally for the 'hygienic materialist', as the fit emblem and companion of his condition, there are reserved the sweet uses and succulent charms of cocoa. I had an occasional, dreadful suspicion that it was to this drink, so little loved by G. K. Chesterton, that

* G. K. Chesterton, "Blake", pp. 98–99.

the Alien Voice, if it had got a palate besides, might have presently become addicted. But I may be mistaken.

By this singular method of testing natural dispositions the interpretation of Allegra's soul that I have put forward was curiously confirmed. I never remember seeing her touch ale or water, unless perhaps under some compulsion of necessity. Spirits she would contemplate only in the form of an occasional cocktail before meals or a still more occasional liqueur after them; and that was not enough to establish any affinity with spiritualism, to which, as Chesterton suggests, they should logically lead. Her real taste, always most moderately indulged, was, however, for wine; and, smoking not at all, she was exceptionally qualified to appraise its merits. On the Chestertonian hypothesis, she might indeed be said to have raised her glass to Rome twice in the day. Of which convergence of thought and palate I may perhaps say in passing that I supposed myself to have found circumstantial evidence in her unqualified approval of a wine that travels ill but is indigenous, or nearly so, in the Eternal City, and excellent. It was that same wine, the power of which to gladden the heart of man is preserved in the name of "Est, Est", bestowed upon it, so the story goes, by the valet of Bishop Johannes Fugger, sent ahead to report upon inns for his master's benefit. 'It is, it is the very thing,' the valet inscribed upon the town-gate of Montefiascone; and the Bishop agreed with him so well that he went no further on his way.

Such gifts of God Allegra was the last person to under-value. The Vine, which has so strong a hold alike upon the mind of the mere pagan and the pure mystic, had certainly a great poetry for her. A fine edition of Fitzgerald's works stood on her shelves; and she was no less sensible than others of her generation to the charm of the Rubáiyát:—

> A Book of Verses underneath the Bough,
> A Jug of Wine, a Loaf of Bread—and Thou
> Beside me singing in the Wilderness—
> Oh, Wilderness were Paradise enow!

I can remember her quoting those lines in a southern garden, where in the spring of the year the roses would have afforded Omar just such a setting as his words demand. And to recall them is to reflect how readily the simplest needs of Humanity merge in the sublime, how easily the life of Man at its purest can become the quest of the Holy Grail. Not a word wants changing in the lines just cited for

the Bread, the Wine, the Desert and the Beloved to become transfigured by the purest mysticism. So far did the world of sense reach
out its hands towards a world not sensual!

The Lower Study in the House had two exits; and, as I think,
Allegra, after she had heard the 'great argument about it and about'
that was carried on perennially between doctor and saint in the book-
cases, would not have come out 'by the same door wherein she
went'. For the alternative mode of egress, which led into dining-
room, had much to recommend it to a person of her spiritual and
social affinities. The Greek tradition, it is hardly necessary to observe, is in favour of an informal dealing with the hard questions
of life either peripatetically, when the body is a little warmed by
motion, or in a symposium, when it is a little warmed with wine.
And she, a child, born late in time, as I have tried to show, of the
Florentine Renaissance with its Platonic affinities, proved herself true
to type in her preference for talk in which Bacchus, but in his
happier hours, might mingle. No Bacchanals in ecstasy, nor Nordic
heroes deep-sunk in their potations, would have made boon-com-
panions at her table. The garden that she loved was no bier-garten.
Nohow can I see her falling under the spell of Professor Teufelsdröckh as he meditates in Weissnichtwo betwixt gulps of beer and
clouds of tobacco. To the learning of any Prussian Dryasdust, of
whom, as even Carlyle opines, nothing comparable in 'darkness,
dreariness or immethodic platitude' * is to be found in Nature, she
would, as I see her, have remained indifferent. His values, for all the
praise our pundits used to give them, would have seemed to her
false and his labours fleeting. If she had had her way, she would, I
doubt not, have caused many learned heads to be gently soused in
butts of malmsey or any other handy product of

> The Grape that can with Logic absolute
> The Two-and-Seventy jarring Sects confute;
> The sovereign Alchemist that in a trice
> Life's leaden metal into Gold transmute.

Not that so fine a palate as Allegra's could have remained long
insensitive to the vintage of some German literature warmed by the
rays of a southern sun. To the charm of Winckelmann when, restrict-
ing himself to the bare minimum of bread and wine required to sustain the body, he sought in Italy the intellectual romance of his life;

* "Frederick the Great", I, i.

or of Goethe as, under the influence of Winckelmann's example, he took the same road and then, in Mignon's song, made his acknowledgments to the land of the orange and myrtle; or again of Heine, as he made good Thiers's description of him as 'the wittiest Frenchman since Voltaire'—she must assuredly have yielded. But all this was to demand the cachet of the Latin mind, and in fact to confess that the paganism of the Latin is not as the paganism of the Nordic genius. Its gods are not racial any more; they have admitted that the Galilean has conquered; they have cried out that Great Pan is dead. Somewhat after the manner described in Malvolti's vision in "John Inglesant", they may be caught creeping up from the recesses of the old classics towards Christian altars, as for example in Plato's cry for some diviner word,* or in Virgil's memorable eclogue; and, indeed, whenever in any man's intellectual soul the good tidings arrive that the true God is near. For the rest, Goethe had himself recognised in his conversations with Eckermann † that the German language became vague, difficult and obscure in proportion as philosophy influenced it; and few condemnations are more damaging than this, if one considers its source and its substance.

Thus to the elephantine efforts of the German philosophers to circumvent the metaphysical stumbling-block so firmly planted by Hume at the entrance to the field of knowledge, Allegra would, I fear, have proved as inattentive as I should have proved myself if, like John Sterling, I had been privileged to hear Coleridge soliloquizing about 'om-m-mjects' and 'sum-m-mjects', whilst gazing out into 'the hazy infinitude of Kantian transcendentalism'.‡ Yet Coleridge, though in these wandering mazes so fully lost that, as Hazlitt observes of his conversation, he started from no premises and came to no conclusions, had doubtless his excuses. For a hundred years have passed since those lucubrations of his upon the brow of Highgate Hill, and even still Kant's thought is described by a capable and lucid exponent as 'intrinsically difficult', Kant's method of writing as 'abstract and diffuse', Kant's meaning as suffering bewildering change, and Kant's very philosophy as containing 'arguments for every philosophical position which the imagination of man can conceive'.§ But if such obscurities form no bar to the recommendation of Kant by Professor Haldane ¶ as a better com-

* "Phaedo", 85, D.   † April 14, 1824.
‡ "Life of John Sterling", c. viii.
§ C. E. Joad, "Guide to Philosophy", p. 359.
¶ J. B. S. Haldane in "Possible Worlds".

panion for the scientist than any other philosopher, it seems to be a
fair inference that physical science is not without its hours—if so
much may be said without offence—of obfuscation—as it gropes its
way along the borderlands of Becoming and Being and of the Pure
and the Practical Reason.

"Philosophy", according to a scientific publicist of the first eminence, "lies in the province of science, and not in that of letters"; *
and this resort to German transcendentalism, therefore, seemed best
regarded as the price that the English mind has had to pay for
its tardy emancipation from the influence of Hume's metaphysic.
Amongst the golden girls and boys that our academies turn out,
few, perhaps, have any clear idea of the part that a sceptical epistemology has played in their education, and fewer still could trace
the intellectual uncertainty in which their studies frequently conclude to preoccupation with the 'perceptions' of the senses and
neglect of that world of 'universals' in which the human intellect
lived and moved and had its being from the days of Augustine
to those of Aquinas. Only Macaulay's precocious schoolboys had
achieved any acquaintance with the history of philosophic doubt;
and they had remained schoolboys still in their egregious contempt
for the Schoolmen. Thus none but pedants were left to search the
lumber-rooms of philosophy for the secret of our present intellectual
discontents. Yet how confusing had been the effect of Locke's
attack upon the existence of innate ideas, and how confounding, if
properly considered, his plausible distinction between the primary
and secondary qualities of objects—between their extension and exterior solidity on the one hand and such delicate attributes as scent
and sound and colour, supposedly conferred upon them by animal
senses, on the other! And how singular—to conclude the tale of
these surprises—the fate of our opaque English thought after it had
been sifted by the subtle idealism of an Irish Bishop to show the
existence of God, and then strained anew by the pawky humour of
a Scottish sceptic until the idealistic proof of a Universal Mind
looked little better than a piece of imported blarney! Idealism, as
one could see, had been pushed just far enough by Berkeley to
require objects, if they were to retain objectivity at all, to be
thought of as continuously present to the mind of an all-perceiving,
always attentive, everlasting Deity, and had then been reduced to
a causeless, solipsist finality by Hume, until no knowledge of an

* T. H. Huxley, "Hume with Helps to the Study of Berkeley", p. 51.

objective world appeared to be available at all beyond what our individual perceptions, themselves not immune from error, afforded us of it.

Rationalised science, on this showing, fell under a closely similar suspicion to rationalised theology; and, as Professor Taylor had pointed out,* Hume's irony played in even measure, if perhaps with unequal effect, about the foundations of both. A succession of impressions, subsequently remembered and associated as ideas, which formed in his view the whole content of a by no means solid body of knowledge, gave no more countenance to a law of causation than to a law-giver or a final cause. The mind had, in fact, become impaled on a rickety fence. "We have no . . . choice left", he had declared, "but betwixt a false reason and none at all." †

Few pages indeed in the history of man's effort to think for himself had so chill a pathos as those in which this greatest of impressionist philosophers depicts the nemesis of one who has both disdained the 'ancient philosophy' of Aristotle and Aquinas and seen through 'the modern philosophy' of Locke and Berkeley. "The intense view", he wrote, "of these manifold contradictions and imperfections in human reason has so wrought upon me, and heated my brain, that I am ready to reject all belief and reasoning, and can look upon no opinion even as more probable or likely than another. Where am I or what? From what causes do I derive my existence, and to what condition shall I return? Whose favour shall I court, and whose anger must I dread? What beings surround me? And on whom have I any influence, or who have any influence on me? I am confounded with all these questions, and begin to fancy myself in the most deplorable condition imaginable, environed with the deepest darkness, and utterly deprived of the use of every member and faculty. Most fortunately it happens that, since reason is incapable of dispelling these clouds, nature herself suffices to that purpose and cures me of this philosophical melancholy and delirium. . . . I dine, I play a game of back-gammon, I converse and am merry with my friends; and when, after three or four hours amusement, I would return to these speculations, they appear so cold and strained and

* "We miss half of Hume's irony unless we understand that it is meant to hit, not only 'dangerous friends or disguised enemies to the Christian religion', but also 'dangerous friends or disguised enemies' to Newtonian science" (A. E. Taylor, "Philosophical Studies", p. 333).

† "Treatise of Human Nature", I, Pt. iv, Sec. 7.

ridiculous that I cannot find it in my heart to enter into them any
further. . . . Under what obligation do I lie of making such an
abuse of time? . . . If I must be a fool, as all those who reason or
believe anything *certainly* are, my follies shall at least be natural and
agreeable. . . . These are the sentiments of my spleen and indolence; and indeed I must confess that philosophy has nothing to
oppose to them. . . . In all the incidents of life we ought still to
preserve our scepticism. If we believe that fire warms or water re-
freshes, 'tis only because it costs us too much pains to think otherwise. Nay, if we are philosophers, it ought only to be upon sceptical
principles." *

            •   •   •   •   •

"You were trying, I think, to get into the Dining-room," the
Alien Voice would observe hungrily at this point, "when you fell
into a meditation and a monologue."

"It is all apposite," I would return. "In order to cross the
threshold between the Lower Study and the Dining-room with a
clear conscience, it needed the visa of the 'sceptical' philosophy; and
Hume can help us to that. Notice his words: 'I dine, I play a game
of back-gammon, I converse and make merry with my friends'.
This is his recipe for recovering from the rational inconsequence
and pale cast of post-impressionist thought; and his wisdom is the
wisdom of Omar and Horace or, to come up to date, of old Jolyon
Forsyte. He has reverted to feeling as the foundation of common
sense. He turns to food and play and jollity as his saviours from a
scepticism so all-invading that it has even invaded the very citadel of
sensibility. But let us linger yet a moment before we carry the old
Scotsman off to dine away his cares."

"'Tis impossible", he confesses, "upon any system to defend
either our understanding or senses; and we but expose them further
when we endeavour to justify them in that manner. As the sceptical
doubt arises naturally from a profound and intense reflection on
those subjects, it always increases the further we carry our reflections,
whether in opposition or conformity to it. Carelessness and in-
attention alone can afford us any remedy. For this reason I rely
entirely upon them; and take it for granted, whatever may be the
reader's opinion at the present moment, that an hour hence he will
be persuaded there is both an external and internal world." †

            * "Treatise", Bk. I, Pt. iv, Sec. 7.
            † *Ibid.*, Sec. 2.

For all that, it was not, as it seemed to be, without casting a long-ing, lingering look behind that this most rational of sceptics would exchange the study for the dining-room. In spite of the apparently devastating results of his reflections, he seemed to cling to the com-fortable belief that thought was not wasted labour. "Shall we estab-lish it", he would say as we went into dinner, "for a general maxim that no refined or elaborate reasoning is ever to be received? Con-sider well the consequences of such a principle. By this means you cut off entirely all science and philosophy. You proceed upon one singular quality of the imagination, and by a parity of reason must embrace all of them: and you expressly contradict yourself. . . . Very refined reflections have little or no influence upon us; and yet we do not, and cannot establish it for a rule that they ought not to have any influence, which implies a manifest contradiction." *

The cogent old man seemed thus to be admitting the existence of some unidentified residuum of thought—of a principle, somewhere in the soul, qualified to assert itself by acts of faith both in the promptings of common-sense on the one hand and in the worth of subtle and searching reflection on the other. It was not, however, congenial to the English mind, in general detached, as I thought, by the search for working compromises from any serious interest in first or last things, and always, at least since the Reformation, too busily engaged with hortatory and even, sometimes, pharisaical ethics, to bother about the metaphysical catastrophe which Hume's conclusions had illustrated so candidly. He had spoken no less for the compatriots of John Wesley than for those of John Knox when he observed that morality was a subject that interested men above all the rest; † though he did not sufficiently explain why it should do so in a world where knowledge, strictly speaking, was confined to disconnected impressions and the images of them retained and asso-ciated by memory. God appeared, indeed, upon the distant horizon of his philosophy as the principle of the world's order; but the idea of God, as he presented it, could hardly be said to possess the credentials of a previous impression, and doubtless the group of French atheists, whom, all-unsuspecting, he met during a visit to France, could have given him good reasons for dismissing it as a mental mirage. For the rest, so Olympian a Deity as the eighteenth-century intellectuals sometimes permitted themselves to believe in was not calculated to move the many to acts of devotion. "There

* "Treatise", Bk. I, Pt. iv, Sec. 7.　　　† *Ibid.*, Bk. III, Pt. i, Sec. 1.

are difficulties", Voltaire observes in the "Dictionnaire Philosophique",* "in the opinion that there is a God; but in the opposite opinion there are absurdities." His famous allusion to the Lisbon earthquake of 1755, with its obvious suggestion of some blind and brutal fury in the very heart of the earth, had thus at the close been curiously tempered by some lines of which Rousseau's "Vicaire Savoyard" need not have felt ashamed:—

> Un jour tout sera bien, voilà notre espérance.
> Tout est bien aujourd'hui, voilà l'illusion.
> Les sages me trompaient et Dieu seul a raison.
> Humble dans mes soupirs, soumis dans ma souffrance,
> Je ne m'élève point contre la Providence.

It was hard to make quite sure what the creator of Dr. Pangloss was at. As with Disraeli, his biting wit probably at times left him wondering himself how much or how little he believed. Bentham better than Hume knew how to meet the British mind half-way. His inscription of "the greatest happiness of the greatest number" upon the phylacteries of Utilitarianism was a stroke of genius which not all the comments of its critics from Carlyle to Moore † have been powerful enough to destroy. Happiness may be a will-o'-the-wisp as elusive as it appears in the Eastern fable,‡ or the sum-total of a minority's happiness so outweigh that of a majority as to make it the greater of the two in amount, or the sum in itself prove too various and subtle to be politically calculable at all, or again, if calculable, to be altogether incommensurate with goodness; but, for all that, the phrase mightily appeals to the English people. There is morality in it—morality that seems sensible enough—and the most part of the nation still moves to its comfortable measure. If Jeremy Bentham's body has stayed above ground to adorn an academy, his soul goes marching on.

Thus it had been left to Kant to deal with the metaphysical difficulty which Hume had raised; and he did it, after the manner of his countrymen, with no little prolixity and patience. Behind the

---

* Article on the Existence of God.

† Prof. G. E. Moore in "Principia Ethica".

‡ Prof. Henry Sidgwick somewhere recalls the fable of the Eastern potentate who was assured that he could be healed of a disease by wearing the shirt of a perfectly happy man. He sent out messengers in all directions to search for some such. After much seeking one of them found a man who professed himself wholly contented. The messenger thereupon offered him a great reward for his shirt. "Alas!" he replied, "I have no shirt."

phenomenal world—the world of appearance—another world—a noumenal world, a world of substance—was to be morally or mystically discerned; or at any rate so he made out, to his own and some other men's satisfaction. It satisfied him of the Being of God and the Immortality of Man. Yet he had beheld it apart from knowledge. The senses did not apprehend it, neither did pure reason attain to it. It was a thing real, yet not realised; and, as the return of Hegel and other of his disciples to crude idealism showed, Kant's terminology would not stand the strain of a mixed burden of metaphysics. He did not find the just balance between the two worlds, which his philosophy sought to shoulder; and his counsel, as I thought, ended in collapse.

I never attempted to explain these matters to Allegra; nor in all probability was I at all competent to do so. But I see no occasion to regret it. It is a poor service to mankind to invite any soul to lose itself in fog; and Allegra's was too full of spiritual sunshine to have made such conduct other than an outrage. Not willingly would I have seen her exchange the blue skies of Florence for the cloudlands of Königsberg; not easily could I have persuaded myself that she would have been justified in looking for true reason by dim Nordic lights. There are hours when the Latin genius cries out, "Si non vis intelligi, debes negligi". There are days when the observation of Hobbes that absurdity is a privilege peculiar to man, and that, of all men, philosophers are most prone to it,* returns to mind. There are weeks when the Island of Laputa floats full into view. And such times and seasons perhaps most commonly coincide with the study of German thought. Truth, if Allegra's understanding afforded any key to it, was lightsome; and indeed every correspondence between thought and things should at least, when pointed out, spring to the eye. She would have drawn no conviction from contemplating the monstrous spectacle of minds too long in labour. Some thoughtful words of Walter Bagehot's might, perhaps, be aptly introduced to vindicate such a poise of spirit. "The mass of a system", he remarks,† "attracts the young and impresses the unwary; but cultivated people are very dubious about it. They are ready to receive hints and suggestions, and the smallest real truth is ever welcome. But a large book of deductive philosophy is much to be suspected. No doubt the deductions may be right; in most writers they are so; but where did the premises come from? . . . In a word, the superfluous

* "Leviathan", I, c. 5.   † "Physics and Politics", pp. 190–1.

energy of mankind has flowed over into philosophy and has worked into big systems what should have been left as little suggestions."

"Who is prosing now in manifest emulation of German thoroughness?" the Alien Voice would at this juncture interject; and I never felt quite sure that its words did not find a sweeter-sounding echo in the depths of the House.

"I was only trying to make a case for keeping the Germans out of the dining-room," I would plead, "for they have a gross way of dealing with the nectar and ambrosia of human thought. After all, it is not only I who have found them troublesome. See how the development of their philosophy affects such a critic as Santayana, who finds their egotism devastating.* Let me repeat that Goethe declares that philosophic speculation is a drawback to them since it often renders their mode of expression vague, complicated and even incomprehensible.† Consider that Kant has been called 'the greatest disaster in the history of philosophy'; and, as for Hegel, has he not himself affirmed that 'the coasts of the happy isles of philosophy . . . are covered only with fragments of shattered ships' and that we behold no intact vessel in their bays?"‡ Well did a British Ambassador § to Berlin observe that 'the Germans prefer to hear all the arguments rather than to select the best'.

"Surely we have waited long enough for our symposium?" the Alien Voice would coldly reiterate. "Are we not all 'mustered' now, as you well know Mr. Gladstone is reported to have asked when dining with the Colmans?"

"All", I would rejoin, "save only the Germans. They are sadly to seek in some things beside Greek; and I was just throwing them another bun or two for fear they might start gate-crashing and even end by demanding a bouquet. But probably I was wasting my time, They are pretty sure to get into the room somehow, if it be only by proxy; they are so dreadfully diligent. Not, however, in my judgment, with such philosophical aid as theirs is Hume's cool scepticism going to be banished, nor with such defenders will the Humanities that humanise be saved. By all means let their poets and musicians be admitted to the floors above, for they can sing charmingly when they like. But to have their philosophers in at

* "Egotism in German Philosophy".
† Conv. with Eckermann, April 14, 1924.
‡ Hegel, "Werke", I, 166 (quoted from Wallace, I, 170).
§ D'Abernon.

meals portends a social disaster. The more lively ladies will be leaving the dining-room long before their time is come, and the more prosy gentlemen remaining there long after theirs is up. Besides, if we were to admit the German idealists, it would be unjust to refuse the German pessimists a hearing; and to give pessimism a full run would require a millennium of thought. Do you recall Chesterton's conjecture that 'if every human being lived a thousand years, every human being would end up either in utter pessimistic scepticism or in the Catholic Creed'?"*

"Even if that were true," the Alien Voice would observe, "there is no reason to assume that Schopenhauer or Hartmann might not prove entertaining."

"I would give way and admit them", I would answer, "if they would only despair. Despair, you know, is said to be silent. But German pessimists luxuriate as much in schadenfreude as British optimists in self-congratulation. Where one could do with, or even delight in an Obermann or an Amiel, a young Werther, or, worse still, an old one, would be intolerable. Anyhow, the German soul consorts ill with that of Allegra, and not too well with your own. We are in need of fine instruments, as I said at the beginning, and not of coarse ones, for the detection of truth."

"I felt sure I should catch you excluding the coarse side of life from your survey," the Alien Voice would mock back at me, "and now I have the proof of it. The Germans, you say, are too coarse for you. But God, if there be a God, made them—and a good many of them, too. You recollect Lincoln's saying about common people in general."

"You misrepresent me," I would reply. "The Germans are too coarse for me, not because their manners do not happen to be of the best, but because their minds are wanting in that fineness of quality— that esprit de finesse—that seems to me essential. Their thought is in fact neither simple enough nor subtle enough to contribute anything particular to a criticism of life depending upon delicate instruments. Do you chance to remember Dr. Johnson's reply when his biographer complained of the expulsion of Methodist students from the University of Oxford? "Was it not hard to expel them, Sir," Boswell pleaded, "for I am told they were good beings?" Johnson: "I believe they might be good beings; but they were not fit to be in the University of Oxford. A cow is a very good animal in the field;

* G. K. Chesterton, "William Blake", p. 208.

but we turn her out of a garden." * So it is with the German philosophers. They have, as Buffon long ago pointed out, no power of selection, devour everything they see and chew it interminably. Their mastications are therefore in my view best confined to the Lower Study, where they can browse at will. A dining-room demands finer fare and more agreeable wines than they can do justice to. Do not, however, on this account accuse me of bowdlerising the facts of life. So little is this the case that I propose to call Rabelais into counsel and appoint him, if not to be the presiding genius in the chair, at least to be the principal guest at the table. That ought to satisfy the most critical observer that nothing of the grossness of human nature is going to be deliberately excluded from view. Rabelais, however, let me observe, is not merely Rabelaisian. 'Saluez de ma part', wrote the eminent Budé, 'votre frère en religion et en science. . . . Saluez quatre fois en mon nom le gentil et savant Rabelais.' "

To these observations I would get no answer, perhaps because no adverse answer was easy. For there is no man who has looked the human body so straight (I suppose I must say) in the stomach ('l'estomac'—I refrain, in spite of Master Gaster, from saying 'le ventre'), as Rabelais, and none probably who has better understood the secret reflections of 'l'homme moyen sensuel'. An eminent living critic has, indeed, told us that it would decrease his reverence for Cardinal Newman, if he learnt that the Cardinal had kept an edition of Rabelais locked away in a table drawer. He explains that the 'distinctive beauty of Newman's nature and life excluded cosmic or absolute humour', and proceeds to place Rabelais beyond the reach likewise of Jane Austen, who, he observes, had she looked into Rabelais's works, would have thought him 'not only excessively nasty, but very silly'.† It seems, however, a rash assumption to suppose that minds as subtle as these were blind to facts that all can see for the looking. 'Toute vérité n'est pas bonne à dire'; yet a catholic mind should blink at nothing. The English Cardinal was of the same profession as the Curé de Meudon; and the Curé de Meudon was somewhile physician to a prince of the Church. Time, but not circumstance, opposed their meeting in the flesh. But has Panurge made more 'cosmic' fun than Falstaff, at whose sad size, solid sufferings, shrewd humbug and foiled flirta-

---

* Boswell's "Life of Johnson" (ed. G. B. Hill, 1887), II, p. 187.
† Desmond MacCarthy in the *Sunday Times* (16.12.34).

tions, surely even Newman must have found it in his soul to laugh; and is there 'absolute humour' keener than Mistress Pistol's account of the old rogue's last hours or humour better meriting a Cardinal's smiles and sighs? The Psalmist, for the rest, is not alone in praying to be delivered from his 'necessities'; yet does a Saint contemplate 'Brother Body' with both mirth and pity. And, if to "laugh and shake in Rabelais's easy chair" * involves some increase of coarse fibre even beyond the demands of Swift's keen satire, Sterne's subtle lubricity, and Fielding's genial cynicism, the common indictment of Rabelais still requires some qualification. Not only was it Rabelais's strange lot, as one of his biographers has noted,† to be persecuted by monks and theologians and protected by prelates and princes; but Coleridge can be quoted as saying that 'he could write a treatise in praise of the moral elevation of Rabelais's work which . . . would yet be truth and nothing but the truth', and still later critics can be found asserting that 'the tone and accent of Rabelais's writings betray no morbid obsession of any kind, but quite the opposite'.‡ Rabelais is not read for the reasons on account of which men read Casanova. His indelicacy is not indecency. He speaks where others prefer to be silent, but he speaks for a large constituency. There is nothing perverted or abnormal in his views. For the purpose of any survey of the whole of life his evidence, or its equivalent, would have to be called and reckoned with. To consider his credentials is to confess his competence.

A physician of the soul by profession and a physicist inspired, much like Leonardo, by the piercing rather than prurient curiosity of the Renaissance, Rabelais was even more definitely, as his work at the Hospital at Lyon shows, a physician of the body. His book is in fact essentially a doctor's tale, broad and unblushing in its detail, yet in its general purport kindly and entertaining, and in its counsel sage and sane. European society, always ailing and distressful, had under his eyes begun to discover symptoms of disintegration amounting to disease. The chosen Continent of evolutionary knowledge seemed stricken with intellectual confusion. Human nature was dislocated. Its spirit turned towards hatred; its soul towards uncertainty; its body towards restless or sanguinary adventure. Hamlet,

* "Dunciad", I, 22.
† "Nouvelle Biog. Générale" (Art. on Rabelais).
‡ Nock and Wilson, "Francis Rabelais", p. 225.

as the ubiquitous, enduring appeal of his character makes clear, spoke for generations to come, as well as for his own, when he declared that the time was out of joint—and all the more certainly so, if the conjecture that Shakespeare extracted him from Montaigne * be correct. Mankind had in fact been brought to the verge of insanity by beholding its natural face in a glass and the mysterious reflection of Nature behind it.

The shock brought on a sickness that has lasted to this day and returns like a tertian fever. There have been many consultations and many diagnoses. But among the very finest consultants—to judge from the attention paid to their opinions by the aristocrats of the Republic of Letters—are three sons of that brilliant race whose genius has to many eyes seemed like the Greek, both in its subtlety and simplicity.† Of these masters in modern Humanism, Rabelais is one. In the same clinic, where Montaigne treats of men primarily as works of mind and Pascal as creations of spirit, Rabelais probes them as things of flesh. And, if it be true that every European has two homelands—his own and France ‡—then their diagnoses should serve not only the children of the Church's eldest daughter, but all that Continent which was once the seat of Christendom. Their work, it is safe to say, will never be vanquished with a sneer, nor their insight gainsaid with a smile. For, if their intellects be balked of truth, what hope of it can their critics entertain?

* See G. C. Taylor, "Shakespeare's Debt to Montaigne", p. 40.

† Cp. "Sooner or later the genius of France always comes back to see that the subtly simple—the secret of French greatness as of Greek—outweighs all the ponderous complexities that take in the Teutonic mind" (F. L. Lucas, "Studies French and English", p. 278).

‡ *Sunday Times*, May 7th, 1939.

Chapter VII

THE DINING-ROOM

"HOW can these people strike dignified attitudes and pretend that things matter, when the total ludicrousness of life is proved by the very method by which it is supported? A man strikes the lyre and says, 'Life is real, life is earnest', and then goes into a room and stuffs alien substances into a hole in his head. I think nature was indeed a little broad in her humour in these matters."* The words were penned by one of the best humorists of the present century, but to produce their best effect they need to be placed in the mouth of one of those pompous personages who, before and after grace is said at public dinners, roll out the names, styles, titles and dignities of the persons subsequently and in due course to be heard praying and speaking. But, if Rabelais were of the company, then to Rabelais, in preference even to a toast-master, should those words have been assigned, for of Rabelais were they born and to Rabelais do they return.

I had sometimes wondered what my feelings would have been if that eminent man had, in deed as well as in truth, entered the room which, as being symbolically situated on the level of his philosophy, I had after a manner devoted to the consideration of it. Would he have seemed more fleshly still than his works were wont to make him appear? Or would some glance or gesture have told me that amongst those whose thoughts had been preoccupied with bodily matters there was none with a better claim to be styled 'il penseroso' than this brooding genius, ribald at the expense of ribaldry? However that might be, I could at least feel sure that no framework fitted his criticism of life half so well as that of a dining-room. For by his own account it was actually whilst eating and drinking that he took the measure of his surroundings and composed the monument of his fame. And if, as a result, some element of Dutch courage had entered into his estimates, this would have represented no more of a bias than we found to be necessary to roll the balls on every bowling green of thought in to their target. Where the body of man becomes his counsellor, the heart of man can no more be denied the wine that makes it glad than the bread that strengthens it.

* G. K. Chesterton, "Napoleon of Notting Hill", p. 179.

Nor should any reproach be suspected. "The rule of the body", an eminent physician once observed to a clerical friend of mine, "is the rule of the Church. You must feast and you must fast. But take care", he added, "that you do feast as well as fast." It was not surely without significance that the first wonder in the Gospels was worked at a feast, and that that wonder should have been the conversion of water into wine. The Curé de Meudon, if he ever preached to his flock, had an obvious text all ready to his hand.

Rabelais, then, would, as I supposed, have been most at his ease on the ground floor of the House. I could fancy him turning a curious eye, as he passed through the hall, upon the black and white squares of marble pavement that formed one of its salient features, and observing, as he entered the Dining-room, that just such a flooring would have served for the fantasy, conceived as occurring in the palace of Queen Whims, where the game of chess had been raised by his narrative-power to ballet-rank and all the vicissitude and retributive justice of human conditions been supposedly exemplified by actual men and women, clad in shimmering costumes of gold and silver and taking the parts of pawns and pieces on a chessboard. I could imagine him maintaining that the pageant of life was in fact best illustrated by just such a dance of death as this royal and ancient game provided. And I could see in my mind's eye Allegra approving the man for his great love of what was fine and fair, and liking him well for his bonhomie, and setting him down as one whose company added something appreciable to the gaiety both of men and nations. And I would fancy that, while he spoke with her, all coarseness dropped out of his talk and every baseness fled away, much as if he had been Lysimachus in conversation with Marina or had undergone an unconscious regeneration, like Mr. Max Beerbohm's Happy Hypocrite, beneath the magic mask. But, maybe, I was mistaken; for to me he spoke always as a man will do with men. His broad humour, which explained the easy rendering of his thoughts into the English tongue, was very apparent. In his Humanism, indeed, that sense of the comic, alleged by an eminent philosopher of our time 'not to exist outside the pale of what is purely human',[*] had full play. He seemed to be rocked by what Chesterton has called 'the beautiful madness of laughter'[†]; he was not so much funny, Mr. Hollis[‡] has remarked, as full of fun; and the resonance

---

[*] Bergson, "Le Rire", c. 1.   [†] "The Everlasting Man", p. 35.
[‡] "Erasmus", p. 208, "Erasmus was funny; Rabelais was merely full of fun".

of his voice, multiplied in volume by the echoes of four centuries, would fall upon the ear, as Victor Hugo declared, like an 'éclat de rire énorme'. Epstein's conception of Adam would not have fitted amiss into Rabelais's vision of human life; and I could fancy him roaring with amusement at the spectacle of that ungainly giant with head thrown back, as if to catch a glimpse of the God who walked no more in man's garden, but had withdrawn into the sky. Yet, for all this, I suspected behind that mask of fleshly humours the existence of a fastidious soul, rejoicing in fair women and well-groomed men and in beautiful things not to be found in monasteries. For what else was that abbey of Thélême, which looms so large in his criticism of life, but an academy postulating in its inmates a partnership in every natural virtue and in all earthly perfection? Of that, however, in its place when we come to speak of Gargantua and Friar John and some other creatures of his fancy, not so greatly divided in fact from some outstanding inhabitants of our own world.

Rabelais's presence, you must suppose, was all this while permeating the room, which, having nothing gothic about it to offend him and just such a shade of green, picked out with gold, upon the wall and of pink in the carpet and curtains as I flattered myself—I know not why—would have approved themselves to his taste, had its own part to play in the æsthetics of the atmosphere. In spite of the scientific revolution which coincided with the advent of the present century and was alleged by some to have tossed physical science into the arms of the mystics and metaphysicians, I remained very conscious, when Rabelais was present, of the sensible properties of matter. It was all very well to say to myself that space and time had become mere personal attributes and that it needed a world of at least four dimensions to give them impersonal existence; that motion at a high velocity could change our physical shapes in one another's eyes; and that in fact, as a competent critic has picturesquely suggested, the material world, seen through the eyes of Einstein, had the look of a masked ball where "we ourselves . . . have made the black velvet masks and the gay costumes".* Such reflections doubtless gave furiously to think; yet seldom, while Rabelais was, so to say, in the ascendant, would this too, too solid flesh of man consent to melt into metaphysic. During these 'quarts d'heure de Rabelais', if I may misuse that famous expression, man could appear to me much as I suppose many doctors and physicists see him all the time—a thing,

* C. Nordmann, "Einstein and the Universe", p. 69.

that is, fearfully and wonderfully made out of matter and kept in some sort of mechanical operation by animal and vegetable fuels.

With the body thus in command of the imagination, history would begin to tell its tale grossly. I would catch glimpses of a primæval workshop; and at first it had for me rather the look of Mr. Wells's "Island of Dr. Moreau", where, as the reader will remember, the particular parts of many animals are grafted on to alien forms so as to manufacture unimaginable monsters. But beyond the Island I would catch sight of a waste of waters and cry "Thalassa, Thalassa!", like one who has been delivered from imminent peril. Not all the cunning of the Greeks, however, could yet make Venus rise in beauty from the sea, or the ocean-surface scintillate with countless smiles. There were aspects of that nursing cradle of life that I could not contemplate without a shiver. To this day I recall with disgust the impression left by an octopus which I had watched with Allegra in the aquarium at Monte Carlo. What gulfs seemed to gape between such existence and our own, what miracles of metamorphosis to be required to establish any kinship between those cold, tentacular approaches and the warm embrace of human arms! But, in all the pedigree of the human form that I contrived to swallow on the word of the scientist, there was one thing at least about this sea-faring collateral that, so to say, sprang to the eye of æsthetic sensibility. The very last reproach one would be likely to address to it was lack of significant form. It was at least as artistically satisfying as a Medusa's head and postulated an artificer, and no mean one either. If the Alien Voice persisted, as it usually did, in pointing out that this was one of a series of forms in process of development, and thus the equivalent of a sketch in an artist's notebook, it became obvious to rejoin that the so-called 'descent' of the Human Race from such or similar marine ancestry was in reality an ascent, even if a broken ascent, in beauty of feature and force of intelligence. Then at a certain point in time, mysteriously fixed by the consummation of the human form in a genus, had art, in conjunction with that twin-sister of science whom men call conscience, taken over the story of our vile bodies and converted it from a treatise on zoology into an essay on the sublime and the beautiful.

To all this Rabelais would seem to assent almost as a matter of course. No priest, as I thought, had ever been so well content to watch in time's waters the reflection of the family-tree—not yet a tree of Adam, and still less of Jesse—among whose boughs the latest

antics of some monkey or tarsier were adumbrating the form of man.
"Life in the trees", observes a modern writer with the Montessori
method in her thoughts, "was a splendid school."* With Rabelais
at one's side it was the easier to look on at the magical transformation
of the image in the pool below when a wind, blowing whence it
listed, agitated the tree above. The animal form would seem to
straighten itself under the impulse until it grew erect. Then a vague
expression of humanity would come suddenly into the face of the
hominid; and there would appear that paragon of animals . . .
noble in reason, infinite in faculty, admirable in form, angelic in
action, god-like in apprehension whom Hamlet had thus poetically
defined in detail but whom anthropologists have been content
prosaically to style 'homo sapiens'. It was at best only a reflection.
The incident itself had happened very long ago at some unknown
spot, if the background of vegetation behind the image could be
trusted, between the Tigris and the Nile.

It remained neither more nor less than a miracle that any body so
little formidable as man's, with hardly more than a headpiece to its
credit in the way of weapons, should have been able to establish
ascendancy over remote collaterals armed to the teeth, not to say to
the claws. But already, as one looked, miracles had come to seem
too common to excite surprise; indeed, if only the mathematical
philosophy of the Cartesians had not taken such hold of human
minds, the whole business of the evolution of species might have
appeared to be miracle from start to finish.† Had not the biologists themselves surreptitiously confessed the fact? Had they not
asked us in the same breath to believe that a man's brain had
grown out of a monkey's and yet, with no better than these simian
credentials, to regard it as capable of affording us conclusive truth?
Here was miracle indeed, if animal instinct did of its own initiative
grow into godlike wisdom.

For the rest, carnal glances into the green-room of humanity left
one or two impressions which seemed not irrelevant to a just criticism
of life. I could not but notice how oddly local seemed man's capacity
for pain. Where warning was to the purpose, it appeared like a red
light; but, where needless, the red light would be absent. Stretching
the stomach, for instance, caused pain, but not pricking or cutting it.

* Dorothy Davison, "Men of the Dawn", p. 16.
† Cp. W. MacNeile Dixon in " The Human Situation".

"This reminds us", some well-qualified witnesses* observe in drawing attention to the peculiarity, "that our senses, like the rest of us, are suited to the work they have to do." 'Nature' had evidently a wonderful gift for playing Providence, if in fact she had never learnt her rôle or rehearsed her part. One might as well suspect the presence of an impresario with a whole staff of angels to show such shapes as men had been the way in which to grow.

There was another point that fixed the eye in the colossal expenditure of energy behind the world's stage. One could not but be struck at the way in which sex had supplanted parthenogenesis. Apparently it was quite within the capacity of mammals to have followed the latter method of generation,† and, had they done so, who could even begin to envisage the consequences? But, with the world's green room as it became under the conditions of love and marriage, the complexity of the problems and the multitude of the possibilities involved seemed to confound thought. The gametes of the parents would spread out before one like a fortune-teller's pack; the genes, determinate and recessive, would swarm before one's eyes; genius and its reputed kinsman madness, latent alike in the association for better or worse of similar factors, would raise clouds of doubt; whilst the thyroid and pituitary glands—prime instruments, according to an interesting conjecture of Sir Arthur Keith's,‡ of evolution—would seem to temper the broth of destiny, like the dissevered limbs of frog or newt in the seething stew of a witches' caldron. No haunts of magic—not the heath in Macbeth, nor the heath beside Haworth where the Brontës wove their webs of fate—seemed more ghost-ridden, as Ibsen had foreseen, than these labyrinths of heredity.

I marvelled the more at the boldness with which eugenists propounded their theories, since I doubted whether they had cleared their thought even so much as to know what organic types they

* Andrade and Huxley, "Simple Science", p. 267.

† See on this F. E. A. Crew's article on sex in Rose's "Outline of Human Knowledge", p. 259. "Examination", he observes, "of large numbers of ovaries of rats . . . has shown that in all probability unfertilised eggs begin to develop into embryos and, although the development does not proceed very far, nevertheless such instances clearly demonstrate that, in principle, the origin of a new individual in the rat can occur in the absence of any influence contributed normally by the sperm of the male".

‡ See Seligman's essay on the characteristics and distribution of the human race in Rose's "Outline of Modern Knowledge", p. 433.

wished to perpetuate. Ought budding Napoleons, for instance, to be reared at all, and, if so, should they be of the Corsican, pocket or Notting Hill variety? And, ought the anti-types of that other war-monger, whose face had launched a thousand ships, to be propagated with the zeal that would undoubtedly be thrown into the experiment, if men realised what charms were in the making? Eugenics soon became buried beneath eupsychics.*

Before I had distended the problem to this extent, however, Rabelais would break in upon my cogitation with loud laughter. "Why," he would say, "I don't believe for a moment that these eugenists of yours would even be able to agree whether or not Panurge ought to have been married to the valiant woman of Proverbs. Panurge was, as you know, an amusing fellow, making his contribution to the gaiety of nations, but he was a rogue, a sot, a bit of a coward and an unconscionable practical-joker; and on your principles it would seem doubtful enough whether one had any business to breed from his vile body. Reinforced, however, by the genes of the valiant woman, his chromosomes might perhaps have yielded a tolerably desirable progeny. I could at any rate pile up a list of possibilities longer than the lengthiest of those promiscuous lists of mine that once amused, but now bore my readers."

Here I would be tempted to interject a sound and sounding platitude. "Life", I would say, "is short, art long, and statistics are, not only interminable, but suspect. A relative of mine, who was some while ago Finance Minister in Egypt," I would add, "once told me that, when a hard question was asked him, he would consult his oriental experts as to whether an answer could be found to it, and would be met with the reply 'Yes, certainly! On which side do you want it to come out?' And then there was Sir William Harcourt with his allegation of three mounting degrees of mendacity —viz. lies, damned lies and, finally, statistics."

Rabelais, after doing justice with his jaws to this last penetrating jest, pursued his predication. "It is a great grace", he would say, "to be able to see man's place in nature simply or, which comes to the same thing, sapiently. Your world appears to suffer from scientific specialists who can no more detach their minds from their laboratories than the monks of my own time could deflect their eyes from their oratories; and this habit of balancing oneself, so to speak,

* "There must be eupsychics, and much more, as well as eugenics." Prof. Sir J. A. Thomson in Rose's "Outline of Modern Knowledge", p. 223.

on one leg instead of two has its manifest disadvantages. Ora et
labora is the true path of reformation. Erasmus had the penetration
to see the two sides of that issue with detachment; and in his hands
and Thomas More's the Renaissance should have eventuated in a
healthy development and not ended in a bogus reform. But, as is
usual, the Left-Wing Reformers had no patience and took a mounte-
bank for their teacher. What could I do but laugh at the whole
business, since it was never my way to cry?"

It was characteristic of the man, as it seemed to me, to share Plato's
conviction that a divorce between the physicians of the soul and of
the body would prove disastrous to mankind; and it made me think
better of him than I could have once supposed possible. Yet, for
all that, remembering Pierre Boulenger's remark that Rabelais would
be an enigma to posterity, I felt no certainty that I had seen him
plain. And indeed he never seemed to give me the chance to make a
friend of him in the same way as, upon other planes of thought, did
Pascal and Montaigne. Bon viveur, bon raconteur, he made a boon
companion, but nothing beyond. Acquaintance, not intimacy, was
to be had on the dining-room floor.

Rabelais's story, as I gleaned it from his talk, ran somewhat thus.
His father, a man of substance, had had no use for another son; and
his mother, if she were not already dead, had put up no effective
opposition when, in the same year in which Henry VIII came to the
throne of England, he was pitched into a Franciscan convent at
Fontenay-le-Comte. Not at all a contemplative, but very much a
scholar, Rabelais found the monks ignorant and their manners
beastly. In the multiplicity of prayers he saw rather vain repetitions
than accents of love again and again repeated. A priest by ordination,
he continued to be only a clerk in spirit. His happiest hours—perhaps his only happy hours—were passed among books and friends.
Consumed by rational curiosity, he sought, like Bacon after him, to
take all knowledge for his province. Mathematics, medicine, astronomy, humane letters, all interested him; and Erasmus became his
idol. But his learning gave offence and his knowledge of Greek
aroused suspicion. Had not an old school friend, the Bishop of
Maillezais, come to his rescue, he would have been damned for his
studies. By the Bishop's good offices, however, he was translated
from the uncongenial order of St. Francis to the more sympathetic
order of St. Benedict. Even still vocation seemed lacking; and
eventually he fled the monastery and, by the Bishop's favour, lived,

to all intents and purposes, as a secular priest, in the episcopal palace at Ligugé. There at last he found himself, and thence he had set out to see the world. He had visited the great cities of France, had, as it appeared, travelled in Italy, Savoy, England and Germany, studied medicine at Montpellier, and then, about the year 1532, arrived at Lyon, the libraries and life of which made it at that time the intellectual centre of France. There he had mixed with learned men, worked in the hospital and qualified as a physician. There, too, in the pages of a stupid little novel, he had first met Gargantua, and had quickly perceived the literary possibilities of the character. His work as a doctor had taught him the value of a bedside book; and he set out to supply it out of the material that the thought of Gargantua conjured up. Of such parentage was born Pantagruel, the King of the Dipsodes or thirsty souls; and thus was the philosophy of Pantagruelism launched into the world. The venture had succeeded; the book had been widely read; and the author had become famous. In the sequel he returned to Gargantua, 'the swallower', and wrote up his history likewise. Thus were created two popular heroes, two princes of food and wine; and together with them Grandgousier, their forbear.

About this time in Rabelais's life a new opportunity of seeing the world had presented itself. Another old school-fellow, du Bellay, Bishop of Paris, and one of the leading diplomatists of the day, had been commissioned by Francis I to visit Rome in the hope of bringing about some accommodation between the views of the Holy See and the King of England respecting the latter's marriage with Catherine of Aragon. Du Bellay volunteered to take his old friend with him as his physician; and in this manner Rabelais visited both Florence and Rome. The wonders that he saw did not apparently cause him to refrain from observing that the marbles of Florence were not worth the fleshpots of Amiens. No more did fear (whether justifiable or not) of Rome operate to prevent him from lecturing at Lyon upon the anatomy of a criminal's corpse and in this way acquiring a name as the precursor of Vesalius. An illegitimate son had about this date been born to him. The lapse is believed to have been unique, and was for long as little suspected as that of Wordsworth. His reputation in any case was good enough when he returned to Italy in the suite of du Bellay, now a cardinal, for the Pope to absolve him from any professional irregularities 'in view of his zeal for religion, science and literature, and the honesty of his life and morals'. He enjoyed, in fact, high consideration in Rome, for, though his eyes were busy scanning the politics of the Holy See in odd conjunction with the properties of leguminous plants, he was prudent enough to make his letters discreet even to the point of dullness.

On Rabelais' return to France a canonry, which he obtained the Pope's permission to accept, had been given him at the secularized Abbey of St. Maur, and at the same time he received Papal authority to practise the art of medicine. In his medical, rather than ecclesiastical capacity he was summoned to William du Bellay's death-bed, where the prophetic utterances of the dying man, subsequently verified by the event, made a deep impression on him. Two cures—those of Saint-Christophe du Jambet and Saint-Martin de Medun—came about this time into his hands, though he did not apparently go into residence at either place. He was still preaching in his own way to a wider audience, not, however, without opposition. He had made powerful foes in the doctors of the Sorbonne, and, if it had not been for the yet more powerful friends he had found in King Francis the First and the Bishop of Tulle, it might have gone hard with him. With their countenance he had got the third and perhaps the greatest book of his immortal narrative published in spite of the condemnation of it as heretical by the Sorbonne, no longer under the humanist influences of Fichet and Heynlin. A new reign, however, had threatened him with new trouble; and for a time he had become a physician at Metz and, subsequently, a refugee in Rome. Then once more he had been received into favour at the French Court. A licence was obtained for the publication of the fourth book of his prose epic, and a new victory won against the hostility of the Sorbonne.

It was after this last turn of fortune's wheel that, somewhere about the year 1553, Rabelais found himself confronted with what he is commonly supposed to have called 'the great perhaps', but a later writer has more felicitously described as 'the last curiosity'. For him the drama of man's life had been played out; and, maybe, for a final jest, he called it a farce and let fall the bed-curtain.

The last book of Rabelais's great work was thus a posthumous publication and edited by an unknown hand; but it is not necessarily, any the more for that, an untrustworthy record of his final dispositions. I doubted its verisimilitude as little as I doubted that his face, could I have seen it clear, would have shown me the inner man.

"There's no art", cries the disillusioned Duncan in "Macbeth", "to find the mind's construction in the face." Yet no amount of mistakes will ever persuade Humanity that this is really so. Always we search each other's looks to ascertain one another's characters. Always we assume that the truth is written there, if only we could read it. We are never persuaded that such a miracle as Oscar Wilde has imagined for Dorian Gray has been worked to our discomfiture. Upon that part of our person which vanity prompts or necessity compels us to show nature paints more inexorably than Sargent's brush—so inexorably, indeed, that to critics, skilled in reading the lines of face and hand, the flesh becomes the best story-teller in the world. Perhaps that was the reason why Rabelais rated the body so high. For him at least the story it had to tell was no tale told by an idiot, signifying nothing, but the direct indelible mark of mind's mastery over matter. Like Rubens, whose compère he is, Rabelais painted grossly, but, if the admiration which, as artists, they have received from l'homme moyen sensuel be any index, these two Catholics knew their business and painted man accurately. Doubtless coarseness has always paid, in the way of helping to get a book read, by giving satisfaction to contemporary devotees of the smoking-room or water-closet story. But there is more to it than that. There was in Rabelais something of the eternal boy; and there were moments when the middle state of man between animal and angel would strike him in all its force and make him laugh at its intense incongruity. Yet his medical interests did something towards raising this broad, sometimes bawdy, humour to the rank of science; for in his own peculiar way he was diagnosing the human body, as a man must be content to do who is resolved to see all things steadily and whole.

Contact with the ills that flesh is heir to, so far as my small experience went, tended to make men sceptical and women religious. I had, indeed, known two Catholic doctors in the course of my life; and one of them was a President of the Royal College of Physicians*; but on the whole I should suppose that intensive preoccupation with disease rendered doctors as doubtful about God's existence as intensive preoccupation with pain renders nurses confident of it. Want of time for wide reading and constant contact with humane literature doubtless contributed to this doctors' dilemma. An eminent and charming physician once recommended me Winwood Reade's "Martyrdom of

* Sir Norman Moore.

Man" as if it were the last word on the subject; and from that I
drew my inferences. Rabelais, however, was a scholar; and to the
scholar, except in moods of paradox, the part does not appear greater
than the whole. I presume that he saw through a glass darkly what
Samuel Butler, whose unorthodoxy is quite unimpeachable, said
in so many words. "I submit", Butler wrote, after reviewing
Paley's argument from design with especial relation to the human
body and particular reference to the tendons of the human leg and
the band that binds them back at the ankle, "that there is hardly
one of my readers who can be considered as free from bias or
prejudice, who will not feel that the idea of design—or perception
by an intelligent living being, of ends to be obtained and of the
means of obtaining them—and the idea of the tendons of the foot
and of the ligament which binds them down, come together so
forcibly, that no matter how strongly Professors Haeckel and Clifford
and Mr. Darwin may try to separate them, they are no sooner pulled
asunder than they straightway fly together again of themselves."*

The designer in Samuel Butler's view was apparently Humanity
itself; and I could not but suspect that in this matter of the evolution
of species Humanity in Butler's exposition played the part of Mrs.
Gamp, and Nature that of Mrs. Harris. Neither had really produced
the baby; and poor Mrs. Harris was but a scientific myth. Rabelais,
though I dare not pretend to have discussed the matter with him,
would, I believe, have been of much the same mind. When Henri
Quatre suggested to Cardinal du Perron that the Curé de Meudon
was really an atheist, the Cardinal replied that he had seen in Rabelais's copy of Galen, and written in Rabelais's own hand, this note
with reference to Galen's statement that the soul is material: "Hic
vere se Galianus plumbeum ostendit" (Here truly Galen shows himself stupid). Such good sense as this is unlikely to have deserted him
in the dissecting-room, and may do something to explain the
Cardinal's alleged extraordinary observation that the story of Pantagruel was 'le livre par excellence, la vraie bible', as well as his
reported insistence upon the reading of it by such as fed at his table.
Risky as all this may appear in a prince of the Church, it is fair to
remember that one reputable modern critic has categorically declared
Rabelais to be 'the first complete incarnation of good-sense', and
another that "Rabelais almost more than anyone else is the very

* S. Butler, "Evolution Old and New", p. 23. I give Butler's words, but hold
no brief for his English.

personification of what will die if Europe dies".* Rubens did not fatten the carnal man to finer effect nor Hogarth shrink him to more deadly result.

Through the tangled tale, with its endless digressions, of the two giants, there ran, in fact, the notion of the value to the sane mind of the sound body. What an appeal from the cloister to the hearth can be read into the account of Gargantua's transformation from a rather dirty and disgusting little boy (who combed his hair 'with an Almain comb which is the four fingers and the thumb' because his preceptor declared that 'to comb himself otherwise, to wash and make himself neat was to lose time in this world') into a smart, presentable youth, accustomed to rise at four a.m. and to be dressed, combed, curled, trimmed and perfumed, whilst the previous day's lessons were repeated to him! With the Renaissance the body had come again into its own—at what peril to the intellectual soul the exclusive cult of the athlete would at one distant day reveal. For the moment, however, this spring-cleaning of the body might well appear pure gain to one bred in a monastery and bored, as one can see by his allusion to 'dunsicle breborions', with prayer propelled by the telling of beads or the beat of the metre in chant and psalm. "Consider", his contemporary, St. Teresa, was telling her discalced Carmelite nuns of the primitive rule, " . . . that you do much more by making from time to time a single petition of the Paternoster than by hastily reciting the whole prayer many times."† It is perhaps a little difficult for either scholar or saint to do justice to the artifices—and especially the globular artifices—of athletes in spiritual or physical training. Had Rabelais lived in an age when men were tumbling over one another to chase, or even watch a ball in motion, he might have experienced a surprise analogous to that of the late Lord Salisbury when he found himself compelled to postpone the meeting of a Cabinet because, as he is alleged to have put it, "Hartington had to go and see whether one horse could run faster than another". But the concomitants of a world at play had not in Rabelais's time superseded those of a world at prayer.

Before the vision of a monastery, as he had found it in fact, had faded, Rabelais would carry me away in spirit to his ideal abbey of

* Stapfer, "Rabelais", p. 360. Hollis, "Foreigners aren't Fools", p. 63, and see his "Erasmus", pp. 250–252. "Had there not been Erasmus, there could hardly have been Rabelais. This was the egg that Erasmus truly laid."
† "The Way of Perfection", c. XXXIII.

Thélême. A gift from Gargantua to that forcible Friar John of whom something must be said later, it indicated pretty plainly a monastic foundation as the proper basis of a well-constructed society. Nothing, in fact, in all Rabelais's table-talk seemed to me more striking than this circumstance, all his anti-monkish predispositions seeming likely to draw him the other way. The Abbey no doubt was very differently conceived to monasteries in general, but an abbey it was, though so ordered as to prove a school for the humanities. Architecturally reminiscent, perhaps, of Cardinal du Bellay's palace at St. Maur, and, perhaps too, conversationally indebted to the circle of savants associated with Bishop d'Estissac's château of Ligugé, Thélême presented the spectacle of a vast academy where elect youths, between the ages of twelve and eighteen, and elect maidens, from ten to fifteen, grew together in wisdom and stature. In this antechamber of life those values which men mostly prize only as they approach the time of death were already perceived and assimilated. Within its precincts all material things—the food, the wine, the decoration, the costumes—were of the best and put to the best uses, so that it seemed in very truth a school of golden girls and boys, and of the purest gold at that. The Abbey, in short, was a home of beauty, a house of mirth, a palace of art, a companionship in every virtue and in all perfection; and its assortment of children might have paced very prettily through the pages of "Love's Labour's Lost" or of Tennyson's "Princess".

It required no great insight to perceive in this dream-cloister the protest of the human body against its expulsion from Eden and a passionate plea for the recovery of the loveliness that it had lost. Not willingly was the creature made subject to vanity. Yet Rabelais knew too much to leave the matter there. So soon as the oracular utterances which terminate the charming description of Thélême were concluded, Gargantua, we are told, 'fetched a very deep sigh', as well he might, for they had discovered to his understanding apparently nothing better than a prospect of mob-rule and bigoted fanaticism. "It is not now only, I perceive," meditated the fleshly giant, "that people called to the faith of the gospel and convinced of the certainty of evangelical truths are persecuted. But happy is the man that shall not be scandalized, but shall always continue to the end in aiming at that mark which God, by His dear Son, hath set before us, without being distracted by his carnal affections."

So, as Rabelais proceeded, would the eugenist's dream be ruthlessly dispelled, and mankind, trailing no more its morning cloud of glory, seem to set forth once again upon its earthly pilgrimage. Yet sometimes it would be borne in upon me that Allegra, passing so gaily through the world, yet with a certain cloistered charm about her, had, quite unconsciously, moulded her earthly life upon the pattern depicted in Rabelais's description of Thélème and shown me, so to say at leisure, that plenitude of gifts and graces which Herrick, or another, had caught sight of only in a lady 'passing by' and, with Purcell's aid, translated into music.

Such a knocking as falls upon the ear in the memorable scene in "Macbeth" and recalls the mind to the visible world would seem at this point to make itself heard; and I would guess that Rabelais had struck a blow with his magic wand and brought me back to my senses. A din of battle had succeeded the cloister of peace, and, though the scene was still an abbey, it was that of Seuillé, not of Thélème. Before me, as Rabelais talked on, I beheld that Friar John of the Funnels, the muscular monk, whom some have identified with the Cardinal of Lorraine or the Cardinal of Châtillon and others with Luther. Catholic or Protestant, Friar John at all events impersonated Force championing Love whilst he laid about him vigorously with a heavy cross in his hands; and Rabelais chuckled at the inherent irony of it.

War, it appeared, had broken out between King Grandgousier and King Picrochole; but Rabelais had not been recounting the causes of the outbreak above a minute or so before I recognised that he was describing a war of any time and a battlefield of all existence. Was this really Grandgousier's Ambassador who was apostrophising Picrochole, or was it some more familiar, some contemporary voice? "What rage of madness", I heard him say, "doth now incite thee, all old alliance infringed, all amity trod under foot, and all right violated, thus in a hostile manner to invade his country without having been by him or his in anything prejudiced, wronged or provoked! Where is faith? Where is law? Where is reason? Where is humanity? Where is the fear of God? Dost thou think that these atrocious abuses are hidden from the Eternal Spirit and the Supreme God who is a just rewarder of all our undertakings?"

That, however, appeared to be just what Picrochole did think; for his reply showed that he was a past master in power-politics. "Come and fetch the stolen cakes", he sneered; whereupon Grandgousier's Ambassador reported that Picrochole 'was quite out of his wits and forsaken of God'. In vain did Grandgousier attempt to appease his adversary by a lavish gift of cakes far in excess of those stolen. Picrochole was assured by his captains that fear had prompted this overture. "He is not skilled", one of them urged, "in warfare, nor has he any stomach for it." And thereupon Small-Trash, Swashbuckler and Dirt-tail, as Urquhart renders their names in English, proceeded to tickle Picrochole's ears with as fine a promise of world-domination as literature has on record. Grandgousier, he was told, would at the very first shock be routed; and that would mean getting money by heaps. An army would march through Gascony and beyond it, taking what it wanted without resistance. Picrochole would coast along Galicïa and Portugal, seizing all the ships and all the stores that he required. Spain would yield, for the Spaniards were nothing but a race of boobies. The Straits of Gibraltar would be crossed; and Pillars more stately than those of Hercules be erected there in honour of Picrochole's triumph. In Morocco Barbarossa would yield himself a slave. Tunis would be over-run, and Barbary as well. Italy would be conquered; Rome would fall; and the Pope die of fear. So, by way of Naples and Sicily, would the victor come to Cyprus and Crete. Soon the Morea would pass into Picrochole's hands and Jerusalem lie at his disposal. Let him advance slowly, and he would have Asia Minor as far as the Euphrates. Meanwhile another army would have taken the North of France, Holland and Belgium; and in due course Picrochole's empire would extend to Britain and Scandinavia. His invincible forces would capture Poland and Prussia in their turn and push down to Constantinople; and so Picrochole would end as Emperor of Trebizond. "But there was present at that time", Rabelais would continue, "an old gentleman, well experienced in the wars, a stern soldier who had been in many great hazards, by name Echephron. He, having heard this discourse, observed: "I do not greatly doubt that all this enterprise will be like the tale or interlude of the pitcher full of milk wherewith a shoemaker made himself rich in conceit but, when the pitcher was broken, he had not whereupon to dine. What do you pretend by these large conquests ? What shall be the end of so many labours and crosses ?"

"Thus it shall be," said Picrochole, "that, when we are returned, we shall sit down, rest, and be merry."

"But," said Echephron, "if by any chance you should never come back . . .! Were it not better for us to take our rest now than unnecessarily expose ourselves to so many dangers ?" "

Both in the little engagement at Seuillé, when Friar John rushed out and routed Picrochole's troopers, as upon a larger scale in the rest of the war, power-politics were defeated and the moral foundations of the world thus confessed. But all Friar John's righteous indignation, so far as I could see, never had any particular effect on Panurge; nor, for the matter of that, did Pantagruel's common-sense. And Panurge represented a type agreeable to a good number of men—a little funnier, a little naughtier, a little smuttier, and a little more roguish and disingenuous than they are themselves.

Rabelais would describe how this amusing rascal had entered Paris by the Bridge of Charenton; and there were those who read a certain significance into his route and believed that the Cardinal of Lorraine was indicated and had traits in common with this exceedingly profane person. Be that as it may—for it is quite likely no more than fancy—there could be no doubt that Panurge had found a god in his belly to vie with Falstaff's, and that, being a Frenchman, he had carried sensuality to satisfaction and with due regard for the claims of logic. He must be reckoned the patron of all those who believe that their senses of touch, taste and smell tell them all that is really worth knowing about the world. It was in vain to remonstrate with such a fellow, as Rabelais would point out to me, about the slitting of purses or sullying of clothes or robbing of offertories or other more indelicate enormities! Such things seemed to Panurge to be excellent fun; and, given his principles or lack of them, he was quite rational in treating mankind as pawns in his game or pieces to his purpose. "My friend," he would have answered Kant, who argued so wisely that all men ought to be regarded as ends in themselves, "thou hast no pastime at all in this world. I have more than the king, and, if thou will join thyself with me, we will do the devil together."

The person to whom, according to Rabelais's account, these observations were actually addressed, was somewhat less serious-minded than Kant, and merely replied, "No, no, by St. Adaurus, that will I not, for thou wilt be hanged one time or another!" But Panurge was at no loss to meet this anticipation of the argument from 'the policeman round the corner', and rejoined, "And thou wilt be interred one time or another. Now which is more honourable —the earth or the air? Oh, you big blockhead!"

Panurge, though he gained his point at the time, proved no more able to hold it as his last criticism upon life than did Falstaff.

Long before he lay on his death-bed, he was crying out "God, God, God!" It had been enough for the base matter of his body to be tossed in a heavy storm at sea to cause him to send for Friar John in order to hear his confession. But, as we all know, the devil that will be a saint in the hour of sickness, the devil a saint is he in the hour of recovery. Panurge was no exception to that rule. Nevertheless he had betrayed his scepticism in respect of the creed of sensuality; for the base matter of his body had confessed under trial the secrets of his soul.

At that point in the conversation I might try to introduce a story that I fancied would tickle Rabelais's humour. It related how a certain learned member of the Anglican Bench of Bishops had once gone down to preach in a remote country church. With all the resources of scholarship at his command he expounded to the simple congregation that it was the fool who had said in his heart that there was no God. The parson, taking the freedom of an old friend, observed in the vestry, after all this eloquence was concluded, that he was afraid the discourse had been above the heads of the congregation. The Bishop disputed it. They resolved to put the matter to the test, and enquired of the first old woman they chanced to meet what she had thought of the learning to which she had just listened. "It war' a very fine sermon, my Lard," she answered the Bishop, "but I don't agree wi' ye, my Lard; for I do think as there be a God."

"That old body", I could hear Rabelais saying, "had the hang of the thing. She felt the fact, as you English say, in her bones. And Panurge, had he been hung, would have got the hang of the thing as soon as the noose was round his neck."

"I suppose one might say", I would suggest magnificently, "that he had recovered his sense of the numinous."

"We had a simpler word for it," Rabelais would return. "Panurge, you see, was a most entertaining sophist. Do you recollect the motif which announced his advent?—'Comment Pantagruel trouva Panurge, lequel il aima toute sa vie'. It was vastly amusing to watch the morality of circumstance finding Panurge out and to listen to all the ingenious humbug that he would emit the moment he felt its pressure. There was nothing he would not say to make a case for himself; nor did he stop short of the most magniloquent language in dishing up his nonsense. His apologetics, for instance, included a defence of debt (into which, needless to say, he had fallen); and he would make out that it was 'a union or conjunction of the heavens with the earth . . . of such virtue and efficacy that the whole progeny of Adam would very suddenly perish without it'; that, in a word, it was 'the great soul of the universe'. A world without this relation of creditor and debtor, he would declare, must collapse. "The moon would not give her light, for why should the sun shine upon her; Lucifer would break loose, the earth would become a dog-kennel, men would neither render aid nor ask it; and in short faith, hope and love would be quite banished." Panurge had much of the charm of Villon; an amusing rascal.

"After this manner, you see, is charity, with its companions, justified of the meanest of mankind as something latent in the very nature of things. But Pantagruel, sagacious though amused, was no more taken in by the rogue's sophistry than one might expect a well-instructed member of your Charity Organisation Society to be by the plausibilities of those whose craft lies in plucking the rich and pauperising the poor—beggars or politicians, as the case may be. He knew that true charity has a greater concern with a man's soul than his body; and all the ingenuity of Panurge did not persuade him that a debtor's fine words buttered a creditor's parsnips.

"To obtain victuals under cover of cosmic theories or Christian morals did not, however, exhaust the fleshly preoccupations of Panurge. He was greatly concerned to know whether he ought to marry. Totally indifferent himself to a husband's rights or to a woman's virtue, he was illogically sensitive to the fear of being cuckolded. "Do not marry, then," Pantagruel advises him, "for, as Seneca observes, what we have done to others, others will in turn do to us." "Is that true", Panurge enquires, "without exception?" "Without exception," Pantagruel replies. The perplexities of the carnal mind are not, however, thus simply solved. "Is it not better", Panurge asks his mentor, "to marry some honest, lovely and virtuous woman than to pay promiscuous attentions and run the risk of being bastinadoed or becoming diseased? For never, be it spoken by their husbands' leave, had I enjoyment yet of an honest woman." "Marry, then, in God's name!" replies Pantagruel.

"Panurge, however, continues dissatisfied and resorts to the counsel of quacks, and then, after he had finished with sortes Vergilianae, lotteries, dreams, sybils, rhymesters, and deficients, turns, on Pantagruel's advice, to professional men. A theologian, a physician, a philosopher and a lawyer are all invited to give their views on the tormenting problem of Panurge's espousals. The theologian recommends marriage to an honest woman as the best safeguard in the circumstances. "You would have me, then," says Panurge, twisting his whiskers on either side with the thumb and forefinger of his left hand, "to take to wife the prudent, frugal woman described by Solomon. Without any doubt she is dead; and truly to my best remembrance I never saw her." Discarding the counsels of the physician of the soul, Panurge grasps his nettle by the root and addresses himself to a physician of the body. Rondibilis, the doctor, after summarising the five methods known to him of dealing with carnal desire—viz., drink carried to the point of stupefaction, drugs, physical exercise, mental preoccupation and finally indulgence—concludes by drawing a portrait of Panurge as a married man of mature age and appearance, in good heart and the father of a fine family. Panurge, however, remains preoccupied with his dominant fear of being cuckolded. "By the haven of safety," cries out Rondibilis, "what is this you ask of me? If you shall be a cuckold? My noble friend, I am married, and you are like to be so very speedily: therefore be pleased to write in your brain with a steel pen this subsequent dictum: 'There is no married man who doth not run the hazard of being made a cuckold. . . . The shadow doth not more naturally follow the body than cuckoldry ensueth after marriage to place fair horns upon husbands' heads.' "

Rondibilis, so Rabelais continued, had gone on to fortify his thesis by giving an apothecary's diagnosis of the feminine constitution. "When I say womankind," he told Panurge, "I speak of a sex so frail, so variable, so changeable, so fickle, inconstant and imperfect that in my opinion Nature . . . did in a manner mistake the road which she had traced formerly and stray exceedingly from that excellence of providential judgment by the which she had created and formed all other things, when she built, framed and made up a woman."

Panurge, finding no comfort at all in these generalisations, then seeks out a philosopher, a prolix and ambiguous person whose professional futility in respect of the real problems of life Molière was one day to study in "Le Mariage Forcé". So at the end Panurge comes for advice to the attorney, Bridlegoose by name, who confesses to him that he reaches his own decisions by the toss of dice, and observes further that the results afford general satisfaction. After that, it was but a short step forward to ask counsel of Triboulet, the

Fool, who, indeed, in so crazy a world, promises to prove the best of advisers. Panurge opens the proceedings by offering Triboulet a drink; and Triboulet, after draining the flask to the dregs, pointedly hands it back. Panurge draws the conclusion that wine contains the answer to the conundrums. In vino veritas! And so originates the famous quest of 'the holy bottle' which supplies the concluding episode of the fleshly picture of human life that Rabelais had planned to paint.

Accompanied by Friar John, Pantagruel and Panurge set out in search of the vinous oracle; and there was nothing of which they took a more ample provision than of the herb, Pantagruelion. Rabelais would pause at this point, as if awaiting a question, and then explain that this herb was no other than hemp from which ropes 'exceedingly odious and hateful to thieves and robbers' were made. Pantagruel, so malefactors declared, held them by the gorge. Yet, Rabelais would continue, it was not Pantagruel 'the idea, pattern, prototype and exemplar of all jovial perfection and accomplishment', but rather Pantagruelion which provided the criminal's cravat. I gathered that, like Joseph de Maistre, he had found the figure of an executioner at the basis of human society; and I saw that, whilst setting his heroes to search for the holy bottle, holy grail or whatever it might be in which the mystery of life's meaning lay hid, he was in no doubt himself that the carnal philosophy of Panurge and his kind hung by a hempen cord, and in the nature of things would fall to the ground, were this wanting. Of so much could the stupidest make sure.

Meanwhile in Rabelais's fable the voyagers were making for some land situate between India and Cathay—the wonderland of the mediæval, the lost horizon of the modern world. They passed through a shattering storm in which Panurge lost his nerve and by which Pantagruel was strangely moved to relate how a pilot, sailing the Mediterranean in the days of the Emperor Tiberius, had heard a voice crying in terrible tones to him in the night that Great Pan was dead—a story wherein he seemed to find the turning-point of time, interpreting as he did the announcement of the death of Pan to mean, not so much the death of Nature, as of Nature's God, the Great Shepherd of Humanity, Jesus Christ.* Having ended this extraordinary discourse, Pantagruel, so Rabelais said, had remained silent and deep in thought.

* "Pantagruel", Bk. IV, c. 28.

The travellers had sailed on, coasting past many islands where the foibles, the fallacies and the futilities of mankind were duly exposed and damagingly described. They had sighted the so-called Isle des Tapinois,* where, under the name of Shrovetide, there reigned Anti-Nature as exemplified in bigoted ultramontanes and demoniacal Calvinists. Over against it they had come upon the Wild Island, where dwelt the Chitterlings, "females in sex, mortal in condition, some of them maids, some not". "Physics, that is to say Nature," Rabelais assured me,† "at her first burthen begat Beauty and Harmony, without carnal copulation, being of herself very fruitful and prolific." And so, leaving the exact definition of beauty and harmony out of the discussion, it had apparently been, according to our latest authorities on the physical world; for parthenogenesis, rather than cohabitation, had served as the instrument of propagation. But, as Rabelais continued, Anti-physis, the antagonist of Nature, out of spite begat Deformity and Dissonance. The Chitterlings, for the rest, were very oddly connected; the Giants who piled Pelion upon Ossa, the Serpent who tempted Eve, and the Swiss, not to speak of the Ethiopians, being all of their kinship. Against these distorted creatures, Pantagruel, assisted by Friar John, two colonels—Colonel Maul-Chitterling and Colonel Cut-pudding—with a company of chefs, had gone out and won a famous victory, which I assumed, from Rabelais's manner, had discomfited the kill-joys of the world, whether Puritan or Calvinist, whatever other matters it may have left undecided.

The travellers had coasted on past the Island of the Winds, where the wind-bags dwell, and had landed upon that of the Pope-figs, who cared not a fig for the Pope until their pope-figgery brought them ill-fortune and calamity, after which they cared for him no more than they had need to do. Proceeding, the voyagers had tried the Island of the Pope-fans, whose perfervid ultramontanism came near to mania. The Bishop there, one Homenas, prophesied much, in the vein of other more secular prophets, of brave new worlds, declaring what good things would come of exterminating recalcitrants with fire and sword and applying oneself closely to the study of the decrees of supreme authority. "Then," he predicted, "uninterrupted and eternal peace through the universe, an end of all wars, plunderings, drudgeries, robbing, assassinations, unless it be to destroy these cursed rebels, the heretics!" The good man had anticipated the revolutionary and

---

* Island of Impostors.   † Bk. IV, c. 32 (tr. Urquhart and Motteux).

other idealists of our own day. So little does human nature change from age to age.

"Spoke like an organ!"* quoth Panurge sceptically, "but for my part, I believe as little of it as I can." The Bishop, however, gave the voyagers a feast and a present of pears at the end of it. Pantagruel, it appeared, had decided to name this fruit "bon chrétien", perhaps because no fruit desiderates greater circumspection in the choosing and none is more delicious, if wisely chosen. Friar John, I was not surprised to learn, had observed that he would have preferred a cartload of buxom lasses. I conjectured therefore that Rabelais, like One he sought in his strange way to serve, had come in the guise of a husbandman seeking ripe fruit among his contemporaries; and that, not finding it either among the Pope-figs or the Pope-fans, he had wished to warn mankind to sample the fruit of Christianity only in its best specimens and at its ripest. Corruptio optimi pessima! The least decay rendered Christianity as unpalatable as the most obvious immaturity. But Rabelais was so enigmatic a symbolist that it was always rash to assume one had understood him aright.

The voyagers had held on their way and come into strange seas, where they heard the sound of voices in the air—voices of men, women, children, even of animals—voices, but nothing besides! Panurge had at first grown alarmed, but subsequently became as eager to thaw all this talk into comprehension as if it were a handful of sugar-plums that could be melted into sweetness with the mouth. The tapsters and topers of Rabelais's time could hardly have been more intent upon hearing the words of the Reformers or undertaking the interpretation of the Scriptures. But the prudent Pantagruel bethought him of the opinion of Antiphanes that Plato's philosophy was 'like words which, being spoken in some country during a hard winter, are immediately congealed, frozen up and not heard',† since what Plato taught to the young would only and with difficulty be understood by them when they came to be old men. He bade his companions, therefore, search in that region for the lyre of Orpheus, which, after the Thracian women had torn its master to pieces, had floated away, melodiously complaining, to the Euxine. This idea was quite beyond the

---

* Viz., "You have heard others talk thus, and upon that footing you affirm it; and so you do just like the organs which yield a delightful sound when well managed; but for my part, I will not believe you without good vouchers." (Footnote in Urquhart and Motteux's translation.) † Bk. IV, c. 55.

capacity of Panurge to assimilate. He was much more taken with the skipper's view that they were on the confines of a frozen sea where the shouts and sounds of a recent battle had congealed and were now thawing. He desired that these therefore might further materialise. His wish was granted. Pantagruel caught some handfuls of words, red and blue, black and gold and green, and threw them on the deck. But, as they melted, they began to sound like gibberish. Only one in Friar John's hot hands afforded at first any intelligible meaning; and that was a chestnut which cracked like a field-piece. Melted together on the deck, the other words began to behave in much the same way and to produce the din of battle. Some fine sport came of all this; but at the end Panurge began to cry out again for the word of the Holy Bottle and no further prolongation of his pilgrimage.

Pantagruel, meantime, had begun to suspect that they were approaching that equilateral triangle, of which he had heard and where is the abode of truth. Rabelais, I could see from something in his face, was up to mischief and about to spring a surprise no less disconcerting than the explosion of Friar John's chestnut, in which, whether I was right or wrong, I had discerned a symbol of the effect of reading the Bible upon the mind of the many. The party had landed on an island 'which for situation and governor, may be said not to have its fellow'. So charming and salubrious did it appear, once its heights were scaled, that Pantagruel hastily made up his mind that he was about to arrive at the seat of Areté, 'described by Hesiod', but found on further investigation that it was in fact the abode of one, Master Gaster, 'the first master of arts in the world' and a sovereign, imperious, inflexible and invincible. Of him they heard that he spoke only by signs, and yet that those signs were more readily obeyed by everyone than the statutes of senates or the commands of monarchs. 'Do this', he would say, 'or die'. The kingdom of the Somates—that is, of the other members of the human corporation—had tried to throw off his yoke, but in the end had been obliged to submit, for fear of starvation. "What company soever he was in, none disputed with him for precedence or superiority; he still went first, though kings, emperors, or even the pope himself, were present." The Belly—for Master Gaster was, of course, no other—exercised his sovereignty equally over men and beasts. But Pantagruel took exception to the ventriloquists and gastrolaters—forsooth charlatans and the like who, as Rabelais remarks, being the enemies of the Cross of Christ, idolised this powerful monarch—and, disappointed of their hope, the travellers sailed on again. No better satisfaction awaited them, however, in the Island of Hypocrites, where their vessel was for a while becalmed, than in the realm of Master Gaster; nor again in the Island of Thieves, where Friar John wanted to land and execute justice, doubtless with his cross, but which Panurge desired to flee from and Pantagruel decided to by-pass. Still in quest of truth and the Holy Bottle, they came to the Ringing Island, where they heard much ringing of bells and singing of birds —of birds of passage, it appeared working their way from countries named respectively 'Want-of-bread' and 'Too many of them'. There were clerg-hawks and kites and bigottelloes, representing none too favourably, as judged by the places where they fed and their manner of feeding, the monks, the nuns and the friars of the time. There were besides some larger species of these predatory and colourful birds—bishawks, cardinhawks and a pope-hawk.

I am bound to say I thought Rabelais grew a little tedious as he discoursed on this topic, but, then, I had heard in the course of my life overmuch talk elsewhere about the shortcomings and depredations of the clergy of all denominations. "In that house", said an American millionaire, pointing it out, as he spoke, to a friend of mine as if it were one of the wonders of the neighbourhood, "lives a very remarkable man. He's the only parson round here who hasn't asked me for a subscription." Still, as I would comment to myself whilst listening to Rabelais's diatribes, the clergy, on his showing, had in nothing shown themselves more able to share the infirmities of other men than in their alleged acquisitiveness, sturdily grasping in their days of opportunity and sturdily begging still, though by no means always for themselves, in their days of decline. The over-praised monarch with six wives, who in England despoiled them, not content with their abbeys, had even seized, though he failed to retain altogether, the London hospitals of his time; and the new men, who hung about his Court, fashioned themselves after his likeness. As the power of monarchy waned, Whiggery had taken over; and the country-houses, great and small, came to occupy something of the same position as the monastic foundations as social centres of enlightenment. They, too, in their turn found the door wide open for selfish appropriation—or ought we to say for enlightened economic enclosure? But opportunity passed on, and presently the People got their chance of plunder, and were taking it now with a vengeance.

"I am not sure", I would insinuate in imaginary conversation with the grand old jester, "that if, as some people say, you had England in mind when you described the Ringing Island—and people do ring their bells there a good deal, and wring their hands, too, afterwards—you would not have had better fun there to-day with the powers that be than ever you did with the clergy of the Renaissance. The politicians and the publicists are, if I mistake not, a degree more subtly unctuous and several degrees more acquisitive than any of their ecclesiastical predecessors; and you would certainly have discovered that these predatory birds had migrated from a country called 'Want-of-circuses' quite as often as from the one called 'Want-of-bread', and that, if there had been 'too many of them' in monks' and friars' habits in your day, there were coming to be more still now in civil-servants' liveries. You would have been amused, too, by all the little sparrow-hawks that come chirping behind the vultures of larger size and by all the perroquets that chatter 'democracy' or 'equality' or any other word they have heard tittered frequently enough to recall. I can't help doubting whether the monks really gave quite such good openings as the petits fonctionnaires of our time. For, whilst the monks retained some more or less steady notion that they were the stewards of God, however unjust, this new vol d'oiseaux of ours is so 'volage' in its activities that no man can any longer call his house his castle or his children his charge, and scarcely his soul his own. Panurge would certainly have got in with this crowd and taken some of their pickings and stealings; and Friar John, mindful, I daresay, of Luther's exhortation to 'strike, throttle (and) stab'* the rebels of Swabia and the parts adjoining,* might, perhaps, have seized his heavy cross and smitten the complaisant crowd; but our modern Pantagruels, good easy men, are not much more successful in defending their rights against the bureaucrats than were the gentlemen of France in defending their heads against the lawyers. According to the Goncourts, it took all the screams of Mme. du Barry, on her way through the streets of Paris to be guillotined, to make the Parisians realise that it hurts to be decapitated; and it would take more than the silent protests of the English squirearchy to make our reformers realise that it can be pain and loss—pain to the squire and loss to the locality—to uproot the traditions and affections that custom and fellow-service have consecrated."

"I was not writing", Rabelais would reply, with that huge laugh

* See Mackinnon's "Luther and the Reformation", III, p. 240.

of his, "about the occidental Islands of the Blest, where, if I am well
informed, the inhabitants grumble at everything and hold themselves
up as an example to everybody. I was only repeating the story of an
odyssey wandering eastwards in pursuit of truth. I continue my tale.
After the travellers had left the Island I have just spoken of, they
came in due course to another. This was apparently depopulated, but
phallic emblems and venereal diseases had so infected the very
vegetation as to mark the passage of man. Here you might perceive
what, if the physicians of the soul fail to prevent, the physicians of
the body are left to cure. I was at pains to disguise the disgust with
which the beastly business inspired me, but you in your virtuous Isles
of the Blest will feel, I presume, that my words are superfluous.
Perhaps, however, you may deign to study them with lofty detachment. Not, of course, your women! I needn't tell you that I
didn't write my lives of Gargantua and Pantagruel for them; since in
my time they had better occupations than to eat extensively of the
tree of knowledge. All the same, they knew quite enough. My
poor travellers were still, as you saw, some way from getting a
drink from the Holy Bottle. Panurge and Friar John, like the fools
they were in their different ways, fell into the hands of inquisitors on
Condemnation Island through the matter of some hats one of the
ship's company had imported from the Isle of Games and Cheats;
and they had no sooner bribed their way out of the hands of the
canon-lawyers than in the Island of the Apedefts or ἀπαίδευτοι they
fell into those of some common-law attorneys, whose long claws and
crooked paws proclaimed their character. However, they extricated
themselves from the toils of these likewise, and entered the dominions of Queen Whims. There, thanks to the jargon of pedants about
quintessences or whims, charlatans prospered greatly; and there, after
much talk and feasting, hospitalities ended with a ball where men and
women moved like pawns and pieces on a chessboard, which is what
they mostly do in fact as well as fiction. After that the travellers
touched at the Island of Clogs or Sandals, where the inhabitants
were friars and no better than they should be, and so went on to the
Land of Satin, where men lived by Hearsay and had Aristotle among
their company. And now, at length, they made the Port of Lantern-
land, where, on a high tower, the high lantern light of La Rochelle
appeared, and beside it the lesser light of Athens. People may
suppose if they please that the former was that of the Bible (which
the Huguenots took for a special creation instead of a compilation of

scriptures slowly and carefully effected by the Church), but I would have you notice that La Rochelle lay in the diocese of Maillezais, of which the Bishop and Lord was my good patron, Geoffrey d'Estissac.

"Guided thus, then, by lamps of learning, the travellers came at length to the 'Temple of the Holy Bottle', with its vineyards without and its flagons within. The Lantern that had led them explained that in pagan times Jupiter's priestess, for a very good reason, could not have guided them under the pergola of over-arching vines that they needed to pass through. The grapes above her would have gone to her head, whereas the contemplation of divine things postulated a tranquil mind. The presiding Priestess, Bacbuc, however, filled their shoes with vine-leaves so that they might tread the grapes under their feet. 'Though no scholar,' commented Friar John, 'I find by my breviary that in the Revelation a woman was seen with the moon beneath her feet, which was a most wonderful sight. Now, as Bigot explained to me, this was to signify that she was not of the nature of other women; for they have all the moon at their heads, and consequently their brains are always troubled with lunacy. This makes me willing to believe what you said, dear Madam Lantern.' "

Cherchez la femme!—in high matters, as in low ones, the advice apparently held good. I wandered on wonderingly in the wake of the enigmatic rhapsodist,* whose love of symbolism became, if possible, more and more marked as the tale drew to its conclusion. Descending steps into a subterranean cave, where Panurge's heart naturally began to fail him, they reached at length the very gate of the temple, over which was written in Greek ἐν οἴνῳ ἀλήθεια—'In wine is truth'. There the Lantern of Learning left them with an exhortation to be of good courage. The gates opened of themselves by virtue of a hidden mechanism; and upon the pavement and walls of the building the triumphs of Bacchus were depicted with a prospect of Egypt at the end. The Temple was of great beauty, with its floor of precious stones; and in the centre hung a crystal lamp, casting a comely light like that of the sun and seeming to diffuse all the colours of the rainbow. Beneath lay a lovely fountain, with fantastic properties; and from it flowed water which turned into wine, and such wine as each man had a mind to drink. Panurge took the wine to be Beaune, Friar John compared it to Greek or sparkling wine, and Pantagruel to the wine of Mirevaux. Let them change their fancy, the Priestess told them, and the wine would change its flavour; and let them not presume to think anything impossible with God.

* Cp. Sophocles, "Oedip. Tyr.", 391—"the riddling sphinx".

Panurge, after much ritualistic ceremonial, was then led by the jolly Priestess into a chapel, where in the midst of a fountain of water stood the Holy Bottle in a crystal vase. Whispering in his ear, she made him sing some ritual verse, of which the following lines formed the conclusion:—

> Bottle, whose mysterious deep
> Does ten thousand secrets keep,
> With attentive ear I wait;
> Ease my mind, and speak my fate.

Then, after some more witchery, came on a sudden the oracular word 'Trinc'. Simultaneously the bottle, to judge by the cracking sound it made, seemed to burst; and Panurge, on his own admission, found himself as wise as before. He had learnt at last all that a man of his kind is likely to learn of life's mysteries and, when he returned to the centre of the Temple, was given his fill of Falernian out of a flask that had all the look of a breviary.

The Priestess observed that drinking, not laughing, was the distinctive trait of man, but added the cryptic observation that she meant not drinking merely, but drinking cool, delicious wine. "For you must know, my beloved, that by wine we become divine; neither can there be a surer argument or a less deceitful divination. Your academies assert the same when they make the etymology of wine, which the Greeks call οἶνος, to derive from vis, strength, virtue and power; for it is in its power to fill the soul with all truth, learning and philosophy. . . . The Goddess Bottle, therefore, directs you to the divine liquor; be yourself the expounder of your undertaking."

Panurge understood nothing of what she meant and became very foul-mouthed, and Friar John likewise rather profane. But Pantagruel had an inkling of what was intended in that age when men had made the very Eucharist a matter of filthy jest and fierce dispute. Meanwhile, the Priestess, so Rabelais continued, had filled three glasses with the water of fantasy and, giving them into the travellers' hands, observed: "Now, my friends, you may depart; and may that intellectual sphere whose centre is everywhere and circumference nowhere, whom we call God, keep you in His almighty protection. When you come into your world, do not fail to affirm and witness that the greatest treasures and most admirable things are hidden underground, and not without reason." God, she went on, was a God who hid Himself, and they would need good lanterns to find Him. Two such, she said, were available: "His own gracious guidance and man's human assistance".

Rabelais closed his doctor's tale in so impressive a manner that, when, at a later date, I met with the opinion in exalted quarters that "drinking is . . . in all ages, a symptom of the soul's thirst",* I felt that not only did I know already what the author meant, but that she had spoken even truer than perhaps she knew. For Rabelais had seemed to say that the senses, if only we drank delicately enough of the elemental water of life, would make us aware of some social or sacramental mystery lying hid in wine. Perhaps, in a finished ritual of thought, one should at this point leave the dining-room and join the ladies. Panurge, however, was in no condition for that. He had drunk of the Holy Bottle without understanding, and lay fuddled in mind and body beneath the table. And that apparently was likely to be the fate of all his sort.

I would keep Rabelais talking in the hall and on the staircase for as long as I could, so as to draw him out a little more upon one or two topics pertinent to the theme of the conversation. The current of thought had been running in his day from the sublime to the ridiculous, but now it was flowing from the ridiculous to the sublime. The body had become lord of all. So much was this the case that in the theory of psycho-analysis the very 'wealth of nations' itself was analysed into a product of the less comely functions of the flesh. Quite solemnly and seriously our psycho-analysts invited us to regard money as 'culturally the most important sublimation of anal erotism'.† On this showing it appeared that 'Lombard Street' had been raised upon a privy and that our pundits of finance were no better than permanent officials attached to the Cloaca Maxima. Not even primitive Christianity had held riches in such slight esteem, nor had sublimation ever taken a more daring flight than in causing the corporation of city-princes to emerge from the garbage-patch of the scavenger. The world of the surrealist, where such objects as palanquins and porridge-bowls, tortoises and top-hats lay together in inexplicable proximity, put no greater strain upon one's manners than the world of the psycho-analyst. But it would have been easier to maintain one's gravity if the witnesses had at least agreed together. Adler laid, however, as much stress upon aggression as the dominant impulse in mankind as Freud had done upon sex, whilst Jung broke

* Dr. MacAlister Brew in the *Times Educ. Sup.*, Feb. 21 and 28, 1942 (quoted from the *True Temp. Quarterly*, Aug. 1942).

† J. C. Flügel, "Theories of Psycho-Analysis" in Rose's "Outline of Modern Thought", p. 379.

away, as one critic complained, into 'somewhat mystic generalizations' reminiscent of Bergson's élan vital.*

I had no great success in drawing Rabelais on to talk of such dubious matters. He looked as whimsical as Barrie; and I got the idea that the only part of the theory of psycho-analysis that made much impression upon him was the notion that sins or shortcomings could only be prevented from becoming a dangerous burden on the mind by some process of confession. "Panurge", he would remark, "did, you see, send for Friar John at the height of the storm; and that is apparently the only piece of common sense that the psycho-analysts have recaptured. I do not set myself out to be a particularly fastidious man, as you may have observed, but I am bound to add that, in spite of what your Oxford Groupists say on the subject, I think confession is the better for being auricular. 'Sharing' has rather the look of a tasteless joke, to my prurient eyes." And that was all I could ever get him to say upon the subject.

How morals had got so deeply embedded in the human body that Pantagruel was instinctively recognised as a better man than Panurge, and the dark counsels of the Holy Bottle seen to contain better sense than the powerful arguments of Master Gaster were questions I dared not press, lest Rabelais should turn upon me as he had done upon Galen and observe that I was showing myself a fool. The things I have mentioned were, as I felt, too obvious for his consideration. He saw them just as facts of life. As there was a supposed gravity in the body pulling it earthwards, so also there appeared to be a certain levity in it urging it towards higher things. And, as a priest, he would not, I presumed, have had any quarrel with the remark of a modern writer that "if the Christian doctrine of original sin is found by many people difficult of acceptance in our day . . . it certainly requires some explanation how it is that all over the world to follow the good impulses has seemed like going uphill and to follow the evil ones like going downhill."†

We would be by this time well advanced up the first flight of stairs and following the elegant turn of the staircase on to the first landing. There, on some pretence, Rabelais would always take leave of me. It rather surprised me, indeed, that I had been able to lure him so far. But on reflection I saw that he had acted just as I might have expected of him. I recalled a remark of Galsworthy's in that

* Flügel in *op. cit.*, p. 366.
† Edwyn Bevan, "Symbolism and Belief", p. 63.

finished study of an old epicurean, which he had rightly named 'A Stoic'. "The French", Mr. Heythrop, the stoical epicurean in the story, is credited with saying, "were the fellows for eating and—looking things in the face! Not hypocrites—not ashamed of their reason or their senses!" Mr. Heythrop had seen the fact, but had been too English to draw the conclusion. He supposed, or acted as if he supposed, that the banquet of life was best terminated by a bottle of brandy on the dining-room floor. The nature of things, as Rabelais perceived, required that the consummation of a dinner should be sought in the conversation of the drawing-room. In France, indeed, the finished manner of a great society required the gentlemen actually to lead the ladies from the room; but in England port-wine or eighteenth-century fashions had led them to be content to join the ladies at their leisure. Rabelais, though, like Talleyrand, he was capable, as I thought, of indulging in post-prandial ablutions at the sideboard, did not lack the fine perception of the Gaul that good taste does not permit the senses to be wholly disconnected from the sensibilities. Indeed, as I passed on into the Chinese Room, I doubted whether the course of true logic should not have brought him to its very threshold. Yet I think he acted considerately and in accordance with his better feelings by keeping away from that room. He might not have been able to control the frolic and rollick of his tongue, had he once come inside. I could fancy his great laugh expanding as he started to quote maxims from a Chinese writer of our time. "Confucius", observes this authority, "reduced the great desires of human beings to two: alimentation and reproduction. . . . Many men have circumvented sex, but no saint has yet circumvented food and drink. . . . Even the most spiritual of men cannot forget about food for more than four or five hours. . . . The pattern of Chinese life is such that we not only settle disputes at dinner, after they have arisen, but also forestall the rising of disputes by the same means. . . . As for war, Napoleon showed the essential depth of his wisdom by saying that an army fights on its stomach. . . . How a Chinese Spirit glows over a good feast! How apt is he to cry out that life is beautiful when his stomach and his intestines are well filled. . . . The Chinese relies upon instinct, and his instinct tells him that, when the stomach is right, everything is right. . . . A Chinese poet says, 'A well-filled stomach is indeed a great thing; all else is luxury'."* "With all the animals and plants," continues this

* Lin Yutang, "The Importance of Living", p. 49.

curious commentary on the paganism of the bodily-minded man, "the proper point of view is how we humans can enjoy them, and not what they are in themselves. The song of the bird, the colour of the flower, the petals of the orchid, the texture of chicken-meat are the things that concern us. The East has to learn from the West the entire sciences of botany and zoology, but the West has to learn from the East how to enjoy the trees, the flowers, and the fishes, the birds and animals, to get a full appreciation of the contours and gestures of different species and associate them with different moods and feelings. Food, then, is one of the very few solid joys of human life."

Rabelais would have paused there, got his laugh out of the company, and then added:—

"You see, it is just as I told you, all the world over. Master Gaster reigns supreme from China to Peru. Now listen to this!"—and his laugh would have grown louder still:—" 'The Chinese have no prudery about food or about eating it with gusto. . . . When a Chinaman drinks a mouthful of good soup, he gives a hearty smack.' " But there I should have stopped the old mocker. On his Chinese friend's showing, it was either Behaviour or Behaviourism that had got to go; and for myself I preferred it should be Behaviourism. So, in spite of what has just been read, had Confucius thought, and had therefore seen in manners the making of man.

Chapter VIII

THE CHINESE ROOM

I HAVE already had occasion to say something of the room that took its character and its name from a Chinese wallpaper which, in the fashion of the eighteenth and early nineteenth centuries, covered its walls. Into the making of it, Allegra, during her brief tenancy, had put as much of herself as into any room in the house; and there, more than anywhere, the touch of her hand might still be felt. With its walls illumined by the gorgeous plumage of some eighty varieties of unclassified and indeed unidentified birds; with its delicate, white-lacquered furniture; with its suggestion of something cunningly transferred across centuries and continents and as cunningly transformed to suit a lighter taste and a darker sky—with, in a word, its substitution of chinoiserie for the purer Chinese art preferred by the connoisseur, it seemed to possess some peculiar qualification for that meeting between East and West which an eminent poet (not, if I had judged rightly from observation of a casual encounter, wholly indifferent to the charm of Allegra's personality) had perhaps too hastily declared to be impossible.

That such a rapprochement between the Orient and the Occident should have occurred in the eighteenth century will astonish no one who considers that at that period in western Europe the mind may be said to have taken such a hold on the human situation as the spirit by some accounts enjoyed in the thirteenth century and as the body has acquired in our own. The age of Voltaire was, par excellence, the age of rationalism; and the Chinese, as a popular novel of our own time assures us, 'are a rational people—the most rational probably on earth'.* Pure reason, to those who, with minds aroused by the Encyclopedia or the Aufklärung, rebelled against the unedifying aspects of the eighteenth century, might well seem to borrow the wings of the morning and betake itself to the confines of the Celestial Empire, where benevolent despotism and intellectual aristocracy had, or appeared to have achieved reasonable and tolerable expression in the person of the Son of Heaven with his Court of Mandarins. In the elegant form and fashion of its silken raiment, just as in the quiet distinction of its landscape-painting or the

* " Pekin Picnic."

lovely glaze of its porcelain, China seemed to illustrate the wisdom of Confucius, with its mannered behaviour, serene response to surroundings and deportment beyond reproach. Lord Chesterfield was in line with Chinese philosophy at its best when he bade his son sacrifice to the Graces; and one could see in Englishmen as differently sensitive as Lowes Dickinson* and Havelock Ellis† how that superbly natural rendering of the rhythm of life still affected western critics. Not surely quite without reason had a writer on Chinese Central Asia quoted an observation of Guglielmo Ferrero respecting the horizons lost to Europe but still in his day at least capable of being regained through contact with China. "We have need", Ferrero had pleaded,‡ "to rediscover, to admire, to save the remains of the old qualitative civilisations which every day we pitilessly destroy to increase our wealth and our power. There—one can never say too often—lies the tragedy of the modern world. The old qualitative civilisations had as their aim perfection, and not power, and are our Paradise Lost."

I liked to fancy that some breath of that lost love of perfection for its own sake had permeated the Chinese room under Allegra's influence. I liked to suppose that the atmosphere there had become surcharged with this magic fragrance from the very day when I first watched her urge the accomplished old expert in Chinese decoration to the use of a gayer green for the groundwork of the paper and to a more lavish distribution of water in the landscape. I liked to believe that a supersensuous air still pollinated every lovely flower and lifted every gorgeous wing. I liked to feel that the wind, playing among the trees of the garden, cast a peculiar loveliness of light and shade across the path of all discussion, and that all things, both high and low, that were spoken of were treated without irreverence and yet without reserve. I even dared to hope that in some such dream-garden a man might still walk in the cool of life's evening and encounter the Artist of all the earth, and by Him be led to the exact standpoint where the signature of all things should appear and the world be seen for a creation no less simple than sublime. "La Chine obscurcit," Pascal had written,§ "mais il y a clarté à trouver; cherchez-la." His eyes had rested there before Voltaire's and so, perhaps, had in some measure obviated Voltaire's criticism that

---

* "Letters of John Chinaman." † "Dance of Life", p. 22.
‡ Quoted by C. P. Skrine, "Chinese Central Asia", p. 167.
§ "Pensées", 593.

China found no place in Bossuet's Catholic rendering of universal history.

However that might be, the Chinese, in my view, were far too sensible of the realities of human life as we know it to be anything but dualists. The music that they made had no resemblance to those pipes of Pan in which some earnest minds, as well as some pagan dispositions, have found salvation, or what they took for such. In Allegra's sinological chamber I detected no echo of the higher pantheism which permeates the monistic and melancholy thought of Spinoza and has been crystallised by the genius of Walter Pater in his imaginary portrait of Sebastian van Storck. Rather did I catch there the accents of that beat, now soft, now strong, of 'yin' and 'yang', which a grave historian of our time* has wrought into his philosophy of history. The subtle play of light and shade as it crossed and re-crossed the room would seem to move to a measure à deux temps and, as if in response to a dualism worked into the very rhythm of all things, to come forward, to pause, to retire and again return with the grace of a minuet. Under the influence of such airy fancies the moon might seem to advance to greet the sun; the night to retreat before the day; cloud, as if driven before the wind, to clasp the hand of sunshine and betray the silver lining of its cloak; and death, like a great gentleman, to lead dying life towards the seats of the lowly and leave her there with a gallant bow.

To the music of such motion it was easy to yield. It possessed the manifold enchantments of the house of Circe, and would tempt one to make an odyssey of existence and to drift without design across many seas of thought and time. Only some strong apprehension of ideas of good and evil latent in the very heart of things forbade the luxury of a criticism of life where the stage seemed to conjure all the pain out of circumstance and the opera to sing the likeness of a design into the art of living. I suppose I began to feel the force of this critique of life first when, an undergraduate still, I read the late Lord Rosebery's book on 'the last phase' of Napoleon. The Emperor, as already indicated, was there treated as a-moral; and all the circumstances of his career were privileged accordingly. War became 'the gambling of the gods'; the prisoner of St. Helena took on the air of a new Prometheus chained to a rock by an unjust fiat from high Olympus; and the prosaic Bathurst and the ungracious Lowe obediently assumed the unlovely parts of Zeus and Hermes.

* Arnold Toynbee.

Such power had Drama, when left to its own devices, to obscure the lines and lift the face of ugly fact. Intellect, even of the keenest, was not always proof against its meretricious skill, as I recognised in Rosebery's graceful periods. Its strength I had long ago learnt from Herbert Fisher's lips, when, plunged at the time in the study of Napoleon as an administrator, he spoke to me of the detrimental effect upon one's moral outlook of studying such stupendous talent. Its fascination I noted afresh whenever in girlish enthusiasm or youthful minstrelsy, in heroic romance, epic or ethic, some softer feeling was betrayed towards the murderer of the duc d'Enghien, towards the donor of a legacy to Wellington's would-be assassin, towards the monster who could tell Metternich that to such a man as himself the lives of a million of men were of no account. But the climax of these considerations seemed to be reached in the surprising admission of a brilliant Gifford Lecturer of our time that "Satan, if we understand matters, is the ally rather than the enemy of Michael, and both are God's servants".* The limitations as well as the perils of the merely dramatic outlook upon life seemed fully exposed in that strange sentence which covered crime with glamour and clothed a-morality in shining garments. If the devil did not exist, it was clear that, for the Gifford Lecturer and his sort, the devil would have had to be invented, or else life would lose one half of its savour. Theologians and idealists, this high authority complained, had alike strangely overlooked the fact that 'the conditions of our present lives simply do not and cannot permit of the unbroken felicity we crave'. That disposed well enough of the idealists whose houses, swept free of experience and garnished with optimism, were commonly seized upon and subsequently inhabited by devils seven times more numerous than before.† The theologians, however, were hardly open to the same reproach. They had spoken of a fall of angels and of a fall of man; of a world good enough to be beautiful, yet shot through, like Circe's house, with wiles; of a human nature needing to be born again, but desperately wounded; of a possibility of perfection, but only in connection with a God incarnate. They did not appear to have been rash, like the infelicitous idealists; nor had their statements ever foreshadowed any unbroken felicity upon earth.

* W. MacNeile Dixon, in "The Human Situation", p. 211.
† Cp. *ibid.*, p. 310, '. . . Idealism, that wolf in sheep's clothing of the philosophic schools'.

So far, in fact, from feeling that both Satan and Michael were alike God's servants, and that the essence of tragic drama, in accordance with the Hegelian formula, lay in the conflict of right with right, not of right with wrong, I became certain that any such critique of life had lost its way or, perhaps, which was much the same thing, its canons of judgment. The truth appeared to be both more simple and more profound. The recollection of standing, a boy then of no more than sixteen, before Napoleon's tomb at the Invalides and of looking from the monument to the Corsican interred below to the figure of the Galilean hanging on His cross above, would return and vividly possess my mind. I would fancy my father again at my side as contemptuous as he could be—old soldier though he was—of the adulation of the supposititious hero at our feet and equally well satisfied of the justice of the adoration paid to Him whose body needed no tomb to hold it. I did not feel, however, that the force of the antithesis had come home to him as it had to myself. His strictures upon Napoleon were those of a gentleman very much alive to the truth of Wellington's terse and caustic comment that a gentleman was just what Napoleon was not. That was a plainer issue than the one upon which my mind had begun to work, for it left the soldier still in line with Christianity, without touching the problem which the Gifford Lecturer had stated with such alarming force. To maintain that it needed devils as well as angels to make the universe dramatically satisfying was at a short remove from saying 'Here is Yin' or 'There is Yang', like the imperturbable Chinese.

Such detachment, not to call it fatalism, was perhaps congenial to Chinese art, and had certainly had some place in Chinese history. But in the Chinese Room, where the very term chinoiserie confessed the presence of western influences, it seemed rather a pose than a persuasion. The antithesis that I wrestled with could set all symbolism swaying. It was no refreshing shower that lurked in the soft skies of the Chinese paper, but a tempest sufficient to lay low both tree and flower and to swell lake and river into flood. As one's thoughts formed, the air would seem to grow heavy with secrets old as humanity itself; and Hegel's tribute in his "Logic" to the profound truth of the Eden story would come forcibly to mind. The mystery of evil would make its way even into that garden of delight which, in Allegra's day, had seemed little less than an earthly paradise. Yet the sky, for all the rising menace of its appearance, was of so grand an aspect as to need a Turner to do it justice; and the serpent that came slithering through the grass seemed to have lost nothing of its title to figure as a symbol of that wisdom which some of us had learnt to suspect in it from looking as children upon its emblematic representation on Queen Elizabeth's robe.

The whole situation had, in fact, come to seem as enigmatic as it could well be. The Chinese Room was alive with eastern mystery. Evil was in the air, yet every material manifestation of it appeared full of wonder and often of beauty. It was only in the juxtaposition of things, not in the things in themselves, that one seemed aware of its presence; and it passed one like a wind blowing where it listed. There were, as I had learned, three classical explanations of its existence. There was the Persian theory that the spirits of good and evil were engaged in even combat; there was the Indian theory that the world itself was bad, a cosmic disaster; and there was the belief, which had spread westwards from the confines of Asia, that man's excellent dominion had been assailed by some enemy striking with all his strength, yet with strength falling short of his full requirements. I could remember Allegra toying with the first of these notions, and I could see how it might appeal to a mind eager to see love triumphant and slow to believe that good would not have quickly closed the conflict, if good had possessed the power. Yet as a reading of the riddle it did not tempt me. An even combat, if that were all that was going on, should long ago have brought the world to irremediable chaos. Yet there was no chaos visible except such as prudence could remedy. Law and order were, in fact, so obvious as to have persuaded some scientific men that they were ubiquitous. Neither did the Indian solution appear to satisfy the facts. Men, whether they came from the East or from the West, still set too much store by their individual lives to make it even plausible to suppose that they regarded life as an evil. A general, if not a universal expression of experience was compressed into George Eliot's remark in "Middlemarch" that Mr. Casaubon's outlook had been completely altered by the substitution of the particular consciousness 'I must die—and soon' for the general proposition that 'We must all die'. Suicide, it is true, denied these conclusions; but suicides must, numerically at least, be reckoned as eccentricities, even if not always the eccentricities of unsound minds. And, if rumour spoke truly, experiment had shown that persons afflicted by incurable and painful disease discovered no disposition to act upon the cryptic advice, sometimes discreetly insinuated through the information that an opiate, placed within their reach, should be treated with caution, lest an overdose prove fatal.

Thus, if only by a process of elimination, was the mind driven to that third opinion regarding evil, which supposed the world to have been assailed by some enemy. Spinoza, no less than St. Thomas Aquinas before him, had blocked the road to the belief that evil had anything positive about it. All things, considered separately, appeared good in themselves and by themselves; even dirt, as Oscar Wilde had observed, being no more than matter out of place. And, at the other end of the scale, Satan, though God's servant no longer, was God's creature still. An angel yet, though an angel fallen, the devil discovered just such a dualism in his personality as corresponded with the facts of which the mysterious moods of the garden—its light and darkness—had appeared to be the tokens. Milton, indeed, had so notoriously become subject to the devil's fascination as to have made, all unconsciously, a hero out of his villain. And certainly all the fiction of crime had furnished no figure more sinister or more intriguing than that of one who, to his titles of Lucifer and Prince of Darkness, added that also of Prince of this World. Here lay a possible explanation of that intense interest in the occult and the macabre which was so common a feature in human nature as to pass almost unnoticed. Apparently men found life dull without the devil and the search for him more exciting by a good deal than the search for God.

Who was sufficient for these things? Not certainly myself, for I seemed to lack all that apparatus of instinct, intuition and psychic sensibility by virtue of which some men and women contrived to pick their way through the perplexities of the human situation. I could arrive at nothing, as Allegra once intimated to me, except by mental process, and maybe at not so very much even by that means. It may have been this infirmity that led me at length to seek the companionship of one whose humane and critical soul seemed particularly congenial to a room consecrated to the pleasures of roving thought and free discussion. I am speaking of Montaigne. Que sais-je? In that famous utterance I found humility, not presumption, enquiry, not scepticism. If I had tried to paraphrase it, I should have said that it signified "Who is sufficient for these things?"

The story of Montaigne's mind as I learnt it by degrees from his writings had something for me of the same charm as Gibbon's. There was to be found there the same well-considered withdrawal from the world, the same singleness of purpose, the same well-employed leisure, the same wealth of meditation over the affairs of men and the absurdities of things. Only I would find in him a grace that Gibbon lacked, a sustained feeling for some more excellent way than even the best gifts Humanism could supply, an interest much more than platonic in the observances of that Church which Gibbon joined and subsequently forsook. Not many of Montaigne's readers had done justice to this trait in his character; and some, not liking it at all themselves, had even denied its existence in him. But, even were no external evidence of it available, I think I should have known that it was latent in his soul, so catholic was his interest in the issues of life, so free from prejudice his vision of mortal things, so urbane his citizenship of the City of God. I shall return to these aspects of the man in due course, but to assure to his criticism of life its proper weight in the argument of the Chinese Room, his personality needs to be seen for a short while against its background of circumstance.

Outstanding in that background was the Château de Montaigne. Rebuilt during the Second Empire and burnt down under the Third Republic, it might indeed seem to have lost the best part of its title to figure in the landscape, if it were not for the fortunate preservation of its famous western tower. Rather a dependence than a part of the Château, this building illustrated even by itself all that was most significant in the association of Montaigne's mind with the things of time and circumstance. Here, in ascending order, lay his chapel, his bedroom, his library, and, beyond, the snug little cabinet, adorned with scenes from Ovid's Metamorphoses, where he made a fire and took refuge in cold weather. In these apartments, then, the scholar may still be surprised (or, at least, supposed) with his books; the 'sceptic' at his prayers; the man of the world with his reflections; and the philosopher, in the older and better sense of the word, at his meditations. As for the country around, its prospect from the windows was not out of keeping with the spirit of the Essays. Beneath, lay the basse-cour, a modest reminder of the homeliness of human life as well as of the place held by the farm in the philosophy both of the French physiocrats and the French peasants. Beyond, stretched the delectable Duchy of Aquitaine, whose soft and salubrious wine, warming the soul without exciting the senses, remains admittedly the drink of the epicure; whilst all around spread that pleasant land of France, where good living has been admirably correlated with high thinking and the play and penetration of the mind enriched by the well-being of the body.

To this fair heritage the great gentleman, whose casual thoughts were to seem to many ensuing generations to contain the considered wisdom of European civilisation, had, after his father's demise, deliberately returned. Forsaking for it the life of courts, he made of it, not only his residence as a seigneur, but also his home as a human soul. Here, where he had been taught, almost literally, to babble in the Latin tongue by virtue of his father's instruction, he became the most effective modern exponent of a Humanism, one of whose foremost apostles among the Ancients had declared that, being himself human, nothing human was alien to him.

France, to be sure, stood in Montaigne's time in much need of humanity. The easy-going old libertine, who had ruled so long as François Ier, had, when Montaigne was still in his teens, made way for the stern and melancholy, yet, at his best, gracious and even charming prince who was perhaps the original of Rabelais's Pantagruel. Henri II was both the husband of Catherine de Médicis and the lover of Diane de Poitiers, though perhaps, as some recent investigation indicates, and as her own cryptic device of 'omnium victorem vicit' suggests, a platonic lover only. A hostage in Spain during part of his boyhood, and consequently familiar with the religious intolerance of Spanish state-policy, he was perhaps the readier to countenance the disposition of the French lawyers to persecute which his father, in less anxious times, had contrived to restrain. His reign saw the establishment of the chambre ardente, the French equivalent of the star-chamber, and also a codification of the laws against the Protestants; but of that severity, symbolised by the herb Pantagruelion, there was no more striking example than an incident at Bordeaux when the rebellious Bordelais were compelled to dig up with their finger-nails the corpse of the Governor whom they had killed.

Montaigne, as likely as not, had watched that grim scene, for he was at the time a law student in the University; and the operations of justice not only demand the attention of lawyers but deserve that of students of human nature. For a time, however, legal avocations seemed to block Montaigne's path to humane letters. Following in his father's footsteps, he became conseiller-du-roi dans la Cour du Parlement de Bordeaux, and was presently entrusted with a mission from that august body to the Parlement de Paris which brought him to the metropolis. The hour happened to be one of the deepest political anxiety. Catherine de Médicis, left Regent of France by the death of her husband and the youth of her son, was attempting to adapt the comparatively mild methods of the fourth and fifth centuries after Christ to the fierce controversies of the sixteenth. Advised by Michel de l'Hôpital—a man great enough to perceive that zeal is the beginning and not the end of love, and rash enough to suppose that truth is so great that it must prevail—the Queen-mother issued in 1561 an edict of toleration. The Chancellor had, however, entertained too favourable an opinion of mankind, at least as exemplified in his contemporaries.

Neither Catholic nor Protestant, neither clerk, nor layman, nor lawyer, could find the way of peace. A colloquy of contending theologians at Poissy, with the King in the chair, concluded in intellectual confusion, whilst, as Faurin's diary effectively shows, Catholics and Huguenots alike resorted freely to physical violence to put an end to mental strife. The Chancellor, however, refused to despair. In 1562 a still more tolerant Edict amplified the Edict of 1561 and conceded to the Huguenots, what they had in fact already seized, equal rights of worship. It was a fine gesture in a land where, that very same month, the protestant magistrates of Castres had forbidden mass to be said within their jurisdiction; but Montaigne, whether under the influence of his profession or because, as Champion supposes, he had at the time an exaggerated admiration for the statesmanship of the Guises, became associated with its critics the lawyers. He swore, when, so far as one could see, there was no sort of need for him to swear, an oath of orthodoxy required of the Parisian lawyers by the Sorbonne but not imposed upon the Bordelais; and the act was so unlike him as to be remarkable. Later on he regained that faith in the Chancellor's methods which Catherine de Médicis was, quite excusably, losing, as France sank ever deeper into faction and misery. "It is you", the Queen-mother told Michel de l'Hôpital at last, "who, with your fine words about moderation and justice, have landed us where we are." And so from fear rather than fervency Catherine took the turning which led in due course to the massacre of St. Bartholomew.

A year, however, before politics came to that fearful pass, Montaigne had resigned his magistracy and abandoned for ever the direct service of the State. His motives have never been in doubt. In solemn, almost majestic phrases he placed his decision and the reason of it upon record. "In the year 1571, at the age of thirty-eight on the last day of February, the anniversary of his birthday,

Michel de Montaigne, already a long while bored by the slavery of the law-courts and of public affairs, retired to repose himself on the bosom of the virgin Muses in calm and safety and will pass there the remainder of his days. Hoping that destiny may allow him to re-fashion this home of his, this sweet ancestral retreat, he has dedicated it to his liberty, his tranquillity and his leisure."

If Montaigne had not despaired of the State and adopted Seneca's opinion that, given a certain degree of civic corruption, the wise man will not waste his time in futile political effort, he had at least preferred the service of the Republic of Letters to that of the Kingdom of France. Entailing as it did the substitution of larger vision for local views, of remote purposes for tangible aims, of the preparation of the paths of peace for the stir of controversy and contention, such an act must at any time show character. In the age which was to produce Henri IV and Sully, with their dream of a United States of Europe, it had some universal as well as some particular significance. It showed how much more humanity an accomplished scholar and gentleman, if he has the good fortune to catch the ear of mankind, may sometimes hope to promote, even in a world like ours, by a private life rather than by direct public service.

There was one significant inscription adorning Montaigne's library—a tribute to the friend who had both formed his character and filled high, as no other affection ever did, the cup of his felicity. As Arthur Hallam was to Alfred Tennyson, so was Étienne de La Boétie to Michel de Montaigne. A little older and a little graver than his friend, the young lawyer poet had come for a brief lustrum into Montaigne's life more like an inspiration than an influence. So far-reaching, indeed, had this intimacy seemed that Sainte-Beuve, as he seeks to take its measure, pauses to speculate what benefits such another friendship might not have conferred upon Voltaire in the way of moderating, mellowing and moralising the operation of his trenchant genius. This, of course, can no man tell. All that we dare say is that Montaigne could not have been the Montaigne that we know without the sweetness and light that he drew from the recollection of Étienne de la Boétie. In their intercourse he believed that he had tasted the finest vintage of love, declaring, like such as have known mystic ecstasies, that the communion of friendship in its deepest realisation is unimaginable by those who have not experienced it, and declaring, too, like such as have passed through some momentous parting of friends, that the loss of it had turned all his days to darkness. But let him speak for himself: "Menander of old time said that he was fortunate who had met merely the shadow of a friend. He had reason enough to say so . . . for in truth, if I compare all the rest of my life, soft, easy and secure (as by the grace of God it has been except for the loss of this friend), exempt from grave affliction, and full of contentment and tranquillity of mind, to the four or five years that it was given to me to enjoy the sweet company and companionship of this person, it is but smoke, a night tedious and obscure. From the day that I lost him—that day always bitter; yet always held in honour as by the gods decreed—I do but drag myself languidly along, whilst the very pleasure to come, instead of consoling me, duplicates my sense of loss. . . . So much was I already in the habit of being doubled that I seem to myself to be halved."

It had been thus only the ashes of a heart that Montaigne had offered to the excellent woman—Françoise de la Chassaigne—whom he took to wife after his friend had died. Yet, as her letters to her confessor showed, those ashes satisfied her expectations. Thirty years after his death she could declare that from him had come all her felicity, and, if their union was rather a ménage than a marriage, it is clear, as Madame de Sournay asserts, that she loved him with 'a very warm conjugal affection'.

The famous Essays, however, came to birth, not in his wife's apartments, but in that book-lined tower where Montaigne dwelt with the memory of his departed friend. Here, as in some reliquary, was preserved against the touch of time that grace of full humanity which Voltaire never sought, or at least never found. Étienne de la Boétie, with the superb constellation of the Pléiade shining in the contemporary sky, may seem to us no more than a pale and ineffectual fire; but to Montaigne's loving eye he appeared 'the greatest man of his time', had time only allowed him to prove it. The inclusion of some of La Boétie's odes among Montaigne's essays is the more interesting for that. For Montaigne too is a poet, though a poet who hides himself. It is not Montesquieu only who recognises it; it is Sainte-Beuve also who declares that of all French writers, the poets by profession not excluded, Montaigne possesses the highest poetic sense. And this music in his mind enabled him to frame a style which the same august authority affirms to be 'a continual epigram and renascent metaphor'. Now feathering the face of the waters with his oars, now shipping them and drifting with the flow, now letting his boat lie still in some dreamy backwater to watch the pellucid reflections, and then again striking into the main stream to test the strength of the current, that unconquerable oarsman manoeuvres his boat down the river of circumstance with a poetry of motion at that time all his own and even still, perhaps, unrivalled.

Not only in poetry had the soul of La Boétie anticipated or advanced the mind of his friend. Among the young man's writings lay a plea for popular government as austere as Brutus might have entertained or Algernon Sidney prescribed. The contents of the treatise are epitomised in its alternative titles "Discours sur la servitude volontaire" and "Le Contre'un". It aims at rousing men from the political servitude into which they lapse from personal indolence or are lured by political bribery. Its sentiment has become stale, its argument is laboured, but its conclusion may still be admired by those who have not yet reached Pope's conclusion that the efficiency of the administration, rather than the form of the government, is the thing that really matters to the most part of mankind. "For my part," writes La Boétie, "I am convinced, and not mistakenly, that, since there is nothing so contrary as tyranny to God, all generous and good-natured(tout libéral et débonnaire) as He is, He reserves yonder some special punishment for tyrants and their accomplices."

The pamphlet was published in the days of Henri III; and certain derogatory references in the text are so entirely appropriate to the character and reign of the last Valois king that a good case has been made out for supposing that Montaigne himself inserted them, La Boétie having been some ten years dead by the date of that monarch's accession. The interest of the conjecture lies in the support it affords to the suggestion that Montaigne, for all his retirement and detachment, kept his eye still upon politics, and lent a helping, if a hidden hand to the forces of toleration. Once a follower, at least to some extent, of Guise, subsequently a friend to Henri of Navarre, he was peculiarly qualified to appreciate all the strong points in the religious controversy. He sympathised, that is to say, with the conviction of the Catholics, which has never faltered from that day to this, that the maintenance of one body as well as one spirit is an essential element of the faith once delivered to the saints, and also with that of the Huguenots that feelings, so pious and sincere as their own, merited a respect and a toleration which, unfortunately, they did not always themselves display. Thus, though he did not live to see the submission of Henri IV to the Church or the concession of the Edict of Nantes to the Huguenots, he may be regarded as the forerunner of a settlement which was the best that such unhappy divisions allowed of. I inferred from what he said that he had perceived that the Catholics were fighting with the fury of artists, defending a masterpiece of political construction, and the Protestants with the fanaticism of adventurers in ecclesiastical idealism or the economic redistribution of wealth. To a historian like himself it would have been obvious that the primitive Church could never be restored in Renaissance France, Protestant England or anywhere else, and that the avaricious, and not the pious, would be the principal profiteers in a general scramble.

Through a critical period when, as he observed, every Frenchman had seen himself every hour for thirty years on the edge of an entire reversal of fortune, Montaigne had kept so clear a head that his estimate of human life has become a classic of the first consequence in any critical study of it. As one turned over the pages of his famous essays, soiled and tattered though they be by the hands of a dozen generations, one could fancy that one heard the scratching of his quiet pen to the distant accompaniment of armies, carrying banners with legends of love, but marching away into the mists of mortal hatred. Once only, however, was his own peace seriously disturbed. A troop of soldiers, some twenty-five or thirty in number, descended upon the Château de Montaigne with the intention apparently of effecting a treacherous surprise. But Montaigne displayed such generous hospitality and absence of suspicion that the captain in command was, on his own admission, quite disarmed, and so remounted his horse and rode away with his troopers. It was not the first time in history that quietness and confidence have turned violence from its designs, but their power in Montaigne was evidently exceptional. He must have had a wonderful way with him indeed, since, with no stronger weapon, he apparently persuaded a robber on another occasion to release him and forgo a ransom.

Amidst so great a commotion of events, then, had this Socratic soul pursued its way towards self-knowledge. "I study myself", he declared, "more than any other subject; it is both my physics and my metaphysics." The physics of his personality, in that fulness of his intellectual powers when I made so bold as to fancy I had come to know him, revealed an oldish man once handsome but looking a little the worse for wear and enduring with philosophic patience, if not altogether without mocking allusion to the ineptitude of doctors, the pains of stone and colic. Preoccupied though he was with his reflections, his senses were exceptionally acute, and his sensibility was such as to cause his features rather to announce than repeat his sentiments. As for his mode of life, it was not altogether unworthy of the Roman tradition that he placed so high. If his malady compelled him to add to the clothing of the upper part of his person in cold weather, he did not change that of his legs with the seasons. Winter, in fact, he preferred; as his eyes suffered much from the glare in summer. And if, in comparison with other of his contemporaries, he rose late, breakfasted late and dined late, he slept, and slept soundly, for eight or nine hours at a stretch on a hard bed which he would not allow to be warmed for him. His diet, though he declared that at times he would eat greedily, was simple. No fastidious feeder, he had from childhood disliked delicacies—sweets and jam and suchlike—and in mature life he was accustomed to start his meal after others had begun, to eat the first thing offered him and to discountenance a succession of courses. Fish he liked; and, consequently, he welcomed days of abstinence. If he had a weakness, it was for sauces, not excluding that of good conversation. But his wine, both white and red, he mixed with water.

To put the matter in a nutshell, I could never imagine Montaigne taking his meals with Panurge. Happily, however, that apostle of flesh-pots and punch-bowls, though I would sometimes fancy I saw him grinning like a gargoyle at the corner of some larder or closet, kept severely to the ground floor of my house of memories and impressions; whilst in the Chinese room Montaigne seemed to smile approval of my own lazy habit of taking my meals on a tray with perhaps a volume of his essays at my side. These last were a constant reminder of my companion's Latinity. No compliment, as I saw from the fact that he had been at so great pains to get himself made a Roman citizen, was more acceptable than a reference to his proficiency in the classics. Though, on account of the mud, he disliked walking far too much to have made a willing legionary, he had undoubted reserves of endurance which would have carried him a long way on horseback, and, indeed, did so, in spite of the painful disease which troubled him. I noticed how susceptible he was to the charm of soldiers—how he would praise their youth, their activity, their good breeding and their artless conversation. Recluse and student though he might appear, the soldier's varied life made a great appeal to him. He liked the sound of military music and, if the truth be told, was not indifferent to the romance of war, which he made bold to say was 'the most useful, just, and universal of all things', inasmuch as it secured both the safety and greatness of one's country—a sentiment which, perhaps, I was justified in regarding as no more than a paraphrase of the ancient adage, so unwisely ridiculed by the politicians of our time, that, if you wish for peace, you must prepare for war. He was in truth up to a point a Roman citizen in both senses; and his Humanism had led him to worship at pagan shrines before he adored the true God. Having made heroes in his time of Epaminondas and Alexander, he had subsequently transferred his veneration to Socrates, and early enough in life to incur the chaff of La Boétie, who styled him a new Alcibiades.

Insensibly I have been substituting the metaphysical for the physical aspect of the man; and I can only hope that the reader has not found the transition too abrupt. In any case, the change has been all to the purpose, if Montaigne is to take over, so to say, from Rabelais and play showman to the human mind as Rabelais has done to the human body. To converse with him was, as it seemed to me, much as if a man were to place himself at one of those so-called rond-points in a French forest and allow his eyes to wander now down one, now down another of the roads converging there. At the end of each glade would be seen some god or satyr—one of those old Roman deifications of moral virtues, malignant forces or capricious powers—and about each deity Montaigne would have an anecdote to relate or an aphorism to propound. Never unctuous, never dogmatic, never doctrinaire, he seemed to avoid with guileless art the habits that commonly provoke one in the earnest talker; and his judgments were instinct with kindly tolerance as well as with cool observation. Thanks to its élan and its ease, his conversation was, in fact, of the best. The living voice, it is true, was wanting; but I did not regret that so much since I learnt that it had sounded at times a trifle loud.

I felt little doubt, as I listened to this observer of mankind, that, so far as mere man might hope to accomplish it, he had founded his erudition upon a rock. Following Socrates, and after a manner anticipating Descartes, he had built his house upon the incontestable fact that on the face of it one knows, or at least can know if one chooses, more about oneself than about any mortal man, or than any mortal man can know about one. Perhaps on that account he seemed to me to speak, not as the psychologists or the psycho-analysts do, but with that peculiar authority which is born of candour and humility and requires no other credentials. He got, as the saying is, other people right, because he really knew himself. Let me illustrate that with a little remark that I heard him make, if I remember, near the beginning of our intercourse. "I have", he said, "an astonishing weakness in the way of pity and pardon." It was as if an artist had been surprised, whilst at work upon his own portrait, into an admission of man's true descent from a soul naturally Christian. Consider again, and with particular reference to the notion that we have in him the true original of the melancholy Jaques,* the assurance that he was among those least afflicted by sadness.† He was indeed a perfect humorist, conscious of the grave and the gay, and blending them with so fine a sense as to make tragedy tolerable. How much there was to be found in his remark that our affections carry us beyond ourselves so that we are never truly at home in our mortal lives, but are swept forward continually by our fears, our wishes, and our hopes into the future!‡ By brooding observation and quiet reflection he had come to an understanding of the human situation which men commonly reach only through passionate tribulation. That heart's restlessness, which St. Augustine felt as a great call for God; that boredom which Bossuet, thinking on a lower plane, noted as a proof of man's fall from grace; that despair which drew from Hamlet the exceeding bitter cry that the goodly earth had become for him no better than a sterile promontory, and heaven's roof, fretted with golden fire, a pestilent congregation of vapours—these for Montaigne were rather facts of life that a critical intellect must reckon with. I did not doubt, however, that he perceived their significance. For the possession of faculties, calculated to carry us beyond ourselves, produced an enigma more insoluble than any other, if there was not hidden in the nature of things something to match it. It was like Allegra to touch, however lightly, the pulse of every throbbing question; and I have some reason to know that she laid her finger here. She must, indeed, have lacked something of the fine feeling which I have claimed as part, and great part, of her personality, if she had not felt the moral impossibility of supposing that a being noble in reason as man, and possessed of those other distinctions already cited from Hamlet's magnifical phrases, could in the last analysis be dismissed as no more than an energy of dust. That, however, as the Alien Voice would quickly remind me, was, whatever it might seem intuitionally, still, speculatively speaking, the question. "A question framed", I would hazard, "not without some presumption of design inherent in it." "Not proven!" the Voice would coldly rejoin.

In Montaigne, however, as I gratefully recognised, there lay no disposition to arrive at any hurried or categorical answer to the riddle

* See G. B. Harrison, "Shakespeare at Work", p. 172.
† "Essais", I, 2.   ‡ *Ibid.*, II, 3.

of life. Experience was too many-sided for that. A born spectator, as his much-criticised inaction, when the plague reached Bordeaux, sufficiently shows, he blamed himself for his fastidiousness, his indolence, his indecision, his preference for a life 'smooth, obscure and silent'.* But I had no reason to quarrel with this detachment, for it is a commonplace that spectators see most of the game. I asked no more of him than that he should illustrate, with all the richness of his personality, that trinity of being which an admirer has perceived in him 'the unashamed Adam, the thinker and the artist'. If he seemed static, his critical poise was yet so admirable that he could play with the spheres of past, present and future like the balls that a conjuror throws up in quick succession but never allows to fall. It was after this manner that he seemed to deserve the name of a spectator of all time and all existence.

Musing, then, mostly without method, Montaigne had surveyed the human scene and asked himself what the mind could make sure of in a world so distracted by contradiction. That was a question presently to be answered to the general, if not the universal satisfaction of the four following centuries by Descartes's 'Cogito, ergo sum'; but Montaigne might, perhaps, have preferred St. Augustine's kindred remark that, if a man can be certain of nothing else, he can know at least that he doubts. Every doubter has so much affirmation to his credit. If there were no exterior world to be known, he must still confess that he himself was there to doubt its existence.

How fully the Latin Doctors of the Church had recognised the difficulties of the doubter had been, as it seemed to me, too little noticed by those who spoke of them mostly from hearsay. "It seems", says St. Thomas Aquinas, putting the ultimate case for all his doubting namesakes, "that God does not exist, because if one of two contraries be infinite, the other would be altogether destroyed. But the word God means that he is infinite goodness. If therefore God existed, there should be no evil discoverable; but there is evil in the world. Therefore God does not exist." The answer returned may or may not satisfy a modern mentality, but at least nothing is wanting to the challenge of the objection. It is difficult to excel scholastics in the dispassionate, business-like marshalling of the arguments on either side; and in that they continue to be an example to us all. Within my own life-time the English estimate of Scholasticism had, indeed, undergone an astonishing change. It is an English

* "Essais", IV, 10.

metaphysician of mark who so far follows Pope Leo XIII as to
say, "I feel convinced that, if we would make progress in sound
theory, we cannot do better than to go to school to St. Thomas",
and proceeds to characterise the Thomist philosophy as 'a masterly
synthesis of both Plato and Aristotle, effected by original insight of
the first order'.* It was consequently the more interesting to find
that Montaigne, so typically modern in his unsystematic approach
to the problems of philosophy, should have noted that the foundations of the apologetic which elicited his own observations upon
religion were laid, as he tells us he had reason to believe, in Aquinas's
teaching. The "Apologie de Raimond Sebond", where the method
of the Spanish mystic, Ramon Lull, is alleged to mingle with the
mind of Aquinas,† had impressed him so deeply that, though it had
been placed in his hands by his father only for translation into French,
he had made it the basis of an essay showing us all his mind about
first and last things. The book was a doctor's book, a 'religio
medici', the work, in fact, of a Spanish physician. "I found the
images (les imaginations) of the author fine," Montaigne would say in
explanation of his own commentary, "his work well constructed, his
object full of piety. His aim is bold and courageous, for he under-
takes by natural and human reasons to establish and prove against
atheists all the articles of the Christian religion, in which, to tell the
truth, I find him so forcible and happy that I do not think it would be
possible to put the argument better, and I believe that none has
equalled it."

That sentence alone might be held sufficient to dispose of
the common notion, somewhat disingenuously propagated by the
enemies of the Church, that Montaigne was in fact, and in our common use of the term, a sceptic. It does not, however, protest alone
against this absurd misconception. Montaigne's private chapel, his
visit to Loreto and his reception of the Last Sacraments, all tell in
the same sense. But, as an acute critic has pointed out, it is his essay
on prayer which is conclusive on this point. For if that essay, "with
its casual allusions to his own special fondness for the Pater Noster
and for the Sign of the Cross, is all a cunning piece of stage-craft,
then, instead of the sincerest, he was the insincerest of men".‡

* A. E. Taylor, "Philosophical Studies", No. vi, "St. Thomas Aquinas as a
Philosopher". Cp. W. R. Inge, "God and the Astronomers", p. 13.
    † See the article on Sebonde (sic) in the "Nouvelle Biographie Générale" (Paris,
1864).
    ‡ F. L. Lucas, "Studies, French and English", p. 118.

And that would be to reverse the universal verdict of mankind. "Apologiste de Raymond Sebond, il croyait fermement en Dieu", * observes Motheau, with quiet conviction, in a classical edition of Montaigne's Works. Natural reason, on his own showing, would, in fact, have allowed him to do no less. "Of all the ancient opinions of men regarding religion, that one", he wrote, "seems to me to have had the greatest look of truth and excuse which recognised God as an incomprehensible power, the origin and preserver of all things, all goodness, all perfection, receiving and taking in good part the honour and reverence that mankind rendered him under whatever appearance and in whatever manner it might be. For the gods to whom man of his own invention willed to give form are harmful, mistaken and impious. And that is why of all the cults that St Paul found in favour at Athens the one devoted to an unknown and hidden divinity seemed to him the most excusable." †

Shock as it may be to many who in his name have cast out theologians, the fact is that it had been science rather than theology which roused Montaigne's critical talent to its highest power. The remark that 'the opinion of science is the curse of man',‡ which I one day caught him making, was more, I think, than an obiter dictum. No small part of his study of Sebond's apologetic is a damaging criticism of the world's claims to knowledge combined with some genial mockery of the differences and contradictions that have chequered the history of human thought. "I think", he would observe, "that man would admit to me, if he spoke the truth, that the only acquisition obtained from his long quest was to have learned to recognise his own vileness and weakness." §

I felt that I ought at this point of our intercourse to have urged that physical science had done much to ameliorate the lot of man. But my courage failed me; for I knew that he would have blandly pointed to the great wars of our time and to all the science that had gone into them and to all the inhumanity that had come out of them. And, had I protested still, then he would have overpowered me with quotations from our own journals to show how vilely we treated one another and how weak we were in our Christianity, hold-ing up our hands as we did in horror at the very thought of the wars of religion in his time, and all the while proclaiming that our own savage conflicts were nothing less than crusades against the devil.

* "Essais", IV, p. ii (ed. Motheau). † *Ibid.*, II, p. 210.
‡ *Ibid.*, p. 184. § *Ibid.*, p. 198.

No! The argument was not to be risked with a man of Montaigne's address; and, besides, the science that he had in view was less applied science than that science of ethics which Leslie Stephen and some of his sanguine contemporaries had fondly hoped, at the end of last century, to raise on an agnostic foundation without recourse to theology.

Montaigne, in truth, was never more dangerous than if one began to make much of the wisdom of man. He took a gentle pleasure in deposing the mighty from their seats and exalting the humble in mind. "It happens", I remember him saying on one occasion, "to the truly wise as it happens to the stalks of corn: they go on raising themselves and holding their heads high so long as they are empty; but, when they are full and swollen with grain, they begin to abase themselves and to lower their eyes. Similarly the men who have tried everything and plumbed everything, since in all this mass of knowledge and presentation of so many different things they have found nothing solid and firm, but only vanity, have renounced their presumption and recognised their natural condition. The wisest man that ever was . . . when asked what he knew, replied that he knew nothing." * Philosophy, he would add, affords three possibilities—to find, to seek or to give up seeking. He had no unkindly word for those who, by taking the last course of these three, demonstrated their belief that men's minds are unequal to the search for truth; yet it was towards the second class of thinkers that his own conclusions tended. His attribution to Aristotle of the high-sounding but obviously half-ironical titles of 'prince of the dogmatists' and 'god of scholastic science' was as significant in one way as his observation that the great peripatetic, by virtue of his treatment of certain questions such as immortality, merited the name of a pyrrhonist. Perhaps owing to Pascal's fault, this pyrrhonism of which Montaigne speaks is sometimes misconceived. As he defines it, it is 'a perpetual confession of ignorance, a judgment without bent or bias on every occasion'. It bears, in the usage he makes of it, the stamp of humility. It makes fun of man's pretensions. It recognises his limitations. It betrays a Socratic irony, but, like Socrates, it comes out on the side of the angels. "It is", to use Montaigne's own words, "a clean slate prepared to receive from the finger of God such figures as he is pleased to inscribe there." Reason could hardly ask more eloquently for the light of faith.

The march of human knowledge during the three centuries and

* "Essais", II, pp. 198, 199.

more that have passed since Montaigne wrote his essay had not, as it seemed, done anything to weaken the strength of his position; but rather the reverse. The magnitude of the scientific revolution which our age has seen gave him at the start some good points in debate. Physical Science had never been so sure of itself, perhaps, as at the close of the nineteenth century. It had affirmed the reign of law throughout the world of sense and staked out a claim for it over the world of spirit. It had located ultimate reality in what a popular novelist of the time designated as 'the mighty atom'. It had pointed to the theory of gravitation as a truth established beyond the possibility of dispute by a series of tests extending over a period of time to ensure their validity. No one of these views was now entirely tenable. The conduct of electrons, so far as it is understood, was not consistent with a reign of law; if, as is supposed, they leap capriciously from atom to atom. The atom itself had ceased to appear an indestructible solid, and become an energy of electrons revolving round a nucleus, and with such vast spaces interposed between them that a man's body, if condensed, would, we are told, be scarcely visible to the human eye.* Even Newton's famous law appeared to be no more than a working rule for bodies rotating at low speeds; and gravitation only a phenomenon due to the curvature of space, not a force by means of which bodies act upon one another at a distance.†

A mechanical view of the world thus found its level as no more than a working hypothesis; and a mathematical one, wherein the Universe might be said to take leave of man's senses and place itself at the mercy of his abstractions, rejected any essential difference between time and space as a psychological peculiarity and declared for a four-dimensional space-time continuum. The only reality that this latter analysis appeared to allow human beings to share was, thus, a certain unperceived spatio-temporal relation or 'interval' between events. For the old common measures of time and space it had no use; and it reduced mechanics to a convenient fake and mathematics to a kind of magic emporium with an assortment of

* J. W. N. Sullivan, "Limitations of Science", p. 48.

† J. W. N. Sullivan (*ibid.*, pp. 69, 70), after observing that 'Newton's theory of gravitation . . . was regarded for over two hundred years as the most perfect and perfectly established of human laws' and 'that great mathematicians have been unanimous that Newton's discovery and development of it was the supreme achievement of human genius', continues, "It is not only that the Newtonian theory leads to results which are incorrect in detail; the whole method of thought on which it reposes has been abandoned, root and branch".

geometries in stock to match every new freak of scientific discovery.

In these circumstances the Roman Congregations of the seventeenth century who condemned Galileo might have found something to say for themselves even to-day and may conceivably have less to reproach themselves with in the way of error than the scientists of the nineteenth century. For, since the doctrine of relativity appears to make it as true to say that the sun goes round the earth as that the earth goes round the sun, Galileo's famous discovery is, perhaps, more accurately described as an astronomical assumption than as a physical or metaphysical truth. Poetry, in any case, has never recognised it; and for the poet, who has all of us, here at least, in his grip, the sun rises and sets as of old. But let that be.

With twentieth-century science in such a state of convulsion, an attitude of philosophic doubt in respect of its conclusions appeared to be even better justified than ever; nor could it escape notice that in a universe where physical knowledge appeared so largely to depend upon the pace at which people and things were travelling through space, psychological knowledge might fairly lay claim to the benefit of analogy, and intellectual and spiritual discernment require to be related to the speed at which a human soul is moving towards its goal. There would, then, be nothing curious any more in the fact of a scientist proving incapable of seeing certain things that appeared obvious enough to a saint. A mind, cultivating a frigid detachment and seeking to hold all things, so far as possible, at a standstill for the sake of experiment, could not reasonably be expected to have the same intellectual vision as one fully alive to the considerations advanced in Bergson's "L'Évolution Créatrice" and warmed by love to a great glow of spiritual fervour. True science, as Henri Poincaré had argued, was a luxury reserved to those who could afford to pass beyond the pace of the mechanical science sufficient for ordinary life. How much more, then, was a high velocity of the soul likely to be required for the perception of eternal verities and values.

I would fancy that I saw Montaigne secretly smiling as I produced this modest commentary upon his estimate of scientific knowledge. Not, however, that his sceptical attitude towards human conclusions had rendered him an incurious or unobservant spectator of human things! His account of a child monster with one head and two bodies, which he saw and examined, was as precise, cold and detailed as a doctor's diagnosis, and compelled his interlocutor to look straight at facts as disconcerting as any that the mind of man has to master or the spirit of man to meet.

Much of Montaigne's wisdom, as I came to appreciate, arose from his being content to use a lantern and not clamour for the light of a mid-day sun. This seemed to me a very great grace in him and one very consistent with his modest estimate of human knowledge. He saw things well enough not to stumble or to walk clumsily, but he was often content to see and not understand. As in the case of the child-monster, he had cultivated a habit of looking and passing on where another might magnify an incident or an exception into an event or a rule. Had anyone stopped him to suggest that the particular monstrosity just indicated resulted from imperfect constriction in the isolation of blastomeres during ovular segmentation, he would doubtless have listened with considerable interest and proper respect; yet I suspect that in his heart he would not have felt that these fine words had buttered any parsnips of his. It was, as the phrase goes, the "why" of the phenomenon rather than the "how" of it about which he would have been wondering; and it would have been precisely there that he would have found the information given him to be wanting. A child with two bodies might be a portent or a prodigy, as the Ancients supposed; or a prodigality, a mutation, or a muddle, as the Moderns might variously argue; but anyway one needed to know a great deal more about the general structure of the universe than physical science was in any position to impart before one could arrive at any conclusive opinion. The only person with whom it was really worth while to converse on the subject was clearly God (assuming that there was a God); and the Book of Job had recorded the result of so doing in terms with which scientific men might be expected to sympathise more than they always confessed. "Show me something here that I can understand", a relative of mine once asked an eminent scientist at an exhibition of scientific marvels, only to receive the engagingly candid reply, "There is nothing here, I think, that you could understand". So in effect was Job answered out of the storm. "Where wast thou when I laid the foundations of the earth? Declare, if thou hast understanding. Who determined the measures thereof, if thou knowest? . . . Shall he that cavilleth contend with the Almighty?" I believe that Montaigne's wise man, who confessed that at the close of his researches he knew nothing, would have been better satisfied with that reply than any other, postulating, as it significantly did, the high velocity of a whirlwind, for its delivery. I was not therefore altogether surprised that it had escaped the hearing both of Mr. Bernard Shaw's "Black Girl" and E. V. Lucas's "Typist".

For all that, Montaigne's unpleasant story halted my mind and enhanced my sense of a mystery of deformity perhaps more baffling in some respects even than the mystery of pain. The problem covered a great area, from a slight defect, whether of mental or physical capacity, to a gross monstrosity of shape; for everywhere within that area things, without fault of their own, fell short of that perfection in their kind which nature appeared in general to prescribe for them. The cases of Cinderella and the Ugly Duckling had elucidated the question, when one thought as a child; and perhaps one might do worse than continue to peer through the darkened panes of one's nursery-window in the hope of some day seeing a fairy coach come swinging round the corner into the street below, or the muddy duck-pond over the way grow suddenly alive with swans. Yet there were times when the child within one would insist upon breaking loose and running out to pluck half-ripe fruit from the old tree of knowledge. One was all the readier to do this that now and again a bitter apple would seem to turn sweet in the chewing. Such a diet for thoughts on deformity had once come in the shape of an epitaph communicated casually by a friend; and I grew to like it so well that I could have begged for its inclusion in every intelligent man's guide to religion. It ran, if I rightly remember, thus:—

> Hard by this stone beneath a grassy hump
> A little crooked priest awaits the trump.
> He loved his life but gladly down it laid,
> And praised his Maker, though so strangely made.

The crookedness was in this case so lovingly entwined with faith that to have straightened the priest into a comely shape would evidently have been to ruin his charm and destroy his character. Never had gnarled bough so proved its title to belong to the true vine. But beyond that sacerdotal figure rose a warrior form much more clearly defined. No literary creation of our time had, as it seemed to me, touched the romantic grace of Cyrano de Bergerac. Rostand, with his magic verse, had raised the ridiculous to the sublime and of an ugly feature made the genius of a face. Who could read without emotion the passage in which Cyrano describes his sense of solitude as he sees other men walking with their mistresses or their wives, or regard, without suspecting the existence of a world beyond the grave, the last and loveliest scene between him and Roxane? To-

wards the end, then, of the sombre avenue down which Montaigne
had led my thoughts by his story of the monster-child, I had found
a figure more to my mind—more filled, that is, with grace—than the
Hermes of Praxiteles which I had seen long ago at Olympia or
that statue of Antinous which had caught my vagrant fancy in the
museum of the Vatican. Thus did the essence of perfection ever
seem to detach itself from the stranglehold of matter and fling itself
headlong into some spiritual embrace more subtle and more sublime.

I have digressed, though not I believe unduly, from the path,
itself full of twists and turns, along which Montaigne led me by
the magnet of his mind. But, however that may be, I now return
to the guidance of that companionable soul.

"Shakespeare", a critic of delicate perception * has remarked,
"hints, by his well-known preoccupation with Montaigne's writings, that just there was the philosophic counterpart to the fullness
and impartiality of his own artistic reception of the experience
of life." Montaigne's essays, as the same writer proceeds to point
out, constituted in themselves 'a life' in which the rude matter
of sensible perception had been traversed and illuminated, fused
and organised by beams of seemingly benevolent design suggesting a providence shaping character to ever finer effect. I sought
the more earnestly, therefore, to see whither all this talk of
Montaigne's tended. A casual observation of his to the effect that
Catholics had accentuated the troubles of his time by compromising
with the Reformers upon points of difference of which they did not
always understand the import, gave, in the hackneyed phrase of his
countrymen, furiously to think. And that much thinking grew to
more when he added: "I can say this from experience, having formerly taken the liberty on my own initiative to dispense with certain
practices of our Church which seemed on the surface empty or
strange, only to find, on reference to men of learning, that these very
things had a massive and very solid foundation and that it was
stupidity and ignorance that made us depreciate them." † Montaigne was evidently that rare being, a man not prevented by prejudice from supposing that the clergy might possibly be right, nor
precluded by pride from admitting it, should investigation prove
it so. A layman himself, he was, as a result, able to pursue in
apologetics a style of fence admirably calculated to counter the a
posteriori thrust of the new secular learning. There was enough in
his method, as he remarked, 'to prove that man has no more know-

* Pater, "Gaston de Latour", p. 83.   † "Essais", I, c. xxvii.

ledge of his corporal than of his spiritual side'.* But, masterly as was this riposte, he had no illusion about its nature. "This pass", he would say, "must be used only as a last resource. It is a desperate stroke in which you have to let go your weapons to compel your adversary to lose his; it is a secret trick of which one must make use seldom and with reserve." † To minds as finely tempered as his own and the late Lord Balfour's a dexterous thrust with the rapier of philosophic doubt will always make a peculiar appeal, not merely because it results in running the enemy through with the most graceful weapon in a gentleman's armoury, but because that weapon is also capable of cutting gordian-knots that it might otherwise take an unconscionable time to untie. The world's coarse challenge to the Christian doctrine of the Incarnation or the Resurrection can, for instance, be quite effectively met, and the sceptic forced on to the defensive, by such mild observations as that, since according to science parthenogenesis is a commonplace in nature, and corpseless immortality, accompanied by morphological change, by no means unknown in the humblest organisms,‡ it appears hard that theology should be required to reject as contrary to physical law testimony of the highest consequence to the virgin-birth and rising again of Christ. If such astonishing phenomena as those just mentioned are credible at one end of the scale, and that end the lower, they should enjoy equal consideration at the other. To add that the use of the weak things of the world to confound the things that are mighty discovers itself as a historical principle may seem no better than foolishness to a Greek or a stumbling-block to a Jew; but it is not out of line with a dispassionate scepticism. It is the unexpected that happens, as many historians have had occasion to observe and many politicians to discover.

It is important to observe that Montaigne did not pretend to substitute this brilliant pass of his for the solid, traditional swordplay of the Scholastics. "Sustain your Sebond", he observes, "by the dialectic you have learned . . . keep to the high road; it is not good to be so subtle and so ingenious. He who refines too much pulverises himself. I counsel you in your opinion and conversation, as much as in your manners and in everything, moderation and reserve and the avoidance of what is new and strange." §

* "Essais", II, p. 256.   † *Ibid.*
‡ *E.g.*, the Clavellina, of which marine creature some account may be found in Prof. Julian Huxley's article on "The Meaning of Death" in "Essays on Popular Science".   § "Essais", II, pp. 256, 257.

Scholastic philosophy, the approach to which Montaigne was thus defending single-handed against the advancing tide of the Reformation, was in fact a very powerful structure of a priori thought, built into that doctrine of universals which we owe to Plato, and converted by Thomism into an impregnable fortress defending the mind's integrity and the body's freedom. As conceived by much modern science, a universal is no more than a medley of the characteristics apprehended by the senses in objects of similar appearance. But the Schoolmen were artists in thought, somewhat in the same way as Cézanne is held to be an artist on canvas, in that they perceived, not the common phantasm, eclectic and ill-defined, of things that looked alike yet were never in bodily shape identical, but the finished intellectual image behind the resemblance, the essential idea from which the object drew its nature and its name. Avoiding Peter Bell's memorable approach to things, they saw a primrose as it was in deed and in truth; and the eye of their mind pierced to the significance of pure form, to the mystery hidden behind matter, which Kant could only grope after sentimentally and blindly recommend. A world invisible thus sprang into clear view and spread before the Schoolmen like a wide champaign. In that Eden of the mind the intellect might presume that it was perceiving things and persons, to some degree at any rate, after the pattern which first gave them being. Design on such an assumption could no longer remain in doubt, for the mind of the observer would in a modest way have made mental contact with that of the designer. It was as if teleology had come to the aid of cosmology to make deity plain; as if the alpha of the evidence for God's existence had been completed by the omega; as if the mind's dependence on the thought of a first cause resulting from the fact of development had been increased by dependence on the thought of an ultimate plan resulting from the study of creative evolution. Causation might be questioned by a scientist reproducing Hume's argument in the light of the quantum theory, or harmony be ridiculed by a sceptic arguing that the beating of a tom-tom might seem lovelier to one ear than an oratorio of Handel to another. Yet causation appeared an inescapable assumption if we busied ourselves with matter, and beauty if we interested ourselves in mind. Creation without a creator and design without a designer thus fell alike into the same class with the famous representation of Hamlet without the Prince of Denmark.

In accordance, then, with Montaigne's advice to keep in touch with Sebond, I would begin to re-shape for my own use and in my own fashion those old cosmic and purposive proofs of a deity which it seemed to need only the so-called ontological argument to wind into a triple cord not easily to be broken. The last named of these lay still, perhaps, beyond real apprehension, prize as it was of the whole nature of man at one with itself and in passionate pursuit of Perfect Being. On Montaigne's intellectual plane the cosmological argument might well appear the most cogent. It was easy to see that the principle of causation led one to a first cause and not too difficult to perceive that, on the principle of sufficient reason, a first cause must be likewise, so to say, an effect and contain within itself its own rational sufficiency. It was the teleological argument—the argument from design—which seemed to be most adversely affected on this particular plane of thought. No one who studied it closely could continue long unaware of the apparent waste and hardly disputable pain involved in the scheme. In the astounding productivity, requiring an almost equally astounding mortality to balance it, of animal life, as in the unconscionable conduct of certain creatures like the cat, when it sports with a mouse, or the ichneumon, when it devours a living caterpillar piecemeal, the critic of a planned universe could find abundant opportunity for his talents. But these things, which impressed some people so much, constituted, so far as I could see, rather a criticism of the method than a disproof of the design. I felt no competence to criticise the designer, and all the less that I had occasion at least twice in my life to see immeasurable misery inflicted and prolonged by some of the best men I had known, with ends fully within my understanding, and constituting, according to them, a complete vindication of the means employed to realise them. To Newman, with the righteousness of God in his thoughts, it had seemed that the extremest agony of earth was less appalling than a venial sin; and to man, with the wickedness of man in his mind, it seemed that, within the limited scope of human effort, breaches of faith should be avenged at no less cost. If men could do one another such mortal mischief for offences utterly incommensurate with their consequences, was man in any strong position to arraign the author of nature on account of proceedings very imperfectly understood? To be judicial one had to have all the facts before one, but in regard to nature one knew very few facts indeed compared to those that evidently existed. Something had pretty clearly gone wrong with the scheme of things; but it was quite conceivable that no use of force could put the matter right again, and that it had to wait upon the slow processes of love. Force was no remedy for some things. It had proved a wretched remedy for the troubles of Montaigne's time and no remedy at all for those of our own, though it had been recommended by the politicians who were indeed for the most part ignorant of any other.

Meanwhile it was undeniable that 'Nature' had satirised evil to brilliant effect in her zoological exhibits. We should hardly be able to discern what manner of world it is that we live in, or to imagine what moral and mental dangers it contains, without the generous aid provided by fox and pig and snake, by wasp and ass and all the rest of those admirable actors engaged in the performance of Nature's morality-plays. But the very excellence of the acting rendered it all the more astonishing that man should still remain content, like Ajax in "Troilus and Cressida", to rob many beasts of their particular additions, and not only to rob them himself, but to set them tormenting each other for his own particular amusement. The sport of the cat with its victim seemed a trifle beside productions like that of the bullring, or the cockpit, or other scenes of pleasure tempered by pain with man as the impresario. I could not think of these without feeling that the darts aimed at the deity by mankind on account of the suffering in nature had much the look of boomerangs.

It was at this point that Montaigne, who had been somewhile silent, whether because, like Pitt after reading Butler's "Analogy", he thought the argument had raised more difficulties than it had solved, or because he thought all argument on the subject unprofitable, would break in upon my reflections in a manner more suggestive of conclusion than conversation. " 'Oh! what a vile and abject thing is man!' he would cry out, quoting a pagan author, 'unless he raise himself above humanity.' The Stoics never said a truer thing than that. But to make the grip greater than the fist, the embrace than the arm, and to hope to bestride more than the legs can stretch across, that is impossible and monstrous. Man cannot climb above himself and humanity; since he can see only with his eyes and apprehend only with his grasp. He will raise himself, if God gives him His hand; he will raise himself by abandoning and renouncing his own means and allowing himself to be uplifted by divine grace, but not otherwise." *

I was listening, as it seemed to me, to the voice of the purest reason—to reason, that is, erect upon its throne, but clothed in humility and with faith and hope for supporters. One might sup-

* "Essais", II, pp. 316, 317.

pose that some such word of God as Simmias in the "Phaedo",* two thousand years before, had desired to hear, had come to the speaker's aid. Montaigne, indeed, had heard it only with the hearing of the ear. It would have been straining language to say of him, as of Job at the close of his troubles, that what his ear had once learnt from others, his eye had now seen for itself. But I liked his evidence none the worse for that, and all the better because he had passed through the tribulation of a period when old beliefs and traditions had been cast violently into the melting-pot, when controversy had risen to fever pitch, and when charity had grown pretty nearly stone-cold. If in such conditions his faith had endured to the end, it owed something almost beyond question to the fact that he had valued his intellectual integrity and maintained it in the manner of the great gentleman that he was.

Few things, indeed, struck me more in all his talk, though many struck me much, than an observation that Montaigne made about the religion of the English; and I have sometimes wondered, in consequence, whether the English mind has ever entirely recovered from the intellectual degradation into which, as it seemed to him, it fell at the Reformation. "Since I was born", he would say, "I have seen the laws of the English three and four times changed, not only in the matter of politics, where inconstancy must be allowed for, but in the most important matter that there can be—I mean religion. I am vexed by and ashamed of it, and all the more that here is a nation with which the people of my part of France had once so special an intercourse as to have left traces of the connection in my house. What then does philosophy enjoin in such a predicament as this? That we follow the laws of our country, in other words the unstable sea of a people's or a prince's opinions? . . . I cannot entertain so flexible a power of judgment. What sort of goodness or right is this which I saw thus held in esteem and then in a day so greatly changed as to have become vice?" †

It was, as it seemed to me, impossible to answer him. The English under the Tudors had for the most part shown a religious pliability betraying an intellectual indifference of which, as Macaulay pointed out, the combination of a Catholic liturgy with Calvinist articles of faith in the book of Common Prayer remains the lasting memorial. I blushed a little to remember that Burghley had been twice a Catholic and twice a Protestant. It seemed just twice too

* 85, D.   † Bk. II, p. 285.

much to be convincing; and I could not feel Montaigne unfair if he regarded such opportunism as intellectually intolerable. Though, as a disciple of Michel de l'Hôpital, he had sought a middle way of safety for the ship of state, he was not the man to mistake it for the thread of the golden mean in the labyrinth of religious philosophy. A Humanist of the school of Erasmus; a reformer with a small 'r' and not a large one; an intermediary between Henri III and Henri IV, whose friend he was; a citizen, by every title that the mind can give or a sovereign authority confer, of the Rome that from her seven hills had for some seventeen centuries given light both to the pagan and the Christian world, he would have seemed to himself to renounce the plain pattern of history, had he taken the road to Wittenberg, the power of which to disintegrate human thought he understood so well as highly to approve Sebond's diagnosis of Lutheranism as a wasting decline that would easily terminate in an execrable atheism.* But, whilst the religious settlement in England contained so much in its antecedents and in its character to cause him intellectual distress, the settlement in France, though he did not live to see the promulgation of the Edict of Nantes, might well have been of his making. There was in the latter neither infidelity to the historic faith of Rome nor persecution of those who in good faith rejected the historic evolution of the Church.

I could not find it in me, however, to admit that the reproach which Montaigne brought against the English of the sixteenth century was ever true of their finest minds. I could not believe that what was so clear to Thomas More at the beginning of the English Reformation was wholly hidden from William Shakespeare at the close of it, or that the poet, who had looked so close into the Saint's mind as to draw upon More's study of a death-bed for his description of Falstaff's death,† had not also perceived the full significance of the Saint's defence and martyrdom. For it had grown to be a cardinal conviction with me that the finest intellects had only to look long enough and steadily enough at the last things, and even perhaps at things less than the last, to rid themselves of baffling contradictions. To the marriage of true minds I would no longer admit impediment, nor rest fully satisfied with the comfortable doctrine of the eminent dyspeptic that a disagreement with a friend could be in opinion

* "Essais", II, c. 12.

† I owe this suggestion to a speech of Prof. Read's I had the good fortune to hear.

only. And thus it became difficult to believe that the deepest intellect there ever was in England had been at variance with the
wisest and most poetic mind there was then in France. Not all the
water that has passed between the Straits of Dover, nor even that
silver band of sea that so encircles our souls, as well as our
island-shores, as to prevent the most part of us from conceiving
any kingdom of God, or even commonwealth of nations without a
British landscape at its back, seemed enough to have separated
Shakespeare from Montaigne. They appeared to share a humanity
beyond the Humanities; and I could not but fancy that in
Shakespeare, despite the major poet's paucity of Latin and poverty
of Greek, Montaigne, great classic though he was, might have found
all and more than all that he had lost in Étienne de la Boétie.
Was it tolerable to suppose that such souls had been really sundered
by a contemporary controversy in which a Tudor had driven his
English subjects one way and the French had driven their Bourbon
king another? There must, anyway, be some presumption to the
contrary; and there is, in fact, some evidence to sustain the presumption. As it is alleged that Shakespeare lay under literary obligations
to Montaigne, so, too, it is alleged that he died a Catholic and
surmised that his father was a recusant. It was not, however, in
their attitude towards revealed, so much as to natural religion that
I looked to find the point of closest contact between two men who
were alike stronger in mind than spirit; and there, as it seemed to me,
I found it. Like-minded in their criticism of life, in their approach
to death they were not divided. No less clearly than Prospero had
Montaigne affirmed that his ending were despair, unless it were
relieved by prayer.

Prayer, that is, in which presumably adoration or orison had a
greater part than petition! "A prayer of God", then, such as God
Himself had taught! A prayer requiring, maybe, some such Christianity as St. John's Gospel suggests for a condition of success—some
previous abiding, that is, of man in God and of God in man, for
lack of which many petitions had served as arguments against themselves and many critics found occasion to mock. A prayer certainly
far removed from any process suggestive of putting a penny in the
slot, or reminiscent of the Quaker's petition of which I used to hear
tell, that he might be granted an income of £3,000 a year, to be
paid, as he carefully observed in order to avoid mistakes, in
quarterly instalments! Who had transfixed the gross fallacy latent

here with a keener lance than Shakespeare? Not even Claudius had remained blind to the futility of what he was doing. "My words fly up, my thoughts remain below. Words without thoughts never to Heaven go."

My mind had been, so to say, located in the Chinese room during the passage of these reflections. For that room was the place in all the world where I had found intellectual beauty, by which I mean nothing, as the reader will understand, of the sort that the world styles 'high-brow', but rather a grace, imparting transparency to thoughts and things, so that one began to perceive the hidden essence of reality in a certain correspondence between them, somewhat as the relativist supposes himself to have found it in that intimate four-dimensional union between time and space which he denominates 'the interval'. But, just as all the wisdom of Montaigne and Shakespeare seemed to resolve itself at last in prayer, so the room could lose its diaphanous quality and its glory depart from it. It was then that it would take on the appearance, as I thought, of Swinburne's Forsaken Garden; and I could have fancied that even the flowers on the walls were drooping like Shelley's sensitive plant when its mistress had left it. No longer did I believe that the birds flew from perch to perch for the very joy of living, or sang their vesper hymns to colour as the lamps lit up their plumage. The shadows that fell across the room at nightfall seemed to be cast, like the shadows in the cave in Plato's myth, by the passage of far-off things interrupting the glow of celestial firelight. Gradually, as my mind came to occupy itself with this phenomenon of prayer, I realised what had happened. I had crossed, so to say, the indefinite frontier between soul and spirit; and therewith the room had begun to lose its magic. I had, in other words, become intensely aware that Allegra's spirit had left it and that I was looking for the living amongst dying memories that at my own decease would drop completely dead. I must look for her now elsewhere. I must search the house even to the housetop.

There was, I need not say, a latent sadness in the knowledge that I must seek another framework for my thoughts, so great a mind had I had to let them rest for ever upon that room. But I remembered something that a friend had once said to me about the operation of inevitability in life; and that, platitudinous as it may seem in the light of general experience, is yet a shock and a discovery when it first comes home to oneself. So little goes according to plan, and it is so often the unexpected that happens, that at last one learns to surrender with tolerable grace to the mystery of the unanticipated. "Time and circumstance and opportunity", as a British Prime Minister once expressed it, "paint with heedless hands and garish colours on the canvas of a man's life; so that the result is less frequently a finished picture than a palette of squeezed tints." *

Yes! life was like that, coercive and inexorable to the point of making some men profess themselves fatalists. One had to go on, and oftentimes, like Abraham, to go out, not knowing whither one went. The strongest minds had, perhaps, been the most sensible of it. None of the Greeks had recognised its place in self-knowledge more handsomely than the wisest of them all. In his condemnation of suicide as an act unsuited to beings who were, after all, the chattels of the gods, Socrates had seemed to extend his own faith in the particular providence of his daemon to a general confidence in the moral value of destiny. And great men in great crises still acted accordingly. "We did intend to finish ourselves when things proved like this," Captain Scott had written to Sir James Barrie with reference to moods and matters in the Antarctic, "but we have decided to die naturally without." † There was, in fact, a higher subsequent authority than Socrates, not to speak of experience, for supposing destiny to be, not a blind, but a binding force. Some words spoken beside a lake in Galilee nearly two millenniums ago to one upon whose crucified body was to be reared the strangest and strongest of all sovereign states, had endorsed this mystery of faith in a manner not to be disregarded by any observer of mortal things. "When thou wast young thou girdest thyself and walkest whither thou wouldest; but, when thou shalt be old, thou shalt stretch forth thy hands and another shall gird thee and carry thee whither thou wouldest not."

Most of us had no call, or perhaps no character, sufficient to accept this companionable sense of destiny which seemed to serve the best men for a guiding star and to lead the worst men on like a will-o'-the-wisp into some pit of destruction. Rather did we for the most part tie ourselves to fortune's wheel and let ourselves be broken by its blows, until at length, as the circle was completed, we came round from youth to age and from one childhood to another. Few things in all the passage of the soul from birth to death struck one as more ironical than the way in which one's faculties

* Rosebery, "Pitt", p. 10.
† J. M. Barrie, Rectorial Address on "Courage" at St. Andrews, May 3rd, 1922.

thus returned at length to the point from which they started. Whilst the body pined and wasted, the mind grew simple again, as if all its long journey in pursuit of knowledge had gone for nothing at all. Was this resumption of the childlike mind just a brutal mockery on the part of whatever gods there be? Or was it an inexorable but not unjust reminder on the part of nature of the condition upon which alone true wisdom could be obtained? Christianity, always challenging, was particularly so on the subject of little children. Our minds, it might quite well be, were thus gently and firmly, whether we would or no, being clothed with humility. And, if Nature laughed a little as she slipped on our nightgowns, looking as they did so much like winding-sheets, could we reasonably blame her? After all the experience of life we were still such children— children who, as in Newton's classic comparison, seemed to have spent their day gathering pebbles on the shores of time; children who, as that inconvenient chatterbox, Lewis Carroll, had confessed, were reluctant to go to bed and not a little frightened of the dark :—

> We are but little children, dear,
> Who fret to feel our bedtime near.

All this time I must be imagined as trying to take leave of the Chinese room, the spirit in me straining forward, whilst the mind in me strove hard to linger. But the very stair had now taken the look of a celestial staircase, and in my heart of hearts I knew that sooner or later I had to make an effort to climb it. With its graceful curve and its high dome of light above, it had been one of the features of the house that Allegra most delighted in; and I don't think that for a modest London house the design could well have been bettered. But, despite its charms, I cannot deny that the steps were a little steep, or forget that an old friend had once with unacceptable candour complained to me about their gradient. His legs, it is true, were not of the best, but neither had I any great confidence in my limbs when it came to the Jacob's ladder of the spirit. If only mankind had had wings—the wings of a dove!

Chapter IX

ON THE STAIRCASE

I HAD climbed in thought to the head of the staircase, and stood now upon the landing, which turned one way towards Allegra's bedroom and the other towards a little flight of steps leading to the attics and the roof. I confess to having felt sometimes a little dizzy as I looked back over the bannisters and paused to collect my ideas before peering up through the domed skylight at the stars. The hall with its marble flooring lay far below me; and the once apparently solid foundations of an atomic world seemed that far distant from the present perch of my mind in respect of things both human and divine. On the first floor some large mahogany doors, which were older than the house and recalled its considerable debt to the eighteenth century, had closed upon the Chinese room and upon the witness that it bore to quality and design rather than power as the end of human effort. With its disappearance from view the memories of a day that was gone, when Allegra would take her seat there by the hearth, seemed to fall back into haze; and more and more, the chill of the naked stonework on the stair entered like iron into my soul. It was then that there would mingle with my thoughts a recollection of that old analogy, Saxon in origin, between the life of man and the swift flight of a bird through a firelit hall—through a hall, as the fable required one to suppose, beyond which at either end there spread the darkness of winter with whirling eddies of snowdrift and storm. It seemed no great wonder that that simple comparison, introduced into a critical debate, doubtless with rude eloquence, by some Saxon councillor whose very name is forgotten, should have turned the scales in favour of Christianity in the eyes of the wise men of Northumbria. Assuredly the pain of man's ignorance and his passion for sky light had never been more vividly depicted or more feelingly expressed.

It seemed to me that I had been present at just such another scene; that animation, in the fairest form it was given me to imagine —'half angel and half bird'—had flitted past me through the lighted room; and that now I stood looking into the darkness into which it had passed out. I could have staked my whole intelligence, for whatever that might be worth, that the spirit I had seen was but a bird migrating and had never perished in that wintry pall of snow without. I could have sworn that nature, whatever that term might signify, was no such fool as to create lovely things and let them perish everlastingly. If there were conservation of matter, energy or whatever substance the world might be made of, how much more probable that there was conservation of spirit! Probability, as the sagacious Butler had assured us, was the guide of life. But probability seemed an inadequate leader in face of the blinding darkness stretching across the path which Allegra had taken. Louder and louder grew the cri du coeur—"Oh, that I had wings like a dove!"—which the forsaken garden on the walls of the Chinese room had had power to evoke. Would that I could follow and see what lay beyond the snowstorm!

There were those, I knew, who professed to have eyes that could see and ears that could hear amid that obscurity and silence. And I had known some of them well enough not to be disposed to dismiss their witness to a spirit-world cavalierly. There was far too great an accumulation of evidence, indifferent, fanciful or faked as some of it might be, to permit one to dispose of unfamiliar appearances and auditions, as an old uncle of mine used to do, by a reference to the malignant operation of pork-chops or some similar agent of gastric disturbance. The possibility, however, remained that such phenomena were the work, not of beings like ourselves, but of beings with superior faculties who were just amusing themselves at our expense by impersonating or imitating the dead. No one could prove to demonstration that he was not being deluded in this way, any more than anyone could prove beyond discussion that the outer world of matter is more than a dream of mind. There might be the laughter of gods or devils everywhere in the background; but I failed myself to detect on the face of these glancing waters more than the numberless ripples of a smile, the more enigmatic of course that the tears of things seemed also to be flowing freely.

I could recall once talking to Bateson, the biologist, about psychic phenomena, and, as I remember the conversation, he tapped his forehead gently when we spoke of Mrs. Henry Sidgwick.* I marked his action the more that, though he did not, I feel sure, think of it, she was a near relative of my own and his judgment of her judicial capacity curiously at issue with that of those who had better oppor-

* Née Eleanor Balfour and sometime Principal of Newnham College, Cambridge.

tunities of knowing her well. But his gesture lived in my mind as a symbol of what are perhaps best characterised as the inhibitions of scientific men. Some compartments of the intellectual soul appeared in certain scientists to atrophy from want of employment, as for example did Darwin's, on his own confession, in respect to music; and they grew to despise those who retain open minds and unimpaired faculties. Crookes and Lodge and Barrett were exceptions; and there have been others of equal or greater consequence. Yet the generalisation seemed to be justified. Mrs. Sidgwick was, in fact, one of the most conscientious and dispassionate of investigators; and her character and qualities alone should have acted as a solvent of prejudice against any psychic phenomena which she was prepared to authenticate.

Among the reports of the Psychical Society there are two at any rate of outstanding interest from the hand of Mrs. Sidgwick's brother, the second Lord Balfour, whose qualifications for forming an opinion are as difficult to dispute as her own. One, which goes by the name of "The Ear of Dionysius",* is very well known; and I suspect that few careful readers of it would disagree with the observation of an eminent scientist, possessed of all that incredulity could demand or experience acquire in the way of scepticism, who told me that he did not see his way round its argument. There was reason enough to say so. The reporter was one of the most distinguished Cambridge men of his generation—and a very sceptical generation at that!—the medium was above suspicion; the communicators, according to their own account, were the brilliant spirits of Dr. A. W. Verrall and Professor S. H. Butcher; the communications took the form of a series of allusions to knowledge so erudite or so personal as to preclude the supposition of collusion, conscious or unconscious, on the part of incarnate minds. The austere and intricate narrative thus produced was broken at one point by a ghost story, more or less in the traditional style, but free from the common suspicion of having been improved by time. Mrs. Willett, who wrote down her experience on the day after it occurred, claimed to have seen Professor Butcher on January 21st, 1911, a few weeks after his death; and she expressed what she had felt in the following terms:—

"Last night, after I had blown out my candle and was just going to sleep, I became aware of the presence of a man, a stranger, and—almost at the same moment—knew it was Henry Butcher. I felt his

* *Proc. of the Psychical Soc.*, Vol. XXIX, March 1917. And see Vol. XXVII.

personality very living, clear, strong, sweetness and strength combined. A piercing glance. He made no introduction. So I said to
him, 'Are you Henry Butcher?' He said, 'No, I am Henry Butcher's
ghost'."* A communication, apparently intended to act as a link in
an intricate chain of evidence for personal survival, followed.

Another set of scripts made, however, a deeper appeal to me, for
they combined a certain humour with poetry and pathos. They
pivoted upon the idea of a traveller too irresolute to risk the crossing
of a river in flood, even though the inn which he wished to reach
stood upon the farther bank. The language, no less than the subject
of these communications caused them to be attributed to the spirit
of Dr. Verrall. So striking, in fact, was the similarity of expression
that in the opinion of an old and intimate friend—the Rev. A. M.
Bayfield—the traits of personality and tricks of manner disclosed
eliminated the possibility of their having originated in the mind of
a medium but slightly acquainted with him. "All this", Bayfield
observes of one passage of the communications, "is Verrall to the
life." By so much, then, did the reference to the timid traveller
become more interesting. The recondite allusions, advanced by degrees as if to suggest a considered design, led deviously to some lines
of Dante upon Statius, once analysed by Verrall in an essay, yet at
the same time so significantly that the application of them to his
own case became irresistible. "Could the River", as Lord Balfour
puts it, "which the Pilgrim was afraid to cross, and which for Statius
was the River of Baptism, have been for Dr. Verrall the River of
Faith in a life hereafter and in the reality of communication from
'the further shore' ?" It well might. The passage in the "Purgatorio"†
alluded to in the script recalled Statius's admiration for the persecuted Christians and declared that their righteous lives had made him
despise all other sects 'mentre che di là per me si stette'. But, whereas
this phrase was generally rendered 'while by me yon world was
trod', Verrall in his essay had given strong reasons for rendering it
'while I lingered on the other side' and so making it mean, as is
argued in the report, 'while I abstained from joining the Church'.

So much, then, in passing, for what psychic phenomena had to say
of the spirit world! The reports seemed to me to possess all that one
could reasonably ask for in the way of credibility with reference to
matters peculiarly hard to test, whilst demonstrating at the same time

* *Proc. of the Psychical Soc.*, Vol. XXIX, p. 211.
† "Purg.", XXII, 85–8.

the evidential difficulties attending anything out of the ordinary course of experience. There was another aspect of these occurrences to which the late Dr. Schiller had drawn attention and which seemed of wider significance. The testimony to them, he pointed out, was in the nature of a wasting asset. "The reason", as he said, "is quite simple. The strength of our evidence depended on our securing first-hand records from trustworthy witnesses and getting them competently examined and criticised by honourable investigators. So long as our witnesses and investigators are alive, therefore, they can confront the hostile sceptic in person, and will have the support of those who know them and believe in them. But as the original witnesses and investigators pass away, their evidence inevitably undergoes a serious and progressive loss in value. Coming generations have nothing to go by but a paper record. . . ."* That was a consideration not always weighed in the appraisement of 'gospel truth', but it is nevertheless weighty.

It had begun, as it seemed to me, to feel cold on the stairs; or was it that the intimations of immortality conveyed by psychic research had turned the mind chilly? If that which they implied were all, what then? What if one just went on and on, a ghost in a dim world such as Homer or Virgil had conceived—aimlessly, interminably? I looked at the staircase again; it had precisely the charms of Limbo, as Dante depicted them. It was open and luminous and high—'luogo aperto, luminoso ed alto'. Here one might stay and sit talking on the stairs, as people used to do at London balls in the spacious houses of the vanished Victorian era—talking sense, it might be, or drivel, for there would be people of many sorts and kinds hanging about in this supposititious ante-chamber to Hell, and one could find what company one liked, from Homer singing or Aristotle perambulating, to a girl from a corps de ballet, with whom one might be whirling away in some dance after death without hope or fear that the delectable moments would ever pass. There lay the fantastic aspect of the whole business as seen by the aid of psychic phenomena. It didn't end, for the river of time found its way no longer safe to sea, but flowed on wearily, endlessly, eternally. One had what one had striven for, and one had it always; and the having it was hell just on that very account. The incandescent walls in Poe's tale did not close in more inexorably on the dreamer than this truth closed in on me. It was indeed a burning thought, and scorched the soul like fire.

* *Proc. of the Soc. for Psychical Research,* Pt. lxix, Vol. XXVII, p. 195.

Every palace of art inhabited by merely human minds alone must, it appeared, at long last become a prison.

A favourite, though doubtless transient doctrine of the time seemed to enforce the point. Serialism rests upon the incontestable fact of self-consciousness. The self is always detaching itself from the world, and perceiving the world, inclusive of the spectator's own brain and body, as a thing apart from itself. It can even dissociate itself to so great a degree as to know not merely that the body is diseased, but that the mind is going mad. Man perceives the world, therefore, like an artist, imparting line and colour to its content, and, to make the scene inclusive, introduces himself, with brush and easel, into the foreground. But, as often as he steps back to contemplate his work, so often does his self-consciousness come afresh into play, detaching him again from the scene and making him once more a mere observer. It is a process without end—an infinite regress —and may be enough to prove to such as have a taste for the dry wine of mathematics that man is not entirely finite and will not altogether die. Yet, like all operations suggestive of an animal engaged in pursuing its tail, mathematical involutions appeared as well calculated to drive one mad as to give a man his bearings. I felt more stimulus to paint, however badly, some Madonna of the future against the background of the universe than to attempt any piece of self-portraiture. One might—who could say?—find eternity in a Madonna's eyes; but I should never read it, I felt sure, in my own.

I was all this while deviously approaching, as I knew, an ontological argument for the existence of God which, if Dr. Matthews is right,* is in reality raised upon St. Anselm's more famous but less satisfying foundation; and I suppose its peculiar power came home to me as I sat in spirit upon the stairs. As the Finite could have no meaning without the Infinite, so could Imperfection have no meaning without Perfection. The mind's certitude of the one compelled it to an equal certitude, though not to an equal perception of the existence of the other. It would have been odd indeed to credit one's own poor instrument of an intellect with finished powers of apprehension. Yet, since personality, with its implication of a self-conscious spirit detaching itself from its surroundings, was the condition of evaluating with success, however indifferent, the beauty, truth and goodness in the world about us, the

* W. R. Matthews, "The Idea of God" in Rose's "Outline of Modern Knowledge", pp. 56–57.

very idea of perfection as an inescapable fact in thought seemed to guarantee the existence of a perfect personality to perceive it; and there, then, was demonstrably God.

It was interesting to see how forcibly the argument of Anselm had struck the mind of Descartes, as rigorous and egotistical in his logic as was ever Mrs. Battle at her game of whist, and, if not always right, still capable of disposing his mass of manoeuvre with Gallic skill in conflict. One might, he had urged, endow things of an inferior order to humanity, such as earth and sky, with higher qualities than they possessed, but, when it came to the idea of a being of an altogether higher order than one's own, one could not excogitate him out of oneself, and still less out of nothing. The cogency of clear thinking required one rather to attribute to some divine source the presence in the soul of those sublime and beautiful thoughts which went to make up our image of perfection. It was, as he pointed out, in line with such reasoning to suppose that doubt, inconstancy and sadness were not of God, inasmuch as one would be glad to be without them. And, even though one were to become sceptical of the whole world of sense, the mere existence in the mind of this thought of perfection had ever to be reckoned with, and would force one back inexorably to seek its origin in some intelligence equal to the conception itself and, therefore, unconditioned.

Medieval contact between the Gallic and Caledonian minds has doubtless had its influence upon the formation of the hard-thinking Scot; and Scottish comments on French thought are the more worth hearing. No one, perhaps, has contributed a more pertinent criticism of Descartes's ontology than the late Principal Caird in his book on Spinoza.* To him it was clear that Descartes perceived himself that the ontological argument could not be ultimately rested on the pin's point of a finite personality and was all the while reaching out after some larger foothold. "Whether", as Caird expressed it, "the proposition, 'I in thinking am', or more briefly 'I think', is to be fruitful or barren, depends on the part of it on which the emphasis is thrown. . . . In the empirical fact of his own self-consciousness there is nothing which enables the individual to transcend his own individuality. Thought that is purely mine can build for itself no bridge by which it can pass to a world that lies, by supposition, wholly beyond it."† Thus the idea of the Infinite latent in the individual consciousness appeared to sweep each spirit out from all contingent

* John Caird, "Spinoza", pp. 94–111.   † *Ibid.*, p. 97.

and finite existence into some soul of things beyond; and one could detect the pull and power of this strange force as readily in Napoleon's egotistical confession that his nerves were in sympathy with the feeling of God's existence* as in Spinoza's altruistic bent towards pantheism. Like a firefly flashing through the darkness of our night, this winged word, this burning thought would seem to race to and fro within the confines of our little world in search of some mystical body, some larger flame wherein to plunge and lose itself. The onto-logical argument pursued, desiderated, even demanded the cosmo-logical argument to meet and match it. And ever, as it ran and returned, the searchlight of Pascal's genius would seem for a moment to catch it and hold it captive. "Nature", he would interject, "has perfections to show that she is the image of God, and imperfections to show that she is His image only."†

The so-called Symbolists, with their confessed purpose of bring-ing the life of art—and no less, perhaps, the art of life—to the con-dition of music, had seen to a rare degree both the peril and adventure of this quest of perfection and the penalty of failing through some chill rarefication of the atmosphere into which they aspired to climb. Pater's imaginary portrait of Sebastian van Storck had in our time been surpassed as an illustration of the nemesis awaiting Spinoza's disciples by Paul Valéry's portrait, not perhaps so imaginary, of "Monsieur Teste". "Son âme", Mme. Teste had written of her husband, "sans doute se fait une plante singulière dont la racine, et non le feuillage, pousserait, contre nature, vers la clarté! N'est-ce point là se tendre hors du monde?—Trouvera-t-il la vie ou la mort, a l'extremité de ses volontés attentives?—Sera-ce Dieu ou quelque épouvantable sensation de ne rencontrer, au plus profond de la pensée, que la pâle rayonnement de sa propre et misérable matière? Il faut l'avoir vu dans ces excès d'absence. Alors sa physionomie s'altère—s'efface! . . . Un peu plus de cette absorption, et je suis sûre qu'il se rendrait invisible. . . . M. l'abbé, qui a une grande et charitable curiosité de mon mari et une sorte de pitoyable sympathie pour un esprit si séparé, me dit que M. Teste lui inspire des senti-ments bien difficiles à accorder entre eux. Il me disait l'autre jour: Les visages de Monsieur vôtre mari sont innombrables! Il le trouve

---

* Quoted by Nielsen in his "History of the Papacy in the Nineteenth Century", Vol. I, p. 233. I do not know what is his original authority.

† "Pensées", 580. The reference here, and in general, is to Brunschvicg's edition.

'un monstre d'isolement et de connaissance singulière', et il l'explique, quoique à regret, par un orgueil de ces orgueils qui vous retranchent des vivants, et non seulement des actuels vivants, mais des vivants éternels;—un orgueil qui serait tout abominable et quasi satanique, si cet orgueil n'etait, dans cet âme trop exercée, tellement âprement tourné contre soi-même . . . Alors j'ai dit à M. l'abbé que mon mari me faisait penser bien souvent a un mystique sans Dieu."*

The nemesis of mysticism, when treated as a means to intellectual satisfaction instead of as a partnership in every virtue and in all perfection of the society of saints, or—which is the same thing—as an adoration of God, can seldom, if ever, have been more subtly analysed. By just so much did the pursuit of the Absolute and the Unconditioned as an abstraction fall short of the pursuit of God as a perfect Being. Nothing less perhaps than the pure eyes of a Madonna and the extension throughout the world of some corpus mysticum— some Word made flesh and consummating the order of charity—was sufficient for these things; and, without them, the ontological argument could even assume a terrifying aspect. Gale and earthquake and fire were the symbols of what the soul must suffer before it could hope to know itself or hear any still, small voice revealing the hidden path of human destiny.

It was a woman's words—if indeed she had been a woman and not rather an intellectual hermaphrodite—that would recall me from these cogitations. Emily Brontë, in an adult life of the briefest, had not missed much of the tragic, the terrible, or the sublime in the human situation; and her vivid confession of faith, with its independence of the cosmic and its suggestion of the ontological approach to theology, used to fall on my ears like an envoi to St. Anselm's argument. Familiar though the lines are, they do not weary or grow old.

> Oh God within my breast,
> Almighty ever-present Deity,
> 　Life that in me has rest,
> As I—undying Life—have power in Thee.
>
> With wide-embracing love
> Thy spirit animates eternal years,
> 　Pervades and broods above,
> Changes, sustains, dissolves, creates and rears.

---

* Valéry, "M. Teste", pp. 89–99.

Though earth and man were gone,
And suns and universes ceased to be,
And Thou were left alone,
Every existence would exist in Thee.

There is not room for Death,
Nor atom that His might could render void,
Thou—Thou art Being and Breath
And what Thou art may never be destroyed.

I was looking up now at the stars through the domed skylight. To all intellectual purpose I had reached the top of the house: and I felt something akin to fear. "What is there beyond that starry vault?" Pasteur had asked in his address on reception into the French Academy. "More starry skies? And beyond them? . . . It serves no purpose to answer. Beyond are spaces, times and magnitude without limit. . . . He who proclaims the existence of the Infinite, and no one can escape from that, heaps up in that affirmation more of the supernatural than there is in all the miracles of the religious: the notion of the Infinite has the double character of imposing itself and of being incomprehensible. The notion of the Infinite—in the world I see everywhere the unavoidable expression of it. By virtue of it the supernatural is at the base of all hearts. The idea of God is a form of the idea of the Infinite."*

It was but a short step from Pasteur to Pascal.

"Le silence eternel de ces espaces infinis m'effraie." I had come to the top of the house, within sight of Pascal's starlit dwelling, and his famous sentiment inevitably sprang to mind. Yet, frightening as was the unheard music of the spheres, the desire was strong in me to hear what he had to say.

It was as I reached this point in my argument—and so exactly so as to prevent me ever after from reducing the circumstance to the level of a coincidence—that a bolt from the blue broke in upon my stellar reverie and recalled me to earth. Whilst I had been gazing at the floor of heaven and letting my mind wander idly amidst those suns and universes of which Emily Brontë had written, a bomb had fallen from the sky—in no merely symbolic sense—and made of the House, within which my thoughts had hitherto been confined, "nothing more", as the report declared, "than a heap of rubbish."

* Quoted from Boissarie's "Lourdes. Histoire Medicale", pp. vii, viii.

Chapter X

SKYLIGHT

SO that was the latter end of all the loveliness that Allegra had been at such pains to create! No wonder I had shrunk, instinctively as well as rationally, from the philosophy of the Germans; no wonder I had had the gravest doubts about the saving virtue of Luther's Bible and Kant's transcendental philosophy. There was a lie, as Santayana* had seen so clearly and warned the world so wisely, deep seated in the German soul. It was not, as with the Italian school of Machiavel, a short-sighted, but plausible acceptance of evil as a more paying proposition than good. It was not, that is, conscious wrong-doing of the sort committed by people who understand very well all the while what wickedness it is. The surrender had been rather to the devil than to the world or to the wisdom of the world. Evil, be thou our good, the Germans had urged, until the very colour of their souls was changed and they had grown to believe in their own sophistries, to see the bad as the better reason and power and fate as stronger forces than grace or truth. Goethe had done well to take the legend of Faust from Marlowe and clothe it in German dress. Only the German nation perhaps could do it full justice.

Blind and brutal as the whole business in Bryanston Square was in respect of the perpetrators, and maddening as it became whenever one reflected that a little wisdom, not to say a little common-sense, in high places might have preserved Britain from plunging almost unarmed into a conflict beyond her province and her power, I believe that I recognised almost from the first that the spoilt design of national and individual life left still some larger purpose untroubled and untouched. Not the Alien Voice itself, even in that hour of shattered hopes and desolated memories, could have persuaded me that the catastrophe had exhibited the intrusion of a pointless universe into my personal existence. This was not just an intuition. The synchronisation of the catastrophe with the attainment in thought of the summit of the house was too striking to be dismissed as coincidence. I had no need to inquire, like the spectator of the fall of the Bridge of San Luis Rey, why the collapse had come

* "Egotism in German Philosophy."

188

just when it did. It seemed obvious. The genius of the house had said its say, had told me all that it had to tell, had guided me to the head of the stair, and then had left me looking up at the stars. With a strangely human consideration, it had even seemed to spare me the sadness of farewell. Always for me a dream-house since Allegra entered it, it had proved itself in the end to be of such stuff as dreams are made. Like an unsubstantial pageant, it had faded; and all its music, even to those haunting voices calling different ways, had been turned to silence with catastrophic effect. Nothing but dust remained of the enchanted vision. I should never be able to seek Allegra there any more. Noli me tangere—touch me not. The mystical injunction had become imperative. I had to look for her, and for all she stood for, only in the world of spirit.

Of the profound significance of self-consciousness I could now no longer feel any doubt at all. I was a very conscious spectator, not indeed of all time or all existence, but most certainly of that modest part of them which had come under my eye. My mind, as I had tried to make it, seemed to lie buried beneath the ruins of the house, where it had once feasted on reason, like the body on roast. The self—the spirit in me—had retreated from them and was regarding its shattered sensations and possibilities of sensation from a great way off, yet not as if it had loosed its hold upon them for good and all. There were, as it appeared, intimations of immortality to be found even among the fragments of catastrophic dissolution.

Young men, it is said, become preternaturally aware that death is not the end of all when they see a friend killed on the field of battle. But even in older men, the contemplation, even at a distance, of such a holocaust of youth as our times have seen can afford something very like assurance that the soul of man reaches beyond the grave. There were few minds of his time, if any, with a keener edge or deeper thrust than Arthur Balfour's; and there are few passages in his biography, if any, of more arresting interest than the confession, wrung from him by the impact of war, of an absolute confidence in man's survival of bodily death.

"For myself", he wrote to an intimate friend after the death of her sons in the Great War of 1914–18, "I entertain no doubt whatever about a future life. I deem it at least as certain as any of the hundred-and-one truths of a framework of the world as I conceive the world. It is no mere theological accretion which I am prepared to accept in some moods and reject in others. I am as sure that those I love and have lost are living today as I am that yesterday they were fighting heroically in the trenches. The bitterness lies, not in the thought that they are really dead, still less in the thought that I have parted from them for ever; for I think neither of these things. The bitterness lies in the thought that, until I also die, I shall never again see them smile or hear their voices".*

Goethe, as he watched the sinking sun one evening in the May of 1824, had expressed a somewhat similar assurance of immortality. The thought of death, he told Eckermann,† left him completely peaceful, so firm was his conviction that man's spirit was of an indestructible nature. Yet it was, as it seemed to me, Lord Herbert of Cherbury who, in the hey-day of the Renaissance, had most effectively cleared the case for life after death of adverse presumptions.

". . . As I found myself in possession of this life", wrote this thoughtful and talented man, "without knowing anything of the pangs and throes my mother suffered, when yet doubtless they did not less press and afflict me than her, so I hope my soul shall pass to a better life than this without being sensible of the anguish and pains my body shall feel in death. . . . And certainly since in my mother's womb this Plastica or Formatrix which formed my eyes, ears and other senses, did not intend them for that dark and noisome place, but, as being conscious of a better life, made them as fitting organs to apprehend and perceive those things which should occur in this world; so I believe, since my coming into this world, my soul hath formed or produced certain faculties which are almost as useless for this life, as the above-named senses were for the mother's womb; and these faculties are hope, faith, love and joy, since they never rest or fix upon any transitory or perishing object in this world, as extending themselves to something further than can be here given, and indeed acquiesce only in the perfect, eternal and infinite."‡

It might be, as La Rochefoucauld had observed, that neither at the sun nor at death can one look steadily; but these particular testimonies to human survival seemed at least of exceptional interest

* B. Dugdale, "Life of Arthur James Balfour", Vol. II, p. 297.
† Conv. May 2nd, 1824.
‡ "Life of Edward, Lord Herbert of Cherbury", pp. 30–36.

as examples of considered reaction to bodily death on the part of highly critical intellects at very different periods. A French endorsement might be added. Bergson, like Arthur Balfour, had carefully surveyed the human situation in the light of modern science; and to Bergson likewise it appeared that the burden of proof lay upon those who doubted human immortality, not upon those who credited it.* Both men illustrated the spirit of finesse or intuition at work upon the facts of life, but affirmation came more rapidly to the master of debate, who was philosopher rather by occasion, than to the philosopher by profession, who perceived the significance of Christianity rather from contact with a character like Péguy's or a conversation with Cardinal Mercier, and became at long last satisfied with it.†

Intimations of immortality, such as Plato and Wordsworth derive respectively from the study of the soul of man or the sentiment of nature, can never, indeed, finally determine the controversy regarding a resurrection which raged even between the Pharisees and the Sadducees; yet, as it seemed, Shakespeare came as near to do so as is possible, in the familiar observation of Prospero that our little life is rounded with a sleep. Equivocal at a first hearing, this reference to the hidden half of human consciousness would seem at a second more eloquent of immortality than the return of spring. It was so utterly astounding—this strange power in sleep of passing out of our bodies and then again returning into them—and would have appeared so terrifying, had we not undergone it so often and found it so good a friend! It seemed as if some elusive providence were teaching us, like men in constant training for some unfamiliar and alarming experience, to lose consciousness without fear. The words of Prospero or, for the matter of that, the challenge contained in the assertion that death is an eternal sleep—what did they really come to but a tacit admission that the analogy between death and sleep held true? We sleep only to wake, and if, after life's fitful fever, we sleep well, why should that be, unless to wake the surer?

So one might argue, and come to feel with Arthur Balfour that resurrection was manifest in the very nature of things. Yet I knew that I was looking for the intuition of some yet subtler mind, the sensibility of some more burning heart, the companionship of some spirit that had spied still further into the world of mystery. And that led me back in thought to the head of the now fallen stairs, and

* Bergson, "L'Energie-Spirituelle" (Engl. trans.), p. 59.
† See on this some letters in the "Tablet" on Jan. 25th and Feb. 15th, 1941.

to him whose words, as I have recorded, would come to mind as I stood there. I speak of that Pascal whose domesticity was such that he used often, as he tells us, to say that all the unhappiness of men came from one thing—namely, that they did not know how to stay quietly in a room.* I speak of that Pascal in whose personality there met, as one of his numerous editors has observed, 'a marvellous combination of beauty of soul and greatness of genius'; † of that Pascal of whom an eminent logician‡ has declared that 'it might be doubted whether any man possessed a more acute and perfect intellect'. Certainly I could think of no other who had put finishing touches of more satisfying grace to that fineness of thought upon which, as Mr. Masefield tells us, 'all the Renaissance was based',§ or whose faculties satisfied to an equal degree the requirements of penetrating insight into human life. A representative child of France, 'a French Plato', || with all the searching lucid genius of his country in his soul, an artist in letters, a mathematician of great mark, a scholar, a scientist and something of a saint, Pascal seemed to have looked in every important direction, and to have had, so far as a mere man may, the essential facts before him. If his body had wasted under the consuming energy of his mind, his spirit had given him wings when his feet could no longer carry him. Conscious to a degree that perfect sanity was a secret, requiring of man a poise betwixt two worlds and a vision of two infinities, he gave an impression of seeing things visible and vain with so keen an eye for proportion that a dreamer might have been satisfied with his appreciation of man's greatness and a cynic with his apprehension of man's littleness and lowness. He seemed to blink at nothing of the truth, however ugly it might be. Voltaire could have found no human weakness that Pascal had not perceived; and his diagnosis of human nature is as caustic as any we possess. "The maxims of La Rochefoucauld", as Sainte Beuve takes occasion to observe,¶ "in no way contradict Christianity, though they take no account of it. . . . Man, according to La Rochefoucauld, is precisely man fallen, if not in the sense in which St. Francis de Sales and Fénelon

---

* "Pensées", 139. † Faugère, "Pensées de Pascal", I, p. vii.

‡ Jevons, "Logic" (c. xiii).

§ "Shakespeare and Spiritual Life", p. 22. Mr. Masefield observes that "every church is against it". I should not have supposed this to be true of St. Thomas More or of a number of other representative Renaissance saints and scholars.

|| Chevalier, "Pascal", p. 12.

¶ In his foreword to La Rochefoucauld's "Maximes".

understand the term, at least as Pascal does." Pascal, then, was in no danger of falling a victim to those optimistic illusions about mankind that so often nowadays vitiate judgment and confuse counsel. He had learned, perhaps from Montaigne's essays, which he read so much and so critically, to recognise the influence of little things—the shape of Cleopatra's nose or the gravel in Cromwell's ureter—upon large events, no less than the need for accommodation between the justice that is rooted in custom and the secular peace that is of all human needs the greatest, if the life of societies is to become religious in any Christian sense of the word. Yet, with all that, the more one mixed with him the more one realised his incomparable graces. He had a power of fascination as great as that of some dream-hero of spiritual or intellectual romance, such as John Inglesant or Marius the Epicurean. Only, unlike them, he had lived in deed and in truth. The setting of his life was, moreover, worthy of theirs—as rich in romance, more ruthless in realism.

It happened to Pascal to be born a son of France in that animated age of the great Cardinals—Richelieu, Mazarin and de Retz—which moves before our eyes so vividly in the pages of "Les Trois Mousquetaires" or "Vingt Ans Après", in Vigny's "Cinq-Mars" or de Retz's own Memoirs. For the rest, was he not an Auvergnat by birth, with the Puy de Dôme on his horizon; a Parisian by residence, in the days of the Fronde; an habitué of Madame de Sablé's salon; a scientist so distinguished at the age of twenty-four as to attract a visit from Descartes at the height of the philosopher's fame; a resident at Port-Royal-des-Champs; and a familiar of that strange Port-Royalist movement, Catholic in form and faith, if almost Puritan in feeling, which Sainte Beuve thought it so much worth while to study three hundred years after? All this rich field of experience Pascal surveyed like a true Platonic student of all time and existence. Himself a prodigy in youth, a marvel at maturity, a great sufferer and dying young, he tended, moreover, on this account to arouse the rarest sentiments both of admiration and pity. And, if adventure in the common sense was wanting, there were adventures of the mind and spirit which more than made up for it. The Pascal of the calculating machine, the conic sections, and the great experiment of the Puy de Dôme was an explorer; only the mountains that he climbed were the hills of science and the seas that he sailed were the seas of thought.

In these earlier activities Pascal could be clearly perceived at work under the inspiration of that esprit de géometrie which, as the name which he gave it implies, envisages all things in terms of motion, number and space, and is in proportion exact, hard and inflexible. "Let no one enter here", Plato had inscribed over the entrance to his Academy, "who is ignorant of geometry." And the French Plato had instinctively followed that course. Hence there had come to him a temper of mind consorting well with that so-called intellectual conversion of his which occurred in 1646 under the influence of two Jansenist surgeons then attending his father. "There is something geometrical", an American critic* has observed, "in the stern remote god of Jansenism"; and there was perhaps something for a time congenial to Pascal in the conception of a Deity no less well calculated to correspond with the prevailing Cartesian theology than with the modern idea of the world as a thought of the mind of a mathematician. The geometric mind in every age gravitates naturally towards the notion of a predestinated humanity. It is a notion which, to say the least, has plausibility enough; and neither St. Paul nor St. Augustine has failed to do it justice.

There is a story told how Diderot, who knew nothing of algebra, was confounded at the Court of Catherine the Great by Euler's grave delivery of the proposition that $\dfrac{a + b^n}{n} = x$, with the rider attached, 'therefore God exists'. Encyclopaedist though he was, Diderot was, in fact, uncertain whether the existence of God could or could not be demonstrated by mathematics and, fearing a fall, retired in confusion from a contest in which the eminent mathematician had bluffed him into ridicule. Neither the one nor the other had found occasion to suppose that systems of geometry were as much or as little absolute as those of philosophy and that the facts under consideration tended to impose the geometry employed rather than any absolute or universal geometry to impose itself upon the facts. If there were a mathematica perennis, Euclid, at all events, was not much longer to remain its Aquinas. Within a couple of centuries Riemann and others would arrive to dispute his title. Infinity, indeed, as Pasteur had emphasized, lay beyond all signs and symbols, and the puppets of Number, as Minkowski showed, can be taught to dance so prettily as to make the doctrine of relativity assume the appearance of a studied design. But that was all. The story of Diderot and Euler has nevertheless its point and moral; though Pascal possibly saw them

* M. Bishop, "Pascal".

more truly than Prof. Hogben, who retails it * for the benefit of
the million—those mortal millions whom not all the mathematics
in the world will deliver from the 'isolation' where, as Arnold†
asserts, they live, and where, as Pascal, no less poignantly insists,
they die, alone. 'On mourra seul'. All the mathematics in the world
and all the politics based upon mathematics would not alter that.
Unless the order of geometry could be superseded or suffused by the
order of charity, there was not much of value to be hoped from this
world or another. Pascal's thoughts had led him here, if I understood
him aright, along a rather unusual line. I must do my best to make
it clear.

It had happened to the little Pascals as children to possess some
sort of entry into the 'grand monde'. Pascal's younger sister, Jacqueline, had, it is said, sat on Richelieu's knee and won her father's
restoration from disgrace to favour by her girlish charm. It was,
however, mostly through his friendship with the Duc de Roannez
that Pascal himself tasted the crème de la crème of French society.
He had been, indeed, so intimate with de Roannez as to be able to
oppose successfully on religious grounds the Duke's marriage to one
of the richest heiresses of the time, and to encourage the belief that
he thought of proposing himself for the hand of Charlotte de
Roannez, the Duke's sister. His reflections on love had even been
connected with her name, although, without any such reasons as
Hamlet's, he had been found advising the woman he was supposed
to care for to get her to a nunnery. However that may have been, and
whether it was as actor or spectator that he probed the mysteries of
love, his analysis of it and of its place in human thought was as
profound and penetrating as one might have expected. "We are
born", he would say, "with an impression of love in our hearts
which develops as the spirit grows more perfect and leads us to love
what seems beautiful without anyone's telling us that it is so. Who
doubts after that whether we are in the world for anything else but
to love? . . . Man does not care to live with himself; yet he loves;
he must therefore seek elsewhere something to love. He cannot find
it except in beauty; but since he is himself the most beautiful creature
God has ever formed, he must find in himself the model of this
beauty that he seeks abroad. . . . Although he seeks something
wherewith to fill the great void he has made in going out of himself,

* Hogben, "Mathematics for the Million", p. 13.
† M. Arnold, "Isolation".

no kind of thing satisfies it. He has too great a heart for that; he must have at the least something that is like him and approaches as near as possible to him. That is why the beauty that can satisfy man consists not in mere suitability (convenance), but also in resemblance which, by virtue of the distinction of sex, both restricts and confines it. . . . Beauty is distributed in a thousand different ways. The subject best adapted to it is woman. When she has wit she animates and enhances it in a wonderful way. . . . Love bestows wit and sustains itself by wit. There is need of address in loving. One exhausts the ways of pleasing daily; nevertheless one must please and one does so. . . . Love and reason are of a piece. . . . Where one loves strongly, it is always a novelty to see the person loved."*

This sensibility of Pascal's to all that is involved in the grace of marriage had, as his discourse on the passions of love discovered, played its part in enabling him to draw that distinction between the spirit of geometry and the spirit of finesse which figured so largely in his thoughts and writings. Indeed, it seemed to me true to say that in him, as compared with Newman, whose mind and manner resembled his own more than that perhaps of any other English writer, there was a distinction that might be constantly observed. Newman was instinctively a celibate; and his acquaintance with the world, though subtle and penetrating, was more notional than real. His famous analysis of the character of a gentleman would not, so easily, have come from Pascal's pen. For Pascal had felt something of the attraction of the world and had experienced the charm of women; and this had interposed a world of difference between the Oxonian and the Parisian. Mixing with such men as Méré and Miton, the Horace Walpole and the Lord Chesterfield of his time and country, he had neither eschewed the salon or the theatre, nor even the gaming-table, and so had come to value the grace of good-breeding (honnêteté) as that was understood in a capital which gave the law to Europe. He had thus in his early days had some use for money and, as I gathered, had shown himself at one time by no means indifferent to the fate of his sister's fortune. He had argued, too, in his writings that ambition disputes with love for possession of the human soul, and that, whilst their simultaneous presence is incompatible with a great passion, the sovereignty of love at the opening of life and of ambition as life goes on afford humanity its maximum of pleasure. Without being a worldling, he knew in fact very well what the world was like; and his apologetic for Christianity, based as it was upon the

* "Discours sur les passions de l'amour."

Skylight

thought of an approach to religion, no less along the low road of man's littleness than the high road of his greatness, could hardly possess the peculiar power that it has, if he had not envisaged life from the standpoint of the epicurean as well as from that of the stoic and the scientist.

All these considerations rendered Pascal's brief discourses on 'the condition of the great', addressed as perhaps they were to the son of that Duc de Luynes who was the secular patron of Port-Royal, especially interesting. Like Fénelon, and before Fénelon, he was one of the first men in France to be deeply disturbed by the problem, old as the days of Menenius Agrippa, of what Disraeli was later to denominate the two nations—of the rich, that is, and the poor; and he was quick to remind the patricians of his time that they came of no different blood to that of the plebeians. Whilst he believed degree and order to be essential to the conduct of society, he would have no noble suppose himself superior to the common crowd by reason of any honour that was paid him or forget that he was, strictly speaking, 'un roi de concupiscence'. In his view the great only held their privileges and position for the sake and with the consent of their fellow men. What was more, their external grandeur demanded an interior humility to balance it. His political theory had, in short, much use for the hard saying of Thomas à Kempis that we ought not to suppose that we have made any progress at all in the spiritual life until we have learned to feel ourselves inferior to all.

In that most exacting demand of traditional Christianity lay, as it seemed, the real answer to all the shallow modern talk about equality in a manifestly unequal and evidently hierarchical world. Manifestly unequal and positively hierarchical! French logic perhaps faces up to the fact of the grand seigneur and the grande dame which English humour does its best to discredit obliquely by making merry over the snob and the toady. But neither revolution nor ridicule will alter the ways of nature; and the extinction of the aristocrat will only hasten the advent of the despot and the parvenu. Meanwhile no communist has yet been heard to complain of inequality in the garden or to propose that the rose be deprived of privileged soil and service or the orchid ejected from the hothouse. If aristocratic sentiment be all snobbery, then the poets are the worst of snobs. Burns himself, for all his fine talk about the daisy, must needs go and compare his love to a red, red rose! And if, as a popular poem incautiously asserts, we are nearer God's heart in a garden than anywhere else on earth, God was pretty plainly no Marxist. Doubtless He loved the daisies, since He made so many of them—and, if Lincoln's argument from numbers be soundly based, the weeds no less—but there was still no getting away from the carnations and the lilies. He had made them too and made them more beautiful; and the religion of sensible men would make the most and not the worst of the apparently nowadays distasteful fact. Yet, unless the aristocrat became poor in spirit, the whole business seemed likely to give trouble enough; and all the more if equality were to be identified with equity. The Greeks, as it seemed, for all their subtlety, had never really seen their way through the problem any better than the French. Their fine sense of proportion alone was enough to teach them that no country could afford to surrender the doctrine of government by the best men, whoever they might be, for that of government by the pliable and credulous crowd; and they based their much-admired political conceptions upon concessions to aristocracy and presumptions of slavery incompatible with modern ideas of democracy, as Aristotle's magnificent man alone sufficiently shows. From all of which considerations it might be effectively argued that in politics a spiritual world has to be called into being to correct the balance of the natural.

To Pascal, at any rate as I think, this appeared self-evident. The mass of men, he would declare, value good birth; but cleverish people are apt to disparage it as a freak of chance. Really clever men, however, he would continue, honour it, not for the reasons that appeal to the vulgar, but for reasons that amount to saying that manners are the making of man. And he would add that the devout, zealous rather than wise, despised birth, owing to the strength of their conviction of a world beyond the grave. It was only perfect Christians who did it honour by reason of a still more piercing light —the light, if I understood him aright, of Providence working out its design of the world through hierarchies of men no less than of angels. People, he would conclude, only came to see this by degrees.*

To have known Allegra was, as I used to reflect when the conversation took this turn, to have reached the heart of this matter at a leap. She was, as one who knew her well, and the world well too, had observed, the best of arguments for aristocracy.† But, in fact, with

* "Pensées", 337.
† E. Marsh, "A Number of People", p. 199. ". . . if at the Day of Judgment I were called upon to show one cause why the old order in England should not be condemned, but rather praised, for its fruits, I should name Guendolen Osborne."

her the argument can hardly be said to have arisen, for the conclusion sprang to the eye. It would have been as hopeless to contest it as—to revert for the last time to the simile that I have perhaps already worked too hard—to maintain that a garden lost nothing by the absence of the lily or the rose. She was what she was, tradition and circumstance meeting in her and matching; and there was nothing to be said or done but to admit it. No complex of superiority or inferiority troubled her; and none perhaps troubled others in her company. The truth of things had made her free. "Things"—and persons too—"are what they are, and the consequences of them will be what they will be; why then do we desire to be deceived?" Why indeed? Only, perhaps, because, for some reason or other, we choose to think that the world would look better as a great plain—to use Bob Lowe's memorable comparison—with nothing higher thereon than a thistle. Yet who in his inmost heart does not endorse Aristophanes's gibe at Demos* and say to himself in secret, 'Equality—thy hidden name is dullness'? Or who, with any sense of drama in his soul, does not want all the world a stage, with stars as well as supers, and some part at least of the play a pageant? Or who that is truly human would not prefer to follow the undulations of the pilgrim's way with all sorts and conditions of men upon it than multiply labour with all the apparatus of the statistician and produce a race of robots over whose procreation the eugenist and the equalitarian might wage interminable warfare?

Allegra, never attempting to reverse the order and nature of things, but gathering rosebuds as she might, would, I felt sure, have seemed to Pascal's keen eye to have come nearer the heart of this matter than many of those industrious persons who hope to work miracles with file and docket. At all events, she exemplified to perfection Pascal's favourite doctrine, already alluded to, that all the troubles of the world—its agitations, its quarrels, its many dubious enterprises—came of man's inability to live at peace in a room. Quite unaffectedly and unostentatiously she took her house into a sort of partnership with herself; and, had the times been such as to give to the salon its proper place in the scheme of society, I do not doubt that some or, maybe, many would have been found to say that they had found in her the essence of a liberal education. But, then, as I have said, she had qualities reminiscent of times when women were more concerned with distilling the subtle essence of grace at home than of battling directly with the storm of the world's

* Knights, l. 221.

unrest. I make no criticism; for, though I have my own preferences, such criticism might seem alien to Allegra's own profound and instinctive toleration. I am only explaining the presence of a certain distinction in her that a clear eye can discern in the antecedents of the artistic legacy of Europe from the early Italian Renaissance to the eve of the Revolution—a legacy consonant with the intellectual grace and spiritual beauty of Pascal's thought. I could see Allegra, as indeed I have actually seen her, passing like a flicker of sunshine through that lovely Burgundian church of Brou, to the beauty of which Matthew Arnold has paid so delicate and delicious a tribute. I could see her in spirit, as indeed I have often seen her in the flesh, standing radiant against the golden glory of the house at Stanway, which of all houses, I think, she admired and loved the most. Conversely, against the loud emphasis or harsh sensuality which seems to be the outcome of a finished philosophy of sense her being seemed as silently and decisively to protest as a Greek statue against the loss of serenity in the soul of a spectator. But to return from a digression, which, nevertheless, was not an irrelevance!

It was apparently as a result of mixing with the great world of his day that Pascal had first become conscious of the limitations of the geometrical spirit as an instrument of truth—so conscious, in fact, that in an obiter dictum, which Méré reported, he declared that he preferred Miton to Descartes or Plato. The sentiment made Miton laugh, but it was, as Pascal's latest editor observes, distinctively Pascalian. Thanks to Méré and Miton, Pascal learnt to know the beau monde, not merely as a place of corruption and perdition or as the theatre of abominations against which the preacher is accustomed to declaim, but as a society where sentiment is elevated by delicacy of education and conversation and rendered capable of reflecting the subtlest shades of thought and feeling. A keen epigram or penetrating aphorism recommends itself readily in such company, whilst laboured proof becomes superfluous and, if attempted, spoils the effect. For words can have a weight in themselves equal to their occasion and lightly knock an opponent out on the instant as indisputably as if the laws of thought had been pedantically applied by a master-pugilist in the heavy style. This art is no monopoly of the beau monde; but it is there that it has been cultivated with the most effect; and, since nowhere else is life apt to seem so short or art so long, its merits become the more obvious. Here, then, was to be found the cradle of a finer spirit than the spirit of geometry, as well as of a style so finished in its ironic mockery of this world's madness as to make it the acknowledged model of Gibbon's grand manner, yet so direct and delicate in its treatment of heavenly things as to be more than the equal of Newman's in simplicity and grace.

The mental instrument of which this spirit made use might indeed utilise, as in the case of Pascal himself, the spirit of geometry with all that geometry has to give in precision, but it was none the less for that, as Pascal claimed, a distinct faculty. No mathematical reasoning, no rationalistic inference dominated the thought that ripened with greater or less speed into certitude. One saw and believed. Call it sentiment according to the fashion of Pascal's time; adopt the terminology of Newman and speak of an 'illative sense'; or style it intuition as some would do to-day—it matters little. Thanks to this faculty, which was more than any faculty could be, which reached to the very heart of being, which was the very genius of the intellectual soul, doubt disappeared. For it had the power of gathering into its grasp and refining to pellucid truth the result of all kinds of experience. The irksome distinction between subject and object seemed to yield to its pressure. One was surer of its findings than the most elaborate ratiocinations could make one feel—sure, for example, that Napoleon had existed, however ingeniously Whately might argue to the contrary, or that one had lived and loved, however ably some cunning metaphysician might dispute existence or some physical scientist depreciate emotion.

Not everyone, of course, could see the point of an epigram, perceive the significance of a picture or poem, or recognise the beauty of a view. Finesse was needed to seal assurance at every turn. Yet that eye must be dull indeed which did not mark the flash of Pascal's reflections, or perceive at a glance that his were no spurious gems. Generation after generation had tested them; and not all the subtlety of Voltaire had sufficed in their case, any more than in that of Shakespeare's plays, to shake the judgment of the world upon their worth. A particular providence had, happily as it seemed to me, intervened, though at the cost of Pascal's life, to prevent their incorporation in a treatise. Such jewels of thought needed no setting; and we had them just as they were first cut and polished by the fineness of his mind. Dante, it is true, had dared to set jewels of equal worth in a framework; but what a framework it was! The beauty of a woman's neck and hair with celestial light falling upon them and rendering them translucent.

Philosophy, as must be repeated, can clip an angel's wings; yet has Pascal's spirit of finesse a place well-assured in human thought. "Pascal", said the outstanding philosophic genius of our time,* "introduced into philosophy a certain way of thinking that is not pure reason, since it corrects by the esprit de finesse the mathematical part of the reason, and that is not mystic contemplation either, since it arrives at results that are capable of being examined and verified by the world at large." To Bergson's eye, in fact, as he told Jacques Chevalier, this current of Pascal's thought ran deeper than the mathematical current of Descartes's doctrine which until lately disputed with it for the mastery in modern philosophy. It ran on indeed until it reached La Rochefoucauld's maxim, "La trop grande subtilité est une fausse délicatesse et la véritable délicatesse est une solide subtilité". And then it ran on again.

Escape from the insinuating influence of the esprit de finesse is not, let it be said in passing, to be found by any rationalised resistance; for it recognises readily the fact that rationalism only reluctantly confesses. "We must", remarks Lord Russell in a little manual on the problems of philosophy, "sooner or later, and probably before very long, be driven to a point where we cannot find any further reason and where it becomes certain that no further reason is even theoretically discoverable. Starting with the common beliefs of daily life, we can be driven back from point to point until we come to some general principle or some instance of a general principle which seems luminously evident and is not itself capable of being deduced from anything more evident."†

Into such deep waters, then, had Pascal come by sheer force of thinking and living. Yet he was not at a loss, as they must be who have nothing but the spirit of geometry to guide them. He had, indeed, done that spirit full justice, for he belonged in part to the new world of inductive science which came into its own at the Renaissance, and argued from the world to God rather than God to the world. Yet he saw, and no man more clearly, that in itself the knowledge thus obtained was insufficient to pierce to the heart— for heart precisely it was—of truth. "One must have", he would declare in a searching sentence, "the qualities of the sceptic (pyrrhonien), of the mathematician, and of the obedient Christian; and these agree with one another and temper one another by causing one

* Chevalier, "Pascal", p. 15, footnote.
† Bertrand Russell, "Problems of Philosophy", p. 175.

to doubt where one ought, to make sure where one ought, and to submit where one ought."*

It seemed to me, as I listened, that Pascal had forged for himself a sword of the finest steel with which to open the world's oyster—a sword of the spirit, critical, precise and Christian. Yet even so, as I could perceive, it was not tempered to such utter perfection as to satisfy him, and fell still some way short of his requirements. We know on the authority of his sister Jacqueline that he had at one time been troubled by the idea that he was recoiling from human society through mental conviction rather than under divine guidance. It was as he wrestled with this disquiet that there occurred, in circumstances never fully revealed by him and probably past adequate expression or even complete comprehension, an incident which has become an event just because he, of all men, was the subject of it. At the close of a day in autumn, dedicated to the memory of St. Clement, it seemed to Pascal that his spirit was bathed in mystic fire. In that strange night of vision both dark and light, which led him to score the word 'Feu' at the head of his record of it, he perceived God, no longer—so he would himself express it—as the god of philosophers and scholars, but as "the God of Abraham, Isaac and Jacob"; and his conviction of Christianity was therewith changed to full assurance. Twice in his account he used the word 'certitude', and then amplified its significance by the terms 'sentiment', 'joie', 'paix'. There followed in rapid succession a series of staccato phrases. "The God of Jesus Christ! My God and yours! 'Thy God shall be my God.' The world and everything forgotten except God! He is to be found only by the ways taught in the Gospel. Greatness of the human soul! 'Righteous Father, the world has not known Thee, but I have known Thee.' Joy, joy, joy, tears of joy! I separated myself from Him: 'They deserted Me, the fountain of living water.' My God, will you leave me? Let me not be eternally divided from Him. 'This is eternal life, that they know Thee alone as the true God and Him Thou hast sent, Jesus Christ.' Jesus Christ! Jesus Christ! I separated myself from Him. I fled Him, and renounced Him, and crucified Him. Let me never be separated from Him. One keeps Him only by the ways taught in the Gospel. Renunciation whole and sweet! Entire submission to Jesus Christ and my director. Eternal joy in exchange for a day of discipline on earth."

So ran the memorial, sewn into Pascal's clothing so that he might

---

* Quoted from Faugère's edition of the "Pensées", I, p. lxxvii.

always have it with him, of that memorable night in 1654 when, for a space of time extending from 10.30 p.m. to 12.30 a.m., this brilliant and exquisite soul was caught up into some sort of ecstacy and experienced things that cannot be conveyed in any words we know but his own. It is, however, clear enough that Love, visiting him like a thief in the night, had raised his spirit to its highest power, and that therewith he had tasted joy such as had never before been known to him. Doubtless, if the event needed further diagnosis, it would be correct to identify it, as one recent critic does, with that stage of mystical progress which goes by the name of Illumination. But classification of this sort has a slightly frigid effect. It might be simpler and truer to say that Pascal had at last beheld the heart of reason with the reason of the heart.

It was at this turning point in his life that, leaving the society of such eminent friends as de Roannez and de Luynes, Pascal sought the solitude of Port-Royal-des-Champs and the guidance of a director with an exceptionally high reputation for wisdom and prudence. To be the confidant and confessor of Blaise Pascal can have been no slight responsibility; but there seems every reason to suppose that Monsieur de Saci was equal to it. He saw that in Pascal he had to deal with one who had come, by the unusual power of his intellect, to an apprehension of the same truths and an application of the same methods that the Fathers of the Church, notably St. Augustine, and, one might add, St. Bonaventure,* had expounded; and he saw, too, that Pascal, unfamiliar with patristic tradition, had found these truths astonishing. He had drawn Pascal out, as was his way with his spiritual children; had led Pascal on to speak of the part that Epictetus and Montaigne, and more particularly the latter, had had in the formation of his pupil's thoughts; and in this manner had elicited an exhaustive discussion of paganism, both stoic and epicurean, which shows us the esprit de finesse ranging over human conditions and discovering Christianity to be the exact just mean between those two opposing estimates of the meaning of human life. Epictetus had depicted man as a noble creature, equipped with a mind equal to the discovery of truth and a will equal to the choice of happiness. Montaigne, on the

---

* Cp. Gilson's "The Philosophy of St. Bonaventure", p. 470, "Because of a deep-lying analogy—above all because of the Augustinian element so strongly active in both of them—St. Bonaventure's method is closely related to Pascal's. This 'order of the heart', with all the totally unforeseen conclusions it involves, is St. Bonaventure's as well as Pascal's", etc. The point made is that with both the Sacred Heart is at the heart of all thought and can alone co-ordinate thoughts.

other hand, had ridiculed man's ignorance and fallibility—and with this Pascal confessed his sympathy—and by this means had conveyed the impression that for a being so unfortunately handicapped the best thing to be done was to drift with the current of custom or trust to the guidance of inclination.

If this were not wholly fair to Epictetus and Montaigne in themselves, it was perhaps fair enough as an estimate of the influence they had frequently exerted upon others. Along one or other of the lines of thought indicated, men for the most part made their way. The counsel of Epictetus was a counsel of duty and self-assurance, and led easily enough to pride and presumption. The counsel of Montaigne was a confession of ignorance and incapacity, and might lead almost as easily to intellectual indolence and cowardice. Between them these counsellors brought out, as Pascal maintained, the fact that man had fallen from one estate to another. But, as they had not perceived this fact, much less assimilated their teaching to it, they had left the world distracted and anarchical. This intellectual confusion, so Pascal argued, the Gospel, with a wisdom of divine origin, was able to reconcile. Instead of crediting nature both with grandeur and weakness, it had attributed man's weakness to the effects of his fall and man's grandeur to the operation of heavenly grace.

M. de Saci, it appeared, could not refrain from expressing to Pascal at the close of this discourse his surprise at the speaker's power of putting his points. He had compared him to one of those physicians who would prepare the deadliest poisons in order to draw from them the greatest remedies. Pascal had replied that the art of Epictetus was incomparable for troubling the mind of those who seek peace in exterior things, and the art of Montaigne for confounding the pride of those who think to find in the sciences unassailable truth—so much so, indeed, that these latter become at the end so battered in spirit as no longer to be able to pronounce with confidence on the possibility of such mysteries as the Incarnation and the Eucharist.

Those were the days when Pascal dwelt off and on at Port-Royal-des-Champs, living there like a solitary, making his bed, washing his plates, and embracing a squalor which St. Bernard, as his sister Jacqueline suggested to him, would not have commended. Fresh from the world, he had discovered at Port-Royal what long afterwards Sainte-Beuve, with critical, if not spiritual, insight, had also clearly discerned—the beauty of holiness. Protesting against laxity in the Church and in the world to a point which has almost made men class them as protestants, the Port-Royalists at their best seemed to rise on those wings of purity and simplicity which lift men heavenwards. To the eyes of many of their contemporaries they shone as lights in the world; and Pascal, himself lately illuminated and seeking a society of the perfect, lent for a while the burning and shining light of his genius to their constellation. Yet he was never definitely of them. No one, in fact, could have asserted his independence much more clearly than he had done himself in the XVIIth of his "Lettres Provinciales." "I am alone," he wrote, "and, speaking literally, do not belong to Port-Royal. . . . Thanks to God, I do not adhere to anything on earth save the one Catholic, Apostolic, Roman Church in which I desire to live and die in communion with the Pope, its sovereign chief, and outside of which no safety lies." Yet this freedom from binding ties had brought him no freedom from current controversy; and, by a curious irony, he had become entangled as a principal in a quarrel for which he had hardly the qualifications of an auxiliary.

It had happened in this manner. At that precise moment of French history the vexed question of freedom and necessity was revolving upon the pivot of the doctrine of sufficient grace. Man, as theology maintained, was helpless without grace to gain for his moral acts, good though they might be, supernatural merit or to bring them within reach of supernatural reward. For that purpose, however, sufficient grace was accorded to all men and, if this did not prove efficacious, it was because, according to the Jesuits, though not the Thomists, man's will had resisted its operation. Jesuit and Thomist alike guarded, however, the belief in man's essential liberty as well as in God's essential aid. Man, as St. Vincent de Paul observed, had no merit unless he were free, God no justification for command or punishment if grace were granted to some, but denied to others. It was Jansen who maintained (beyond serious dispute, whatever the Port-Royalists may have argued) that for lack of grace some commandments of God are impossible to just men willing to perform them, and that it was an error to maintain that Christ shed His blood for all men without exception.* So melancholy a view of man's condition has now for a long while been condemned, not only by the Apostolic See, but by the common sense of Christians. Yet,

---

* Hatzfeld, in his "Saint Augustine" (p. 92), puts the point very simply: "St. Augustine expressly asserts that God gives all men a sufficing grace and that their goodwill can render it efficacious. Jansenius admits only efficacious grace which God gives to some and refuses to others."

as St. Cyran, the great apostle of Port-Royal, had been Jansen's friend, the Port-Royalists had considered it necessary after St. Cyran's death to continue to champion Jansen's orthodoxy; and Pascal, in his turn, being as he was under such great obligations to Port-Royal, had begun to champion them.

This had been the genesis of the famous "Lettres Provinciales". Whether their delicate irony—a quality certainly not absent from the Gospels themselves—had lapsed at points into 'médisance' is a matter about which opinions will doubtless differ. But the world's satisfaction at seeing certain fine distinctions of the religious casuist turned into ridicule seems to need tempering by the reflection that the mockery of Pascal would become devastating if applied to the casuistries of the world itself. Who would not fear for the fate of some of even our most respected politicians and jurists if their doctrine and practice were to be sifted by such a winnowing-fan as Pascal's wit? Were there ever men who so regularly justified their means by their ends (in the crude sense, that is, commonly given to the phrase by the world, though not intended by the Jesuits who used it only in connection with things indifferent*)? What Foreign Minister, for instance, might not tremble if a Pascal were to handle the case of a Christian, bound, as such, to seek to save every human soul from sin, yet, as a statesman, condoning the purchase of some venal creature ready, for the sake of a handful of gold, to betray his country's secrets? Falkland, as Clarendon records, refused as Secretary of State to employ spies or give any countenance or entertainment to them;† but what evidence is there that any other politician has allowed himself to be troubled seriously about such a thing, either before or since? Traditionally shocked at the subtlety of the Jesuit and the secrecy of the confessional, politicians nevertheless live, move and make their mark in an atmosphere so thick with 'casuistry' that one may catch them loftily refusing so much as to

---

* As Fr. Martindale, S.J. ("The Faith of the Roman Church", p. 104), points out, the phrase, "The end justifies the means", in its theological use relates merely to neutral acts and is only properly understood when balanced by the converse statement that "The end vitiates the means". If, as I think Herbert Spencer argues, there is morality in the shutting of a door, it is only e.g. because one might keep it open to get fresh air or, alternatively, to eavesdrop.

† "Great Rebellion", vii, 226. Clarendon adds: "I do not mean such emissaries as with danger would venture to view the enemy's camp and bring intelligence . . . but those who, by communication of guilt or dissimulation of manners, wound themselves into such trusts and secrets as enabled them to make discoveries for the benefit of the State".

consider negotiation with one ruler, whilst entering into close partnership with another, whose crimes and tyrannies are no less notorious, whose eligibility for trial in some international court of justice, if such existed, is no less assured, but whose big battalions procure for him in the confessionals of Whitehall and the chambers of Fleet Street the immediate absolution of his past sins, and even maybe, besides, some little licence to commit sin at a future date, if the temptation should happen to return. Escobar, as Pascal saw him, is never very far away from any one of us, but, if one had need to look for him, a walk from St. Paul's to the Houses of Parliament might prove the surest way to track him down.

Casuistry, meanwhile, of the better kind is old as conscience; and the science of casuistry at least as old as Aristotle; and no man—not even a Pascal—does wisely to make broad his own phylacteries when he speaks of it. "All the basic principles of the entire Jesuit moral philosophy", observes a modern writer,* "can be traced back to the Nicomachean Ethics." Doubtless! And much other moral philosophy as well. John Morley's essay "On Compromise" is a piece of casuistry as fine and fair as one can well ask for, being well calculated to dispose, not only of any lie in the soul, but of cant on the tip of the tongue or the nib of the pen as well. No book, it might be said in passing, unless it be Leslie Stephen's "Science of Ethics", has, perhaps, shown more clearly, in the light of the event rather than in the intention of the author, that the moral standards of Christianity survive dogma by one generation, but no more. If the creed goes, the standard follows after; and then there is little place left for the casuist. The only question remaining is whether a man should be a law or no law unto himself; and that is no complex consideration.

Pascal, however, like Plato and Augustine before him, belonged in heart and mind to the society of the perfect; and the Order of Charity is often impatient of moral economies. "Dilige et quod vis fac"†—"Love and do what you will"—is a sword that in the hands of a saint cuts a good many Gordian knots which the casuist can only at best laboriously untie. But most of us are not saints; and the sword of our spirits is neither sharpened nor ready for use. And so Escobar, or a better than Escobar, enters on the scene, much as Aristotle appears in the wake of Plato.

It would be an error to suppose that Pascal had intended any attack

* Fülöp-Miller, "The Power and Secret of the Jesuits", p. 158.
† Augustine, "In Joan.", vii, 8.

upon the confessional. "Could one imagine anything more charitable and gentle?" he would ask, after alluding to the nature of
auricular confession and the inviolability of its secrets, and then
would add, "Yet such is the corruption of man that he still finds
some harshness in this rule; and it is one of the chief reasons which
has made a great part of Europe revolt against the Church."* And
certainly such as feel a private confession, once in the year, of grave
sins, of which the sinner has full knowledge and to which he has
given full consent, to be an indignity or an outrage, might appear to
have still some way to go before they reach the temple of humility
and take their stand there beside that publican who knows no hours
of pharisaism.

Meanwhile Pascal's exposure of the excessive subtlety of the
casuist discovered all too close a correspondence with the complexities
of things as human society has contrived to tangle them up; and this,
rather than the attack upon the ethic of the Jesuits, made, as it
seemed to me, the really terrifying aspect of Pascal's indictment.
The irony of the "Provinciales" concealed a loud and bitter cry for
simplicity of intention and purity of affection in our dealings with
one another no less than with God. Not the Port-Royalists themselves could, in fact, escape casuistical problems. The defence of
Jansen, as the event proved, caused them to resort to a device which
Pascal himself had countenanced in his Letters. They coupled their
repudiation of the errors alleged to be contained in Jansen's book
with a mental reservation that the errors in the book were not in fact
there. Such a mental reservation is not perhaps inconsistent with the
distinction which theologians draw between the deposit of truth in
which the Catholic Christian is bound to place full credence and the,
so-called, dogmatic facts which fall outside the deposit. But Pascal's
super-subtle sensibility had fled before a stronger sense of the
subterfuge; and, when the question arose of the signature by the
nuns of a formal declaration of faith, he seems to have held that
the document tendered to them pledged them to an admission of the
publication of the errors in question no less than to a rejection of the
errors themselves. The issue between what is owing to authority
and what is owing to private judgment seemed for a moment to
menace him; and it looked as if he might come into collision with
the spiritual powers of his time precisely on a case of conscience.
But, as I gathered, a stronger love and humility than was apparent

* "Pensées", 100.

in the controversial days of the "Provinciales" had made themselves felt in his inner life; and the evidence of the parish priest who attended him in his last illness is, if it be admitted, conclusive on the point. All echoes of the conflict that had once made his name so famous were, in fact, dying away from his own hearing as the trumpets began to sound on the other side. He had never really been a Jansenist. He had only wanted to give full weight to each side of every question. "Truth", he had even written in his latter days, "is so obscured at the present time and falsehood so established that, unless one loves truth, one cannot know it. If there ever is a time when one ought to profess two opposing opinions, it is when the reproach of omitting one is made. Therefore the Jesuits and the Jansenists are wrong to conceal them; but the Jansenists are the more wrong, for the Jesuits have better put forward the two sides of the question."*

Thus, at least as I came to know Pascal, had the influence of Jansen's "Augustinus" yielded to that of the Augustine of the "Confessions" and of the "City of God"; thus had the trenchant irony of the "Lettres Provinciales" been exchanged for the truth and beauty which pervade the "Pensées". Heresy—that choosing for oneself, as the term implies—is at best a second-rate thing. As it had been with Arius and others, so it was to be with Jansen. The wind of time, to borrow Mr. Belloc's words, was to blow him and his doctrine all away. Nobody bothers to read the "Augustinus" now; and the Jansenists are interesting chiefly because Pascal thought so much of Port-Royal. But Pascal is interesting because his finished intellect could at long last be satisfied with nothing less than catholic truth.

A wonder had, however, occurred during the publication of the "Letters Provinciales", which the Port-Royalists took as a sign of divine approbation to themselves, but which might with as much plausibility be regarded as a particular providence vouchsafed to the family of Pascal. The miracle of the Holy Thorn, though it may not appear specially remarkable or exceptionally well authenticated to those who are familiar with the literature of the miraculous, is nevertheless well attested and entirely credible. The world, convinced from time to time against its will by the presence of such phenomena in its midst, tends, however, to remain of the same opinion still, and to discard them as pious, superstitious or unscrupulous inventions. For myself, I do not think it is any longer in the power of an honest historian to

* "Pensées", 864, 865 (freely translated).

reject such testimony to the miraculous as may be found in Boissarie's and Bertrin's medical histories* of the occurrences at Lourdes, or inferred from Zola's disingenuous treatment of the case of Marie Lemarchand and pusillanimous refusal of Dr. Boissarie's challenge to a scientific inquiry into another sudden cure.†

However that may be, Pascal's reputation must, on the strength of such nineteenth and twentieth century evidence, be relieved of any suspicion of undue credulity. Letters written in the week of the occurrence declare that on the very afternoon when she had been touched by the relic, preserved at Port-Royal de Paris, Marguérite Périer, Pascal's niece, was cured of a lacrymal fistula, the size of a hazel nut, which had been on the point of being surgically operated. Four physicians and four surgeons checked and re-checked the evidence, and reported the event to be miraculous. Obviously, at some point in any process of healing the human body by miraculous means, what we call normal forces must take over control of the event from those we regard as abnormal. It is the speed and circumstances of a cure, even more than the cure itself, that are impressive. The secretions of dacryocystitis may apparently dry off through the nose as a result of necrosis of the bone, but it is, to say the least, improbable that the sac containing them will burst on the day required by the use of the relic and the prayers of the faithful, or that, if it does burst to time, the foetid matter will clear away so completely as, not only to give the patient immediate relief, but also freedom from any return of the trouble. Whilst, therefore, some minds unaffected by any bias of probability are able to believe in a coincidence resulting in an instantaneous cure, others may perhaps in the circumstances be excused for their scepticism in respect of such singular vagaries of chance and change.

Pascal, eminently rigid and skilled investigator as he was of the secrets of natural science, had at all events been fully satisfied that a notable miracle had occurred and, accepting their interpretation of its significance, had defended the Port-Royalists with the greater zeal. Yet, as was indicated, neither the miracle, nor the dialectical victory that his polemics brought him, prevented him from confessing in the end that the Jesuits had been fairer than their opponents in putting the two sides of the question at issue between them.

* Dr. Boissarie, "Histoire Médicale de Lourdes": Bertrin, "Lourdes".

† The case of Marie Lemarchand (Elise Rouquet), which Zola travestied in his novel, was one of lupus. The details of it can be found in Bertrin's "Lourdes", p. 221, and the details of the challenge, *ibidem*, p. 191.

From the date of the miracle, as I guessed, the dual aspect of the deepest problems had struck him with increasing force, and led him to realise that in the search for truth poise was everything. Our intellectual difficulties, as he came to believe, were to be traced, not to any contradiction in things themselves or to any want of correspondence between thoughts and things, but to the natural infirmity of the human mind resulting from an immature and illicit attempt to consume the fruits of the tree of knowledge before they were ripe for human digestion. He seemed thus to escape by anticipation those errors in German philosophy which once had so much vogue in English universities—Kant's disastrous conclusion that pure reason, by virtue of the oppositions that it created, could reach no assurance on matters of ultimate consequence, and Hegel's still more paradoxical doctrine that Being and Not Being were the same thing. Pascal was far too sound a scientist not to stick to the facts, and had far too humble an intellect to take any pride in systems. The cause of mistakes in the work of human apprehension had, in his view, to be laid at the door of a fallen nature. It was of a piece with this to notice, as he did, that the Church had first looked at the facts with which it was chiefly concerned intuitively, and only afterwards sought to clarify them intellectually. Christ—to take the most obvious example—was both God and Man: and that should be obvious enough to anyone who chose to give the facts their proper value. But the intellectual expression of this conclusion could be reached only by degrees through the suppression of error—Arian or Apollinarian, Nestorian or Eutychian—and to a rude mind, watching this process of refinement, it might well appear that the world at the date of the Arian controversy was divided by no more than an iota. Yet the iota had to be eliminated before any adequate reflection of the diaphanous vision of the God-Man could be perceived by the mind; and in this there was work and to spare for the esprit de finesse.

Whilst the perfect vision of these things was, in his view, committed to members of what he would have called the order of charity, I think Pascal believed that reasoned conviction lay within the reach of every man of liberal education (honnête homme). Anyone who was content to study the facts of history could attain the moral certitude of the juror who is asked to decide questions of life and death. Only good sight, he would say, is needed to get at the truth of things; but that sight must be really good. He was repeating his sustained plea on behalf of the esprit de finesse, his old protest, so particularly required on the threshold of an era dominated by the Cartesian philosophy, against putting one's trust in the virtue of the spirit of geometry. The force of the plea was doubled, of course, by the fact that it came from this brilliant scientist and mathematician. Not that the spirit of geometry was a false spirit, but that something still was wanted to give it cogency for human beings. To listen to Pascal was thus in a manner to take the measure of his contemporary, Descartes, the dominant influence, and most of all, perhaps, in medical theory, from that day to one not so long ago.

It had been, and is still, the iron strength of the Cartesian metaphysic that its author would not willingly allow anything to pass into his philosophy which did not satisfy his cold canon of certitude. Yet the proofs of God's existence and of man's immortality, after Descartes had let them through the lock-gates of his mind, have at best only the charm of a limpid river that has been frozen in its flow. It is not surprising that he had felt the need of ensconcing his body in a heated room before his thoughts could gain momentum, and that he has put this fact on record in the opening of his famous discourse on method. Pascal's delicate intellect, like the very different minds of Hume and Keats, did not fail to feel the chill of philosophy. "The metaphysical proofs of God", he would observe, "are so remote from the reasoning of men and so involved, that they make little impression; and, though some people may be thus aided, it is only during the moment of demonstration; an hour later they are afraid that they have deceived themselves."* His own reflections could never be made the subject of a similar reproach. They were so far from being ice-bound that I used to think of them as drops of molten gold falling from some celestial furnace. 'Feu'—the key word in his cryptic script—would come back to mind and seem charged with fuller meaning. Vision, as he continued, seemed to become purified, strengthened and indefinitely extended. A new perspective imposed itself. A new appearance spread over the face of things. Intellectual concepts melted into intuitive certitudes. The 'order of charity' made itself felt at every turn.

Thus would Pascal persuade me of the truth of what he was saying as he piled thought upon thought. And I could understand him well enough and had sufficient education to know that he was not excogitating brilliant nonsense, but all the while consolidating his hold upon realities. It seemed to me that he spoke, not like those

* "Pensées", 543.

who pursue truth just for the pleasure of possessing it, but like one who loved it for all that it held of grace and goodness. There was a cogency of life as well as of argument in all his logic; and, when he would declare in words that have echoed down the ages that the heart has its reasons of which the reason is unaware, I recognised that he was not substituting feeling for thought, but urging the intellectual soul forward to that mountain height whence the pure in heart already see God.* The cult of the Sacred Heart was the deepest answer of the Church to the error of Jansen; but, like many well-considered replies to powerful currents of thought, political and religious, it represented, not a damming of religious emotion, but the direction of it into a safer channel. Pascal, as his thoughts deepened, seemed to draw nearer to his eminent contemporary, St. Margaret Mary Alacoque, the sponsor of the famous devotion to the Heart of Jesus. "C'est donc par le coeur," says St. Cyran, "que nous croyons comme il faut et que nous acquérons la vraie justice et la vraie piété."† In some burning sentences that have been reckoned the finest in French prose, Pascal had applied this science to the diagnosis of man.

"The infinite distance", Pascal would say, "between body and mind symbolises the infinitely more infinite distance between mind and charity, for charity is supernatural. . . . The greatness of men of intellect is invisible to kings, rich men, fighting men who are great according to the flesh. The greatness of wisdom, which is nothing if not of God, is invisible both to the carnal and to the intellectual. Here are three orders differing in kind. Men of great genius have their empire, their distinction, their majesty, their triumph, their splendour and are in no need of material greatness, with which they are not concerned. Their eminence is visible, not to the sight but to the mind; and that is enough. The saints, too, have their empire, distinction, majesty, triumph, lustre, and need neither worldly nor intellectual greatness, to which they stand in no relation, since they neither add to nor take away from it. They are seen of God and the angels, and not of carnal men nor by curious minds. God is sufficient to them. . . . Jesus Christ, without wealth or any exterior work of science, is in his Order of holiness. He made no invention, he did not reign; but he was

* "Pensées", 277–8.

† Quoted from Brunschvicg's edition of Pascal's "Pensées et Opuscules", p. 458, footnote.

humble, patient, holy, holy in God's sight, terrible to devils, sinless. Oh! in what pomp he came, in what a vast magnificence, as seen by those eyes of the heart which discern wisdom."*

So the voice would run on, causing me to raise my eyes, until the three Orders stood before the mind like the peaks of three hills, one green and grateful; the next brown, yet beckoning; the last and highest snow-clad, but with such a radiant glow upon it as one sometimes sees at sunset. Pascal, however, had not stopped speaking; and, after I had looked for a little at the hills, he would regain my full attention.

"There are those", he would perhaps be saying, "who can only admire carnal grandeurs, as if there were no intellectual ones, and others who admire only intellectual ones, as if there were not others infinitely higher in the region of wisdom. All material bodies, the sky, the stars, the earth and its kingdoms, are not worth the lowest mind, for it is cognisant of all that and of itself as well, whilst matter knows nothing. All bodies together, and all minds together, and all their products are not worth the least motion of charity; for it is of an order infinitely superior."†

Was Pascal still sticking to the facts, as his method demanded, or was he mesmerising me with the magic of his style ? "Le style, c'est l'homme même." Was there, then, really this order of charity, or had he conjured it up out of the flame of his desire ? Men appeared to deceive themselves, as well as others, to such an extent that it was hard to rid any testimony completely from suspicion. I am not thinking of the Tartuffes and the Pecksniffs whose hypocrisy is nothing, as the famous aphorism reminds us, but a tribute of vice to virtue. What was intriguing was the unconscious intellectual insincerity of many a professed unbeliever who would sometimes act as if things, which he doubted or disclaimed or denied, were true, and so appear more Christian than Christians themselves. These intellectual freaks so persisted in taking the side of the angels as to remind me of Sir Anthony Absolute's memorable rejoinder, when debating the subject of education with Mrs. Malaprop, that she showed herself a truly moderate and polite arguer, since every third word she said was on his side of the question. The sceptics whom I had in mind seemed to bring no logic at all

* "Pensées", 793. I have used a little freedom in translating, in some faint hope of catching the English idiom.   † "Pensées", 793.

to bear upon their conduct of life, and would even renounce their goods and sacrifice their lives, as if they were fully convinced that they had treasure in heaven. Charming sentimentalists, they had apparently parted company with the facts of life as they professed to know them; and their philosophy contradicted their science at every turn. One could but salute them in passing for showing so much heart when they had so little mind.

Pascal, however, was clearly no eccentric of this kind. His soul moved on the most logical and lucid lines; and what he believed he acted upon with startling precision. To doubt his complete intellectual consistency was out of the question. All that he did, all that he became in the last years of his life, postulated precisely the existence of this order of charity of which he wrote so eloquently. The conclusion of his course, as traced by the hand of the curé de St. Étienne du Mont, who attended him in his latter days, suggested, in fact, some such development of the soul as the works of St. John of the Cross, with their sublime, unearthly music, have made familiar of late to many curious enquirers; and this would be quite in keeping with his admiration for the holiness of heart, independence of mind and submission of will which he himself noted in St. John's compatriot and contemporary, St. Teresa.* It seemed reasonable to interpret the charitable sale of his effects—of his silver and carriage, his tapestries and furniture—as the act of a traveller whose spirit, just as St. John's mystical symbolism demands, had stolen out of its mortal dwelling, whilst its desires lay slumbering, through the dark night of sense, and so found means to follow the pilgrim's way of the saints, into the darker night of the soul. Also, though not unaware of the Catholic's right of conscience to appeal in the last resort to the tribunal of Jesus Christ,† he made in that final phase his full peace with the Church on the vexed question of Jansen's orthodoxy.

I had tried to understand, if only from a great way off, how all this might come about in correspondence with the inmost truth of things. One point at least Pascal had made clear. One must expect everything that one was seeking—no matter whether it were God or love or the meaning of history—to be concealed. It had even come to seem to me quite unreasonable to expect anything else in a world so plainly stricken and so obviously mysterious.

* "Pensées", 499, 866, 917.

† *Ibid.*, 920. Cp. Newman's Letter to the Duke of Norfolk ("Difficulties of Anglicans Considered").

Somewhere in Froude's life of Carlyle there occurs a passage where the biographer records a conversation between the sage and himself in which the former, discoursing on the subject of God and suffering, exclaims, with an exceeding bitter cry which the hearer could never forget, that God does nothing. Pascal, I thought, would have asked for no better illustration of his own remark that "One can know well enough that there is a God without knowing what he is",* and might well have gone on to dismiss the wisdom of Chelsea, like the philosophy of the Cartesians, as 'useless and uncertain'.† Deism, and even theism, as he thought, did nothing to lift the veil of the temple or discover to view the unknown god. And that surprised him the less that he was in general distrustful of philosophers and inclined to suspect that they were in search of admiration and had in proportion lost competence for communion with God. Knowledge of God, he would say, without knowledge of one's own misery, made for pride; knowledge of one's own misery without knowledge of God made for despair.‡ Thus in the hour of illumination he had specifically acclaimed 'the God of Abraham, of Isaac and of Jacob, not of the philosophers and the men of learning'. For only such a God was really alive and could inspire both hope and fear. Love would suffer no less. "Love, like fire," says La Rochefoucauld, whose maxims I had come to look upon as the world's commentary on and confirmation of Pascal's thoughts, "cannot continue without continuous movement and ceases to live once it ceases to hope or fear."§ Yet, as the same keen analyst remarks, "If there is a pure love, exempt from admixture with our other passions, it is that which is hidden at the root of the heart".‖ Of these things Pascal was fully aware; and they reduced the god of the philosophers to an abstraction. Natural reason could provide the thought of God, but only the secret sanctuary of the heart could give Him a real personality.

Intellectually ruthless, as was the way with him, Pascal would therefore make game of the rationalist's shortness of thought. There is mystery, he would reiterate, at every terminus of thought—mystery so deep that our human minds cannot fathom it anywhere; the mystery of number where we lose ourselves in the consideration of the infinitely great and the infinitely little; the mystery of antithesis through which we can only find our way, so to say, negatively, by 'regarding as true only those things the contrary of which seem to us

* "Pensées", 233.   † *Ibid.*, 78.   ‡ *Ibid.*, 527.
§ "Maximes", 75.   ‖ *Ibid.*, 69.

to be certainly false';* the mystery of error (and it was thus that he would in a manner obviate Kant's transcendental scepticism) that comes, not of matter nor from the nature of things, but of mental defect in ourselves. Here lay part of the blight fallen upon man when he fell, and hence it was difficult for us to see things as they really are. Nevertheless, as he would insist, everyone is driven to act upon some assumption; and, therefore, however unwilling or sceptical one might be, one had in practice to lay a wager for or against the truth of religion. He had become himself so much a creature of spirit that for him there could be no question where to place his bet. It astonished him the more, therefore, to see the worldling backing the wrong horse and putting his money on the things that were visible and vain, rather than on those that were invisible but to his eyes so much more real. St. Paul did not deride the calculations of the god-less with greater vigour, when he accused them of saying "Let us eat, drink and be merry, for tomorrow we die".

As the words came to mind, I could have fancied they brought with them some mocking echo of the Alien Voice lingering still among the ruins of the stricken House and carried to my ears by vagrant breezes. So strong, indeed, was fact or fancy that I could have shaped my account of this adventure of ideas to fit the likeness of that scene where Childe Roland comes to the Dark Tower, and all the hills around reverberate to the sound of a bell tolling ever more loudly for the souls of the lost, whilst between the hills the dying sunset kindles with eerie light. But Pascal's soul seemed to ride on into the twilight with all Childe Roland's fearlessness and, as he reached the spot where men must make their venture to win or lose it all, his intellect seemed clearer than limpid water and his thoughts to shine like stars reflected in its depths.

* "De L'Esprit Géométrique."

Chapter XI

TWILIGHT

IT may be presumptuous, in a world so preoccupied with devastation both spiritual and material as our own, to say so, but I doubt whether any other poet before or since has reflected the impression of waste land more effectually than Robert Browning in his description of Childe Roland's ride to the Dark Tower. And, if that record of wild country, twilight quest and dauntless challenge does not serve to convey some idea of Pascal as he came to grips with the powers of evil, I know of no other that will. He had stopped at no half-way houses, such as afford deists or agnostics lodgings for the night, on his way. He was too subtle not to see that the ultimate issue of the conflict, when it is pressed home, must turn on the person of Christ: and he made straight for the mystery of evil, in full assurance that it could be matched only by the mystery of Jesus. I supposed that he had marked Browning's 'hoary cripple' or the like of him, posted at the crossways and pointing down the track that led off the main road to the Dark Tower, and had read in his 'malicious eye' all the world's amusement at anyone so temerarious as to court the only adventure in life that appeared to be certainly worth while. But neither saturnine old age nor cripple's crutch would ever have held Pascal back from this emprise. The not inconsiderable resources of his own derision seemed hardly to suffice him when he spoke of those who sought 'de faire le brave contre Dieu'; * for to his eye inconsequence and cowardice could no farther go. So, as I say, he had to me the air of one pricking across the waste land after the manner of a knight with wisdom in his wallet and temerity at his sword-point, and, when he came to blow the slug-horn at the gate of the Dark Tower, he might have been sounding one of the last trumpets, so clear was the note of finality, so calm the note of confidence.

"Before entering upon the evidence of the Christian religion"—in such terms Pascal couched his challenge—"I find it necessary to show the injustice of the men who do not trouble to seek the truth of a thing that is so important to them and touches them so nearly. Of all their mistakes it is beyond doubt this which convicts them

* "Pensées, 194.
219

most of folly and blindness and wherein it is easiest to confound them
by the first opinions of common sense and by the sentiments of
nature. For it is indisputable that the time of this present life is
but an instant and that the state of death, of whatever nature it
may be, is eternal. From this it follows that all our actions and
thoughts require to take such different roads according to the condition of this eternity as to render it impossible to make a move
with sense and judgment unless one adjusts it to the truth of a
consideration which ought to be our ultimate object. There is
nothing so clear as that; and therefore, according to reasonable
principles, men's conduct is altogether unreasonable, if they take
another course. Judge, then, thereby the case of those who live
without thinking of their last end, who follow their inclinations
and their pleasures without reflection or anxiety and, as if they
could annihilate eternity by withdrawing their thought from it,
do not seek happiness except in the present moment. Yet eternity
subsists; and death, which threatens them perpetually, must infallibly
put them in a short time under the horrible necessity of being
eternally annihilated or being eternally unhappy without knowing
which of these eternities is preparing for them. . . . To repose in
this ignorance is a monstrous thing, the extravagance and stupidity
of which ought to be brought home to the perpetrators by confounding them with the sight of their folly." There followed close upon
this challenge a sharp sword-thrust, "These people lack heart".* It
was the unkindest cut of all, and went deepest. The sarcasm was
savage, but the core of the question, even if there were no heart in
the hearer, had been reached.

"What reason", Pascal would pursue with caustic energy, "have
atheists to say that one cannot rise again? Which is more difficult,
birth or resurrection, the coming into being of that which has never
been, or the revival of that which has been? . . . What have they
to say against the resurrection or the Virgin-birth? Is it more difficult
to produce a man or animals, or to reproduce them? And, if they
had never seen one kind of animal, could they divine whether it was
generated by association or not? How I hate these stupidities—not
believing in the Holy Eucharist and so forth? If the Gospel is true,
if Jesus Christ is God, what difficulty is there?" †

The quality of Pascal's mind was such that it found its way without effort through all the armour of sense to the heart of the problem,
or, as in the summing up of an inexorable judge, threw into strong

* "Pensées", 195, 196.   † *Ibid.*, 222–4.

relief the outstanding issue of fact upon which everything else depended. The deity of Christ, there lay the vital point; the resurrection of Christ, there was the essential issue. Christ, indeed, had not left in any doubt the place of these matters in an adequate criticism of life. He had asked His disciples: "Who do men say that I am?", and immediately after: "But who do you say that I am?" And, with that question answered, He had constituted His apostles' witnesses in the first place to an event.

It was thus, as always with Pascal, a fact rather than a theory that had to be dealt with; and here a fact of history in opposition to a theory of physical science. In other words, a miracle had to be proved against those who argued à priori that 'miracles don't happen'. The theory made no appeal to Pascal as a scientist. Like T. H. Huxley long after, he saw that the physical world was too full of wonders to make any wonder impossible; and he would readily have endorsed the opinion of a recent Gifford lecturer that the whole world was alive with miracle at every turn. But men have tended from the first to prefer a familiar assumption to an attested fact; and the fact had to be insisted upon to confound the theorists. It was not, of course, as he saw things, a fact that should be expected, so to say, to spring to the eye. God was always for him a God who hid Himself from the eyes of the curious, the proud and the profane. It was never God's habit to compel continuous attention. One would understand nothing of the works of God if one did not take it as a general principle that it was His will to let some men be blinded and to enlighten others.* "Nature had such perfections as to show the image of God and such defects as to show that it was only the image."† So Pascal had warned me in words calculated to explain both the ambiguity of nature and the cecity of man. The truth of God, as he observed, was not just to be had for mental satisfaction. So conceived, it would become no more than an idol. The heart had to be associated with the mind in the order of charity; for the idea of God, dissociated from the idea of love, fell short of truth.‡ It could not be coldly conceived.

I felt that Pascal was forcing me back upon that old simile of truth which I had found for myself in a game of bowls. Charity was as the bias in a bowl, without taking account of which it would never roll in true to the jack. Let it be added, lest the simile should seem too trivial, that the bowl to my eye became as a golden bowl, capable of being broken, but, whilst intact, symbolic of life moving with a

* "Pensées", 566.   † *Ibid.*, 580.   ‡ *Ibid.*, 581–2.

greater power of thought and feeling than I should otherwise have deemed possible. Pascal had merely taught me, by means of his order of charity, in what way exactly love could place itself, as one that serveth, at the disposal of truth.

Subtle at its best beyond imagination, yet, even when grossly conceived, a cupid dodging the eye and darting his arrows without warning, this impalpable essence could never be denied its place in any realistic conception of human affairs. Pascal had perceived that; no man more clearly. "He who would know the full extent of man's vanity has but to consider the causes and effects of love. The cause of love is a 'je ne sais quoi', and its effects are terrifying. This 'je ne sais quoi', so trifling that one cannot even recognise it, moves everything—kings, arms, the entire world. The nose of Cleopatra— had it been shorter, the whole face of the earth would have been changed." *

'Cherchez la femme'—it seemed, then, to come pretty nearly to that, and so to scatter all the dry-as-dusts of history like the keen wind of March. If the face of woman had the power to launch a thousand ships or change the course of events, what prepotency must not the genius of her soul possess? What chance had the spirit of geometry, though fortified by a whole arsenal of statistics, against the subtle magic of this strange, incalculable force? Who so dull as to doubt the substantial truth of the first great scene in the drama of human history? "The woman gave me of the tree . . . and I did eat." Take Eve away; and we should have another "Hamlet" without the Prince of Denmark in the cast.

Was it not, then, to be expected that a woman should also require to be found at the consummation of human history, and a woman full of grace? Was Mary less obvious to a fine understanding than Eve in the general body of knowledge? Foolish, as Pascal urged, though the doctrine of original sin must appear to the wise of this world, whose sweet reasonableness was evidently impaired by its presence, it appeared to be indispensable to any real comprehension of the present condition of man which hung upon this imperceptible point.† The mind of Mary had recovered by its humility and purity what the mind of Eve had cast away by its curiosity and impatience; and the theme of Cleopatra had thus been, as it were, surpassed, transfigured and returned for the consideration of the historian. A dream fairer than Helen's face had launched myriad ships now sailing the world's sea. Dante had, of course, set out this theme with

* "Pensées", 162.   † *Ibid.*, 445.

a beauty which knows no equal in poetry of man's making. Beatrice, just as she leaves him at the mountain pass of heaven, speaks of the 'pure light, light intellectual, and full of love' that lies ahead of him; and the words are as the commendation of a spirit by heavenly wisdom to the care of Mary's diviner grace. A moment later, in the form of a river flowing between banks aglow with all the wonder of spring, Dante perceives the light that Beatrice spoke of; and it suffuses an understanding, already sublime, with finer powers of vision. He perceives at last, white and mystical as the petals of some radiant rose, the spirits of just men made perfect; whilst angels, like bees, climb and descend again the lovely flower. One of these roving ministers of sweetness seems incandescent with the living flame of love. It is Gabriel, singing the 'Ave Maria' with his eyes fixed on her who, as St. Bernard, standing by, declares, alone has strength to fit the human mind for the sight of her Son. Then, as if in contemplation lost, the Saint observes that, if there were any that would have grace yet not through her, they were as men that sought to fly without wings. Thus did Dante pass up the last steps of the ladder of life into the courts of Heaven.*

Pascal, however, thought in aphorisms and not in lyrics. But, if before his inward vision there flowed no river of light, throwing up from the depths of its mobile waters a rain of gems that fell like rubies into the golden flowers of heaven's springtide, he looked ever, as it seemed to me, into a crystal pool where the full face of history was mirrored and where in the bed below there lay, white and lovely, a pearl of great price worth the whole world's ransom. I could even fancy that the air above the silence of those still waters was full of sweet sounds; that David could be heard there touching his harp-strings to make music for Pascal's recitation of his much-loved one hundred and eighteenth psalm, and the son of David causing his great canticle of love to soar like a skylark's song into the supersensuous air. Yet Pascal never forgot that the God he sought was one who hid Himself; that things could be visible to us only through a glass and darkly; and that in the very consciousness of mystery lay the making of man. A numinous haze, obscurely bright, spread over the vast campagna of his thoughts and, as one has put it in words I dare not tamper with by translation, 'mieux que devant une realité imposée, achevée, concrète, l'esprit aime à s'exalter et à rêver devant le chaos des Pensées de Pascal ou les ruines du Colisée'.† Pascal's was in

* "Parad.", XXX to XXXIII.
† Maxime van der Meersch, "L'empreinte de Dieu", p. 221.

fact an artistry beyond the reach of art for art's sake, beyond the reach of anything but truth rooted and grounded in love—or so, at least, it seemed to me in the hours when, so far as one could judge, one's faculties were at their best.

In one of Carlyle's essays there is a reflection upon the blindness of Tacitus to the supreme event of the era that he has so brilliantly portrayed. Subtle and searching historian as in many respects he was, he records the fact that one, Christus, had lived and died and left behind a body of disciples, with a nonchalance worthy of Pilate as drawn by Anatole France, in perhaps the most telling of all his tales.* Though time enough had passed to make truth easy to attain, if only there had been love enough to give light to the eyes, Tacitus had not the faintest suspicion of what was already apparent to the inferior mind of Josephus—that in Christ he might have to do with something more than man. Centuries before Carlyle was born Pascal had commented on the blindness of these two eminent historians.† Thus could 'le mystère de Jésus' escape the historian's eye, even when that eye was as keen as that of Ernest Renan; and the outstanding figure of all time be still presented as a deceiver or a self-deceiver, an eccentric gentleman, a poetic dreamer, or an amiable philanthropist, according to the taste of scribe or pharisee or philistine at work upon the portrait. One had to reckon with this curious preternatural blindness in respect of spiritual things.

Such lapses were unimaginable in Pascal. His mind, with its sure grasp of salient facts, seized as easily upon Christ's place in history as upon the mystery of Christ's personality, and grasped with equal power the psychological background and the historical event. None had seen more clearly that the weak things of the world had in the case of Christianity confounded the things that were mighty; and none had recognised more quickly that a psychological explanation, adequate to the historical magnitude of this phenomenon, had to be looked for. The objectivity of events must, in other words, be met and matched by the subjectivity of selection, and the spirit of geometry transcended by the spirit of finesse. Only so can that 'provinciality' of which Prof. Whitehead ‡ has accused modern writers of history be avoided. Facts, whatever persons claiming to be impersonal may choose to maintain, are no more free and equal than men themselves. Some are outstanding, some hide their force; some that were once thought mighty are in time deposed from

* "Le Procurateur de Judée", in "L'Étui de Nacre".
† "Pensées", 786–7.   ‡ "Adventures of Ideas", p. 4.

their seats. Everywhere the spirit of finesse is needed to estimate them aright.

To a mind attentive to the seemingly weak things of the world there was no difficulty in looking for the last word upon life to the tiny state inhabited sixteen centuries before Pascal's time by a people evidently gifted with a rare and singular genius, yet, as their own historians were never tired of testifying, curiously wanting in constancy to the God whom they worshipped and acclaimed as an unique power making for righteousness. It was only, however, as one continued to gaze at Judea, that one's eye became riveted by the fact that this locality seemed to be situated at the very focus of humane ideas during their most critical, most adventurous conjunction. Behind it lay the Orient, where tradition and research tended alike to place the nativity of homo sapiens and whence in the pregnant sixth century before Christ there had sprung the three most influentially wise men of the East—the Buddha, Lao-Tse and Confucius, kings of thought and leaders in religion. Then, to one side of it lay Egypt with its dark sense of immortality; and to the other side Greece, clear shining with its humanism, its exquisite sense of proportion, and, in a word, its pagan grace. Finally, to the West, beyond Homer's wine-dark seas, rose the hills of Latium, pregnant with an ordered civilisation of which the pagan world brought forth none greater in the plenitude of its majesty and power, nor any so moving in the pathos of its decline and fall. The idea of chance did not seem equal to sustain all this conjunction of circumstance—or at least it was too hard for Pascal's scientific soul to suppose so. He saw, as Dean Church was one day to phrase it, that Christianity was a harder thing to explain, if it were not, than if it were, true. He recognised that in Christ he had to deal with a manifestation of Humanity that beggared all comparison and with a claim to allegiance that rendered all other pretensions no better than those of thieves and robbers.

The most modest acquaintance with the science of comparative religions seemed enough to establish Pascal's position. A 'way'—even in one or two cases a mystic way—was indeed indicated by Asian teachers; but where were truth and life? Not surely in the creed of the Buddha, who found life so full of pain that man's best hope was to lose all desire, if not all consciousness, in the calm of nirvana, whatever that term might exactly signify. Not in the words of Lao-tse, though he had fine things to say about the making of a contemplative and the hidden spirituality of the Being to be contemplated. "We look for Him and see Him not, for He is in-

visible. We listen for Him and hear Him not, for He is inaudible.
We grope after Him and grasp Him not, for He cannot be grasped."*
Not in the positivism of Confucius, since he admonished his followers that, as life was incomprehensible, it was useless to ask questions about death. Nor again in the theology of Zoroaster, where
gods of good and evil contended on equal terms, though apparently
without producing the utter chaos which might have been expected
to follow.

These doctors, it was plain, were of the number of those with
whom, if one were young enough, one might have great argument
and yet evermore come out by the same door wherein one went.
All that such conferences made clear was the perpetual demand
of man for religion in some shape or another and the numerous
sources of supply that existed to meet the demand. Socrates,
with his subtle irony and sublime ignorance, afforded more conviction than the rest in respect of the truth of his conclusions, such
as they were. One could not doubt that he emerged from all his
logomachy on the side of the angels; that his death, if not also his
life, contained a confession of other-worldliness; and that, in a word,
he had superimposed upon or substituted for the sophistical tendency of the Greek genius in philosophy something to which Bergson
has given the name of 'l'attitude du sage'.† "The question is"—to
quote the same searching critic—"to know exactly what this very
practical genius would have done . . . if the Greek that he was had
not checked in him the Oriental that he wished to be." ‡ Under his
influence the Greek soul (to retain the Bergsonian terminology) was
on the way to exchange 'la morale close' for 'la morale ouverte',
which at length found full expression in the Sermon on the Mount.
Even Platonism could not take the step needed to pass from a mixed
society of bondsmen and freemen to the liberty of the sons of God.
"One had to wait for Christianity before the idea of universal
fraternity, implying equality of rights and inviolability of the person,
could become active." § The Chinese, the Stoics, and Socrates himself had pointed that way. Yet "their formulae were those of an ideal
conceived, and conceived perhaps as unrealisable".¶ Christianity,
building after the design of which Judaism had traced the outline in
the Messianic monarchy, had produced a city of God, super-national
because it was supernatural and, therewith, a new urbanity unknown

---

* Quoted from O. Karrer, "Religions of Mankind", p. 38.
† "Les Deux Sources", p. 60.
‡ *Ibid.*, p. 61.   § *Ibid.*, p. 77.   ¶ *Ibid.*, p. 77.

before. It was the personal element in Christianity that had effected this. At the heart of the Christian polity lay the undying life of its Founder. A patriotism wide as the world was sustained by a loyalty beyond the touch of time.

Pascal's presentation of the mystery of Jesus was consonant with such considerations. "Tout vient à point à qui sait attendre." There comes a time in every complete intellectual development when the questions 'What think ye of Christ? Whose son is He?', 'Who do you say that I am?', 'Why do you call me good?' become inescapable and can no longer be put off by the cloudy evasions of the sentimentalist or the latitudinarian. The Gospels showed that Christ had early pressed the dual nature in His person upon those about Him. The distress that His mother discovered when He remained behind in Jerusalem could not be met by any plea of mere human obligation; nor was the authority that He assumed in the synagogue to be easily vindicated by any credentials of man's giving. The mystery of His being would suffer no simplification which left Him a moral man, but deluded; a model man, but a megalomaniac.

So much might be gathered from the brief account that we have of those moments when Christ stood at the bar of this world's judgment. Caiaphas, the Jew, had cried blasphemy; but Pilate, the Roman, whether or not he jested to cover his confusion at silences or replies more searching than his interrogatories, so little disputed the prisoner's sanity as to stress His innocence. "I find no fault in this man," he told the Jews and proceeded to insist with powerful irony upon the recognition of the prisoner's claim to be the Jewish sovereign. He had chanced upon something that he did not really understand and, unless appearances are greatly at fault, he knew it.

Pascal, asking the same question as Pilate, "What is truth?" and perceiving how cunningly truth hides itself behind seeming contradictions from the diseased eyes of men, had declared, after Augustine, that one only arrives at truth by charity.* Truth was to be had for the seeking, but not for the asking. Most of all was this elusiveness of truth to be anticipated when one reached the core of the world's mystery. A book, as he put it, had been thrust into the hands of the Jewish scribes; but, when they turned to read it, they could not make it out.† Their carnal mind was at such enmity with God that they could not see Him in their midst, though they had been consciously

---

* "De L'Esprit Géométrique." Cp. S. Augustine's 'Non intratur in veritatem nisi per caritatem' (Contra Faustum Lib. XXXII, cap. xviii).

† "Pensées", 737.

awaiting One who would inaugurate the reign of righteousness. This blindness of the Jews in the midst of light had impressed Pascal profoundly. He could see clearly the full force of the double entente in Messianic prophecy; and he declared that anyone, with no more than eight days left him of life, and therefore presumably disposed to take life seriously, must see at least that here probability told against the presence of chance.* For the evidence of the expectation of a Messiah was overwhelming. "It is a whole people", he would cry, "which announces it." † And, as he sketched in the long course of Messianic prophecy, it was hard indeed not to recognise that, whatever blending of the prophetic soul of a people with the dream of a Saviour there had been and whether the prophecies of Daniel had been put into shape in the days of Nebuchadnezzar or of Antiochus Epiphanes, there had been shadowed forth through the chiaroscuro of visions, sublime as they were beautiful, the likeness of one godlike, gracious, suffering and strong, beyond any imagination in all these points of the sons of men. That was as obvious in the twenty-second psalm as in the fifty-third chapter of Isaiah; and no identification either with the Hebrew people or the Hebrew monarchs, both of them so unfavourably depicted as a general rule by their prophets and chroniclers, satisfied the allusions contained there. So intelligent an anticipation of events or estimate of occasions might have provoked the envy of the most astute journalist or attracted the attention of the most sagacious statesman. Even though repetition had long dulled the significance of the dark speeches from Israel's harp, yet still, in listening to Pascal's talk, the marvel of it all would return to startle and amaze. The regeneration of the sense of wonder was not, perhaps, after all, so far beyond our reach as we sometimes supposed. They say that, not long ago, at a congress of modern philosophers, there were two present who took occasion to declare how, when they first read the Gospels somewhat later in life than most of us, they became convinced of Christ's divinity; and this, not because He fulfilled their own ideal of supreme goodness, but because His goodness so outstripped any previous conception they possessed of the good as to show them for the first time what moral perfection meant.‡ The incident tells in favour of the superiority of a historical to any metaphysical demonstration of perfection. Man at his best can recognise the Perfect intuitively in an incarnation, whereas it dissolves rationally into endless disputations.

* "Pensées", 694.   † *Ibid.*, 711.
‡ M. D'Arcy's, "God and the Universe", pp. 132–3.

It was characteristic of Pascal that there was no part of the Gospel drama, or at least of its Passion play, which so discovered to him the divine perfection of the hero as the garden-scene at Gethsemane. "Who taught the Evangelists", he would say, "the qualities of a soul perfectly heroic, so as to paint it to perfection in Jesus Christ? Why do they make Him weak in His agony? Do they not know how to paint constancy in death? Yes, for St. Luke himself paints that of St. Stephen as bolder than that of Jesus Christ. They make Christ capable of fear before the need for dying has come, and then utterly courageous. But, when they show Him in distress, it is because He distresses Himself; whilst when men distress Him, He is courage itself." * There was matter indeed at Gethsemane for unexampled distress, unless Christian theology were strangely at fault. Perfection was about to make the closest contact it has ever made with evil: immortal being to endure the pains of death: the Lamb of God to atone for the sin of the world. Here was matter, then, for an agony beyond the reach of man's imagination. "Nowhere perhaps", says one with a high title to an opinion, "does the unique and incomparable character of Christianity break out in a manner more profoundly touching. Here were concentrated upon a real person the most exalted and universal feelings in the heart of man—its spirit of renunciation and its spirit of charity." † If that be so, then the power to appreciate Pascal's "Mystère de Jésus" may well afford as searching a test as we have of the modern man's capacity of apprehending perfection when it is shown him.

"Jesus", Pascal would say as he recreated the scene, "is in a garden, not of delight like the first Adam who lost himself and all mankind besides, but in a garden of suffering where He saves Himself and all the human race with Him. . . . In His Passion He suffers the torments that men inflict on Him, but in the Agony those that He gives Himself. It is suffering from no human, but from an all-powerful hand, and one must be all-powerful to endure it. He turns for some comfort to His closest friends, but they slumber; He prays them to support Him a little, and they leave Him utterly neglected—alone with the wrath of God. He is alone upon earth, not merely the only one who feels and partakes of His grief, but who knows of it: only the Heavens and Himself are aware of what is happening. He suffers this pain and abandonment in the horror of night. I think Jesus never gave expression to His grief except this once, but then He expressed Himself as if He could no

* "Pensées", 800.   † Brunschvicg's note on Pensée 553.

longer restrain His extreme distress: 'My soul is sorrowful to the point of death'. Jesus will be in agony till the end of the world: one must not sleep at such a time as that."

"In agony till the end of the world!"—the continuation of the event at Calvary, the abiding presence of Christ in the Sacrament, was never more subtly suggested than by that poignant sentence. It was just like Pascal to start kindling the altar candles for the coming Mass of the Eucharist whilst in the twilight, as the office of Tenebrae advanced, the lights of the world were seen, one by one, to be going out. But suddenly he would seem to pause and ponder, as if a thought of great profundity had struck him. "If God", he would say, "give us rulers, with what loyalty we must obey them. Necessity and events are infallibly that." Then, as if the Figure, whose grace of suffering had made His deity so clear, had marked the soul watching Him in His pain and made answer to its thoughts, there followed some words of memorable beauty and supreme consolation: "Be comforted; you would not seek Me, had you not found Me already. I was thinking of you in My agony, I have shed drops of blood on your account. . . . Let yourself be guided by My rules; see how well I have led the Blessed Virgin and the Saints who let Me act in them. . . . I am more your friend than this man or that; for I have done more for you than they, and they would not suffer what I have suffered from you, nor die for you in the time of your infidelities and cruelties as I have done, and am ready to do, and do do in My elect and in the Blessed Sacrament."

One had not to wait for Pascal's reply—"Lord, I give you all"— to be sure that for him the inescapable wager had been made in the Garden at Gethsemane rather than beside the Empty Tomb. His evidential assurance of the Resurrection was, as will presently be seen, all that it could be; yet it was clear that the die had been cast on the earlier occasion. Thus he might almost be said to have made the venture from which the timid disciples had fled, to have courted the blessing belonging to those who have not seen and yet have believed, and, if the metaphor may pass, to have made his wager with the jewels of faith and love rather than with the coin or counters of reason and will.

In the same hour in which he wrote "The Mystery of Jesus", Pascal had, as it seemed, for the second time struck the mystic way and seen all the wonder of it. His artist's vision of Gethsemane, lost in gloom yet with high lights falling on the Angel of the Agony, the symbolic chalice of pain and the bowed figure of the Suffering

God, invested the dark night of the soul with a significance so vivid and detailed as to make the world's taunt—justified, perhaps, in respect of some other Asian mysteries—that mysticism is but mistiness, look curiously absurd. No one, perhaps, with the grace and genius of that garden-scene full in view, could doubt its proffer of an adventure in thought and life compared to which that of a Columbus must seem trivial and that of a Socrates trite. "From no material thing—earth or empire or starry sphere—" as Pascal put it, "can one draw one little thought, nor from all matter and mind, one motion of charity! It is an impossibility. Charity lies in the order of supernatural things."*

There is an hour, following close in the order of logic upon the disappearance of the physical world behind enigmas of energy, when the consideration of life in physical or metaphysical or mathematical terms seems all alike a cheat. It is then that the mind, be it ancient as Plato's or modern as Bergson's, resorts to myth or turns to mysticism rather than surrender to the mocking suggestion that it is, after all, in no better case than the blind man in the dark room hunting for the object that is not there. It is then that it begins to substitute graces once little prized for faculties too greatly trusted. It is then that the fading memory seems ready to lose itself in radiant hope, the clear understanding to clasp the hand of kindly faith, and the good will to become possessed by burning love. It is then perceived, to borrow the words of one who has been idly named a 'professor of nothingness', that while "sense cannot grasp or attain to more than the accident . . . the spirit, purged of the clouds and species of accident, penetrates the truth and worth of things, for this is its object".† It is then that the way of perfection, along which, as the same Spanish mystic declares,‡ the spirit of man was carried at God's swift pace in baptism, opens out before the eye like the long stages of a road adapted to man's slow endeavour—stages for which no more adequate figure has ever been found than that of a bridal procession moving at foot's pace from the betrothal to the consummation of the spiritual marriage. Then, but not before, does it become plain that the dark night of Gethsemane was indeed no time for sleeping, but the immortal hour of all Mortality's romance. Then, but not before, is the secret significance of the search for perfection, set in the heart of man, yet so often rendered ridiculous by man's

* "Pensées", 793.
† St. John of the Cross, "Ascent of Mount Carmel", Bk. 3, Chap. XX.
‡ *Ibid.*, "Spiritual Canticle". Commentary on Stanza 23.

insensate vanity, made plain, and with such cogency that one must either flee or follow.

Some acquaintance, however inadequate, with Christian mysticism appeared, thus, to be essential to any historian who sought to assess Christ's place in history; and it is to the credit of a high master in the school of modern sceptical criticism that he has frankly faced the fact. "To understand the thought of Jesus", Goguel remarks, "one must have or make for oneself the soul of a Christian. Erudition is indispensable. But, where there is no more, something essential is wanting. The Jesus that erudition elaborated alone would not be the true Jesus." * Such an opinion went a long way towards admitting the old claim of the Church to be the true interpreter of the Gospel; but, however that might be, it was certainly in line with Pascal's insistence on the spirit of finesse in addition to the spirit of geometrical accuracy. Only an artist in Christianity, as the same writer perceives,† could be expected to recognise, much more transmit, the moral dignity, the searching thought, the superb grace of the authentic portraits of Christ, just as only a Christian mystic could be expected to penetrate any distance behind the cloud of unknowing which hides the inner life of one claiming to be the true Light of the World. Thus the historian, intent upon rectitude in the perspective, value, and tone of his landscape and portrait, might reasonably feel that his ending must be despair unless relieved by orison and prayer.

Men being what they are, it was, of course, too much to expect that they should not subject a personality so unique as that of Christ to the utmost tests of critical ingenuity. Though few might be so presumptuously foolish as to suppose themselves capable of plumbing the depths of a soul so obviously superior to their own; yet few could fail to see that the whole moral standard of historical judgment was involved. To probe the matter to its foundations might at moments seem to be in no better taste than to peep and botanise about a grave; yet, since some minds are girt with triple brass and some feet will seek to scale the heights of heaven, the endeavour at its crudest could be understood, extenuated and excused. It was an investigation, moreover, that had not been discouraged by the subject of it. "Which of you convicteth Me of sin?" and "Why callest thou Me good?" were questions whose challenge had echoed down the ages.

* Goguel, "Vie de Jésus", I, p. 197.   † *Ibid.*, p. 263.

It was clear at a glance that the white robe of holiness refused all comparison with the shining armour of success. With those—and they were many—for whom the glories of blood and state appeared to be, not shadows, but substantial things, and for whom the line of the Caesars, from Julius to Napoleon and beyond, retained its charm, the old argument of Thrasymachus did not fail. With them justice remained the interest of the physically stronger. Love had picked up this glove, flung down upon the field of history, and tossed it contemptuously back again. In the duel each combatant had his own choice of weapons. Force armed itself with violence, Love with loving-kindness. Criticism could not hope to show that loving-kindness had failed, for that could only be settled at the end of time, but just to prove that Christ Himself had failed to manipulate His chosen arm to perfection. That was not very easy. "Son parfait idéalisme", Renan had observed of Jesus, "est la plus haute règle de la vie détachée et vertueuse. Il a créé le ciel des âmes pures, où se trouve ce qu'on demande en vain à la terre, la parfaite noblesse des enfants de Dieu, la sainteté accomplie, la totale abstraction des souillures du monde, la liberté enfin que la société réelle exclut comme une impossibilité et qui n'a toute son amplitude que dans le domaine de la pensée."*

Whilst all men's motives on every occasion can, of course, be debated, two incidents in the life of Christ had especially attracted the attention of critics—the destruction of the swine at Gadara after the exorcism of the demoniac, and the fate of the barren fig-tree. The former, as the subject of a memorable duel between Gladstone and T. H. Huxley, had perhaps been as much discussed in England as any act recorded in the Gospels. A dispassionate spectator of those crossing swords might perhaps have been tempted to observe that, if one of the combatants appeared to be more than usually well acquainted with the counsels of the Almighty,† the latter was more than prudently confident of the weight of his agnosticism. "I repeat," Prof. Huxley observed, "without the slightest fear of refutation, that the four Gospels, as they have come down to us, are the work of unknown writers." ‡ That was written in 1889; during the reign of Baur and Strauss and before the advent of Harnack. Men

* "Les Apôtres", p. xliv.
† The phrase is borrowed—perhaps, as a friend suggests, from Lowes Dickinson.
‡ T. H. Huxley, "Essays upon some Controverted Questions", p. 340, footnote.

less knowledgeable than Gladstone or less sceptical than Huxley might well, then, have paused before attempting to assess the significance of the obscure event at Gadara. On the confines of a world (as Gladstone would have said) unseen, and (as Huxley would have added) unknown, one had great need of caution. Huxley's ethics, moreover, show in the retrospect some signs—to borrow a convenient colloquialism—of 'dating'. They presuppose a somewhat higher regard for private property than in general obtains to-day: for, putting aside altogether the question whether the Gadarenes, if they were Jews, had any business to be owning swine, the liberation of a human soul from bondage and of a district from a madman would appear to be a first charge upon a philanthropist. A disciple of Mill might, perhaps, deplore the loss of so many porcine carcases, but, as Gladstone shrewdly observes, the fact that "the Gadarenes should have done no more than ask for our Saviour's departure, affords of itself the strongest presumption that the action in which He co-operated, and which was certainly detrimental, was not illegal." * All said and done, it is idle to argue with a physician over the cost of a cure, unless one is oneself in a position to effect it at a cheaper rate. There is no reason to suppose that the demoniac would have remained anything but a demoniac if Professor Huxley had been called in, whilst, on the basis of the facts as we have them, the locality was cleared of a curse and the man of a disease by the sacrifice of a few animals of a kind that we habitually consume.

If they had the look of being embarrassed for an argument who turned to the fate of the swine to find some flaw in a character long esteemed perfect, those who made much of the incident of the barren fig-tree fared even worse. Christ had chanced upon that showy yet slovenly shrub, already in leaf, though it was not the season of figs, in an hour when His mind must have been preoccupied by the failure of the Jews to respond to His mission. The fruit, like the land where it grew, had not been ripe for the day of its visitation. The sight provoked a comparison and invited a moral. Like a good husbandman, Christ condemned the tree for its worthlessness, and, like a great prophet, compelled it to serve the claims of parable. The fig-tree, so it is said, withered away after His visit. There was nothing in this to offend either the science of a horticulturist or the soul of a symbolist; yet, as all things can be turned to adverse account, if only one knows the trick of it, one militant rationalist

* Gladstone, "Later Gleanings: the Swine Miracle".

took occasion to compare the incident to Xerxes' celebrated chastisement of the sea.*

Beneath the reflections to which Christ's action in these two cases has given rise in the mind of the world lies hid significantly the suggestion that any association with or assent to destruction, even in respect of the animal and vegetable creations, is unworthy of a perfect man. So crudely disingenuous is the world, which, when convenient, ennobles and even glorifies the use of violence, not against beasts or plants, but against mankind, yet finds occasion, in estimating the character of Jesus, to animadvert upon the fate of a herd of swine destroyed or a rotten tree struck down!

Simple truth and honest thought will find their way through such perversities or, as some would say, profanities of criticism. But, though the action taken in both the cases considered above can be shown to be consistent with that which a good man might take in the circumstances, it needs, perhaps, the authority of One who could lay claim to be Lord over the animal and vegetable world to place the apology on a plane where its argument becomes unassailable. A Creator could evidently do what He would with His own, and a Redeemer what He pleased with a world irreparably ruined but for His intervention. Divinity, let alone Humanity, had thus ready its answer to criticism. Who art thou that answerest against God? Canst thou make Leviathan; and, if not, canst thou pass judgment on the use made of him and his kind? I was bold enough, however, to believe that Humanity could reply with no less effect that, as one grew (if one grew) more humane, any debatable features in the acts of Christ, like the debatable touches in a masterpiece, would fall into line with one's idea of humane perfection. The converse of this act of faith was to be found among Pascal's thoughts. "Not only", he declared, "do we only know God through Jesus Christ, but we only know ourselves through Jesus Christ." †
It was the judgment of a supreme connoisseur, a master in the spirit of finesse. It happens to endorse the judgment of that part of mankind which, humanly speaking, created the culture of Christendom.

In a manner not always clearly perceived, the moral perfection of Christ's character, if admitted, bears upon the decisive issue of the Resurrection. It can no longer be plausibly urged that it goes against all common experience that a man morally perfect should rise again

* Winwood Reade, "Martyrdom of Man", p. 191.   † "Pensées", 548.

from the dead, if in fact we have had none but men morally imperfect under observation. On the hypothesis of a divine incarnation and the presence in the world of a perfect man, there exists no law of nature to impede the free operation of human testimony. The evidence for the Resurrection, in other words, has to be taken on its own merits or, more accurately, on the merits of the witnesses. No predispositions are permissible, for no comparisons are valid. Hume's familiar argument against miracles, based on the notion that it is more probable that men are mistaken than that wonders occur, is thus put out of court at the very outset; and Hume's somewhat inconsistent thesis that, metaphysically speaking, nothing in the nature of cause and effect can be securely inferred from experience, restored to its place in thought. If no man had convicted Jesus of sin, there could exist no customary sequence to distract or deny our observation; and history could not be expected to repeat itself in conditions hitherto unknown.* The facts, unobscured by probability, would thus be absolutely at our disposal. If the apostles could not be discredited as men, they should have it all their own way as witnesses. Their testimony went, in fact, unchallenged by any natural law, and was the more worth considering that it might disclose a supernatural one.

Pascal as usual had gone straight to the point. "The hypothesis of the Apostles being cheats", he argued, "is very absurd. Consider its full implications. Suppose these dozen men assembled after Christ's death and plotting to declare that He had risen again. They would thereby be challenging powers of every kind. The human heart is oddly inclined to levity, change, promises, bribes. If one of them had been discredited by yielding to any of these attractions and, what is more, to imprisonment, torture or death, they were all lost men. Follow up that line of thought. The Apostles were either cheated or cheats. The former hypothesis is as hard to believe as the latter. It is not possible to make a mistake about a man's resurrection from the dead. Moreover, whilst Jesus Christ was with them, He could give them power of initiative; but, after He was gone, if He did not appear to them, who gave them character to act?" †

There, stated with precision, was the critics' dilemma; and even yet they find themselves impaled upon the horns of it. For, if the

---

* "What we want to know, if we are to write or read history," says Professor A. E. Taylor, "is not what a given man finds credible, but what we ought as rational beings to pronounce credible or incredible, and the philosopher of pure experience can give us no guidance here." ("Philosophic Studies No. IX—David Hume and the Miraculous.")   † "Pensées", 801–2 (freely translated).

Apostles perpetrated the fraud, their well-simulated corporate conviction is as hard to explain as the failure of their foes to confute or
confound them by the production of Christ's body; and, if they were
taken in by the Holy Women, it was only, by all accounts, after an
initial scepticism regarding the alleged event as contemptuous as
that of the critics themselves. According to Pascal's reading of the
nature of things, no man is compelled against his will, by the mere
pressure of facts, to believe in the religious truth of Christianity; but
in this matter of the Resurrection, once predispositions of any kind
in judging the evidence had been ruled out, it became uncommonly
difficult, historically speaking, not to believe. All things considered—
which is not always done—the attestation of the event was as good
as could possibly be expected. The Apostles were plain men, slow-
minded men, timorous men before the event, and fearless men after
it. Their number satisfied, perhaps even dictated, the requirements
which, in its considered wisdom, English law still imposes in
matters of life and death. They had, moreover, the advantage of
becoming eye-witnesses of the miracle, as well as of being jurymen
in respect of the event; whilst the essential point to be decided was
so straightforward as to need no judge to formulate it. It was quite
rational to wonder whether the verdict of a group of contemporary
scientists, had that been possible to obtain, would have carried
anything like so much weight at this distance of time as that of
the Twelve Apostles. Cleverness, it has to be remembered, is not
generally reckoned the best title to confidence. An expert, for one
thing, is not infrequently found to be at fault. And not only so,
but clever men have in general an unfortunate way of exciting dis-
trust in ordinary people, and it was for all sorts and conditions of
men that Christ professed to have come into the world. To ordinary
men, clever men appear, as the saying goes, too clever by half.
Their motives become open to doubt, and their integrity to suspicion. They are easily credited with low ambitions and hidden
designs. And then, later on, when they have been supplanted by a
younger generation of intellectuals, their methods of investigation
are apt to be pronounced defective and their conclusions to be
regarded as out of date. And so, one way or another, the testimony
that once seemed so unexceptionable comes to be dismissed as
inadequate, and the issue that once seemed decided is reopened anew
for discussion.

Had the Resurrection of Christ been attested by the Hebrew
sages of His time, it is as likely as not that this very circumstance

would have suggested to many minds the presence of a deep-laid plot against the Roman Government and the intention to substitute for the crucified Messiah an impostor—the Perkin Warbeck or False Demetrius of his day—who should re-awaken popular feeling; whilst critics of a subtler cast would have complained that, in comparison with modern methods, the tests applied to the risen body of the Lord had been insufficient. Though such ingenious objections can never be repelled with the inexorable finality of formal logic or mathematical demonstration, they lose all verisimilitude where the witnesses are so evidently without guile as any just psychology must recognise the Apostles to have been. The candour of these witnesses springs to the eye; and this candour of theirs permeates the narratives of the Resurrection in the highest degree. Never at any point is it easy to forget that one is dealing with a plain fact about which no serious mistake was really possible and with plain people to whom it was as natural to confess their own cowardice and incredulity as to recognise the stupendous event itself. Little or nothing in this world can be called morally certain, if the Resurrection is dismissed as rationally doubtful. Seldom, if ever, can witnesses have satisfied so fully, and yet so artlessly, the requirements of initial scepticism, painful hesitation, ultimate certitude and mortal assurance. In the hour of Christ's peril they flee; in the day of His death they despair; on the morning of His Resurrection they doubt; in the years of persecution that ensue, rather than deny Him, they die. No conceivable mode of reaching the truth about an unusual occurrence seems less open to exception.

The written record of an event, so long as the evidence of those who can say 'I was there' is available, can never seem but of secondary merit. Everyone prefers to hear the witnesses for himself, and to form his own opinion of their reliability. So doubtless it was with the first Christians. And so it came about that Tradition took precedence of the Gospels. Whatever legends might gather about the amazing story of Christ's life, the truth could still be ascertained by referring to those human sources of knowledge who had traced the course of events as eye-witnesses from the beginning. But such evidence was limited by the length of human life. Fortunately, however, for the historian, within a few years of the Resurrection an enquirer, as adversely inclined at the start as the most sceptical critic could desire, and as pungently critical himself, both by disposition and training, as the most exacting judge has any right to demand, placed on record the result of his investigations into the alleged miraculous event.

St. Paul did not, however, give his conclusions to his converts without adequate preparation. Spiritual things, as he observed, are spiritually discerned; and he no more assumed that the secrets of the psychical world would surrender at discretion than those of the physical. The oratory and the laboratory have this at least in common: that they both demand infinite pains. It was only after three years' consideration of the tremendous psychic experience that he had had on the road to Damascus that the future apostle of the Gentiles made his way to Jerusalem to compare his mystical vision of the risen Christ with the facts of exterior history. The best sources of information were still at his disposal; and he was careful not to let them be polluted by less direct testimony. St. Peter, who, as the Acts of the Apostles significantly remarks, went throughout all parts, and St. James, who presided over the local community of Christians, were resident at Jerusalem. St. Paul stayed a fortnight with the former, and saw something, too, of the latter. Better authorities could hardly be had; and St. Paul took his account straight from their lips. The evidence thus obtained and summarized for the benefit of the critical Greeks of Corinth satisfies all reasonable demands of the historian. It is precise, definite and sufficient. Christ had been seen after His resurrection by Peter; by the Twelve; by five hundred brethren at once, most of them still alive at the time of writing; by James; by all the Apostles at the same time. An appearance is an uncertain term. It may be, as we are accustomed to say, subjective or objective. St. Paul in the immediate sequence of his statement made clear what he had in mind. The appearances of Christ had been of such a nature as to guarantee to men in general in some future state a possession of bodies transfigured and incorrupt, yet, not the less for that, substantially identical. It was this that he proclaimed as truth; and his statement, therefore, postulates the idea of the empty tomb and is quite irreconcilable with any other.

Fortunately for the conscientious historian, the evidence of the Gospels is completely in line with St. Paul's account of the mysterious event. Some powerful hand, as they show, had rolled the stone away from the Sepulchre where Christ's corpse had been laid; and the tomb contained no body. That important fact was as clear as the yet more important fact of the appearances. As for the incidents framing the great event, whilst one might expect them to give rise to a good deal of pedantic commentary, one could see that they presented no serious problem for a man of the world. Thucydides, four hundred years before Christ, placed on record his estimate of the difficulties confronting any historian even of his own times in discovering the truth; and there was no reason to suppose that these difficulties had diminished. "The endeavour", he observes of the occurrences of the Peloponnesian War, "to ascertain these facts was a laborious task, because those who were eye-witnesses of the several events did not give the same reports about the same things, but reports varying according to their championship of one side or the other or according to their recollection." Nevertheless he claimed—nor is his claim denied by competent judges—to have produced a history deserving the description of a possession for ever.

St. Luke, whilst not underestimating the difficulties confronting the most excellent Theophilus in arriving at "Gospel truth", had had himself from the beginning, as he informs us, personal knowledge of the relevant events—events falling within a field of observation very restricted indeed in comparison with that of the Peloponnesian War. That field had lain likewise in full view of St. Peter, whom there is both reason and tradition enough to credit with having supplied St. Mark with his facts; of St. Matthew, to whom there seems no occasion to deny a single personality, and of St. John, who is indicated as the author of his Gospel, no less by its intimate local detail and final explicit attestation, than by a certain divine grace of thought and expression unmatched in history and postulating to all appearance both the closest possible contact with the mind of Christ and years of reflection upon it. With these three memoirs the Gospel of St. Luke showed as nearly as can well be imagined that essential harmony which tends to produce confidence and that diversity, as distinct from contradiction, in the observation of detail which disposes of the charge of collusion.

Nothing, indeed, seemed better calculated to illustrate the infirmity of the human mind than its disparagement of the Gospel story, and, if one had not grown so accustomed to its endless vagaries in other fields, one might be still more impressed by the circumstance. The authenticity of the Gospels was much better attested than that of Thucydides's history or Juvenal's satires; yet no Baconian ever sought to salt the tail of the Shakespearean traditionalist more eagerly than the Biblical critic to bring down his quarry with the slings and arrows of outrageous scepticism. Human nature was really very curious. It never made a serious effort to clear its character

from reproach or its record from folly by discrediting the witness of
Juvenal and Thucydides. Yet, when it became a question of believing good tidings of great joy, there was no exertion it would not
make or absurdity it would not countenance in order to render them
void. Knowledge, unattended by understanding or wisdom, was
played off against judgment; and often enough it appeared no better
than that little learning which is proverbially a dangerous thing.
There is an old tinker, going by the name of Shaw, in Samuel Butler's
"Way of all Flesh" who is made to score off the curate, brandishing
inexpertly Whateley's historic doubts about the existence of Napoleon Bonaparte, by observing that one so well able as Whateley to
prove that what was, was not, must be equally able to prove that
what was not, was. Such Shavian dialectics, though they proved too
much in the book for poor Mr. Pontifex, who straightway abandoned
his orders, are not enough to deliver the rationalist from the dilemma
in which Whateley's logic lands him. A rational mind cannot have
one law for Christian and another for secular evidences. Both the
careers of Christ and Napoleon are so astonishing, though in
different respects, as to appear miraculous and to invite enquiry.
Only, whereas proximity to the present time has rendered scepticism
especially difficult in Napoleon's case, the lapse of nearly two
millenniums and a prejudice against unusual events of a particular
character have deprived the proofs of Christ's history of the cogency
that they once possessed for the Latin world of A.D. 325. The conscientious historian appears to be denied any title to surrender to
sentiments so arbitrary or partialities so patent. The spectator of all
time and all existence dare not yield to the local and temporal effects
of proximity; nor, since, as Plato observes in the Theætetus, there is
no other source of philosophy than the quality of surprise, should
the evidence for extraordinary facts be adversely affected by the
emotion of wonder.

It was possible to take the measure of much critical ingenuity in
respect of the story of the Resurrection by noticing upon what sort
of points it tended to fix. One narrative, for instance, recorded that
it was yet dark, another that it was early dawn, and a third that the
sun had risen, when the women first came to the sepulchre. Yet it
is not certain that these witnesses all arrived at the grave together,
nor clear that they all marked the character of the sky at the same
moment, nor doubtful that the gradations from twilight to dawn and
from daybreak to sunrise are extremely subtle. One narrative, again,
vouched for the presence at the tomb of an angel in snow-white

raiment, another spoke of a young man in a white robe, and a third of two men in dazzling apparel. Yet such evidences of diversity of vision or perhaps of diversity of attention on the part of the reporters would not be allowed to invalidate the proof of a murder or a motor-car collision, and should not therefore be allowed to invalidate evidence for a matter of greater moment. Again, it was hardly rational to raise a mountain of difficulty out of the modest fact that Christ is said to have been seen after His Resurrection both in Jerusalem and Galilee. Casually, in his second mention of the matter, St. Luke had let fall, what might not otherwise have been guessed, the fact that a period of forty days elapsed between the Resurrection and the Ascension; so that there was time enough for the Disciples, taking a week to walk each way, to have passed from the Holy City to the Lake of Remembrance and back again, and time besides for all to be said and done that is conveyed in the words 'Ave et Vale'. The retreat into Galilee, if the needs of the infant Church and the conditions of the time were taken into consideration, was as likely a circumstance as the localisation of the first Easter day and of the first Pentecost at Jerusalem.

For the rest, modern history has not been so free from distortion at the hands of eminent savants that anyone need hesitate to treat the findings or feelings of others on the most exacting episode in all history with considerable reserve. The mentality of the critics requires to be studied and assessed quite as certainly as that of the witnesses. A mind, for example, which, on the strength of a single ambiguous statement at second hand, can substitute a John the Elder, otherwise unknown to history, for the St. John the Divine of external tradition and intrinsic probability as the author of the Fourth Gospel, should not prove incapable of disposing of Wellington, and in due course of Waterloo itself, on the authority of the First Gentleman in Europe who had supposed himself present there, and, presumably, as Prince Regent, in supreme command. It might save a good deal of contention regarding Papias's famous statement if stress were laid, not on the questionable duality of persons, but on the unquestionable duality of tenses * in his account. Some of those mentioned by him would, in that case, be seen to have been classed as having in the past testified to the facts concerning Christ; while others, yet alive, were testifying to them still; and, if this classification be admitted, then there would be no reason for surprise at finding the name of John as a young man in one list and of the same

* εἶπεν : λέγουσι (Euseb. "Eccl. Hist.", III, 39).

John as an old man in another. The advantage of this supposition is
that Papias's statement, whatever Eusebius may have made of it two
hundred years later, would be completely in line with all that we
learn from Irenaeus and others about the Beloved Disciple. The historian has no right or reason to countenance contradictions when he
can get on very well without them. But let that be; for the proof of
the Resurrection does not primarily rest upon the authenticity of the
Fourth Gospel or any other, but upon the tradition that St. Paul
earlier examined and enshrined.

The positive witness of the Resurrection can be tested and
fortified in a negative way by the elimination of every alternative
treatment of the hard fact at the centre. One could in this sequence
exclude with the laborious Keim * as untenable every fraudulent
naturalistic or visionary explanation of the event, and find oneself at
the end even more bewildered by his suggestion that the evidence
that Jesus was alive was best regarded in the light of a telegram from
heaven despatched by His instrumentality under God's will. At that
point indeed one was ready to recognise the force of Edersheim's
conclusion that "the great fact itself . . . may unhesitatingly be
pronounced that best established in history", since, "none is better
attested". † To reject this summing up was in fact to be driven
back upon the abomination of critical desolation reproduced in
George Moore's "Brook Kerith". Only utter despair of accounting
for the actual event can excuse such inartistic fiction. Christ, on
the hypothesis of Moore's novel, never died upon the cross at all,
but, reviving, practised upon the credulity of the unsuspicious
apostles. How artistic beauty of character survives so knavish a
trick is not, if I rightly recollect, demonstrated.

The historian has, however, no need to advance psychological
difficulties in order to dispose of this singular fable; for it tumbles
to pieces at the touch of a little common sense. Among the facts
which St. Luke (if, indeed, he was not himself the companion of
Cleopas on the occasion) carefully verified for the information of
Theophilus, was that of the appearance of Christ during the walk
of the two disciples to Emmaus on the afternoon of the first
Easter day. It becomes obvious, therefore, to observe that the
physical activity involved in this incident would have been wholly
inconsistent with the condition of feet cruelly wounded two days

* Keim, "History of Jesus of Nazareth" (English tr.), VI, p. 364.
† Edersheim, "Life and Times of Jesus the Messiah", Vol. II, pp. 397, 629.

before and utterly beyond the capacity of a body that had hung so recently for three or six hours upon a cross and furthermore been wounded in the side. Even were walking supposed possible, the difficulty and distress entailed could hardly in the circumstances have escaped the attention of the traveller's companions on the road, preoccupied as they were with the subject of the crucifixion. Yet the last thing that they dreamed of was the identity of their companion with Him on whose account sorrow had filled their hearts; though it might well have been the first thing that crossed their minds, had He limped or betrayed exhaustion. In the event, whilst their eyes were holden, their hearts caught fire, until at length, as they broke bread together at the end of the walk, they suddenly perceived that Love had proved stronger than Death.

That burning heart of these first disciples, that sense of faculties preternaturally enkindled, that recognition by love of Love's self, returns, as everyone interested in mysticism knows, again and again in mystical experience. Yet Pascal's terse monosyllabic cry 'Feu' says, perhaps, all that can be told of it. The fact had taken fire in his soul—the same historic fact that had set all the beacons of the Bible alight. It was as if human eyes had left the limpid pools of reason that form beside the river of life and been raised to the everlasting hills, where on that far horizon a line as of fire circumscribed the confines of time. A figure of thought, no doubt, yet apt enough for Lucretius to have caught its reflection in the deep waters of atomic materialism! 'Flammantia moenia mundi'—what could save that arresting metaphor from lapsing into a mere conceit unless the soul itself saw fire as it searched the bounds of thought? Only what to Lucretius, looking into the pools of silence, had appeared a circumambient wall of flame, was perceived by Pascal, conscious as ever that heavenly things are in hiding from the curiosity of the profane, to be a constellation ringing eternity, in the words of his English contemporary, with "pure and endless light".

I could fancy that, like Vaughan, Pascal had come to see all humanity moving within the compass of such supernal fires, and One, besides, walking there among them, whose form was as that of the Son of God. Him certainly Pascal saw with a great clearness as the cosmic centre, the metaphysical source of history. I could feel that behind all the Pensées; but I could hear it, too, in what I came to think of as his consummating cri du coeur: "And so I stretch out my arms to my Liberator, who, having been foretold for four thousand years, came to suffer and to die for me on earth in the times and all the circumstances predicted; and by His grace I await death in peace in the hope of being eternally one with Him; and yet I live with joy, either on account of the good He grants me or the evil that He sends me for my good and has shown me how to endure."*

That was Pascal's thought of thoughts. In it was registered the reaction of the finest human mind (if we accept Jevons's valuation) to the firmest fact of history (if we assent to Edersheim's estimate). Professor Whitehead has commented on the absence of foundations in the modern historian. "This notion of historians", he has observed, "of history devoid of aesthetic prejudice, of history devoid of reliance on metaphysical principles and cosmological generalisations, is a figment of the imagination. The belief in it can only occur to minds steeped in provinciality."† Pascal's aesthetic prejudice, metaphysical principles and cosmological generalisations were alike to be found in the study of the life, death and resurrection of Christ. These facts, in his view, drew all other facts to them, and revealed the true character of grace, the finished standard of goodness, and the real nature of things or, if that makes the matter clearer, of the design of things. Master of them, the historian might hope to do accurate work in the selection and presentation of events. Indifferent to them, he became a vagrant on the vast terrain of history.

The transition, however, from the dark night of Gethsemane, or the twilight and dawn of Easter morning, to the light of common day is the most difficult imaginable. The poets, as it seemed to me, could do more for the historian here than most people. They had genuine perception of subtle intelligences operating behind the scenes and of a magic music in the air that, with its sweet influences, could sweep men off their feet, or with wilder notes, set them dancing like feux follets. The Poets of the early nineteenth century were particularly good at making one conscious of the passion and mystery that the politicians have little or no eye for, and the Buckles, Winwood Reades and Wellses who are made after their likeness. Coleridge was unequalled at making the world feel eerie, Byron at revealing Satan's invisible world, Shelley at showing one the power of siren-songs, Wordsworth at teaching one to hear the voices of hill and dale and river. It was, however, a more recent poet who in some lovely lines seemed to me to have suggested a metaphysical and aboriginal background adequate to a world whose ultimate values have to be sought where Pascal found them.

* "Pensées", 737.   † Whitehead, "Adventures of Ideas", p. 4.

I heard it all, I heard the whole
Harmonious hymn of being roll
Up through the chapel of my soul
And at the altar die.

I stood and stared; the sky was lit,
The sky was stars all over it,
I stood, I knew not why,
Without a wish, without a will,
I stood upon that silent hill
And stared into the sky until
My eyes were blind with stars and still
I stared into the sky.*

Sublime mysticism indeed, yet assuredly not nonsense! For all their surplus stock of charming conceits and luscious fancies, the poets have looked deeper into the heart of history than those who seek the soul of things amongst fossils or dead men's bones; and, as had happened with regard to the Golden Age, their intuitions, though discredited for a time, had a way of renewing their strength and regaining their power. At all events in the shadowy world of becoming which preceded the advent of man I desired no better companion than these visionaries. Whilst one tried oneself to keep step with the plodding feet of science, it was everything to have those at one's side who took their course from the stars. There still they hung, those crystal spheres, reminiscent of a history behind the historian, postulating a cosmology beyond the astronomers, causing the human mind to lose itself in the infinities of space and to find itself again in the verities of morals. Why should one treat as fairy tales all that the poets had said of them? It was not so difficult to think of them making music in the vault of heaven, since they made so much music for us on earth; nor was it so improbable that those who first heard that music had shouted for joy. With as much humour as we see tempering the world, it seemed credible enough that wisdom should have sported before God when the universe came into being.† In fact, if imagination was to play any part in a critique of human history, there seemed nowhere more demand for it than in the consideration of these first beginnings of time and space, or of space–time (if that makes us a whit the wiser). Wherever the spirit of geometry fumbled or failed, there was the greater call for the spirit of finesse.

More than beauty and humour might be expected in the first

---

* Ralph Hodgson's, "Song of Honour".   † Proverbs VII, 31.

beginnings of a divine comedy which incorporated so much tragic matter. A battle as old as or older than time had plainly swept across the rose-red sky of heaven—the portent of a conflict apparently destined to find its final occasion and full consummation on this inconspicuous planet. Somehow in that mysterious air, evil had appeared—evil that in the last analysis, as the metaphysicians assure us, is nothing positive, but a privation, the loss of some perfection within the capacity of the creature concerned to possess. Lucifer, an angel fallen, was thus an angel still; his essential nature remaining, even after all grace was gone. And in no being less richly endowed was it easy to imagine that evil, in all its dark negation, could inhere.

Metaphysicians, however, are not always found persuasive and, notwithstanding the support which they have received in this matter from the poets—from Milton and Goethe no less than Dante—the devil had lately been refused any place at all in the drama of human life, or at best been provided with the part of a clown and the face of a gargoyle. So resolved had man been to convert, if he could, this mortal scene into a pastoral, with nothing worse than Pucks and Ariels anywhere about! Lucifer, however, as a sure instinct taught Meredith to see, is best perceived in starlight.

> He reached a middle height and at the stars
> Which are the brain of Heaven he looked and sank.*

The poets had not been more lavish in thanks to the theologians for their vision of God than the scientists to the poets for their vision of Nature; but the historian had to be dull indeed who does not see how deeply indebted they are. Much dogmatic fact had slipped through into common thought under the cloak of poetic imagination, and particularly in respect of the remote origins of psychic life. The physicists had admittedly nothing to tell us about it. Mind, so far as they were concerned, was nothing but a mode of matter or energy. But intelligence had got into the picture somehow; and it was no more surprising to fancy it springing up amongst star-dust than arising from the slime of the earth. The poets, anyhow, had managed to soften a fact that in the hands of the theologians seemed sometimes too intractable. There were those who could get something out of the thought of Lucifer reaching a middle height and falling back into the abyss at sight of the starry brain of Heaven, but who could make nothing of the notion that the devil had occupied an

* G. Meredith, "Lucifer in Starlight".

intermediate post in the polity of the Kingdom of God, rebelled against the Creator and thrown the celestial constitution into disorder. Yet the idea behind the words was pretty much the same. In any case, the fact of a power behind phenomena and making for wickedness had to be faced no less than that of a power making in the opposite direction. It had, indeed, a disconcerting way of turning up in unexpected places. Consider, for example, the remark of a popular writer, with a good title to take stock of current affairs in the political field of action, that, unless his readers believed in the devil, his book would provide no explanation of what was happening in the world.* Or consider the ensuing conjunction of stellar and sacramental thoughts introduced into a singularly subtle and unsparing critique of military psychology by a distinguished soldier of our time. As an epilogue to the description of a casual christening by night at a church in Paris, there will be found in General Spears's "Prelude to Victory" this passage: "As we looked up at the cold, clear sky, lit by myriads of stars, a great peace came over us. We both felt we had been near a truth too great and splendid for us to understand, but, however far we were from comprehending it, we were content, blessed and penetrated in our inmost beings by something impregnated with heavenly beauty. In the light of that afternoon's experience the War seemed utterly despicable and not worthy of a moment's attention." †

Such intimations of worlds not realised could doubtless be conveyed in sunset-touches or fancies from flower-bells; but they were perhaps seldom so importunate or overpowering as when they came straight from the starlit heavens. Kant spoke for many besides himself when, in his classic remark, he associated the starry sky above him with the conscience within him as the two things supremely capable of filling the soul with awe and wonder. The former, though not the latter, was likewise numinous for Napoleon. Thus could the music of the stars hale men's souls out of their bodies and set them thinking on ultimate persons and things—God, freedom, immortality—as certainly as the attraction of the stars could hale the world along its passage through the universe. But that was not all. The astrology (I am using the word in its natural, not its degraded sense) of this stellar music remained as certainly to be studied as the astronomy of stellar forces. Why should starlight arouse such feelings in the

* Yeats-Brown, "European Jungle", p. 30.
† "Prelude to Victory", p. 116.

mind, or wise men feel drawn to follow a bright, particular star, or superstitious men fancy they had their own bright, particular stars to follow? Problems not, perhaps, in this world to be satisfactorily resolved!

There is another light less brilliant and perhaps better suited to mental equipoise in such a time as this. There is twilight. There was a twilight of the Gods, when the old pagan deities turned and fled and were seen no more except as freaks of Nordic fancy. There was, too, a vesper twilight of Christendom when elect souls like Pascaí's rode through the waste land of man's endeavour, blasted their challenge against some dream-gate of horn and perchance re-entered ivory towers. But there may come yet another twilight before dawn when women may be seen wandering out to ascertain whether a certain tomb was empty and, finding it to have been so indeed, may return to renew their perennial conflict with the incredulity or inhumanity of men.

Chapter XII

THE TWO MIRRORS

I HAVE never yet attempted, when wandering in recollection through the rooms of that now-vanished house in Bryanston Square, to bring my reader, if any such there be, into Allegra's bedroom. Were I to be asked what it had looked like, I suppose I should reply, prosaically enough, that the walls were of a blue colour tinged with green; that the bed, with other furniture to match it, was of an Italian design in painted woodwork; that the bedspread (as Allegra liked to have it best, especially in hours of pain and sickness) was of a white silk or satin, very exquisite, and—which says everything needing to be said about it—a present from Mells; that the carpet was in the Aubusson style with the added graceful distinction of family inheritance attaching to it; and, finally, that there used to stand upon a table a small statue of the Madonna more delicate in conception and execution, as it might easily be, than many similar objects of art or devotion displayed in Catholic churches and elsewhere. All these things have perished and, since they were rather characteristic than symbolic, I make no further attempt to recall their presence in the room. The mirrors, or at least two of them, came in the retrospect to possess greater significance for me. Not indeed that Allegra's were, as perhaps they should have been, replicas of the lovely Etruscan mirrors of polished metal befitting the room of a Florentine. Yet every mirror, however poor or mean, has some title to bring to mind Goethe's often-quoted lines—

> Alles Vergängliche
> Ist nur ein Gleichnis*—

for no more cogent witnesses to its truth exists, and none afford better excuse for reflecting that all things vanish away and that nothing remains. All things at last—except only the memory in some man's mind, or in the mind of God, of a motion, an energy, an animation, a transparency that has passed! I think, then, of those broken

---

* Everything that passes
Is only a likeness.

mirrors in Allegra's bedroom as strangely symbolic of the difficulty in general attending all 'recherche du temps perdu', but in my own case accentuated by an enforced change to circumstances very different from those that I had contemplated when this book, now entering upon its final phase, was first begun.

One of the mirrors—the one which stood on Allegra's dressing-table and which, morning by morning, as her hair was dressed, had doubtless looked back laughingly at her, like the looking-glass in "Love in the Valley"—might, with its ormolu frame and ornate decoration of Prince of Wales's feathers, have been (and, for anything I know, was) contemporary with the house itself; and its now shattered image in my mind served to evoke, not merely the gaiety and grace of its last possessor, but that latest dream of fair women who, drawing water from the wells and pools of medieval romance with the aid of the pre-Raphaelite brotherhood, had produced, in the century after Waterloo, côteries of no small distinction which culminated, or at least concluded in the society of the 'Souls'. Of these last, within whose time and orbit Allegra's own brief life had fallen, Sir William Harcourt is reported to have declared, shrewdly if not shrewishly, that all he knew of them was that they had beautiful bodies; and it was, perhaps, all an old Whig lawyer could be expected to know. For they came of the latest grafting of the romance which flowered first under the special care, as was believed, of Notre Dame, in the Roman de la Rose, and had so moved the minds of men by its beauty that, at its earliest efflorescence, piles of stone, as at Chartres, would be converted into canticles of the Queen of Heaven. And even still, during the worst assaults of the philistines—at the Reformation, say, or the Revolution—there was a 'frozen music' to be made out of the romance of such queens of earth as Marie Stuart or Marie Antoinette. Forbear to ask of the young conscript Marthas of to-day, consule Bevin, whether such children of Mary again can be. 'Où sont les roses d'antan?', now that the snows lie thick upon the soil of civilisation all summer long. A broken mirror serves no more, despite the feathers on its crest, to show the face of Beauty, nor even of its scattered fragments makes a cup to toast the sceptred race or form divine. Enough that Clio, when a muse, dreams still her dream of fair women and passes through her gates of horn her statues of polished ivory.

From the transparent depths of the other mirror I drew no lyrics, yet saw there a poem long enough to serve an epic, or provide tales for a thousand and one nights, or furnish the matter of a drama to one, like Raleigh, who took the whole history of the world for his province and travelled round time as well as space, only, as it proved, at the end to get a whiff of tobacco for his pleasure and the headsman's block for his pains. Into this long mirror, too, had Allegra looked, as often, I suspected, as she went out into the world, and never less intently perhaps than when she was wearing one of those so-called 'robes de style' which, recalling a more graceful period than her own, were yet not altogether excluded by contemporary fashion. Readers of Proust's volumes dedicated to the quest of time past may recall how, towards the close, he rejects as too daring the idea of a book planned on the lines of a cathedral and substitutes for it the less formidable enterprise of something modelled after the manner of a dress. . . . "Je bâtirais mon livre, je n'ose pas dire ambitieusement comme une cathédrale, mais tout simplement comme une robe." A dress, above all a 'robe de style', might indeed, as between styles architectural and sartorial, afford the better design to an author; give him a soothing sense of proportion, should his mind begin furiously to panic; hold his thoughts at home, when a house represented his circumference; even warn him obliquely that a wedding-garment was the one thing needful in case, when the book was completed, he should be bidden to some great supper where it was de rigueur to be rightly dressed.

With such reflections in my mind, the magic of all looking-glasses would take hold of me and, like Alice in her famous adventure, I would try to pass through those I had known, so as to see what there was upon the other side; and, being or becoming child enough for this purpose, was in some degree, as I shall explain, successful. "Oh, Kitty!" Alice had cried to her kitten, "how nice it would be if we could only get through into Looking-Glass House! I'm sure it's got . . . such beautiful things in it! Let's pretend there's a way of getting into it somehow. . . ."

And so, like Alice, I pretended, and saw a silvery mist forming on the reflection of the two mirrors, and passed through the mist, and found, like her, the likeness of some of the old things I had known in the House and yet, like her too, 'that all the rest was as different as possible'. Not different, however, quite in Alice's way; for I discovered that the time or place or whatever it was into which I had got, had more dimensions than I had ever thought of, and certainly more dimensions than I can ever explain. I suppose one might convey some sort of idea of it by comparing it to a hall of magic mirrors where convexities and concavities in the surrounding glass were calculated to yield an abundance of comic illusions or tragic disillusionments. Suppose, in addition, that such familiar optics of humanity as clocks and yard-measures were wanting, and consequently that time was no longer the trick of a hand on the face of a time-piece, but the duration of a soul's experience, and that speed had so interpenetrated space as to make shape the sport of pace, and that the size of men, and of events, had assumed quite new dimensions. And suppose, further, that something made one suspect that this fancied hall of illusions might be in reality a palace of truth. For I did suspect that, and was even more perplexed and bewildered, I believe, than Alice when she first got through the Looking-Glass. Bewilderment, however, was all in character with the experience; for I doubt whether anyone ever gets through any looking-glass without becoming a child again, and then swelling to abnormal and shrinking to infinitesimal size by turns (as indeed Alice had found herself doing upon entering Wonderland); and I was a lot older than Alice at the time of her adventure, and such acrobatics were by so much the more painful to me. But whether they rendered me more childish or more childlike in the end I must leave it to the reader to decide, as also whether what I saw is best called pantomime, play, pageant, opera-bouffe, or grand-opera. Anyhow, it was, I feel certain, not half-so-simple as a child's eye makes it in the seeing or a child's lisp in the retailing: and yet, without a child's uncanny, even impish gift of spotting the point, I am afraid the spirit of man is foredoomed, by some devil's device, to fumble for ever with the gift of knowledge, like Dryasdust and Teufelsdröckh of unhappy memory.

Let the reader, then, make what allowance he can for one who has been looking into cracked mirrors and passing behind broken ones. Let him be a little kind to inadequate figures of speech and imperfect similes and strained metaphors. Let him bear in mind that strange 'interval' which, according to Einstein, makes physical reality fourth-dimensional or more. Let him ponder Prof. Whitehead's exposition of the manner in which a sense-object may make an entry into space-time by modal location—a green leaf, to use his own particular illustration, being present, say, behind one's back, but 'modally located' at another point where one perceives it in a mirror.* And let him pursue the same author's meditations on know-

* Whitehead, "Science and the Modern World", p. 88.

ledge until he reaches the sentence * which says that "in a certain sense, everything is everywhere at all times" where he may pause to take breath; and, then, with such aids to reflection thoroughly possessed, follow me into that galerie des glaces, that salle des pas perdus, whither I had somehow come through the medium of Allegra's mirrors.

Suppose the space-time thus reached shaped like a theatre, and my angle of vision something like that of a spectator in a stall; suppose a stage so spread out as to seem wide as the world, so lofty as to seem high as heaven, and so deep as to seem to end in infinity; conceive it as catching through the magic properties of many mirrors a thousand facets of an unending drama somewhere proceeding; suppose past and present and future distinct and yet so miraculously drawn together as to make one feel that history was after a manner all the while repeating itself, that what was was at once that which had been and that which would be; suppose a sound of footfalls at the back of the theatre ever moving up until the images of those who were the cause of them appeared in the mirrors, and then dying away again, with cadences reversed in strength; suppose, in a word, all the world a stage and all the men and women merely players, and myself, like the melancholy Jaques, invested in my motley—a merry man, though moping too at times and mum —and given leave to speak my mind (which most probably will tno be yours) about the foul body of this infected world. To speak it, but without Jaques's expectation that the world would receive his medicine (which is far too much for one fool to expect of another).

Such, then, was the theatre, and presently I shall try to give you some idea of the play. But not just yet! For it was in one respect, if in no other, very like a play by Mr. Bernard Shaw. It desiderated, that is to say, or even demanded a preface twice as long as itself to be understood; and I can only hope I have the Shavian grace needed to gain indulgence for the required prolegomena.

In that remarkable criticism of human life already referred to— "The Education of Henry Adams"—the author observes, with particular reference to his own dynamic theory of history, that "long before history began, man's education was complete".† If that be so (and it is arguable enough), we have to deal with two distinct

---

* Whitehead, "Science and the Modern World", p. 114.
† "Education of Henry Adams", p. 475.

movements in terrestrial time—a long evolution of animal forms, during which man was in the making, and a relatively short, though still unfinished period with a cyclic rather than an evolutionary movement, so far at least as humanity is concerned, after man had been made. Nothing more eminent in mind than homo sapiens has appeared on the face of the earth; and there is no sort of sign, apart from Nordic fancies about blond beasts and Shavian jests about super-men, that anything more eminent is ever going to appear. In other words, the highest operation in nature came to a lineal end and then began to revolve in cycles, even if in widening cycles, with the first syllable of recorded time. Some prophets have even affirmed that man has regressed. Rousseau, perhaps still, as the intellectual forerunner of the political revolution of 1789, more influential than any other European thinker, based his whole system on the belief that man had morally deteriorated from the standard of a golden age—an opinion that had been powerfully reinforced by some recent researches in anthropology by Elliot Smith and others.* But the school of Darwin, working in close association with the progressive ideas of Liberalism, had given the world to understand that man was steadily improving, rather mysteriously, under the influence of a fierce struggle for existence. This idea was the more surprising that under the operation of the second law of thermo-dynamics, the world, regarded physically, was apparently disentegrating beyond hope of recovery. Leaving that matter aside, however, something still appeared to be at fault with conclusions so different. There might be a lost fact or a missing link capable of reconciling them, but it certainly did not spring to the eye in the arguments of philosophers and scientists.

Meanwhile, so far as a mere historian could learn from the sources directly open to him, mankind seemed to have continued recognisably the same political animal at any rate since Thucydides threw out his guarded conjecture that human nature might remain a constant factor in human history. Making allowance for new inventions, changing fashions and varying interests, man, with all his variations, appeared to run strangely true to type, whether one studied

* G. E. Smith, "Human History", *e.g.* p. 199: ". . . so long as he is free from the disturbing influence of civilization the nomad is by nature a happy and well-behaved child, full of generous impulses and free from vice", and again p. 264: "For various reasons we have acquired habits of violence and have adopted vicious habits that were unknown to our food-gathering forebears".

him in Thucydides or Gibbon, in Homer or Shakespeare, in Aristophanes, or Molière, or Shaw—a creature often amiable, sometimes shrewd, generally ridiculous, solemn and silly by turns, now delightfully kind and then again desperately cruel, but substantially stable at bottom. The classics never became just fairy-stories about ogres and heroes long since extinct. They were read, because they amused us by holding up the mirror to human nature as we knew it; and they comforted us a little for our sad condition by showing us that, if we were no better than we should be, we were not, anyhow, much worse than we had been. How, if one came to consider, could it well be otherwise? As Le Play had brutally pointed out, a new body of small barbarians was being perpetually launched upon society under maternal cover. Instruction sometimes afforded some little defence against their attacks, but no assured one. The Germans in the late nineteenth century had been as well instructed a people as any in Europe, and were highly recommended by Carlyle and Arnold and other eminent persons in consequence. Their unprovoked assaults, pitiless massacres and ruthless enslavements have now, however, by a great deal outstripped those of the Athenian pupils of Pericles; and they appear to sustain the thesis that instruction can be in labour with fair words and foul deeds at the same time.

That theme admitted of further expansion. Invention itself appeared to be as morally neutral as instruction. Destructive weapons kept pace with remedial discoveries; and an inhuman servility to the State seemed destined to replace a slavery, comparatively humane, to an individual master. The education of man might thus in some sense be said to have been completed, as Henry Adams opined, before man's historical record began. At all events, however annoying it might be to pedants and pedagogues, man appeared to be incapable of giving himself anything worthy of the name of education as distinct from the instruction that grew in scope with the advancement of knowledge. But instruction went for nothing. Indeed, if the conqueror of Napoleon—and the opponent of all that Napoleon stood for as the child of the Revolution—were right, education without religion, which is precisely what instruction is, produced clever devils. It certainly looked rather like it in the year 1943, though Adams had so little emancipated himself from the optimism of his time as to conclude his criticism of life with the pleasing conjecture that, perhaps in 1938, when, had he lived, he would have reached the centenary of his birth, he might return to this planet and 'find a world that sensitive and timid natures could regard without a shudder'.* It was evident that another quarter of a century had been needed to finish his investigation of the habits of mankind by correcting his notions about progress. Given yet a further twenty-five years of life, and he might have been in a position to complete his education by subscribing to Chesterton's theory already mentioned that one had only to live long enough to end as a pessimistic atheist or a Catholic Christian.

It was Adams's way throughout his book to make intermittent fun of pteraspis, a ganoid fish, which Lyell, on enquiry, had indicated to him as his first vertebrate ancestor; and the blessed word evolution, in the sense of an all-round development of species by fortuitous variations through the medium of a bitter battle for life, evidently failed to satisfy him as a final cause sufficient to account for the course of events. So little, indeed, that his search for a dynamic theory of human history halted between the Blessed Virgin of Chartres and all that she stood for, and the kinetic theory of gases, or at least some similar analysis combining or simplifying the relations between matter and motion.† This was to contrast the operation of dynamic forces upon terrestrial affairs with a vengeance; but Adams, I think, perceived that no true student of homo sapiens dare shirk the problem. Without finding at least some provisional solution, the historian's work in selecting and evaluating facts became hopeless. Bryce, for example, had been at once amusingly and cuttingly criticised as a critic by the observation that all facts for him appeared to be free and equal. The historian, in other words, had to know himself before he could hope to appraise the knowledge that his senses and his studies brought to him. The spirit sending its thoughts and feelings soaring heavenwards in Gothic spirals; the mind exploiting the discovery of printing for more than it was worth; the body propelling itself faster and faster through space by the aid of the internal-combustion engine—here were patent three outstanding phenomena and latent three distinct, if not contending criticisms of life. The historian had to determine which of them was the most worth while; and woe betide his history if he failed to know his mind.

'Wie es wirklich geschehen ist'—How things had really happened! Yes! but what was the real? 'Voyez juste'?—Yes, but what optics enabled one to do that? Rabelais with his jolly eye; or Montaigne

* "Education of Henry Adams", p. 505.　　† *Ibid.*, pp. 427–31.

with his open, searching vision; or Pascal in his supreme, ecstatic hour? To some degree at least one had to reach an a priori opinion about the nature of Being before one ventured out into the wide world of history—of Becoming—to know (shall we say?) which of these men was the most worth knowing, if one were ever truly to know oneself, or find out what was *really* happening in the world around one.

Vico, who, like most men, had somehow satisfied himself of a rational significance in the world's events, had perceived also that, if history were ever to be able to tell its tale to a delicate ear, philology must have a place in the prelude. Language had been at the back of all man reckons life; and all the resources of language, sounding now sweet now bitter, coming down from high heaven or rising up from an earth in pain and travail, were needed to unfold the tale of history so as to enable it to convey any impression of a single eye sifting the sense of it. One had only to glance at Santayana's "Three Philosophical Poets" to recognise how differently events would seem to shape according as man's thoughts were dominated by his body, his mind or his spirit. Lucretius with his eye fixed on the atom; Dante with his eye held captive by Beatrice, and all that Beatrice impersonated; Goethe with his eye pursuing the vagaries of the Time-Spirit—these had all winged their words to very different purpose before, under the blasts and eddies of the French Revolution, all words became wild and whirling. 'In the beginning was the Word'— there lay 'le mot de l'énigme', the key to the riddle of human history, for such as repudiated Faust's audacious alternative 'In the beginning was the deed'. For "Faust" had been called the 'divina commedia of the German people'; and the more valid this comparison in influence, the more suggestive became the contrast in motive. Both Goethe's poem and Dante's were sown in personal romance, and both advanced from the personal to the political adventure of life. Only, whilst the one had been spiritually begotten by a soul with youth renewed through remembrance of Beatrice's virginal beauty, the other was mentally generated by knowledge lusting after an illicit way of mystical affirmation and not ashamed to prostitute to its purpose the body of Gretchen. It followed that the Divine Comedy of Dante rested content with an effective solution of the riddle of life appropriate to man's ignorance, whilst "Faust", demanding, as Aquinas would have said, a 'propter quid' instead of a 'quia' demonstration * of the truth, remained dis-

* "Purg.", III, 37.

satisfied to the end. The Latin mind of Dante reached, and knew that it had reached, the apex of man's mortal knowledge in Piccarda's now so familiar confession of faith that in the divine will lay the peace of humanity, and that towards a sea of love all things created, of their very nature, tended.* But the mind of Faust, knowing neither itself nor the luminous ideas from God that lay behind all knowledge, moved ever restlessly, seeking to become the captain of its soul, seeking new worlds to conquer, and meeting death at last under conditions, as Goethe presumably meant us to understand, of ironical triviality. It was enough to see Faust devoting his dying breath to planning the reclamation from the sea of marshes in the Netherlands to find in this flat finale a mocking echo of his own fine language in the prelude. "Verweile doch, du bist so schön!"—Stay, thou art fair!—thus in his last hour had Faust apostrophised the fleeting vision of his puny philanthropy; and the rash speech had supplied the decisive, contractual word of his pact with the devil:

> When to the moment I shall say,
> 'Linger awhile; so fair thou art!'
> Then mayst thou fetter me straightway,
> Then to the abyss will I depart!†

Word and not deed had, after all, had the best of it.

It is true that Goethe, with, as he confessed to Eckermann, the aid of symbolism borrowed from catholic theology, provided some sort of a happy ending to the story of Faust. Though the more perfect angels were not deceived as to Faust's spiritual condition, some younger angels, according to this account, carried off the immortal part of him and procured him a new job, apparently as a celestial tutor. But, as Santayana icily observes, "Faust is not saved in the sense of being sanctified or brought to a final, eternal state of bliss. The only improvement in his nature has been that he has passed, at the beginning of the second part, from private to public activities." ‡ And that, if Mephistopheles knows anything about it, gets Faust

* "Parad.", III, 85.
† " Faust", Pt. I, 1346–1350 (as given in Swanwick's translation):

> Werd' ich zum Augenblicke sagen:
> 'Verweile doch! du bist so schön!'
> Dann magst du mich in Fesseln schlagen;
> Dann will ich gern zu Grunde gehn!

‡ "Three Philosophical Poets", p. 188.

nowhere, even though political planning is nowadays reckoned to cover a multitude of sins. His diabolical comment follows close upon the flattering unction, addressed by Faust to his departing soul, that the draining of the marshlands will keep him in age-long memory!

> The last worst empty moment to retain,
> E'en to the last, the sorry wretch was fain.*

The 'deed', as opposed to the 'word', had evidently been the devil's delight from first to last.

Contemporaneously with Faust's new scholastic occupations in heaven, the prayers and penances of Mary Magdalen, of the woman of Samaria, and of another Mary, raise Gretchen heavenwards; whilst she in her turn, under the approving eye of the Mater Gloriosa, draws her faithless lover, by some means undisclosed, after her. But this purgation without purgatory had to all appearance as little to do with the plot of the play as Faust's previous escapade among the witches on the Brocken. Still, as Goethe assured Eckermann † that no fundamental idea really lay behind his famous drama, but only, as he put it, a course of action 'from heaven through the world to hell', it would be unfair to treat the concluding scene as more than an excursus imposed by the facts as he found them upon his study of life. So regarded, it constitutes a sufficiently powerful endorsement of Dante's earlier vision. Only, whereas in the "Divina Commedia" the women's part in the argument—the place, that is, accorded to Piccarda, Beatrice and the Blessed Virgin—is perfectly integrated with the rest of the poem, in "Faust" the Holy Women enter like an afterthought, and presumably because the only artistic epilogue to our mortal drama, as Shakespeare had seen and made Prospero say, would be despair unless it were relieved by prayer. So impossible was it even for Goethe's soaring intellect to disentangle the poem of life from the 'Ewig-Weibliche', 'drawing us above', which the Regency of Our Lady had made familiar to Christendom!

Amongst Vico's speculations regarding the origins of man will be found, following close upon what we should call the thought of the numinous, the thought of marriage. In pagan mythology, as he

---

* Den letzten, schlechten, leeren Augenblick,
  Der Arme wünscht ihn fest zu halten. ("Faust", II, Act 5, line 11,590.)
† Conv., May 4th, 1827.

quaintly argues, Juno was apprehended by man immediately after the fear of Jupiter had come to him. Depicted among other symbolisms with two stones at her feet to intimate the indissolubility of wedlock, the Queen of the gods was also represented as barren, to show that women were not the founders of families.* It was a curious myth, and had a curious way of coming to one's mind as one scanned the supersensuous air for the lost horizon of human history. It served the world of the Greeks well enough for a numinous background and might have had to serve us too, had no revelation intervened to bring Eden under consideration. For Eden indisputably discovered a new perspective to be explored and one, if there were any consonance between poetry and truth, bright with intellectual promise. Even Paradise, however, had had its material as well as its spiritual prolegomena; and of these the historical imagination had likewise to take account.

At some point, then, in time a wonder had appeared in space. Somewhat similar things had been seen before, but about this one there appeared to be something exceptional. Out of a sun, swept and spotted by storms that in themselves seemed portents, had leapt the earth, all swathed in incandescent vapour. Let poetry here come to the aid of physics, which appears to have a rather inadequate vocabulary to describe what followed. Behind this veil of mist behold a beggar maid, yet one that on her way had fallen in with some imperial lover. Out of the void she came, with little enough to show by way of dower, yet pregnant with infinite fertility and singing hymns to colour. Her pagan children, when they came to years of discretion, would call her Pandora; for she seemed to possess all manner of gifts and graces, and her wiles and witcheries were beyond imagination. In her hand, they declared, she held a box; and from the rash opening of the box, so they said, there had come a world of mischief.

It was a pretty conceit, and not so wild either. Yet earth's wiser children told a different and, as it seemed to me, a likelier tale. There had been, these said, war in heaven, and its repercussions had spread to earth. To catch sight of tares growing amongst wheat, or to hear the groaning and travailing together of things created, was to attach the readier credence to this story. It seemed likely that all earth's loveliness had been somehow spoilt; that there had been some prince of this world, and that prince no pleasanter than the Prince of Machiavel; and, in short, that the 'beggar maid' was in the nature

* Flint, "Vico", p. 211.

of damaged goods. The two Voices in the fallen House would seem to take up this parable, whenever I let my thoughts rest upon the origins of the human comedy or tragedy, whichever it might happen to be. And I cannot hope to reproduce their effect upon my mind better than by quoting a few lines of verse and then of counteracting prose; and I doubt not that every man's own experience will supply whatever else is wanting.

There is a well-known poem of Browning's which Allegra used to love and draw my attention to, though it was only after her death that I came to give it true value. It is that poem where, under the title of "The Guardian Angel", Browning recalls the impression of a picture at Fano. An angel is seen with an open door behind him and, in front of him, a child in prayer. The exquisite grace of the child's attitude and the lovely suggestion of celestial guardianship, conveyed by the overshadowing wings of the angel, so affect the poet that he represents himself as pleading to be allowed to take the child's place after the angel's ministry is accomplished and, as if he were another child, to be raised and guided through the opening door of heaven.

> If this was ever granted, I would rest
>   My head beneath thine, while thy healing hands
> Close-covered both my eyes beside thy breast,
>   Pressing the brain, which too much thought expands,
> Back to its proper size again, and smoothing
> Distortion down till every nerve had soothing
>   And all lay quiet, happy and suppressed.
>
> How soon all worldly wrong would be repaired!
>   I think how I should view the earth and skies
> And sea, when once again my brow was bared
>   After thy healing, with such different eyes.
> O world, as God has made it! All is beauty:
> And knowing this, is love, and love is duty.
>   What further may be sought for or declared?*

"O world, as God has made it! All is beauty":—the words would return again and again, adding their grace of vision to supersensuous ideas, to the heart's confidence that truth and beauty are ultimately one, to fancies drawn from flower-bells, to lights not seen on land or sea, but, above all perhaps, to the thought of woman brought to so great a depth of mystery as to make the very sun-lit air seem gaudy and to leave only night—the night 'of cloudless climes and starry

* Dramatic Lyrics, "The Guardian Angel, a Picture at Fano".

skies'—for comparison. Was it thus that all things really were, if one only possessed the clarity of a pure intuition so as to be able to behold them rightly? Was it by the single eye alone that the book of nature could be read from end to end, as St. Bonaventure would have had one suppose, without a sigh, and every creature, no matter how small or abject, rendered, as to Thomas à Kempis, 'a mirror of life and a volume of holy doctrine'. Something of this faculty, saved in the flight from paradise and preserved to man under the name of synteresis, had apparently been regained by the poet.

Yet here the Alien Voice would insist that one could envisage the real world so differently from this as to defy any such identification. It was not just that, in Tennyson's formula, nature was red in tooth and claw, food enough for thought as that line contained. It was that something diabolical seemed to lurk amidst its recesses. There was a striking expression of this in a novel by Mr. Somerset Maugham, purporting to be a study of Gauguin; and there the effect of that artist's work upon one of the characters is thus described:—"He seemed on a sudden to have entered a magic world. He had a vague impression of a great primæval forest and of naked people walking beneath the trees. Then he saw that there were paintings on the walls. . . . His eyes grew accustomed to the darkness, and now he was seized by an overwhelming sensation as he stared at the painted walls. He knew nothing of pictures, but there was something about these that extraordinarily affected him. . . . It was indescribably wonderful and mysterious . . . it filled him with an emotion which he could neither understand nor analyse. He felt the awe and delight which a man might feel who watched the beginning of a world. It was tremendous, sensuous, passionate; and yet there was something horrible there too, something which made him afraid. It was the work of a man who had delved into the hidden depths of nature and had discovered secrets that were beautiful and fearful too. It was the work of a man who knew things that were unholy for a man to know. There was something primæval there and terrible. It was not human. It brought to his mind vague recollections of black magic. It was beautiful and obscene. 'Mon Dieu, this is genius.' The words were wrung from him, and he did not know that he had spoken."*

"Is it not strange", as Benedick observes, "that sheeps' guts should hale souls out of men's bodies?"† It is strange, but so it is;

* W. S. Maugham, "The Moon and Sixpence", p. 293.
† "Much Ado About Nothing", II, 3.

and the painter's brush and canvas can, if properly manœuvred, be trusted to make pretty nearly as wild a music of our world as the wailing of a violin. If the Blessed Angelico does not raise our minds to Heaven, it is as like as not that some Gauguin will show us 'Satan's invisible world revealed'. Physics may protest that the physical world is the work of a mechanician or a mathematician or even of mechanics, or mathematics—but perhaps without carrying complete conviction even to physicists. "Cosmic nature", observes T. H. Huxley in his once-famous Romanes Lecture, "is no school of virtue, but the headquarters of the enemy of ethical nature." *
It was interesting, if a little odd, to find so rigorous a logician as Huxley indulging in language which certainly invited one to suppose that he, no less than Disraeli, was on the side of the angels, to the extent at least of reckoning with the intervention of black ones. Physics, it might be inferred, would never long prove able to shoulder the burden of mystery in 'this unintelligible world' without aid from poetics and all its apparatus of symbol, metaphor and parable. In the beginning, as had appeared, was the 'word', however small an initial letter one gave it; and all around the word, like the gauzy mist of an autumn morning, there lay, and, if Einstein could say anything to the point, there ought to lie, mystery. "The fairest thing we can experience", that keen intellect had declared, "is the mysterious. It is the fundamental emotion which stands at the cradle of true art and true science. He who knows it not, can no longer wonder, no longer feel amazement, is as good as dead, a snuffed-out candle." † So, then, as I guessed, Einstein, too, had walked through Wonderland and might, for anything I could tell, be considering the Looking-Glass World from some point of vantage not far removed from that occupied by Newton and Pasteur.

Meanwhile the reflections in the Mirrors were always changing, and the vistas deepening. At the moment apparently a masterpiece of opera, with acting equal to the voices and music, was in progress. I saw, as I fancied, Henry Adams in the stalls, made for him, and asked him and one or two other historians who were with him what the piece was about. They all returned the same answer "God knows!" I had already thought that might prove to be their reply, particularly as neither they nor I had heard the prelude, and without

* "Evolution and Ethics", p. 75.
† Einstein, "The World as I See It", pp. 4–5.

the prelude one could hardly be expected to master the meaning of the play. There were, however, some programmes to be had with, so to say, the divine imprimatur upon them; and I saw 'in my dream', as Bunyan would have said, that I had got hold of one of them, and was soon after studying the argument with rapt intensity.

Chapter XIII

HEBREW MELODIES

THE first section of the Synopsis that I found now in my hands was headed "Proem from Genesis". I read the argument with care and came to the conclusion that it better deserved the name of a revelation than any other literature of the same sort with which I had met. For the Proem was a poem of such rare verisimilitude that any reader, taking account of the date of its first appearance and the character of contemporary cosmogonies, and bearing in mind Thomas à Kempis's admonition that "all Scripture is to be read in the same spirit wherewith it was written",* must be struck with its sublime and singular quality. To the arbitrament of art one might indeed well rest content to see the majesty of its inspiration referred for vindication. Yet, perhaps, seeing that the matter once gave rise to a great debate between Gladstone and Huxley and exemplified to the full that 'hard clash of mind with mind' in which a great debater has seen the express virtue of a university education, I might, if I said no more, be accused of slipping past a critical corner in the fair criticism of life or dodging an engagement at least as memorable in the wars of thought as Towton or Tewkesbury in the Wars of the Roses.

Frenchmen might have shown a finer thrust and parry than the two eminent protagonists just named, but for passes in the best English style between a master of the spirit of finesse and a past-master of the spirit of geometry no man need look farther than that memorable duel. The synthetic ethos of a mind that had listened to the harp of Homer, sat at the feet of Joseph Butler and mixed in the counsels of Robert Peel is as patent in the approach of the one to the subject as is the analytic habit of the laboratory in that of the other. Whilst Gladstone marvels at the evolutionary perception of the author of Genesis in a way to obtain approval from Prof. Dana † (than whom Huxley himself declared there was none to whose authority on geological questions he would more

* "Imit. Chr.", I, 5.

† See his letter printed in Gladstone's "Later Gleanings", p. 39. "I agree", says Dana, "in all essential points with Mr. Gladstone and believe that the first chapters of Genesis and science are in accord."

readily bow*), Huxley is concerned with such exceptions to a progress of animal life from the water to the air and then from the air to the land as is afforded by tortoises, snakes and lizards— terrestrial reptiles presumed antecedent in time to birds.† It is, however, rather with Gladstone's simplification of the account of creation in Genesis that Huxley appears to be at issue than with the account itself, which in truth indulges in no such broad generalisation respecting "a water-population and air-population and land-population" as does the statesman. If the great sea-monsters (tanninim) were, as the word apparently implies,‡ crocodiles, and if the birds were classified, as the Egyptian zoology of Genesis suggests with fishes because they nested in swamps on the banks of the Nile, § the order adopted by the writer becomes an interesting piece of local observation, accurate as far as it goes, incidentally confirming the historic presumption of a Mosaic authorship, and, beyond and besides that, contributing its modest part to a story of creation of which a more recent critic has observed that alone among all creation stories of antiquity it makes some approach to a scientific cosmological conception, 'most prominently apparent in the creation of light'. He finds there in fact 'the first endeavour to establish a cosmological system which is not based on mythological ideas but which follows an evolutionary view based on a religious foundation'‖; and this appears to be a cautious up-to-date estimate of the achievement. Gladstone had gone rather further and ventured to say that he did not suppose it 'feasible, even for Prof. Huxley, taking the nebular hypothesis and geological discovery for his guides, to give, in the compass of the first twenty-seven verses of Genesis, an account of the cosmogony and of the succession of life in the stratification of the earth, which would combine scientific precision of statement with the majesty, the simplicity, the intelligibility and the impressiveness of the record before us.'¶ The covert challenge constituted something better than the cheap retort which seeks to divert the issue from the critic's actual criticism of the thing achieved to the critic's probable incapacity to do any better himself. Huxley himself admitted in so many words his fear that 'if nothing is to be called

---

* T. H. Huxley, "Essays on Controverted Questions", p. 122.
† *Ibid.*, "Mr. Gladstone and Genesis", pp. 100–1.
‡ Yahuda, "The Accuracy of the Bible", p. 159.
§ *Ibid.*, p. 157.   ‖ *Ibid.*, pp. 138–9.
¶ "Gleanings of Past Years, 1885–1896", p. 66.

science but that which is exactly true from beginning to end . . . there is very little science in the world outside mathematics."* And even so, as I had little doubt Montaigne would have genially pointed out to me, Huxley on the very page preceding had taken occasion to remark that, while he conceived ordinary geometry to be science in virtue of its method, and its axioms, definitions and conclusions to be true, there was 'a geometry of four dimensions' which he likewise believed to be science because its method professed to be scientific, but which was for him altogether 'unreal', because he could not conceive four dimensions in space.†

So much being granted, it did not appear that an artist's treatment of the beginning of things, which could elicit such unqualified praise as had been given it by Prof. Dana, had anything much the matter with it. If exact truth, as Huxley averred, was unattainable outside mathematics (and not apparently, since the existence of Einstein's four-dimensional world had been established, even there without falling into some degree of 'unreality'), then a series of dissolving views where the obscurity of night repeatedly inaugurated the dawn of a day of yet more astounding development was as proper a rendering of a great artistic production as a reasonable mind, not in search of a catalogue raisonné, could ask for.

If, on the other hand, God Himself were no more than a mathematician or a physicist, something else—and as I thought something lifeless—must have been looked for in this Proem. In the controversy over the opening chapters of Genesis between these English champions respectively of Humanism and of Natural Science there had appeared more than the hard clash of mind with mind already referred to. There was to be found in the different approach of the controversialists the distinction, subtle and profound, between a university like Oxford, which had not, at any rate in Gladstone's time, lost its spiritual foundations, and a university like London, which had never truly laid them. Huxley was a good scholar, but I think Pascal would have reckoned that the spirit of geometry more nearly represented his habit of mind than the spirit of finesse which Gladstone, doubtless, was not incapable of carrying to exasperating political excess.

Such opposition as had here arisen between minds of a very high order might especially be anticipated at the point where physics and metaphysics met; and, once one had grown to expect its occurrence

* "Essays on Controverted Questions (Mr. Gladstone and Genesis)", p. 125.
† *Ibid.*, p. 124.

just there, one was on the way to explain, if not to excuse, the frequent provoking incapacity of modern intellects to reach any agreement upon premises. The temperamental 'not disagreeing except in opinion' was in fact fast being substituted in the idea of a university for that intellectual agreement upon first and last things which had once governed discussion and prevented it from degenerating into mere argumentation. Even in a mind formed in the sister-university of Cambridge an Oxford man might sometimes become aware of such fundamental disagreement as to make him wonder whether a colloquy between Roger and Francis Bacon might not furnish a new Landor with the most profitable and entertaining of all imaginary conversations. For the rest one could never hope at all to understand the world unless one treated it as a house full of hiding-places and hidden treasure and searched it, as Jerusalem is said to have been searched by God, with candles. The Jews, as Disraeli so dexterously and entertainingly maintained, had been astute beyond other races and were more gifted visionaries than the rest of us. Mysterious in their origins, their Messianic hopes, and their final and fearful fate, they had missed little or nothing that was to be learnt about life from the sages of Chaldæa, the priests of Egypt, or even the philosophers of Greece, and yet had seemed to range beyond all this world's wisdom. If religion be reckoned a science, they had certainly proved it so by their single-handed fight for monotheism; and, if an art, they had equally discovered it in the enduring appeal of their psalms and the profound significance of their sacrifices. Stumbling here, turning aside there, incurring both the wrath of God and the hatred of man, they had nevertheless managed to carry the torches of religious truth, moral aspiration and heavenly beauty through the wilderness of the world until at the advent of the Messiah these burning and shining lights seemed to become blended in a far-flung illumination of radiant Love.

This unrivalled genius of the Jews for religion would in itself have encouraged and entitled a historian, resolved to deal faithfully with the origins of mankind, to give to the story of Eden priority of place and of attention. But the time-honoured tale recommended itself for other reasons. It recommended itself, for example, to any student of psychology who found, from self-analysis and observation of others, no occasion to doubt the accuracy of St. Paul's much-quoted diagnosis of unregenerate man. "The good which I would, I do not: but the evil which I would not, I do"—was it possible to analyse more succinctly the profound malady of mankind?

Something in man's inmost being had seen better days; something that explained the remorse he often showed and the censure he liberally distributed. A being progressing by some evolutionary process—natural selection or any other—and by hypothesis, growing, according to its ability, better and better every day, should have no occasion for repentance and no disposition to blame. It was always, so far as nature and circumstances allowed, as good as it could be; and Leibniz, like Voltaire's Pangloss, might well conclude that all was for the best in the best of all possible worlds. But Leibniz's conclusions were evidently incredible to the most part of men. Mr. Churchill had, doubtless, the best medical advice at his disposal; but he showed no disposition to dismiss Herr Hitler's acts as the unavoidable pains of the parturition of blond beasts or black, or even the man himself as a pathological case.

The verisimilitude of the Eden story fitted in, so it appeared, no less conveniently with recent archaeology than with straightforward psychology. Primitive man, as perceived through the study of the most primitive races—those, that is, which had experienced least contact with so-called civilised man, possessed in general the monogamous and pacific, the honest, humane and hospitable habits, that we can seldom count upon in nations and races that have eaten freely of the tree of knowledge. In the Andamanese, the Negritos of the Philippines, and the Puam of Borneo Elliot Smith and his collaborators were satisfied that they had recovered the evidence for the tradition of a Golden Age, and had gone on thence to the conclusion that "once the innocence of the Golden Age is demoralised, it required the wisdom and magnanimity of the highest form of culture to recover the primitive virtues of tolerance and generosity."*

Perhaps the recovery needed still more than human wisdom and magnanimity. The play, I gathered, had, as it went forward, been suggesting as much. Meanwhile I turned back to the prologue which I had missed and became again absorbed in the argument.

The mise-en-scène had evidently been admirable. In some oasis, for Eden signified or symbolised that,† in the desert of the world, if not in the desert about Egypt—somewhere at any rate between those

* Quoted by Davison, "Men of the Dawn", p. 77, from G. Elliot Smith's "Human History".

† So Yahuda, who rejects the derivation of the word from the Assyro-Babylonian 'edu' as an 'extraordinary aberration of the Assyriologists' ("Accuracy of the Bible", p. 162).

great rivers, Tigris and Euphrates, which are the making of Meso-
potamia, and the Upper Nile, with its 'leaping' cataracts, and the
Lower Nile, with its 'swollen' floods, whose characteristics are
reflected in the names Gihon and Pishon*—Man had come to birth.
It was difficult to conceive a more perfect setting for a being poised
between earth and heaven. Eddington in one of his lectures has
dwelt upon the praeternatural beauty of the Orient as darkness gives
place to dawn; of the sense of a veil that has worn so thin as to seem
transparent; of the expectation that the light mist of morning will
suddenly lift altogether and reveal a world hitherto hidden from
human eyes. Yet it was not only in the East that things seen could
manifest and make felt things that are unseen. It was in Italy that
Browning had minted to perfection the concept of a garden of
delight:—

> . . . . Fresh births of beauty wake
> Fresh homage, every grade of love is past,
> With every mode of loveliness: . . .
>
> . . . . Up and down
> Runs arrowy fire, while earthly forms combine
> To throb the secret forth; a touch divine—
> And the scaled eyeball owns the mystic rod;
> Visibly through his garden walketh God.*

From the first, as I gathered, some secret hid itself behind all
this beauty—the secret of some primaeval catastrophe, of which the
ultimate sources, lying as they did beyond the bounds of time and
space, lay also beyond the utmost reach of human understanding.
A little only was known, but that little was enough to make the
opening garden-scene of the play imaginable. A detailed reconstruction of that, or any subsequent act of the Great Drama, was, however, beyond a late observer's powers. I had seen it only in reflection, down the vistas of the years. What follows must, then, be
treated as mere notes and sketches in a playgoer's commonplace book.

There had, as it appeared, been war in Heaven—a rebellion of
angels, in which the prince, or angel of this world had been involved
as a principal and paid the price of defeat in perdition. The repercussions of that conflict had been felt upon earth and were implicit
in the whole staging of the piece: implicit in the sunlight that
brought things to view as in the darkness that blotted them out or
the moonshine that made them spectral and creepy; implicit in the

* "Accuracy of the Bible", pp. 174–5.   * "Sordello", Bk. I.

uncertain glory of an April day; implicit in the brook now rippling through wood and field, then rising in flood and torrent; implicit in the mountain climbing through verdant slopes to snowy summits whence a pale finger of smoke menaced the whole mountain-side with streams of molten lava. Implicit, but hardly explicit in inanimate Nature and emphatic only as Nature attained a high degree of animation. In all those elemental contacts and chemical combinations that provided the basic conditions of life there was no sanguinary struggle, no battle for existence costing blood. The elements were kindly mixed. Only, when into the water came life, did there also follow with it pain and death. And only as the evolution of things reached that point, could the scenery be fairly accused of sacrificing the pure enchantment of a Turner landscape to the requirements of a problem-play. Long before that, however, the Supreme Artist had stepped out of the world's morning mist of radiant colour. If loveliness or law had any bearing upon design; if calculable change—the change of seasons, say, or the vital reaction of chemical compounds to the revolutions of the earth and the system or systems of which it forms part*—were any indication of almighty mind; if the strange similarity between sidereal and atomic revolutions by carrying the imagination from edge to edge of two infinities—the infinitely great and the infinitely little— imposed the thought of holism, if not of the beauty of holiness, upon an imaginary spectator; then, as it appeared, long before the humblest animal actor in the drama had begun to play, the art and science embedded in the stagecraft had disclosed an impresario of boundless power and genius behind the whole emprise. "Le dernier acte est sanglant," Pascal had cried, "quelque belle que soit la comédie en tout le reste."† But the prologue was just light and shadow, line and colour, with no blood shed.

Certain aspects of the vegetation, depicted in the mobile reflections on the stage, carried the general sense of purpose into convincing detail. Orchids in especial arrested the eye. The process of fertilisation which these plants originally performed for themselves had, it appeared, been gradually transferred to the ministration of insects. A longer lip, serving the insect for a platform; a knob containing cement and fixing a stalk of pollen to the insect's head; a hinge in the stalk coming into play and causing the pollen, as the insect reached another flower, to penetrate the ovary; revolving

* See on this F. Wood Jones, "Design and Purpose", pp. 55–60.
† "Pensées", p. 210.

shutters in this second flower so functioning as to hold the insect's head in position whilst the fertilisation was effected—at all these things botanists, as I gathered, had for some while wondered. But in one North African variety of orchid a further marvel seemed calculated to shatter the last vestiges of doubt about design. Not only had the flower been so finely fashioned as to resemble the female of the insect, but to such perfection that the male insect fondly believed that he was embracing his bride, whilst the advent of the bride was, if the botanists might be believed, so dexterously delayed by the space of a fortnight as to render the lovesick bridegroom as passionate as he was blind.*

I was being fast driven to the opinion that the Jew Apella, far from being a credulous fool, might have been a very intelligent man, if such things were going on in the world of plants and insects. But, then, the Jews had always had some special knowledge of creative evolution.

It was, as I judged, with the introduction of insect life that the Artist, now so convincingly confessed by the charm and character of His work, had begun to let into the scene some new element beyond surprise. Ideas of good and evil, faintly foreshadowed in the play of light and darkness upon the landscape or of calm and swell in the waters, became suddenly pronounced in the disposition of animal types whose generic or individual traits would seem to abstract and throw into high relief the graces and disgraces of man. The effect of these animal studies upon my mind was not unlike that produced by those puzzle-pictures which challenge one to detect a face in the complexity of some vegetable or animal design, amid the branches, say, of an oak or the antics of a farm-yard. So dexterous in fact was the detail of the shifting scenery that human types, or even representative men and women, would suddenly spring to view and, so to say, hit one in the eye out of the features of the scenery at which one had been unsuspiciously gazing. Some fair-haired Niobe (I take outstanding examples) would be revealed in the face of a rock,† or some imperial Caesar discover himself in the head of an eagle; a raging bull might recall Bluff Harry; or an innocuous log, with frogs hard by for neighbours, appear the express image of Louis Seize. Once one perceived it, this lambent genius of the Artist, with its pathos, its irony, its humour and its wit, seemed to be everywhere at play; driving one to tears, to laughter, to a deeper toleration of

---

* There is a full account of all this in J. Langdon-Davies's "Man and his Universe", p. 204.　　　† "Iliad", xxiv, 614.

circumstance and a wider wisdom in judgment. How could one resist a smile when perhaps the face of Karl Marx appeared in the configuration of an antheap, or refuse a tear when the physiognomy of some cat, walking by itself, produced the effect of a disgruntled Spencerian individualist? But I derived more poignant impressions and provoked more lively imaginations from contemplating the spectacle of a parliament of rooks in the foreground, or a gaggle of geese in the distance, and when to this was added the sight, on one wing of the mobile scenery, of parrots in conclave and, on the other, of monkeys in session, all evidently chattering to the utmost of their joint and several ability, I must admit that the Artist's humour seemed to me so vastly in advance of that of mankind in general that I should have been prepared on this account alone to have placed full reliance upon his justice.

It must have been, I think, at some such point in my observations that two old ladies distracted my meditations. They might have emerged, as I conjectured, from such a boarding-house as that in which Herbert Spencer resided; or they might have stood for the White Queen and the Red in Alice's dream, for I think one was a 'dear-old-lady', but I had my doubts about the other. At the moment when I caught sight of them they were neither of them quite at their best, engaged as they were in hot disputation. I had little difficulty in guessing what they were quarrelling about; for their eyes—and not their eyes alone among the audience—were riveted upon an apparently unfortunate grub, which had been so deftly depicted as to enable one to perceive through its semi-transparency that it had been stung to paralysis and was being internally devoured by ichneumonidae. Never, it struck me, had I noticed before quite so telling an illustration of parasites as I understood the term—whether they were the beefy barons, pot-bellied knights, or sturdy beggars of the historic past or the highwaymen disguised in philanthropic harness of the political present. However, I reminded myself that these had all in their time been esteemed 'honourable men' and that England had dearly loved not only a lord, but Jack Falstaff, Robin Hood (or the imagination of him), Jack Cade and Dick Turpin, somewhat to the prejudice of those they preyed upon. The old ladies were, as I guessed and partly overheard, studying the ichneumonidae and their victim from another angle to mine. Such a sight, she whom I have called the Red Queen declared, was incompatible with her theology, which postulated a beneficent creator. But the White Queen replied that for her part she never expected to understand such matters

which were above her comprehension, and she consequently under-
lined her faith in Providence with an emphasis worthy of Queen
Victoria.

I could not myself see how the Red Queen contrived to be so
positive or why the White Queen needed to be so fatuous. Neither
of them could possibly know what pain the caterpillar suffered, or
whether it suffered any pain at all, or, if it did suffer any, whether
this exceeded the irritation I endured from a mosquito-bite or, for the
matter of that, from being converted into a fly-walk. To parasites of
all descriptions I had an aversion, but I had again to pull myself up
and recall the observation of an up-to-date biologist that 'the first
development of life must have been parasitic upon its inorganic
environment'.* It might thus be a little difficult to make sure
which had been the hero and which the valet in these affairs; and
stones might presently be heard crying out against some virus that
had used them. A very enigmatic world it was indeed when we got
down to rock-bottom, or brass tacks, or beyond brass tacks to worms
and graves and epitaphs! Too enigmatic, perhaps, ever to be judged
on any parasitical basis of valuation by caterpillars or queens!
Happily, however, for my two representative Queens, their great
debate was rapidly turned from the conflicts of animals to those
of men; and there they found themselves to be agreed. "There's
nothing to be done with the Germans", the Red Queen said with
fierce conviction, "but to exterminate them. Off with their heads!"
And the White Queen replied with equal assurance, "Yes! that's
quite right, dear. For I hear they do nothing now but cut off one
another's heads—like the French did during their Revolution; and
you know, dear, we have two governesses in this life 'Mrs. Do-as-
you-would-be-done-by' and 'Mrs. Be-done-by-as-you-did'. So I'm
sure you're quite right, because as they wouldn't be taught by the
one, they must be taught by the other."

I fancied that I detected some little contradiction between the
methods of the two admirable instructresses mentioned; but then,
after all, the White Queen's head had never been of the clearest.
So I turned again to the scenery and noticed there something I liked
very much. The scene-painter seemed to have surpassed himself in
mobilising a flock of sheep upon a hillside. They gave one exactly the
idea of sheep without a shepherd listlessly and aimlessly in search of
pasture. There was indeed a bell-wether, but he had as stupid a face
as falls even to a sheep to possess; and the sheep-dog looked more

* Wood Jones, "Design and Purpose", p. 66.

like a wolf. A vignette, in short, of God's silly sheep, most of whom you might reasonably hope to fool most of the time! It was only the lambs that were entirely charming. So much so, indeed, that I could have fancied the shepherd, had there been one, might have had the look of a lamb.

One could not contemplate this scenery long without recognising that some extraordinary mystery of iniquity had met and matched the enigmatic beauty of the landscape. In support of the fundamental 'holism' or integrity of the scene there would come to mind the consideration adduced by a modern apologist for supposing that a 'Satanic corruption of beasts' had preceded 'the Satanic corruption of man'* and that, in fact, animals had been dragged down to the level of the vegetable creation, where the mild competition of plants for soil and space need no more offend the hypercritical mind than does the consumption of them the queasy stomach. Of this fall of beasts, that pre-eminent imp of Satan, the palate of the pugnacious mosquito, appeared to my own unsophisticated eye to afford some sort of confirmation, if, that is, a leader-writer in the always august and in general accurate *Times* might be trusted for the facts. According to him† the sanguinary tastes of this insect had resulted from the perversion to blood-sucking of an organ, originally designed to suck the juices of plants. There seemed at any rate to be no prima facie objection to this idea in reverse. "The digestive system", we have been assured by some modern authorities,‡ "alters with the diet. John Hunter, the great anatomist, made a seagull produce a passable imitation of a gizzard by feeding it for many months on grain only. Few organs escape some degree of modelling by their own activity."

There were doubtless many cognate issues to be considered. Exuberant as was the fertility of Nature, a Malthus might still have questioned whether a purely herbivorous creation could have found adequate sustenance. Were the mouths of lions to be stopped with fodder and their organs adjusted on Lamarckian principles to such food, there must have been the less for the lambs and more lambs left to eat it. The urge of sex had certainly to be reckoned with. It had to be observed, however, as Messrs. Wells and Huxley put it, that "sex intrudes, an essentially anti-reproductive process, and forces

* C. S. Lewis, "Problem of Pain", pp. 123–4.
† See *The Times* of Nov. 22nd, 1941—the last leader.
‡ Wells, Huxley and Wells, "Reproduction &c.", p. 126.

itself on the life-cycle.''* At the outset plants reproduced themselves asexually by spores and shoots, whilst binary fission and partheno-genesis were methods of rapid propagation. Sex, by demanding the co-operation of two individuals to produce a third, acted as a power-ful brake upon fertility. But, after that had been recognised, such a wealth of possibilities appeared that Malthus himself, with a whole army of statisticians behind him, might well have been bewildered. 'Et in Arcadia ego.' Death for all the strange corpseless reproduc-tion of low forms of life, had been seen stalking through the world, causing the flower to fade, the beast to waste away. Resourceful and surprising, he might perhaps have found a way, even without the aid of carnivores, to balance accounts with fertility. Mere changes of climate had swept whole species away; and a world might be imagined where Death would have seemed no more hideous than a lengthening shadow on a summer evening, and his touch have left nowhere an uglier mark than the colour of a leaf in autumn. Whatever Death's powers, Adam, Homo Sapiens, Man fully finished and supernaturally endowed—speak of him as you will—had not at his first appearance on the stage lain within Death's grasp. Let Dickens, whose much-abused sentiment so generally reflects the sensibility of the common man, here add his witness to man's original immunity from mortal doom. Let Dickens tell—for whatever it may be worth to men who trust collective instinct to point out the pathway of reality—of 'the fashion that came in with our first garments, and will last unchanged until our race has run its course, and the wide firmament is rolled up like a scroll. The old, old fashion—Death! Oh, thank God, all who see it, for that older fashion yet of Immortality!''† The theologians have no quarrel with him—nor had the Drama that I was trying to reconstruct.

There must, as I conjectured, have been some tense, breathless moments of expectation whilst the listening world awaited the appearance of the chief actor on the stage. Portents of the impending wonder had cast strange shadows before it. The body of man, if the biologists were correct, had been developed from a mammal origin through the agency of apes and ape-men. Then, sometime towards the end of the tertiary or beginning of the quaternary period, in the so-called palaeolithic age, someone, who had nearly learnt to walk upright and could make fire and was beginning to devise tools,

* Wells, Huxley and Wells, "Reproduction, Heredity and the Development of Sex", p. 33. † "Dombey and Son", c. XVI.

had displayed some sort of a likeness to a human face—something that, perhaps (after making my grateful acknowledgments to the columns of a French matrimonial agency engaged in advertising the merits of an ill-favoured male), I may be permitted to call 'un visage quelconque'. The 'Dawn-man' must not, however, be hastily judged by appearances. 'Ce monsieur avec un visage quelconque' was not, if modern authorities are right, a bad fellow—no more brutal, in fact, than the brutes, from which his body had been in some sense derived, were really in our sense brutish*—even if he fell short, like the cave-men who came after him, of the qualifications required by evolutionary experts to enable a man to be classed as homo sapiens. Upon what principle any being is eventually exalted by the anthropologists from the status of a hominid to that of homo sapiens remains, however, far from clear. Such bodily variations as seeing straight, standing upright, or thickening one's skull, and such mental aberrations as wearing charms or supplying corpses with food for an existence beyond the grave seemed to afford as poor a title as the good looks of the handsome Cromagnons, who succeeded the slouching Neanderthals, to sapience. Sagacity, meanwhile, offers a possible basis for finer distinctions and closer classifications.

Lord Herbert of Cherbury, showing himself as thoughtful as his brother, George, showed himself devout, had long ago suggested that the specific difference between men and animals was to be sought in man's capacity for religion rather than his reason;† and, though this way of expressing, if it amounted to that, the rise of reason to its noblest height would probably fail to satisfy more orthodox theologians, the idea, which likewise appealed to Wesley,‡ cannot be reckoned as wholly uninteresting by an age confronted with the notion of sub-men and the idea of the numinous. If Adam had been the first creature to know God, not as a vague awe overshadowing nature, but as Being, pure, perfect, personal—"I am who am"—then, on this showing, an unassailable title to be called the first man, in the fullest meaning of the term, would have been established for him. And still more fully might that seem so if, in

---

* D. Davison, "Men of the Dawn", pp. 26 and 76.

† See Hallam's "Introduction to the Literature of Europe", II, p. 385.

‡ "I have somewhere read a profound remark of Wesley, that, considering the sagacity which many animals display, we cannot fix upon reason as the distinction between them and man; the true difference is, that we are formed to know God and they are not." Hallam, *ibid.*

the recurrent* phrase "Jehovah he is Elohim", with its suggestion of plurality in unity, the author of the Pentateuch had intended to convey the existence in the intellect of Adam's descendants of some faint perception that, in the very heart of monotheism, there lay the need for a trinity of persons behind unity of substance.

Such speculations might, perhaps, have been excited, but could scarcely have been settled by the tenuous reflections falling upon the stage as the great creative Act of the Drama reached at length its climax with the entry of the principal actor. For a short while, as one imagined, all the eyes in Eden had been turned upon him, and every living thing had watched, wondering, to see what he would do. Then the situation had become tense and pregnant to the utmost point of human possibility. Adam was seen to be living in deathless solitude. Amidst all this multitude of creatures he seemed to stand alone in the integrity of his justice. All Paradise lay waiting for some new sign of providence.

The narrative of the appearance of Eve is said by a modern commentator† to have astonished St. Augustine far more than that of Adam. It might well astonish anybody. "One would look in vain in all Creation stories, whether of the Babylonians or any other of Israel's neighbours, for the background of the idea of a living being having been created from a part of the body of another."‡ Apparently, in Egypt alone was that mythical background to be found; and only, therefore, on the most rationalistic reasoning, in Egypt, or when Israel came out of Egypt, was the Proem to Genesis likely to have been penned. Eight gods in one of the oldest Egyptian myths were said to have sprung from parts of Ptah-Atum's body—from his heart, tongue, teeth and other members. A rib was none of these, but chosen, perhaps, in contradistinctive symbolism from them. 'Rib', however, is a translation that might be less specifically rendered 'something from the side';§ and "from the point of view of the material cause", observes one authority,¶ "we may regard as certain the opinion held by St. Thomas (Summa I q.q2, art. 3, ad. 1) in opposition to Peter Lombard, that the 'rib' of Adam furnished only a very small portion of the matter which served for the building of the body of Eve."

* See Yahuda's "Accuracy of the Bible", p. 142.
† E. C. Messenger, "Evolution and Theology", p. 260.
‡ Yahuda, "Accuracy of the Bible", pp. 154–5, and for what immediately follows.   § E. C. Messenger, "Evolution and Theology", p. 252.
¶ *Ibid.*, p. 266.

Here at all events was material ready for the subtlest dramatic treatment; and the spectator, who was historian enough to bear in mind the now classic admonition 'Cherchez la femme', might well pause to consider what Jewish tradition had to show him. Consider, then, the salient points in the creation of woman as given in the argument of and elucidated in the commentaries upon the plot of the Hebrew Drama. Adam, after being called upon to survey all created things, could find no help-mate among them: the marvel* wrought in him, when he was created in God's image, had to be supernaturally matched before it could come to fruition: the woman's body was but to a very small extent drawn from his own, yet to such an extent that the unique virtuosity of a single super-naturalised human being was thus passed on from the stronger to the weaker sex† and in such manner as subsequently to become the symbol of the indissoluble relationship between Christ and the Church: man's honourable approach to his Creator in Eden, as St. Thomas has already been quoted to show,‡ had been through the ecstasy and fruitfulness of human love rather than through the ascetic demands of a divine Incarnation: and finally there had been no shame, or cause for shame, in that unveiled vision, which, afterwards, when some illicit knowledge of love's mystery had been obtained, caused the two actors in the scene to pluck leaves and make themselves girdles. The Tree of Knowledge from which those leaves were taken, was specifically, if one commentator § is correct, a love-tree—fig or sycamore according to the symbolism required by the thought of the bridegroom or the bride. And, had the fruit of the Tree of Life remained available after the catastrophe, Adam and Eve would, presumably, have substituted the prospect of an unending terrestrial existence with one another for that of the Beatific Vision which they had lost.

I add, but in its original tongue, one word more from a writer¶ whose orthodoxy will not be questioned—"Étant donné l'unité du composé humain et les rapports étroits qui unissent en nous l'âme et le corps, provoquer cette activité, c'est faire passer à l'acte, du

---

* "Mirabilia, non miracula", St. Bonaventure II Sent., Dist. xviii, a. i, q. ii, ad. 5.

† See the treatment of this by Messenger, *op. cit.*, p. 272.

‡ Lib. Sent., II, Dist. 20, art. 3, Expos.

§ Yahuda, *op. cit.*, p. 180.

¶ Mersch, "Morale et Corps Mystique", p. 207 (on 'l'activité organique génératrice').

même coup, l'amour lui-même. Les intentions ne changent rien à ces fonctions primordiales. Qu'on la veuille ou non, l'émotion dont s'accompagne l'activité dont nous parlons est le lieu psychologique par où notre volonté s'engage en notre organisme et y est prise. Cela même qui la rend appétible est qu'elle est l'aspect sensible et corporel de l'amour et qu'elle complète l'homme de cette manière-là; elle ne l'exalterait pas, elle ne l'attirerait pas à ce point, si elle n'était pas, en quelque sorte, le paroxysme de son humanité, le sommet où, devenant principe d'homme, il devient homme au maximum. Cette activité est donc intrinsèquement reliée à l'amour, et on ne peut la provoquer volontairement qu'en conformité avec la loi naturelle qui est celle de l'amour."

The detachment and delicacy of the priest had enabled him to say something which perhaps the modern artist, if Eric Gill's Auto-biography* be any guide, could only handle so crudely as to seem rather to rend than to raise a veil. Yet, even so, the exposition of this sacramental truth was likely to raise men's eyes higher than they mostly cared to lift them. They could not, indeed, in general, keep their minds off the matter, but they would not suffer the mystery to become consecrated in thought; and the oldest of human sacraments, the source and symbol of love's ecstasy, was denied in the divorce-court and mocked and spat upon in the brothel. That is all as might be expected:—

> Some secrets may the poet tell,
> For the world loves new ways.
> To tell too deep ones is not well;
> It knows not what he says.†

Nevertheless Bergson's words regarding love and mystery might well be borne in mind by the student of human origins: "When mysticism is reproached with expressing itself in the manner of a lover's passion one forgets that it is love which started to plagiarise mysticism, which borrowed its fervour, its transports, its ecstasy; in making use of the language of a passion that it had transfigured, mysticism had but resumed its property."‡

Meanwhile out of the fallen world of nature and into the oasis of Eden had slid that subtlest of beasts, the 'companionable'§

---

* *E.g.*, p. 247. "He (Jesus) ordained that our bodily motions should be pleasant and gratifying and that the pleasure of marriage should be beyond the dreams of avarice."　　　　† M. Arnold, "Stanzas in Memory of Obermann".

‡ Bergson, "Les Deux Sources de la Morale et de la Religion", p. 38.

§ Yahuda, *op. cit.*, p. 183.

Serpent. Paul Valéry has supplied a penetrating account of what followed as from the lips of this 'tertium quid'.

> Ève, jadis, je la surpris,
> Parmi ses premières pensées,
> La lèvre entr'ouverte aux esprits
> Qui naissaient des roses bercées.
>
>   .   .   .   .
>
> J'étais présent comme une odeur,
> Comme l'arome d'une idée
> Dont ne puisse être élucidée
> L'insidieuse profondeur.
>
>   .   .   .   .
>
> O quelle prose non pareille,
> Que d'esprit n'ai-je pas jeté
> Dans le dédale duveté
> De cette merveilleuse oreille!
>
>   .   .   .   .
>
> Elle buvait mes petits mots
> Qui bâtissaient une oeuvre étrange;
> Son œil, parfois, perdait un ange
> Pour revenir à mes rameaux
>
>   .   .   .   .
>
> Âme, disais-je, doux séjour
> De toute extase prohibée,
> Sens-tu la sinueuse amour
> Que j'aie du Père dérobée?
> Je l'ai, cette essence du ciel.
>
>   .   .   .   .

There, mindful of Matthew Arnold's warning, one did wisely to leave the inmost of the matter. It was enough to have seen for oneself that the old tale could renew its strength, fortified by archaeology with its returning faith in a golden age; fortified by everyman's familiar self-analysis showing degeneration whenever the doing of evil that one would not was substituted for the doing of good that one would; and fortified even, maybe, by the fashionable Freudian philosophy of the hour in so far as it postulated at the back of man's complex nature a region of subconscious being, swept by storms of desire and tormented by memories of faults and fears.

If physics had no knowledge of a Fall and anthropology only a remote acquaintance, fiction, and fiction of the best, knew, as it seemed to me, a good deal. One way of being 'thrilled' was, apparently, to become aware in some sub-conscious, surrealist sort of way of subnormal terrors, and I knew no better 'thrillers' than Stevenson's "Dr. Jekyll and Mr. Hyde" and Rider Haggard's "She".

The one had exposed the depth of the wound and the venom of the bite from which human nature was suffering. The other discovered, with rare, possibly unconscious subtlety, the passionate desire of woman to regain the earthly paradise she had thrown away and to inhabit it with the man she cared for, untroubled by any dread of death.

Fables, of course; yet surely such fables as materialism itself would have to resort to, if it were seriously to attempt to cover the whole nature of man or deal seriously with the riddle of the eternal feminine! "Poetry", as Flint has neatly observed, "is older than prose" and "the first singing was speaking". And Vico was not perhaps so much mistaken as Flint supposed in regarding marriage as near allied to the apprehension of a divine presence and power in the universe.* "O you wonder!"—Miranda's maiden eyes did not perceive the marvel. Yet there was woman, looking man so hard in the face, that Eden without Eve becomes as inconceivable as Eve without Eden.

Eden, however, had to be relinquished by Eve; and I can only invoke the haunting lines of a modern poet to punctuate their parting and perpetuate her regretful eyes.

> Ach, sie hätte gern in jenem Land
> Noch ein wenig weilen mögen, achtend
> Auf der Tiere Eintracht und Verstand.

> Ah, she would have gladly in that land
> Stayed a little longer and have learned
> How the beasts agree and understand.†

She might well have desired to gain that particular knowledge, for in that supposed fall of beasts to a state of struggle of which I have spoken, there had been little if anything to compare with the singular hatred of his own kind which, developed by pride, anger, avarice or envy, was leading man far beyond slaying another species from lust of possession to a joy in killing for killing's sake and a sadistic pleasure in giving pain. Well might Hobbes fancy that the natural condition of man had been as a time of foul weather, its dispositions continually clouded with menace and intermittently distilling in storms.‡ And well might Gibbon, after those first thoughts on

* Flint, "Vico", pp. 211–12.
† Rilke's "Eva", trans. Leishman (cited from Bowra's "Heritage of Symbolism", p. 63).
‡ Hobbes, "Lev.", Pt. I, c. 13.

history, which caused the precocious young Oxonian to be received into the Catholic Church, had been suppressed by parental pressure, conclude that history itself, if faithfully recorded, was, 'indeed, little more than the register of the crimes, follies and misfortunes of mankind'.* But to return to the scene of Eve's exodus from Eden!

A little incident, which presumably occurred about the time when her boys came to manhood, seemed to justify Rilke's conjecture that Eve had felt cause to regret her lack or loss of insight into the relations of animals, so relatively benignant, in comparison with those obtaining from her time onwards among her own offspring. It was a little incident as modern society sees the world, yet more educative than many a modern statistical report informed by the dogma of progress; and its presence among these prolegomena of Hebrew history invited, like many another passage of Scripture, a search for such a pensée de derrière—such a thought in the background as Pascal† had been wont to recommend in looking at the world. "If thy heart were right," sings the author of the "Imitatio Christi", "then every creature would be a mirror of life and a book of holy doctrine. . . . A pure heart penetrates Heaven and Hell."‡

Eve's loss of vision, ill compensated by her newly acquired knowledge, had, as a long experience has taught her latest descendants to suspect, opened the door to an interminable investigation of the 'how' of things, whilst pulling it to in respect of the 'why' of them. She had, as it seemed, consequently failed to teach her elder son much about the world they now lived in or the truth of the human situation. Cain, seemingly, had supposed that the fruits of the earth would suffice to provide offerings for the service of the Deity. But Abel had the keener insight. And thus, through a difference about the substance and symbolism of sacrifice, fraternity was perverted into fratricide; as happened again, millenniums later, at the Reformation and after. Man had perhaps never been more dangerous to his species than when he wrestled with ultimate problems that he has no sufficiently clear vision to see plain. Or so the Drama seemed to intimate.

I wondered, then, whether the impresario of this stupendous play had introduced the incident that I am recalling on a somewhat similar account to that which led Hamlet to introduce a dumb-show before the insidious play-scene intended to catch the King. "Mich-

* Gibbon, "Decline and Fall", Chap. 3.
† p. p336–7.   ‡ "Imitation" "Pesées", "Christi", Bk. II, c. 4.

ing mallecho!" There was mischief abroad; and Human Nature had to be both convinced and convicted of it. Cain, as was said, came offering an unbloody sacrifice of the fruits of the earth; and Abel a bloody sacrifice drawn from his flocks: and Cain's sacrifice was inacceptable, but Abel's was approved. The vegetarianism of Eden had no longer, it seemed, obtained in man's fallen state. Without shedding of blood there could no longer be any propitiation of the Deity. It had come to that; and Abel had known it, but Cain not. And Cain was angry at that—so much so that he shed the blood of Abel, killed him and fled, no man so far pursuing.

There was cryptic suggestion enough here to tempt one to look on over the argument and see what came of it all. And so I noticed that at the very climax of the piece that had been played, a blood-stained sacrifice, which indeed appeared to deserve the title of supreme, being the sacrifice of an Incarnate God, had been continued and perpetuated through the substitution of bread for the flesh that had been mangled in the Judgment-hall and nailed to the Cross. In this sort of way were motifs, as it seemed to me, introduced, dropped and then repeated, until one gained the impression, or perhaps more strictly the certitude, that the hand of an artist was fully as active in the text and action of the play as in its scenic accompaniments—an Artist, however, who hid himself as certainly behind the facts of human as the harmonies of natural history. Thus did the enigma of sacrifices, both fair and foul, which seemed to haunt the many approaches to human history and beckon the mind down crazy paths to broken altars and valleys of dry bones, suddenly lose the look of a feu follet and become irradiated with kindly light. At worst, given the rationalistic investigator's inevitable postulate that there was reason enough to look for a reason, the prevalence of sacrifice postulated a sense both of something numinous needing to be propitiated and of something gone wrong needing to be put right. All Asia had in some sense felt that once and, if Europe had now lost the knowledge, one could only adopt and adapt Symonds's remark that "if a critic is so dull as to ask what 'Life of Life! thy lips enkindle' means or to whom it is addressed, none can help him, any more than one can help a man whose sense of hearing is too gross for the tenuity of a bat's cry."*

The world had been put out of joint:—Hamlet had said that and so much else to the point in a play which, more, one might conjecture, than any other of human origin—more than the "Prometheus", more

* J. A. Symonds, "Shelley", p. 24.

than the "Antigone"—had seemed to gather into its slight compass all the pain and pathos and perplexity of the world. It was, as Hamlet never doubted, a world, a cosmos and no chaos. And it was out of joint. And, if one wanted to set it right, one conjured up, as Prospero was presently to demonstrate, the baseless fabric of a vision only to abjure it later as rough magic and, lest one's latter ending be despair, to plead for heavenly music.

There, in "Hamlet", as it seemed, one might hear the voice of a Humanity half-stunned, as the mind of Christian Humanists such as Thomas More or Erasmus betray, by the bludgeon of the Reformation. There one might breathe the authentic troubled air of the Renaissance, and feel the recoil of a supreme dramatist from the shock that had been given to the Divine Comedy. I say it only in passing, to illustrate in what way the reflections of the Looking Glass World would seem to move backwards and forwards to the accompaniment of Hebrew melodies.

For the action of the play, as the reader will doubtless have understood, was all this while advancing down vistas of time with a good deal of sometimes hardly perceptible, yet fairly continuous scene-shifting; the piece being mounted in a lavish manner reminiscent of Beerbohm Tree, though of course on an incomparably grander scale and one as different as possible from that which modest circumstances, or perhaps cheap ideas, have lately made fashionable. In some way which I cannot pretend to fathom but which I have tried to explain by the saying that history repeats itself, what I was reading in the Proem to the past would blend with what I was seeing of the present. At moments I would say to myself that the unity of the Drama so exceeded its diversity as to make its retrospect, its aspect and its prospect all one and to render each meaningless without the other. And in that effect lay, I believe, great part of its grandeur and power. It was integrated as plays in general are not.

Meanwhile the character and course of the argument seemed to suggest that Man could no more long keep his mind off God than his hands off his brother. As Mr Langdon Davies points out in a book by no means intended to promote Christianity and striving to be 'modern' with all its might, the search for the unknown God qualifies in every age the research of Nature.* The human intellect, however, has nowadays become so muddled with all kinds of knowledge that magniloquent heights of passion are reached and magnificent deeds of daring done long before it is at all clear that any

* Langdon-Davies, "Man and his Universe", see esp. pp. 238, 241.

sanctions exist to justify indignation or vindicate vengeance. Hegel had, indeed, advanced so far along this path of reflection as to see tragedy as a conflict of right with right; though all such conflict as that might seem rather to merit no more than the epithet of pathetic. Anyhow, great drama, as I came to think, demanded some surer foundation than an ethic based on the voice of nature, of national will or tribal deity. The wind of Hebrew history, indeed, like all other human and patriotic chronicles, carried such sentiments upon its breezes; but its assurance, again and again repeated with rising strength and increasing beauty, that in Hebrew history only had such sentiments an absolute and exclusive right to be entertained, swept with the force of a gale through the valley of human decision. A single scene in the play, but of a supreme quality, seemed in particular to compel assent as only the genius of dramatic truth can hope to do. Not even Moses as he moved down Sinai, his face aglow, the tables of the Law in his hand, and the pattern of holy things in his heart, produced an impression of such majesty as Elijah when, after rejecting the loud, elemental claims of Nature—raging storm and riven earth and roaring fire—to be the authentic voice of God, he passed out, from a cave on the mountain side, under the open sky, and stood still, waiting, his face covered, for the low, soft sound which he would recognise as the true prophetic word, even though it had not yet become that Word someday to be heralded by angels, and seen of men, and known of mystics.

To such a height had the religion of Israel power to conduct the spirit of man; and the scene had obviously fallen with matchless effect into the plot of the play. It was easier by far to imagine the reign of Elizabeth without a Shakespeare than the reign of Ahab and Jezebel without an Elijah. His figure seemed so set in the tapestry of the time that, had it been found wanting there, the design might have been lost. Yet on the eve of his immortal hour he had despaired of his country, confessed his cynicism as regards the Chosen People, and prayed for death at the hands of God. All the anatomy of man's deepest melancholy might be read into Elijah's soul; and perhaps all the anatomy of man's deepest absurdity found in Elijah's mockery of the priests of Baal. Made great enough to be as a happy child laughing with the world about him, Man had, with the Fall, become himself a laughing-stock to Elijah, to Hamlet, to anyone with eyes to see the might-have-been in the make-up.

Let me add, however, in passing that I fancy Chesterton made a mistake in suggesting that Christ permitted His mind to dwell upon the human comedy; and let me say it clearly, lest I should seem to have shirked a difficulty that may seem to people with a fine sense of humour at times acute. By virtue of a common infirmity we all derive some title to become articulate in respect of one another's absurdities; for we may ourselves most reasonably hope to add something to the gaiety of individuals, if not to that of nations. But it would hardly have been in character for One, not Himself afflicted with moral infirmity, to make mock of those who, made in the image of God, so generally spend their time in robbing beasts of their particular additions.* When even a gentleman may hesitate to ridicule a bore, it might ill become Love itself to deride pharisee or philistine. One must be on a level with one's target, or at a still lower altitude, to let one's sense of humour loose; and Jesus, in the Christian view, was never that. Hence it is recorded only that "Jesus wept", but nowhere that He laughed; room being left, one may presume, for many a smile where small children, and not grown-up babies, came into play.

The diagnosis of human nature in the Drama, I was about to observe, when I dropped into this digression, reached far into the bowels of human history—as far perhaps as into those of divine compassion. It reminded me in its historical aspect of an estimate I had come across of the attitude of Christ to those so often adulated as the voice of God under the name of the People—to the most part of men, that is, of whom the best Carlyle could say was that they were 'mostly fools', and Abraham Lincoln, that great democrat, that you could fool all of them some of the time and some of them all of the time, but not all of them all of the time. Here is the estimate:—"Aucun sentiment n'est plus étranger a Jésus que cette vénération admirative pour le peuple, que cette foi en sa sainteté ou en son infaillibilité en quoi consiste, aux yeux de certains, l'amour des humbles. La forme de son amour du peuple, c'est la pitié."† If this estimate were correct, then, as I judged, the Bible was all of a piece politically and its whole argument well-calculated to clear the human mind of a particularly nauseous, though highly popular type of cant. And if there were a difference to be marked between the former and the latter parts of the Drama I was watching, it lay in this —that the former posed the human problem and the latter tendered the solution of it.

* "Troilus and Cressida", I, ii.

† Huby, "Christus", p. 1010. The article quoted is by Huby and Rousselot.

After this manner, then, did the political diagnosis of the spectacle reach to the bowels of divine compassion; and the stage come near at times to taking the look of a laboratory or clinic, so closely were pain and remedy alike under observation. It was, I felt satisfied, all in the design to make one feel that, whilst in powers of diagnosis Jew and Greek differed not so widely but that their thoughts might meet, the Jew in the theory and practice of medicine was immeasurably superior and more skilful. The Greek, like some of his disciples even to this day, believed in reason to the point of turning it into a patent medicine and maintaining that it could cure all ills; but the Jew had found out, what the Greek had missed, that the mind of man no less than the rest of his nature had been desperately damaged. It was this that had given Jewish history a sort of primacy in the study of the Humanities and justified its place in history and in education. The Drama from the first had fixed the eye of the spectator upon the idea of human redemption with extraordinary skill. But for this overmastering consideration the scheme of the play might have wandered wildly over a great range of circumstance. Instead it concentrated its theme upon a focal point which grew as the drama advanced to a great intensity of light.

For this reason the history of the Jews, if it were attentively studied with its hagiographa as commentary, afforded a more telling exposition of the foundations of political science than anything even the Greeks had to give, and closed in no anti-climax, such as one is sensible of when Plato averts his eyes from the illustrious Athens of his time to look for the model of his ideal republic in bleak, forceful Sparta, or when Aristotle's tuition of Alexander as a prospective philosopher-king, or at least as the royal torch-bearer of Hellenic civilisation, ends in the valuation of the "Iliad" by the pupil as a fine military manual and in his entirely congruous ambition to be left with no worlds to conquer.

The Drama before me had had its melancholy surprises, but they were not of this comic sort. The political honours all went to Solomon; and Solomon had been the embodiment of a knowledge, an understanding and a counsel as much deeper than Solon's as wisdom is higher than them all. There was nothing so very surprising about this. Much about Solomon should have helped him to see men and things as they really were. The throne upon which he sat, founded as it was upon the repudiation by the Israelites of the pure theocracy of Moses, was a standing reminder of the fact that the politics even of the Twelve Tribes had become based upon the principle of the 'second-best'. Until the time of the Kings, every Israelite had it still in his power to say what, if I rightly recollect, an Englishman, required to kneel at its bar, did once say to the House of Commons:—"I kneel only to God". The Israel of Samuel, however, had preferred to kneel also to kings; and the Deity had given them their way.

Such were the people, even the Chosen People! What of the Kings, the anointed Kings? Solomon had David to his father; and David had had Bathsheba to wife; and thereby hung a tale. Outstanding as the patriot king par excellence, as the sweetest singer in Israel, as the royal founder of the line whence the Messiah was to come, as one in whom Samuel had perceived a man after God's own heart, David was yet found wanting in the eyes of Jehovah in one all-important respect. High-hearted and (despite the ugly dying admonition to his son to execute Joab—the Bismarck of the Jews—after his death) high-souled, he had failed to qualify as the architect of the house of God. He had shed blood. The builder of the Temple had to be a man of peace. The identity of the God of Jacob with the God some day to be born of the seed of David in the City of Bethlehem was never made plainer than at that crucial point. Jehovah had 'winked at' much ignorance, but not here—not in this matter of Temple-building. The rejection of his father—holy David—as the master-builder had been precisely Solomon's cue to come forward to the front of the stage.

In the skylark's spring of his reign—in that first memorable communion of the young King with God—the wisdom of Solomon had reached to the gate of heaven. Then, as the midsummer of his days drew on, his wisdom had circumscribed the earth, wandering all the ways of men, running to and fro in its curiosity and enterprise to the very limits of Vanity Fair and beyond them—running and returning again in the autumn of his life with a crop of maxims and aphorisms so permanent and pungent that even yet they might serve to raise the chill temperament of a Bentham or reduce the high tempo of a Beveridge. The wisdom of Solomon had evidently been of a very excellent vintage of cynicism; its bouquet fragrant as the spices of the East, its taste dry and mature, its properties apparent in the keen eye and steady hand of one whose champagne had been associated (as I have heard it said is sometimes done in the case of athletes) with soda. In vino Veritas!

Solomon had seen how frail man was, how foolish, how futile; how easily the tedium coming of his downfall drove him toward changes of which he wearied almost as soon as made; and how, at the close, nothing seemed to satisfy him, and the dream of youth ended with the disillusionment of age. He had doubtless watched, as we do still, the pilgrims of futurity setting out upon the golden road to Samarkand; and he had doubtless found how vain it was to remonstrate with men too spirited to stand and wait, too stupid to see that strength oftentimes comes of sitting still.

> We are the Pilgrims, master; we shall go
> Always a little further: it may be
> Beyond that last blue mountain barred with snow,
> Across that angry or that glimmering sea,
> White on a throne or guarded in a cave
> There lives a prophet who can understand
> Why men were born: but surely we are brave,
> Who make the Golden Journey to Samarkand. *

Solomon had no need of golden journeys or silver-tongued prophets to tell him the truth about the human situation. He knew why men were born and what they were here to do; and it would not be too much to say that his political science touched the peak-point that it is given to man to reach under the inspiration of the thought of God but before any incarnation of the Word that was with God and that was God. To this day, if rumour speaks right, the building of Solomon's Temple affords the fundamental symbol in Masonic Societies of the deistic basis of their craft.†

The wisdom of Solomon, as exemplified in his famous judgment, illustrates admirably what happens when justice is identified with what, for lack of a better word, has lately been styled 'egality'. On

* Flecker, "The Golden Journey to Samarkand".

† Such a remark, perhaps, invites a comment. Few things that have been said to me about social service made a more lasting impression on my mind than a casual remark of my father's regarding freemasonry. Having become a Mason himself at the time of the Crimean War, when it was thought that membership of the Masonic brotherhood might gain some special consideration for the wounded at the hands of a foe reputed none too gentle, he told me that he thought, without any breach of the pledges he had given at the time of admission to the Order, he might say to me, who was at the time contemplating a similar step, that he had not cared to carry his own membership further from a certain sense, or perhaps suspicion, of its incompatibility with his Christian professions. He would not of course have intended this remark to a son as any sort of reflection on his friends or relatives, one or two of whom, and probably more, were distinguished English Masons. I leave this digression there—for indeed I have no title to make further comment—with only this rider added, that my father was, as I think most people who knew him would have agreed, a very shrewd man—and so make my way back to the contemplation of a shrewder.

the facts as presented to him the two women were equally entitled to one half of the child. Solomon pretended to decide as our mathematically minded politicians and philosophers now tend to decide all questions in heaven and earth; and, behold! no baby, but a corpse. The judgment of Solomon, by bringing in the affections of the heart, brought out the equity of the matter, and for all men who are disposed to believe that egality supplies the last word in political science it no less points a moral than adorns a tale.

More judicial than the astute Elizabeth, more poetical than the judicious Bacon, the Megalopsychos of the Hebrews had, if the Drama might be trusted, contrived within the limits of his tiny kingdom to try out the common-sense of good government and to present its maxims in the light of a glorified prudence. He had preserved peace; he had entertained good relations with his neighbours; he had promoted commerce; he had planted gardens and built houses; he had pursued variety and cultivated splendour; he had kept public interest alive; he had provided public amusement with apes and peacocks and anticipated therewith the amenities of Regent's Park or the Jardin d'Acclimatation. The Queen of Sheba, as we all know, had seen nothing like it. Yet Solomon himself kept his head and took the measure of his accomplishment. On a long view it proved vanity and vexation of spirit. The fear of God, according to the conclusions of the Preacher, the son of David, King in Jerusalem, constituted the whole duty of man. And in fact the Temple of God, and not the kingdom of Solomon, proved within a little while to be the only enduring monument of the greatest reign in Hebrew history.

One problem—and that the most difficult in political philosophy —had in fact eluded solution even at the hands of the wisest of Kings. The sense of ennui, a mark of the fall of man, had invaded Solomon's life on every side, and after his death had brought his kingdom crashing to the ground. He himself wearied of women, as his crowd of wives and concubines discovered; and women wearied of him. "I find a thing more bitter than death," says the Preacher's commentary, "even the woman whose heart is snares and nets. . . . One man among a thousand have I found; but a woman among all those have I not found. Behold, this only have I found, that God made man upright; but they have sought out many inventions."* The legacy of Eve had been more than a match for the wisdom of Solomon. His politic adventures in matrimony had yielded as little as, or less

* Eccles. vii. 25–29.

than Elizabeth's no less politic adventures in virginity. At the far end of the halls of wisdom, as at its first entry, woman still held the door; and beyond lay Paradise—the earthly paradise with the accursed serpent or the heavenly paradise with the vision of God. Indeed, man had much need of Pascal's esprit de finesse penetrating to the pensée de derrière, if he was not to be lured away by some escalier dérobé into a harem instead of the palace of truth. This great act of the Drama had closed as I gathered with a choir chanting the Song of Songs 'which is Solomon's'—a canticle cryptic enough in its language to set all manner of swine seeking for what they might find among its pearls.

The young men of Jerusalem were as easily bored as the Palace ladies. They too—the young fascists or, which is in practice too often indistinguishable, the young socialists of the day—wanted change, and thought, by the substitution of scorpions for whips, to bring order up to the level of efficiency. The heir-apparent, the egregious Rehoboam, had all the appearance of a conceited ass, and listened gladly to their counsels.

The formulae of such revolutions have become familiar. Everything, doubtless, in the eyes of Rehoboam and his advisers, could be changed for the better; nothing and nobody was to be left alone; and all the maxims of Solomon were to go with the wind, should they fail to be swept away by the whirlwind. The new King immediately upon his accession tossed prudence aside in a manner that has become classic; and the kingdom of Solomon snapped in two. But as the Drama proceeded it became clear that Rehoboam had no lack of short-thoughted successors on either throne. It was in vain that Micaiah, the son of Imlah, warned the Kings of Israel and Judah, for once united, not to make war upon Syria. They put him in prison as a defeatist and hurried off to Ramoth Gilead, where they were defeated, and where Ahab lost his worthless life. It was equally vain, a hundred and fifty years later, for Isaiah to warn the well-meaning but weak Hezekiah that, not in the strength of Pharaoh, but in 'returning and rest, in quietness and confidence' lay wisdom and strength. The King of Judah preferred to put his faith in Egypt, only to find it a broken reed. In his discomfiture Hezekiah thought to buy off the menacing Sennacherib with a bribe; but, whilst the mob went mafficking prematurely at its supposed deliverance, the Assyrian, demanding unconditional surrender, descended like a wolf on the fold. It was then, and only then, after the sheer necessities of defence had thoroughly exposed the ineffectual weaving of impolitic combinations, that Isaiah reassured the frightened, but now repentant and prayerful King. Jerusalem, he foretold, would not fall; and in due course, whether, as Herodotus asserts, a plague of mice devoured their bowstrings or whether a pestilence (of which mice were apparently a symbol) fell on the hosts of Asshur, the might of the Gentile melted away like snow at the glance of the Lord.

The politicians were, however, too timid, the people too stupid to believe and understand. Neither their deliverance nor the carrying away captive of Israel made any deep impression on Jewish minds. If they repented under Josiah, they relapsed again after Megiddo; their faith being in fact no more than an attempt at traffic with the Almighty.

"Savez-vous," Voltaire has observed in an entertaining epigram,

> "Savez-vous, pourquoi Jérémie
> A tant pleuré pendant sa vie?
> C'est qu'en prophète il prévoyait
> Qu'un jour Lefranc le traduirait."

The prophet had, however, other reasons for lamentation. The people had grown more idolatrous, the politicians more presumptuous; and God refused to be mocked any more. Again Judah put its trust in Egypt, and therewith the might of Babylon under Nebuchadnezzar, as formerly that of Assyria under Sennacherib, fell full upon Jerusalem. Jeremiah had warned his countrymen to agree with their adversary while there was time, and had been put in prison, as a defeatist, for his pains. He had, however, being the man that God made him, seen straight. Jerusalem could not meet the challenge which the imprudence of her timid king had brought upon her. The city fell; the King was captured and blinded; and the Chosen People were carried off to Babylon, beside whose waters they sat down and wept. The kingship had dismally failed to make manifest to the nations the glory of Israel or to prepare in Judah for the advent of the Messiah. But in the second part of the word of Isaiah the idea of theocracy, as if in divine compensation for the decline and fall of the monarchy, had reappeared with such a beauty of holiness and wealth of tragic detail that the Prophet, even as he proclaimed that the True God was one who hid Himself, seemed to lift the veil and show the Messiah both in the plenitude of His power and the grace of His Glory. The fulfilment of the vision was yet for an appointed time, but the vision itself had been seen in the dark night of Israel's prophetic soul.

Under the benevolent rule of Cyrus the children of Judah returned to Jerusalem, rebuilt the Temple and exemplified the fate of such as fail to fulfil their destiny. They had never been great enough to pursue that rôle of quiet confidence—or, if you will, splendid isolation—which had been indicated to them from the very time of their entering the Promised Land as the very genius of their policy; and as they neared the final event, which was to sweep them from their place in history, they beheld their country tossed like flotsam amd jetsam upon the tide of empire. During the five centuries that elapsed between the return from Babylon and the advent of the Messiah, they passed from the hand of Persia into that of Macedon, and from subjection to the House of Ptolemy to that of Seleucus. Both by Ptolemy Philopator and Antiochus Epiphanes was the Holy Place profaned; and even the celebrated revolt of the Maccabees led on to that alliance with the might of Rome which in due course was converted into subjection and led Pompey to invade the sacred precincts of the Temple. Thus, six years before the Christian Era, Judaea had been formally incorporated in the Roman Empire and Augustus Caesar become suzerain of the throne of David.

All this, as I could see, lent itself to the theme of the Hidden God as well as to great curtain-raisers like Racine's "Athalie" or to lesser ones like Stephen Phillips's "Herod". The sight, even down the vistas of time, of the Holy City, sitting solitary, in penultimate desolation, whilst an alien governor, with all the pomp and circumstance of Imperial Rome, took possession, produced such a sense of events moving forward solemnly after the manner of a procession to their appointed end as, I thought, could never before have been matched on the vast champaign of history by any impact of secular might upon spiritual decadence. Yet even that catastrophic concussion must, as it seemed, have been lost to the view of any contemplative eye behind a scene that suddenly developed in the very heart of the situation. I must not give the notion that there was anything like the descent of a deus ex machina. The playwright was immeasurably too great an artist for that. Into the heart of the dramatic situation at Jerusalem, where the cause of Jehovah was collapsing so obviously before the arms of Caesar, there slipped, as unobtrusively as the serpent slipped into Eden, the real King of the Jews or, which was the same thing, the unknown God of the Gentiles. Yet not quite unobserved! Voices in the sky, according to the testimony of some poor shepherds watching their flocks by night, proclaimed peace on earth to men of good-will; and from the East there had hurried to the manger of the Messiah sages, who had caught, from the singular appearance and seemingly sudden pause of a star, the music of crystal spheres and the sound, unheard, of Angels' songs.

Chapter XIV

GRAND OPERA

A T this point, as I gathered, the play had leapt of a sudden to the highest point of tragedy—beyond the reach of Sophocles or Æschylus, of Goethe or Racine, even of Shakespeare. If, as used to be maintained by critics, royal personages were a sine qua non of tragic, as opposed to pathetic drama, then pure royalty was here; but disguised, and deeply. The august world, as manifested in Tacitus's pages or Gibbon's critique, had passed Christianity by as a tiresome excrescence or an amiable eccentricity. Yet to the philosophic historian nothing surely in history should seem stranger than that the Founder of Christianity, who has been so often held up as a teacher, a poet, a philanthropist, in whom some have seen a great gentleman and others the champion of the common man, had so rarely been acclaimed, in the direct political meaning of the term, as a Prince. Centuries before Machiavelli made use of that title for his portrait of a statesman and, holding up the glass to nature, had caught the likeness of one who was both a prince of the world and of the Church, who was both Caesar and Borgia, another Prince had laid the foundation of an imperium as much greater than all the rest as its duration has been longer. He had plainly outbuilt all other empire-builders, out-thought all other political philosophers. Dismissed at intervals as defeated, decayed, dying and even defunct; betrayed by its custodians from Iscariot onwards to the latest example of a worldly prelate; angrily identified by its critics with the harlot whom it dislodged from her seat upon the Seven Hills, the imperium of the Christians had shown itself, if History afforded any guidance, to be founded upon a rock. It constituted, therefore, as I judged, an event in history more worth study than all the rest put together. I found, however, that the Drama had taken its estimate and revealed its ethos at least a thousand years ago, when the foundations of Western civilization were laid.

Of the four biographies of Christ supplied to elucidate the second part of the play the first was as plainly preoccupied with the conversion of the Jewish theocracy into the promised kingdom of the Messiah, as was the second concerned to epitomise the dogmatic facts to which St. Peter stood witness, or the third to discover Christ's life from the standpoint of His Mother and the fourth from that of His most intimate friend. The nature and constitution of the Kingdom were in fact so plainly the dominant theme of the First Gospel that the memorable scene which occurred at Caesarea Philippi might well appear to the constitutional historian of Christianity to provide the climax of an interest initiated in the opening genealogy, vastly increased by the great charter or code of the Sermon on the Mount, but consummated only in the interrogation and commission of St. Peter. No one, capable of visualising that dramatic scene, could, as it seemed to me, be so dull as to miss its sublime significance. Christ, it will be remembered, had first inquired of His disciples what men said of the Son of Man; and they had replied that some took Him for John Baptist, others for Elijah, others for Jeremiah. He then asked them directly what they thought themselves. Only Simon, already surnamed Peter, had apparently felt able to frame an answer, and, if he spoke authoritatively for the rest, his answer was none the less singular and conclusive:—"Thou art the Christ, the Son of the living God". For him, as for all his successors from that day to this, the Son of Man had been indeed the Son of God, fully confessed. One of the Twelve at least had shown himself utterly capable of making the decisive act of faith of which the common flesh and blood of the natural man fell short; and that one had been Peter. A blessing, full of divine courtesy, had met his confession; but the matter had not been left at that, as it well might have been if confession were the end in view. "And I also say unto thee that thou art Peter, and upon this rock I will build my church; and the gates of Hades shall not prevail against it. I will give unto thee the keys of the Kingdom of Heaven; and whatsoever thou shalt bind on earth shall be bound in heaven; and whatsoever thou shalt loose on earth shall be loosed in heaven." There had followed a caution to all the disciples from One, still hiding Himself from the world, that they should tell no man, what they now knew, that He was the Christ. Certainly from the standpoint of good drama or good sense, an exaggerated scene with an over-emphatic phraseology, if nothing more was meant than that a strong character made the best foundation for a solemn creed! And certainly—supposing the Papacy was all a fraud or even half an imposture—one containing the most unfortunate speech on record! For the evolution of the cosmopolitan Church had broadened down steadily from precedent to precedent along the evolutionary lines of the memorable utterance; and the supremacy of the Pope, affirmed at the Council of Lyons in 1274 ('perhaps the first and last Council undisturbed by dispute'*) on his way to which Aquinas died and where St. Bonaventure preached, was reaffirmed in yet more explicit terms at the Council held, first at Ferrara and then at Florence, in 1439; the Byzantine Emperor and Patriarch attending there in person for the occasion, so that in fact at the fall of Constantinople in 1453 the Eastern Emperor was in full communion with the Roman See. The Turks, it is true, had, for their own obvious purposes, revived the schism between Old and New Rome: but it required, as I thought, a disingenuous mind to make anything of a breach engineered by the Infidel to promote the division of Christendom and discredit the claims, fully considered and finally admitted at Florence, of the Holy See.

I touch on these matters here, however, only to emphasise that the Drama I was watching in the mirror possessed not merely historic foundation but historic justification according to the canons of Clio. The controversialist might, if he chose, join issue over incidents such as those familiar ones connected with the names of Liberius, Vigilius and Honorius, but only, if I mistake not, to find himself if not first run through by the rapier of the trained theologian, reeling under the impact of a boomerang. He who boasts of the evolution of the Mother of Parliaments must not complain of the evolution of the Papacy; he who swallows the illegality of the trial of King Charles I or the deposition of King James II must not strain at some supposed gnat such as the attitude adopted towards the Popes by the Council of Constance in its earlier, but still unconstitutional† condition; he who affirms that 'the king can do no wrong' must not let his readers suppose that infallibility in definitions of faith and morals is identical with impeccability in the conduct of public affairs or private life. Both the principle and doctrine of Papal Supremacy could then, as I judged, hold their own very well in any court of final appeal where the historic evolution of ideas and institutions on

* Milman, "Hist. of Latin Christianity", Bk. XI, c. iv.

† The Council was in the first instance convened by the Emperor Sigismund with the assent of a puppet anti-Pope, John XXIII; but its legal position in the eyes of canonists dates from the Bull of Convention subsequently issued by the legitimate Pope, Gregory XII, who by this act, with which his abdication was associated, gave the Council its constitution and its authority. The details will be found in Pastor ("History of the Popes", Vol. I, Eng. trans., p. 200) and elsewhere.

the lines explained in Newman's famous chapter on the notes of a true and a false development of types,* was recognised.

"Doctrines", as he says there, "are developed by the operation of principles and develop variously according to those principles. . . . The same philosophical elements, received into a certain sensibility or insensibility to sin and its consequences, leads one mind to the Church of Rome; another to what, for want of a better word, may be called Germanism." The essential thing for any one who desired to see history faithfully told was to avoid the local or national sensibilities such as those against which Rait, as I have mentioned, had warned me. One can hardly stress to any effect the unity of State or Church without conceding to them the claim to a capital or metropolis, and therefore, in the case of the latter, without ascribing to the chair of St. Peter such a presidency of love and authority in matters of faith as had been explicitly done by Ignatius of Antioch and Irenaeus of Lyons in the first two centuries.

It was, however, as I reconstructed the scene at Caesarea Philippi, less of the historic or patristic evidence sustaining the traditional interpretation of the famous charge than of its dramatic aspect that I thought. Without the meaning that had been commonly given to the memorable words, the Drama would have lost point to an incalculable degree. The glove which the world had thrown down by the hand of the Roman Emperor needed, not only for the purposes of good drama to be picked up by the hand of some accredited champion of Christianity—picked up in love, as it had been thrown down in hate —but also to be thrown back on the very site of Imperial Rome and in such a manner that no man, holding fast to facts and preferring length to shortness of thought, could reasonably doubt which in the long run was the stronger power engaged—the Galilean or the Pagan Prince. This seemed an essential feature of the play; and the evolution of the Papacy vital to its artistic execution.

As one looked closely at the text of the argument many things fell into place that had at first seemed disconnected. The institution of Peter as the rock on which the Church was to rise had had a startling sequence in an incident that had almost immediately followed and can have left the spectator in no doubt as to what frailty of man must be anticipated even behind an adamantine virtue of office. The worst that could in principle be said in criticism of St. Peter's successors with any depth of justice had been said of St. Peter himself on the morrow of his appointment and by the Master

* "Development of Doctrine", Pt. II, c. 5.

who chose him. 'Satan', a 'stumbling-block', 'not minding the things of God but of men'—such were the epithets addressed to him. The crude ambition of the man for his Master's exaltation by any and every means could not have been made plainer; and Caleb Balderstone might at that time, perhaps, have found in him a kindred spirit. Yet, rock of fidelity in his care for his Master's honour as he fondly fancied himself already, and had, indeed, the capacity to become, he was a long way from touching rock-bottom in love. "Lovest thou Me more than these?" The question had not at first been posed; and when at last it came, the caution, not to say hesitancy of Peter's reply showed that he felt its searching significance to the full.

"Behind every civilisation", observes Mr. Christopher Dawson, "there is a vision." The vista of Calvary, so repugnant to St. Peter's first dispositions when it was first disclosed, had been followed within a week by another vision, too subtly apposite to have been invented, too artistically conceived to have been interpolated, and therefore the work of a supreme dramatist for whom beauty and truth had actually and effortlessly met and kissed.

Only three Apostles witnessed what occurred at the Transfiguration—St. Peter evidently as Primate-elect; St. John, presumably, as the Beloved Disciple; St. James, perhaps as the proto-martyr of the Apostolic band. For them the veil that hung over human destiny was lifted at last; the 'might-have-been' of Humanity that had been lost in Paradise was shown on the eve of what now had to be in Gethsemane; and, before the Son of Man in power crossed the stage of history carrying His Cross, an anticipation of the advent of the Son of God in glory was seen like a tableau or, if the modernism be not too offensive, like a conversation-picture with Moses and Elijah, just men made perfect, talking to Him as easily as Adam had once talked with God in Eden. It was no wonder that the Chosen Three found the experience overwhelming. In the high altitudes to which they had come the silver lining of earth's clouded sky threw a blinding radiance over the stupefying vision. The Orient has apparently long known how, with the aid of yoga or some other sense-annihilating apparatus, to pass beyond the sphere of sense and achieve some effect that may perhaps be compared to the vision of an empty throne.* But the three Apostles had not only outsoared

* I think Maritain's article on "The Natural Mystical Experience and the Void" in "Redeeming the Time", pp. 225–55, may be the thing most worth reading on what is touched on here.

the shadow of our night and reached a land that is very far off; but had found the throne occupied, and beheld the King in His beauty with Man in majesty standing at his Sovereign's side. "Behind every civilisation there is a vision." This had been a vision of Christ in the Church; and more than one English poet might be needed to provide a catena of words adequate to an experience mystic, wonderful, and ringed with pure and endless light. "And, as they were coming down from the mountain, Jesus commanded them saying, Tell the vision to no man until the Son of Man be risen from the dead." But after that, they were, as it appeared, to tell it to all the world, so that the world might at least understand that mysticism rests on no baseless fabric of a vision but upon dazzling intuition and divine assent.

To dwell upon the two dramatic occasions that carried on the story of Peter—to recall the three shameful denials, the three searching inquiries, the three solemn charges—would be to labour narratives sufficiently observed and perhaps more than sufficiently stressed. They had, however, provided perfect vignettes for the margins of the argument and must have yielded scenes of the most poignant pathos within the larger action of the play, whose cabinet secrets, if I may risk a simile, the keys of Peter seemed so often to unlock. More and more one perceived with what astonishing statecraft the Church had been brought into existence. Its common law codified in the Sermon on the Mount, its constitution defined at Caesarea Philippi, its vision revealed on the Mount of Transfiguration, only the orientation of its policy remained to be observed.

For a moment, then, I must ask the reader to deflect his eyes from the Primate's tragedy, when Peter had warmed himself at the fire and afterwards gone out to weep bitterly, and consider the subsequent conversations of Christ with Pilate. The Drama had plainly laid the utmost stress upon these; and indeed they seemed to me to have reached to the very heart of the matter. I saw the two men speaking, much as Tintoret has depicted them, intimately, almost informally; and if, as Anatole France conjectured in as brilliant a conte du vendredi as even French wit has contrived to produce, le Procurateur de Judée really forgot what had happened to the Prisoner, I doubt very much whether he failed to remember what happened to the conversation. For in that strange, incalculable encounter his fascist cudgel had broken against an armour of honest thought which laid his scepticism open to Bacon's famous rebuke and left him washing

his hands in the eyes of all future generations as ineffectually as Lady
Macbeth. There had been speech of the use of force. At the first
encounter the King of the Jews, so generally silent during His trial,
had puzzled the Procurator by intimating that His Kingdom was so
little of this world that His servants or officers * would not defend
it by arms. At the second interrogation Pilate, after he had discovered to his alarm from the Jewish prosecution that the King of
the Jews had also claimed to be the Son of God, had risked an open
threat to use his power to kill or keep alive, only to be met by the
remark that he could have no power at all unless he had received it
from above. This utter imperturbability in the Prisoner, coupled,
perhaps, with the warning that he had received from a psychic
wife to the effect that he had to deal with a good man, rendered
him indisposed to try conclusions. Caesar's throne, as he doubtless
thought, was not gravely endangered by a King without faith in
force. But the Jewish leaders were too many for him. They pressed
on him the peril inherent in the existence of this upstart prince of
peace to the point of declaring that they themselves had no king but
Caesar; and he, more fearful of not seeming Caesar's friend than of
crucifying a good man, had done as they desired. Force did not
seem to play him false. The so-called King of the Jews, the self-
styled Son of God died upon the Cross. There was no possible doubt
of that; a centurion had seen to it and given Pilate the required confirmation. Nevertheless the Jews had spoken truer than they knew;
and the throne of Caesar was now, if only at long last, in grave and
singular peril.

The nature of the threat was to be found in the essence of the
two conversations between Christ and the Procurator. It was not, as
it seemed to me, too fond a conceit to fancy that the golden thread,
drawn through the symbolism of Solomon's Temple by virtue of the
condition that the builder should come to his work with hands un-
stained by warfare, had been picked up again and worked into the
symbolism of another Temple not made with hands at all. Critics
had often argued as if the question why, if God were truly omni-
potent, He did not offhand make an end of evil, were decisive for
Christianity. To this the Drama, however, returned a convincing
and even a crushing reply. Force, if it sometimes availed to police a
circumstance, never sufficed to change a condition. It was, as some
epigrammatist, trained in the Chestertonian technique, might per-

* R.V. margin.

haps observe, no heavenly use—whatever earthly advantage it might afford. The heart of the sinner was not changed because the hand of justice, covered by the warrior's gauntlet or the policeman's glove, had vindicated the power of the stronger. Force was a palliative, but not a remedy; and there was in the attempt, again and again renewed, of the kingdoms of this world, to take the Kingdom of Heaven by force, a shortness of thought matching the brevity of their own existence. In proportion, however, as they pushed their militant operations, under cover of making safety quite secure, in the direction of Roman triumphs and Carthaginian peaces, of total wars and unconditional surrenders, they sowed dragon's teeth which turned in due course into armed men ready at any cost to ingeminate war and multiply revenge. No political circle, as the age-long relations between such knowledgeable peoples as the French and the Germans show beyond need of further demonstration, was ever more vicious; and the wisdom of God would have looked like the foolishness of men, had it given that fallacy the slightest countenance. Evil must be overcome by good, or it would never be overcome at all. But good, when manifest in pure love, could, if I understood the Drama aright, affect different souls as differently as fire affects different bodies. Some, like Pascal, when he cried "Feu", felt it as a lovely glow; others, perhaps, after a life chilled by hatred and vengeance, when they looked at last with clear eyes upon the Man by whom the world is judged, found themselves scorched by a fire that would not be quenched. To Pilate, however, this new strange power that made nothing of physical force as a foundation for heavenly justice, had seemed, if I mistake not, like some incomprehensible light shining in a darkness that might be felt.

However that may be, the conversation before Pilate's judgment-seat had reached the pith of politics. Human society was confronted, as between the joints and marrow, with a new sanction beyond the range of cold steel to enforce or of sceptical intelligence to apply. It had been placed, like some profound invention, at the service of man, if he chose to use it; but, as we know from Christ's words to His disciples before the event, without any expectation that man would do so. The Founder of Christianity was no ingenuous idealist or fond optimist dreaming idly of the shape of things to come. The Israelite whom He commended as guileless was indeed that same Nathaniel whose knowledge of Nazareth prompted the searching, not to say cynical, inquiry whether any good thing could come out of it; and from the project of a new Jerusalem, of a white-souled city beneath the Syrian blue, He Himself turned away in despair. Yet His sublime irony was, perhaps, never more active than when the use of force was proposed to Him. His warning to the Sons of Thunder, that they knew not of what spirit they were, was matched by His contemptuous acquiescence in St. Peter's appropriation of the two swords. Well-meaning men—not excepting some of St. Peter's successors—have thought to take the Kingdom of Heaven by force; and good men have searched the Gospels to find countenance for the idea. Friedrich von Hügel, for instance, in the year 1916 will be found arguing * that Christ's treatment of the money-changers and the merchants in the Temple constituted some approval of coercive measures. The apologist is hard put to it, if this incident be the best illustration of his argument. There is no evidence in St. John's detailed account that any blow was struck at man even though the offence was sacrilege. The offensive tables and seats were indeed overthrown and the dove-sellers were told to take their merchandise away; but the scourge of small cords was pretty plainly intended for the backs of the cattle. Shame, not violence, was the weapon here. Still to an unwilling and unwelcoming world Christ offered the only policy that could solve its problems, though well aware that it demanded an infinite patience and a voluntary self-abnegation which the most part of men would prefer to devote to secular patriotism and would never consent to place wholeheartedly, if at all, at the disposal of His new kingdom of love. The Drama at this point must have risen to a tragic power seldom equalled or even approached; and there, if its action had ever paused, one might have placed the close of its penultimate act.

There were a good many historians to be seen among the audience; and it was, if I rightly remember, about this juncture in my work of reconstruction that I noticed Renan sitting near me in the stalls. He was talking with a friend, and I caught the words "l'histoire d'un beau jeune homme", and then, as I thought, a remark from his collocutor, "Ça aurait dû finir avec un mariage". So that was how the Drama had struck them. There was certainly no accounting for taste or want of it. All the same, the word "mariage" remained in my memory and recurred to my mind.

Meanwhile, as I read on and studied remote reflections in the long vistas of the stage, I saw that the policy of Christ in regard to Caesar

* "The German Soul", p. 38.

had passed into the hands of Peter to carry on; and I was extremely struck by the initiative that he took. Modern statesmen appear to be agreed, like the men of old time, that every crime should be countered by retribution. The greatest crime in history, on the Christian hypothesis, had lately been committed at Jerusalem when Peter took office. He made, however, no sort of effort to rouse the mob, to bring Annas and Caiaphas to justice, or to expel the Roman usurper. In successive speeches he contented himself with reminding his countrymen of the hard facts. "Ye denied the Holy and Righteous One"—such is the burden of his most telling address—"and asked for a murderer to be granted unto you, and killed the Prince of life; whom God raised from the dead; whereof we are witnesses." * The same dispassionate line was taken even before the high-priest, to the extreme confusion of that dignitary and his colleagues in council. But, beyond this, neither the Apostles nor their followers seem ever to have attempted to go. Time was on their side and Truth; but another element of wisdom entered into their work. Cobden remarked of the Whigs of his era that their love of meddling in European affairs was such that, if gratified, it would leave Providence nothing to do.† St. Peter had anticipated Cobden's good sense. Without the slightest hesitation he left retribution and revenge in the hands of God; and, had it not been for that extraordinary restraint, we may well wonder whether the new movement could ever have overcome the world. His policy in this crucial matter was plainly framed on the example of Christ: and at this point we reach the last of those interior or Christological reasons for the triumph of the Church in Europe which match in number the exterior ecclesiastical causes adduced by Gibbon, "the chief, perhaps the only English writer", as Newman reluctantly confessed,‡ "who has any claim to be considered an ecclesiastical historian". His elaborate mention of the exclusive zeal, the miraculous claims, the austere morals, the immortal hopes and the admirable organisation of the early Christians will indeed satisfy some minds as sufficient causes for the victory of the Galileans over the Julians of the world, but not such exacting minds as have reached the conclusion that the success of Christianity is more difficult to explain if—to repeat Dean Church's remark—Christianity is not, than if it is true. In the prophetic

---

* Acts III, 14, 15.
† Morley, "Life of Cobden", I, p. 309.
‡ In his "Development of Christian Doctrine".

expectation of the Messiah; in the paradoxical code of the Sermon on the Mount; in the tremendous commission given at Caesarea Philippi; in the mystic vision of the transfigured Christ in conversation with Moses and Elijah, lay reasons for the substitution of the Popes for the Caesars more adequate than those that Gibbon adduced. One further reason requires, however, to be added to the other four—the use of the crucifix with all its implications, in the place of the Roman eagles.

Tarde, in a book on "Les Lois de l'Imitation", which made a considerable mark when I was still a young man, has treated of the great place of imitation in sound sociological science and, after commenting upon the use and abuse of statistics, has observed that, whilst they are but a pis-aller, "une statistique psychologique, notant les accroissements et les décroissements individuels des croyances spéciales, des besoins spéciaux, créés originairement par un novateur, donnerait seule, si elle était pratiquement possible, la raison profonde des chiffres fournis par la statistique ordinaire". * It was precisely in its sociological application and psychological understanding of the law of example that the institutional Christianity of the Historic Church excelled all other societies. Spiritually and intellectually the citizenship of the City of God was rooted in and grounded on imitation, and yet in so rare and subtle a manner that one was not tempted to say, as of the victims of our secular statisticians, that, being born men, they died ciphers. Behind the Christian statistic, first of a little flock, then of an elect company in the catacombs, finally of a great society aiming with more or less success at the reproduction of a single superb model, there lay a proof of operative example beyond the fashion of the world, with its shifting admiration for great men, to emulate. The drama that I was reconstructing with ever-rising interest brought out this aspect of Christianity with, as I thought, very telling effect. From the Pauline legend, 'Not I live, but Christ liveth in me', down to the title and sub-title, significantly juxtaposed, of the 'Imitation of Christ or Ecclesiastical Music' belonging to one of the best of 'best-sellers', it may be seen how this particular Christian genius of imitation surpassed and survived all other imitations, penetrating for long ages the thought and life of every Christian man even to the point of provoking the profane to swear by Jesus or Mary, by Heaven or

* Tarde, "Les Lois des l'Imitation", p. 115.

Hell, by a saint or a superstition, and to cry 'hocus-pocus' at anything beyond their comprehension to understand.

The Drama, as I say, brought all this out very well, continually fortifying as it did Gibbon's 'secondary' reasons for the triumph of Christianity with greater. Among the latter the Commission to St. Peter seemed to correspond with, yet, both in tenour and statesmanship, tower above the institution of bishops. Hardly could any man, as I judged, with a keen eye for constitutional history, watch the miraculous rise of the Bishops of Rome without marvelling. It was no question of Catholic faith or the reverse, of ecclesiastical sympathies or adverse sentiments. Here was a fact which no honest student of Latin Christianity or civilisation could avoid. I take the witness best qualified, as I think, to give evidence on the point in this country; an Englishman, a Protestant, a scholar, a Dean of St. Paul's, and the historian of Latin Christianity—Milman. His measured words countenanced and sustained, more truly than perhaps he knew, the grand design, as I conceived it, of the Drama. "The Papacy", he had written regarding the state of the world in the sixth century, when Gregory the Great,* at once the founder of the temporal power of the Popes and the first begetter of the See of Canterbury, came to the Chair of St. Peter, "must re-awaken its obscured and suspended life. It was the only power which lay not entirely and absolutely prostrate before the disasters of the times—a power which had an inherent strength and might resume its majesty. It was this power which was most imperatively required to preserve all which was to survive out of the crumbling wreck of Roman civilisation. . . . Even the perfect organisation of the Christian hierarchy might in all human probability have fallen to pieces in perpetual conflict: it might have degenerated into a half-secular feudal caste with hereditary benefices more and more entirely subservient to the civil authority, a priesthood of each nation and each tribe, gradually sinking to the intellectual or religious level of the nation or tribe. On the rise of a power, both controlling and conservative, hung, humanly speaking, the life and death of Christianity—of Christianity as a permanent, aggressive, expansive, and to a certain extent uniform system. There must be a counterbalance to barbaric force, to the unavoidable anarchy of Teutonism, with its tribal, or at the utmost national independence, forming a host of small, conflicting, antagonistic kingdoms. . . . Providence might have otherwise ordained; but it is

---

* Gregory the Great, A.D. 590–604.

impossible for man to imagine by what other organising or consolidating force the commonwealth of the Western Nations could have grown up to a discordant, indeed, and conflicting league, but still to a league, with that unity and conformity of manners, usages, laws, religion, which have made their rivalries, oppugnancies, and even their long ceaseless wars, on the whole to issue in the noblest, highest, most intellectual form of civilisation known to man".*

Such had been the unseen statesmanship of Christ which, after three centuries of persecution, suffered but not avenged, and three centuries more of prudence, of patience and, in Pascal's sense, of an 'order of love' transcending both in power, had placed the Popes in the seat of the Caesars: and the visible statesmanship of the vicar of Christ, as exemplified in Gregory, was not altogether unworthy of it. He had ascended the Papal throne with reluctance; he filled it with holiness. The music of the Gregorian chant filled the choirs of the Papal Court with divine praises: whilst the austerities of the Benedictine Monk heralded that celibacy of the clergy in which modern authors concur with ancient in seeing a source of unselfish energy beyond comparison. Gregory's bloodless defence of Rome against the Lombard; his assertion that the fear of God forbade him to be concerned in the death of any human being; his unavoidable assumption, in face of the defaulting Exarch, of the secular administration of the city where was already his spiritual See—these aspects of his policy might entitle a historian to say of the Papacy more truly than of the British Empire that it had conquered the world 'in a fit of absence of mind'. Without fleet or army worth mention, by mere force of character carried to the pitch of holiness or the point of martyrdom through the imitation, sometimes no doubt most feeble, sometimes most faulty, yet still always in principle recognised, of Jesus Christ on the part of its pilot, the bark of Peter had been steered from the Lake of Galilee to the port of Rome and had landed its freight on the banks of the Tiber. One could explain all that away by various devices and some inventions. One could query the donation of Constantine and append exclamation marks to the pseudo-Isidorian decretals. But scholarship had come round to the view that the famous fraud was not perpetrated in Rome nor for the sake of the Pontiff, but in France and in aid of a local episcopate, the rights of which were endangered by the ambition of the

* Milman, "History of Latin Christianity", Bk. III, Chap. vii.

monarch and the arrogance of the metropolitans. The Pope was indeed so little the villain in that memorable piece as to appear in fact rather in the light of a hoped-for deliverer. In other words, the place assigned to the Papacy in the spurious or chronologically inexact decretals was very much that which the contemporary requirements of Christendom had in Milman's view demanded of the Holy See from the date of Gregory the Great; nor is it likely that such a place would have been conceded to it in practice without demur unless the documents had been in accord with the general ideas of the time. Poetic justice, however, exacted that Laurentius Valla, an eminent and erudite Papal Secretary in the middle of the fifteenth century, should be the man to show the falsity of Constantine's alleged Donation, and that Cardinal Nicholas of Cusa, about the same time, should repudiate the fraud of the False Decretals.*

Before this reddest of red herrings had swum into sight, the final dispossession of the Caesars by the Popes had been effected in the eyes of all the world at the coronation of Charlemagne. This consummation of Christian policy came in the year 800; the hour was that of the celebration of the Pope's Mass; the day was Christmas Day; the place was the basilica of St. Peter's. There has, perhaps, never been so peaceful a transfer of dominion on a great scale from a hand that had become moribund to another strong enough to receive it and render it the motive of a great spiritual and intellectual idea as this institution of the Holy Roman Emperor by the Pope. The actual procedure has about it still something mysterious, and almost mystical. We do not know exactly how much the Pope intended to do when, after the Gospel had been sung on that eventful day, he placed a golden crown embossed with the cross † on the Monarch's head, nor exactly how much Charlemagne knew beforehand of what was actually intended; but we do know that it was to that act, subsequently protested against by the Byzantine Emperor Basil, though at the time facilitated by the circumstance that the Empress Irene had unconscionably seized the Byzantine throne, that Charlemagne's successors looked for their title. The wondering world forthwith approved this strange, new thing—a Roman Emperor receiving his credentials from the hands of the Vicar of Christ. A thousand years of authority lay before him and his successors—a thousand years during which the Eastern Roman Empire declined and

---

* Mann's statement in his "Lives of the Popes", III, pp. 135–48, gives, I believe, a scholarly and satisfactory presentation of the case.

† "Coronam auream expressam signo sanctitatis . . . posuit."

came at last to dust; a thousand years in which the actual constitution of Christendom was elaborated on lines strangely reminiscent of Plato's dream-republic; a thousand years during which clerks served as the guardians, knights as the defenders, craftsmen as the artisans of a great society, theocentric, functional, compact and much less exclusively concerned than our own with national and provincial culture. To that great society it seemed natural that ecclesiastics should hold benefices anywhere and knights-errant champion causes everywhere; that artists should go carrying beauty from court to court and scholars go seeking truth from university to university: and, if one had to sort out the good and evil of the Middle Age of Europe by studying its graces in such a book, say, as Henry Adams's "Mont St. Michel and Chartres" and its pollutions in such another as Dr. Coulton's "Five Centuries of Religion", one might perhaps find cause to conclude that, during the millennium between 800 and 1800 A.D., the snake which had slipped into Eden had been scotched, though not slain; that the grinning gargoyles outside abbey or minster had been dismayed, if not dispersed by the souls of the saints whose images stood erect and vigilant upon screen or reredos; and that the Devil himself, whilst roaring still, like a lion intent on prey, had been bound for a term of years, though not fast-bound or for ever. The Middle Age—that only begetter of a Christendom, recognisable and to that degree at least real—would not perhaps have quarrelled with such a description of the human situation in its time; for all its strength of line and glow of colour came of ideas of good and evil clearly seen against a background of heaven or hell. It was such a millennium as we may see no more.

The staging of the Drama had, as I gathered, been at this juncture such as one may study still in the cloisters of Santa Maria Novella at Florence or of the Campo Santo at Pisa. Divine equity made good the lack or lapse of human justice; and hierarchy both in earth and heaven had grace and charm for minds not schooled to admire a dead level of equality or affected by 'that disinterested love of dullness which', as Stevenson complained, 'has in our day set so many Peter Bells to paint the riverside primrose'.* Humility, personified in the handmaid of the Lord and Mother of God, sat, as one might say, regent in Christendom no less than regnant in Heaven; and humility is a grace that cannot be, if governments declare that all men are equal and schoolmasters teach us to say "I am as good as you" and lead us on to mutter 'and better too!' "

* R. L. Stevenson, "Fontainebleau", in "Across the Plains".

Chapter XV

OUR LADY'S MIRROR

TO the cult of the Virgin Mother of God the epoch of the Middle Age owed in great part its power. From this cult it drew the singular beauty of its art, the rare lucidity of its thought, the glow of its compassion. Too many elect spirits from Dante downwards have found in the via della Madonna the way of the humane life to leave the matter in much doubt, for all the slush and slime one's shoes may chance to pick up on the path. To enter one of the great churches of Our Lady was perhaps to settle the question intuitively and offhand, so far as art availed to do so. All the tender compassion of Mary's smile, as portrayed in St. Luke's gospel of the poor, seemed to pour down in rays of roseate light through her vast rose-windows upon a people waiting and worshipping in the nave below—waiting for so long a night as it might prove before the lancet-lights of Christ should come again into eastern windows; waiting, whilst the massed candles, gleaming upon the Altar and before the Throne, responded to the waning sunset with their promise of impending benediction. In the ages of faith the Virgin-Mother had shown how worship might be lifted to the level of a grand manner and that courtesy of Christ, upon which the medieval mystics so often dwell, be brought to the knowledge of the humblest of His followers in association with a majesty befitting the King of kings.

I have time and again mentioned Henry Adams; and some words of his return to my mind as I write these lines. "With the Virgin's taste during her regency", he had boldly maintained, "critics never find fault."* It need hardly perhaps be added that, to make his statement good, he had dismissed as 'bourgeois' the taste of Voltaire and Diderot. He would go on to urge that the mind of the Mother of God might be as powerfully felt in the apse to the east as in the occidental romanesque fenestration to the west of her churches. There, behind the High Altar, lay her private apartments, her salon de reception: and thither (though here I venture to prefer my own interpretation to his) they who had adored Christ on the via dolorosa, or reigning from the Cross, or latent in the Tabernacle, or manifest

* H. Adams, "Mont St. Michel and Chartres", p. 107.

312

in glory in the design of some eastern window, might pass on to entertain the 'gracious, tender, reverential' thoughts that speak through every delicate line and lovely colour of a Lady Chapel. As it was said by a good judge of the secular magnificence introduced into France by Le Grand Monarque that those, who had not lived before the French Revolution, had never really lived at all, so is it true in respect of what is magnifical in spiritual life that they, who have had no knowledge or understanding of this so-called 'regency' of the Virgin-Mother during the Middle Age, have never seen nor savoured the grace of a great society moulded to the perfect manners of the humble and meek. Mary held her glorious court beneath the shadow of the Cross; and the Tree of a regenerate Life stood out there as conspicuously as another tree had stood out in the garden from which Eve was ingloriously driven. He who misses that symbolism misses also the meaning of the Middle Age and the genius of the Great Society. If in its essentials it should ever return, it will be because Mary has once more made herself manifest, not as at Lourdes to a peasant girl whose poor home and mean circumstances were analogous to those she herself may be presumed to have found at Bethlehem, but as in the Divine Comedy like a queen distributing intellectual graces no less than remedial favours. It was in the sequence of a movement which had brought down the mighty from their seat and substituted the Popes for the Caesars, that were found the conditions which enabled her to take her proper place at the head of a great society. Such conditions show no sign of recurring.

Meantime it seemed still worth while to notice how such a critic as Henry Adams, who regarded the regency of Mary as a thing as certainly dead as it had been certainly real, correlated woman's place in nature with her intellectual gifts and humanising graces. "One might argue", he would urge, "that Nature regards the female as the essential, the male as the superfluity of her world." And he would proceed to illustrate his meaning by virtue of Garreau's comparison of the sexes at the date of the Crusades, "If we look at their intellectual level," observes that authority, "the women appear distinctly superior. They are more serious; more subtle. With them we do not seem dealing with the rude state of civilisation that their husbands belong to." "Her ascendancy", Adams, still speaking of the medieval woman in general and in particular, would continue, "was secured by her alliance with the Church, into which she sent her most intelligent children."[*]

* For all three quotations see Adams, "Mont St. Michel, etc.", pp. 198, 199.

And at that he would dramatise his argument by pointing out that, whilst, as he put it, "the Virgin was miraculously using the power of spiritual love to elevate and purify the people, Eleanor (of Guienne, the wife of Henry II) and her daughters were using the power of earthly love to discipline and refine the courts. . . . Eleanor and her daughter Mary and her granddaughter Blanche (of Castile, the mother of St. Louis) knew, as well as Saint Bernard did, or Saint Francis, what a brute the emancipated man could be; and, as though they foresaw the society of the sixteenth and eighteenth centuries, they used every terror they could invent, as well as every tenderness they could invoke, to tame the beasts around them. Their charge was of manners, and to teach manners, they made a school which they called their Court of Love, with a code of law to which they gave the name of 'courteous love'."*

Thus may Heavenly and Earthly Grace be said to have passed in together through the cloisters of Our Lady's churches, entered their fabric at the western end and trodden their aisles until, together, they came to Our Lady's apartments behind the choir. It only remained to show that the Churches of Notre Dame were palaces of truth as well as homes of beauty.

The 'intellection', to borrow a French word, of the Great Society itself—the complete penetration by the spirit of man of the objective Kingdom of God upon earth—was left to St. Thomas of Aquin to effect. As Aristotle had envisaged ethics as a branch of politics, so perhaps one might say, had the great Dominican, with that genius of adaptability now no more denied to him by good critics, gone some way to convert the city-state of Athens into a cosmopolitan metropolis fit for the queen of the sciences. His thoughts came late in time yet ripe in season to the court of the Virgin-Mother. They postulated a Christendom where Pope and Emperor had somewhile acted as vicegerents in matters spiritual and temporal for One whose sovereignty seemed to merit all that loyalty had to give and towards whom infidelity was by general consent no less than the direst treachery: they postulated, perhaps only a little less, the imponderable influences of a society—a beau-monde in the best sense—over which no other than Mary, long time resident and regent in the houses and palaces of her Son, presided: they postulated the influence of such a court-chaplain as Bernard of Clairvaux, dominating, by virtue of the romantic strength of his

* Adams, "Mont St. Michel, etc.", p. 213.

devotion to her even more than by the force of his own tremendous personality, the best moral and political energy of the age: as they also postulated such a court-poet as Adam of St. Victor, whose praises of the Queen of Heaven men went sweetly singing through her courts and corridors.

In the Drama Aquinas seemed to enter upon the scene when all had been prepared; and his entry was as much greater than the advent of Berkeley and Butler to the Court of our English Queen Caroline as the philosophia perennis is deeper than the metaphysics of the one or the ethics of the other and the Queen of Heaven higher than any queen on earth. To speak of a system which has survived the tide of time and surge of controversy so effectively as to be recommended after six centuries as the surest guide to sound philosophy, not only by Leo XIII, but by other critics* not of his church or school, would be an impertinence. I only risk the remark, which I think the Drama, as the reflection of Aquinas's large figure seemed to move weightily across the stage, bore out and meant one to take in, that the perennial philosophy desiderates, if it does not demand, the earlier procession of the Virgin-Mother's train with its incomparable colour and delicate decoration, its ground-work of blue and gold and its wealth of lilies white and roses red, thereon embroidered. Only so perhaps can philosophy be seen debating to full advantage: only thus can the dry light of scholastic philosophy play pleasantly upon the life of such a political, but also aesthetic animal as man. Some indeed have tried at different times to import parts and patches of Thomism into other processions of thought than that of the Virgin-Mother's Great Society—its metaphysics, maybe, or its economics, or some other of its incidents—but somewhat ineffectually. Like all finely conceived patterns of thought or dress or decoration, Thomism demands its setting, and that setting is the Court of the Virgin-Mother. It demands it, because it demands the equipoise of a quiet mind within the state as within the soul. Pax est tranquillitas ordinis. It demands tranquillity "because", as Gilson remarks, "it was itself the workmanship of peace".† The divine peace which reigned in the Virgin-Mother's apartments was the true condition of its working. But, as interior peace is a work of great patience, so still more is exterior peace. Pascal, despite his passion for that which is perfect, would one day argue that peace must entail

* *E.g.*, Prof. A. E. Taylor.
† Gilson, "The Spirit of Medieval Philosophy", p. 400.

something at least in the way of political compromise in a world shot
through, as he even more than Aquinas* had reason to know, with
custom. As the nice equipoise of Aristotle's ethic may be seen to
right itself with the aid of casuistry from the shifting impact of the
wind of fashion, so perhaps, within the range of the Virgin-Mother's
influence, might the law of nature, if, as the Romans held, it be
rightly identified with the law of nations, be said to lower its proud
flag to meet the claims of mutual understanding. During the very
years (A.D. 1252–1260) when Aquinas was professor in Paris, St.
Louis, so closely associated with the building both of the Sainte
Chapelle and of Notre Dame de Paris, made a memorable
restoration to the King of England (if only in his capacity as a
French feudatory) of lands in Guienne and Gascony; in order, as St.
Louis assured his counsellors, who no more liked his act than such
men like conciliation or appeasement, that 'there may be love between
my children and King Henry's'—and this, even though he declared
himself certain that the lands had been justly lost to Philip Augustus
by the English.

So once at least might a rare chivalry of thought and mind be
seen moving in the precincts of Our Lady's Court. And so, too, might
a marriage between Aristotle's sagacious common-sense and the
essential humanism of Christianity seem to have been arranged within Our Lady's apartments by Aquinas. No more were the riches of the
Greek inheritance to be wasted on the whims of another Alexander, or
lie idle in the hands of another Averrhoes, or be diverted into the
devil's coffers, as by its compulsory use in the German secondary
schools of our own time. Doubtless it seemed a surprising marriage,
even though surprising marriages can turn out perfect unions.
Aquinas had carried off the master of those who know and married
him to divine wisdom. The most brilliant affair as it was that
ever took place at the Virgin-Mother's Court or, as I judge, ever in
history, inasmuch as it united the two greatest heritages, though of
unequal value, in the world, I do not, still, feel quite sure what St.
Bernard would have thought about it, and I got some idea that St.
Bonaventure did not entirely like it. It was celebrated, indeed, so
truly in Our Lady's Chapel that by its terms and pledges—substance and accident, act and potency, essence and existence—it
seemed to cling to the very horns of the altar and read the ultimate
mystery of love. Yet, for all that, I think the bridal procession,

* See on this esp. Rousselot's "Intellectualisme de S. Thomas", p. 239.

which passed, chanting St. Thomas's great sacramental hymns, up the aisles of philosophy, left to St. Augustine the poetry of the crypt, with its reminiscence of the manger and the catacombs, and of the academy, and to St. Bonaventure the exposition at the High Altar of the Light of the world, whose pure radiance transfigured each humane idea as it entered man's heart and made every wise word falling from human lips seem as if it had dropped from a golden mouth. The Thomist philosophic discussion, even when conducted by Dante under St. Thomas's eye and Our Lady's patronage, never, perhaps, quite accomplished that. For Reasoning remains one thing, ever raising, for some minds at least, as many questions as it resolves; and Revelation is another. And the radiance of the latter had shone at its softest in the catacombs, needing as it did only a little oil from Olivet to make it a burning and a shining light.

There came towards the close of Our Lady's medieval regency a trahison des clercs, just as there came a trahison des philosophes at the latter end of the long millennium of her public influence and as, perhaps, there commonly comes some betrayal by priest or scribe before any great convulsion of society, not excluding that wherein we now reel and totter. Even Our Lady's work was not fool-proof against a German fool nor, as perhaps one might say, 'fan-proof' against a French fanatic. Luther and Calvin, even if one were so fanciful as to see them as the spiritual descendants of the sons of thunder, would still have laid themselves open to the rebuke that they knew not of what spirit they were. Patience and prudence, and such a patriotism of the City of God as befitted Our Lady's Court, would have saved the Great Society. Reform there could have been, for the Counter-Reformation showed it; and reform there would have been, had Luther been willing to strengthen the hands of Adrian VI, the reforming Pope. But violent men as usual carried the day; and it was left to the proof of time to show how gross in kind was Luther's thought, how cruel was Calvin's, and how wise in counsel were Thomas More and Desiderius Erasmus.

The world is seldom able to justify itself against critics like the sagacious Greg, who in his Essays on Political and Social Science* remarks that 'judging from the past history of our race, in ninety-nine cases out of a hundred, war is a folly and a crime . . . the saddest and

---

* Quoted by Acton in the notes to his Inaugural Lecture ("Lectures on Modern History", p. 342).

the wildest of all follies, and the most heinous of all crimes'. In the case of the wars of religion the average man probably understood little and, perhaps, cared less about the first causes and ultimate issues for which he battled; but Old Kaspar had not yet appeared to speak for him. Hocus-pocus dismissed the theology of the Schoolmen by reducing it from four words to two; and in this country the 'King's matter' and the value of the abbey-lands supplied practical arguments of great weight and moment. By degrees a more impressive case was made out. It was argued that the social regency of Our Lady had ended in mariolatry; that the political vicariate of the Pope had proved inimical to freedom of conscience and freedom of speech; and that the effect of the Reformation had been the liberation of the mind. This was all very well, had the facts been there to sustain it; but not so well, if charges that ought in justice to be levelled against all mankind were being brought only against medieval churchmen. Some part of the indictment in this respect looked fishy and has of recent times come to look still more so. Hellenism had killed Socrates; Judaism had crucified Christ; the Augustan age of Rome had been inaugurated by the murder of Cicero; the French Revolution had distinguished itself by the execution of Lavoisier; whilst in the Russia of our time, during the process of creating what some have spoken of as a 'new civilisation', things were done of which it is shame to speak and a polity was framed of which a great historian has said: "All previous experiments in tyranny recorded in human annals pale beside this colossal achievement".* At the height of Our Lady's regency, and through the mouth of one who might well have been styled her lord chamberlain, a lucid statement was made of the best opinion obtaining in respect of the suppression of heresy; and, mutatis mutandis, it was not so different from that which some of us entertain in England to-day. St. Bernard,† following in the steps of St. Augustine, who had been forced by circumstances from an attitude of complete toleration to approve the use of the rod, blamed alike the cruelty which had inspired an execution of heretics at Cologne and the indifference which had characterised the conduct of bishops and others in respect of false doctrine. "Fides suadenda est, non imponenda," he declared; and then "Capiantur non armis, sed argumentis".‡ Let faith come of persuasion, not of force: let heretics be taken with arguments, not with arms. There

* H. Fisher, "History of Europe", pp. 1215–16. † A.D. 1091–1153.
‡ Quoted from Vacandard's "The Inquisition" (English trans.), p. 45.

was nothing here in principle that any man interested in the truth and propagation of Christianity can reasonably quarrel with. The question however remained, as it remains at this hour of writing for a modern Home Secretary, what was to be done in time of peril with those whose ideas appeared to imperil the safety of the state. It is true that serious danger was somewhat differently conceived. Where a modern government is concerned with the occasions of disorder, a medieval one was perhaps more deeply concerned with its ultimate sources. A conspiracy against the theocracy of Christ occupied doubtless in the mind of St. Bernard much the same place that an adverse criticism of British policy has lately occupied in the mind of British Ministers; and in the same way the provision for children of the pure milk of the Word took precedence and would even still take precedence with him of the provision of uncontaminated cow's milk. It was merely a matter of whether one thought the soul or the body mattered the more. But, when allowance had been made for that alteration in precedence, with its implications for thought, the problem of disaffected citizens remained identical, whether one regarded disloyalty to the King of kings, or to the King, or to the Mother of Parliaments as the gravest crime. About the personnel of the sovereign power which determines what is treason, differences of opinion might always arise. Even the honourable gentlemen assembled at Westminster sometimes excite almost as much suspicion in certain minds as ecclesiastics of the Middle Age and after. "There are some gentlemen", I recollect a relative telling me he had heard Spurgeon say from the pulpit, "who are called 'right honourable'; but I call them 'right abominable'."

Let that be; for miscreants, whether they are in open revolt against Our Lady's regency, or a king's government, or a parliamentary administration, have to be dealt with: or so thought King Robert the Pious of France when, in the year 1022, with the mob of Orleans clamouring for action to be taken, he sent some thirteen clergy and laity to the stake for subversive opinions. He might, perhaps, like his Bourbon successors, have done better to use lettres-de-cachet and shut them up to keep them quiet, but he appears to have preferred the method of trial and conviction before punishment. Post hoc, though not perhaps propter hoc, the problems of heresy increased and multiplied, and notably in those regions of Southern France where, in accordance with the 'corruptio optimi pessima' rule, romance had run wild for lack of spiritual grace.

The opinions of the Cathari, as these heretics were generally denominated, were not only a menace to the regency of Our Lady, the traditional faith in the sacraments, and the vicariate of the Pope, but would have been a menace to any state at any time, for they opposed marriage and the procreation of children, countenanced suicide, and condemned the slaughter of animals. The cleverest and perhaps least clerical of all the Holy Roman Emperors, Frederick II— 'stupor mundi' as they styled him—was at one with the Pope in approving drastic action; and the imperial legislation of 1237–1239 condemned heretics to death throughout the Empire. The Episcopate on whom devolved the hateful duty of deciding whether a man were orthodox or not, showed no particular inclination or competence for this task; and thus, with the object of providing abler judges and better justice, the Inquisition was introduced. But Pope Gregory IX, when he passed beyond Innocent III's penal code to recommend to civil rulers the death in place of the banishment of heretics, abandoned in all but name the principle inset in all Inquisitorial judgments:—". . . we strongly beseech the secular court to mitigate its sentence in such a way as to avoid bloodshed or danger of death".

Love had grown blind indeed when such zeal as Gregory's could pass muster as charity. It might have been well for the reputation of the Reformation if it had dealt with such humbug without delay. But consider the illustrious Latimer preaching to Friar Forest to recant the opinions that he himself had but lately held, whilst an iron cage and a slow fire stood ready to enforce the argument of the great Protestant preacher; or consider Calvin assisting in the prosecution of the hated Servetus, who was no more than a visitor at Geneva; and then the charge of mortal persecution would be found to lie, not against medieval churchmen in particular, but against zealots in general. Neither in the Great Society of Christendom nor in secular kingdoms could full conviction be harnessed with fair tolerance unless patience and prudence were joined with them to make a team of four, and that team held well in hand. But when this was done, things could go well enough. The State of Maryland, as Acton* pointed out in a comparison of Catholic and Protestant ideas of persecution, was the pioneer of tolerance in the U.S.A.; and Maryland, though its original ecclesiastical orientation was Anglican,† was

* Dr. Coulton believes that the author of the essay was Simpson and that it was wrongly included among Acton's writings.

† See the D.N.B. on the Calverts (1st and 2nd Lord Baltimore).

founded by Catholics. Yet no fixed frontier-lines between persecution, toleration and freedom could, as the Drama seemed to suggest, ever be found, for they are determined in the abstract by that which divides licence and liberty and in the concrete by the strength or instability of the government in power.

In like manner did the particular charge brought against the Great Society of overriding the claims of private conscience tend to dissolve when brought to the test of fact and circumstance. "Quidquid fit contra conscientiam, aedificat ad gehennam" (He who acts against his conscience loses his soul), says the Fourth Lateran Council; and Newman,* who quotes the words in the course of a careful consideration of Gladstone's idea that the Decree of Papal Infallibility had created for Catholics a divided allegiance, shows how completely the principle enshrined in the words guards the safety of the individual conscience even to the point, in cases of extraordinary difficulty, of being thrown back upon what theologians call 'the Providence of God'. In practice, if one took the case of St. Joan, who died excommunicate, or of Savonarola protesting with his dying breath that, whilst he could be cut off from the Church militant, no power on earth could cut him off from the Church triumphant, it was clear that Catholics retained to the full their obligation to obey 'the aboriginal Vicar of Christ, a prophet in its informations, a monarch in its peremptoriness, a priest in its blessings and anathemas'† within the soul—in other words, each man's private conscience. Only the onus of disobedience to the Pope, like the burden of disobedience to any secular government, lay heavy upon the individual; and any ecclesiastical Hampden had need to show a better case than perhaps the great Hampden possessed against ship-money. Yet, as I judged, the freedom of conscience a Catholic enjoyed was far in excess of that commonly claimed by a soldier or sailor in respect of any modern government. A man-at-arms, almost without exception, appeared to-day to consider that his government had a right to send him to kill his fellow-creatures in any part of the world and that he had no obligation to weigh the rights and wrongs of the quarrel, even though from time to time (as when in 1914 the British Army was confronted with the possibility of having to suppress the Ulstermen) it was plain that some soldiers have had their doubts and that behind their doubts their private conscience was

* "Difficulties of Anglicans Considered", II, pp. 223–61.
† Newman, *op. cit.*, p. 248.

still working. The Great Society, as represented by the eminent
Dominican jurist, Francis de Vittoria (1480–1546), at the very
date of the supposed Protestant vindication of the rights of private
conscience, had entertained a different view. "Soldiers", Vittoria
declared, "are not excused when they fight in bad faith. Again it is
not lawful to kill innocent citizens at the prince's command.
Therefore not aliens either."*

Yet how should soldiers know whether their cause was just? The
politicians knew the facts and communicated so much of them to
their countrymen as they thought convenient; and, whatever the
Pope may have said from time to time in the Middle Age and or
may say to-day, the clergy have shown in every war a facility for
backing up their country (right or wrong, as men may afterwards
think) that seldom, if ever falls short of the benedictions of the
Archbishop of Canterbury and the Bishop of Ely upon Henry V's
prolegomena to Agincourt. The Archbishop indeed spoke for many
of his cloth before and since when, as Shakespeare tells us, he advised
his episcopal brother to listen to the King's discourse of war and hear
'a fearful battle render'd him in music'; but I do not know whether
he should be supposed, like Edward III, when contemplating the
exploits of the Black Prince,† to have smiled to see the hero-king

> Mangle the work of nature, and deface
> The patterns that by God and by French fathers
> Had twenty years been made.

"The good to be attained by war", say the canonists, "must be
reasonably supposed to be greater than the certain evils, material and
spiritual, which war entails",‡ and with such generalities, answered
one way when its occasions and another when its effects are considered, mankind had to remain as content as might be even in the
epoch of the Great Society. It must be doubtful, however, whether
they would have fully met the mind of her who was saluted by the
name of Rosa Mystica and whom, as Archbishop Arundel had observed
in 1399, 'the contemplation of the great mystery of the Incarnation had drawn all Christian nations to venerate'. He added that
"we English, being the servants of her special inheritance and her
own Dowry, as we are commonly called, ought to surpass others in

* Quoted from Eppstein's "Catholic Tradition of the Law of Nations", p. 103.
† "Henry V", Act II, Sc. 4.
‡ Eppstein, "Catholic Tradition of the Law of Nations", p. 103.

the fervour of our praises and devotions".* It might, then, perhaps, be conjectured that, when her roses were appropriated as badges by the contending factions of York and Lancaster, the sentiments of the Virgin-Mother approximated more nearly to those attributed by Shakespeare to the pious, if ineffectual, Founder of Eton College as he wrung his hands upon Towton Field:—

> "This battle fares like to the morning's war,
> When dying clouds contend with growing light;
> What time the shepherd, blowing of his nails,
> Can neither call it perfect day nor night.
>
> .   .   .   .
>
> Here, on this molehill, will I sit me down.
> To whom God will, there be the victory."†
>
> .   .   .   .

And so on with all the lovely rest of that impassioned, despairing lament over the ways of the inhuman children of Adam!

A brighter morning broke for the land of our Lady's Dowry at long last. The sun in its strength shone upon the rose-garden of England; the war between Lancaster and York was buried in oblivion; the red rose was tied to the white; and Prince Charming came of the union. It was said of the Habsburgs in a famous distich that, whilst others waged war, the happy House of Austria married. The epigram might serve for an envoi to the drama of Our Lady's regency of courteous love. It was not her fault if Prince Charming, under the influence of Anne Boleyn, turned into Bluebeard. Katharine, coming out of Castile and the daughter of Isabella, remained true as woman and wife to the best traditions of courteous love; and Shakespeare, true to dramatic truth, at least as soon as Anne Boleyn's daughter was safely dead, gave her at her last end a posse of angels, bringing a crown of bay in exchange for the lost crown of England and beckoning heavenwards with solemn dance and 'reverent curtsey'.

The romance of Christian love had in fact been dishonoured at the summit and in all men's view by the public repudiation of Katharine and subsequent coronation, with bishops attending, of Anne. Therewith Our Lady's benign influence upon her Island-dowry entered upon that slow decline which in our time and before

---

* Quoted from Bridgett, "Our Lady's Dowry", p. 1.
† "Henry VI", Pt. III, Act II, Sc. 5.

our eyes has finished in a fall immeasurable in its effects upon the whole future status and conception of her sex—the conscription of women at the hands of politicians, whose last worst trait, from the French Revolution onwards, has always been their faith in the redemption of society by the indiscriminate use of Humanity as cannon-fodder, providing a proper nadir.

Simultaneously with the withdrawal of Our Lady heavenwards under cover of Queen Katharine's guardian angels the Bark of Peter may be said to have left this sea-girt Isle: and that was virtually the end so far as England was concerned of Our Lady's Regency and the Great Society and the beau monde of courteous love. In Europe of course the great tradition lingered longer. A few years after Katharine was born, in 1493, one, commonly, if perhaps unfairly,* accounted the worst of the Popes, had done his best to anticipate and avert the outbreak of a quarrel between the only colonial Powers of the time by delimiting their spheres of influence—an admirable effort of Christian statesmanship which, needless to say, the world subsequently represented as an arrogant pretension of papal statecraft. Nevertheless chivalry, which had done something to soften the substance of war no less than to embellish, for better or worse, the incidents of battle, was dying. It was in optimistic error that Erasmus had hailed the accession of Leo X to the seat of St. Peter as the inauguration of a new reign of international peace. All the riches of Mary—her lilies and her roses—had failed to outbid, in the markets of Vanity Fair, Eve's legacy of warlike knowledge and Cain's legacy of inhuman hatred. It was but a 'popinjay' talking 'like a waiting-gentlewoman', so Hotspur had reported to Henry IV, that had told him

> . . . it was great pity, so it was,
> That villainous saltpetre should be digg'd
> Out of the bowels of the harmless earth,
> Which many a good tall fellow had destroy'd
> So cowardly; and, but for these vile guns,
> He would himself have been a soldier.†

So gunpowder was once esteemed, like gas to-day, as an inhuman thing unfit for human quarrels! But only by popinjays and waiting gentlewomen! We may, who can tell, get over the thought of gas in time to come, if our Hotspurs grow but a little more inflamed and

---

* See Orestes Ferrara's recent book on Alexander VI.
† "Henry IV", Pt. 1, Act I, Sc. 3.

go on to the use of germs and injections, or if our hearts become the tenth part of a degree colder.

I fancy that it was at this conjunction of past and present—of course in the strange Looking-Glass world of which I am writing—that I had a word or two in the corridor with Froude, who had been so critical in his time of the way our world was going and was now presumably watching the final outcome of the destruction of the Great Society from a seat in the 'Interval'. I said something, I believe, to the effect that the lovely description in the first chapter of his History of England of the change that came upon the world at the close of the Middle Age had seemed to me, as to many, the high-water-mark of his writing. Nowhere had the magic quality of medievalism been so tersely and brilliantly rendered. He picked up one of his own sentences and said that the meaning and direction of the new movement had still been hidden from him at the date of writing that chapter.

"But it is hidden no longer", I ventured. He looked rather uncomfortable and said nothing in reply. "Surely in putting your money on the Germans", I risked again, "you backed the wrong horse; and I can never refrain from suspecting that in some sort of way you knew it all the time. Your shining periods were always at their brightest, if I may presume to say so, when you were writing about the Great Society. Your account of the expulsion of the monks from the London Charterhouse and of the perennial distinction of every Catholic bishop in the passage relating to the earliest Anglican consecrations—Parker's and the rest—are pretty nearly as superb pieces of literature as that lament over the passing of the Middle Age to which I referred. One cannot kick against the pricks all the time, however much one's brother happens to have irritated one." I am afraid my manners were questionable, but in the Looking-Glass world I don't think people minded much about that. The mirrors reflected everything to the last secrets of one's soul; and I had the idea that, in default of any previous auricular confession, people were rather grateful than not to one for saying out loud what they were inwardly aware had become public property. Froude at any rate said nothing, but whether from pride or humility I do not presume to guess.

It was not, however, Froude's eloquent contrast between the Past and Present that took the first place in my thoughts as the Drama, half read and half visualised, left, so to say, Christendom

behind it. A contemplation, rather than an elegy, supplied the substance of a final scene in a period which had run true to design at
least from Charlemagne to Chaucer. For a moment the mirrors
seemed full with what I can only call the speaking likeness of a lamb
—a Lamb that had been slain and yet was come to life again. It was
in the year 1432 that the younger Van Eyck had completed that picture
at Ghent which some have thought, by reason of the superb symbolism
of its subject even more than of the then new technical skill of its
painter in giving life to colour, the greatest painted ever. High upon
an altar the Lamb receives the homage of the hierarchies of Heaven
and Earth; and the very atmosphere seems tense with the spirit of
adoration. In that picture, resting now (or at least in time of peace) in
the cathedral of St. Bavo, there lies half-concealed from our modern
minds such a thing of beauty as is yet, for all our neglect of it, a joy
for ever. A thing of beauty, but of beauty asleep! Still within the
framework of its lovely shutters, where Adam and Eve are depicted
with, as one critic observes,* 'almost brutal exactitude', no less
than masterly power, one may find the image of the Great Society,
even though the breath of its being to be detected seem to demand
a mirror at the lips, so deep is the trance that has fallen upon
it. Requiescat in pace—for peace, however much belied in practice,
was still its significant form.

* Weale, "The Van Eycks", p. 48.

the Puritans or the pardonable prejudice of the Huguenots; and it found a new outlet in the play-houses, where Shakespeare and Racine sustained the connection between real life and high drama which is essential to the true humanity of man. Progressively, however, under the influence of the Reformation, and subsequently of the French Revolution, man allowed his dramatic sense to be isolated from his inner being. As at first the theatre of God yielded place and interest to the dramas of the great poets, so in time were these displaced in public appeal and influence by the equivalent of shows and circuses in the Roman Empire. One could mark the process on its way. Goethe's commendation of Byron as a genius of such mark as had not been before and was not likely to return* owed something possibly to Byron's keen perception that the dramatic element was no accident in human life, but of its very essence. "He", observes a recent writer† in speaking of the Pilgrim of Eternity, "preserves in himself three things which have not been combined in the same degree of intensity and power by any other man: hatred of mass-opinion; delight in the impact of personality; and a sense, so active that it has germinated in the mind of the world, of the truth that hypocrisy does not consist in playing a part but in pretending that the world is not a stage." Let us assume that our author is correct in supposing that a dramatic sense is germinating in the modern world—a matter by no means obvious—and we should still have to confess that it has been put to poor uses, if not prostituted to base ones. Not only is there a conspicuous absence of great acting in the theatres themselves, not only does so-called civilisation increasingly neglect and profess to despise the fine manners, not to speak of the distinctive dress, that makes it easier for men and women to play their parts in the theatre of life; but even the politicians, though deceivers ever, have lately failed to produce a single figure, with the exception of Mr. Churchill, of any histrionic value. The pathetic absurdity of man is stressed in every possible way; and the grand manner, once thought becoming to man from the grand seigneur to the lacquey who rode behind his coach, is ridiculed in proportion. Only in the ritual of the Church is there preserved something of the seemly sense that all the world's a stage and all the men and women merely players. If it be urged that acting breeds hypo-

* Conv. with Eckermann, Oct. 1st, 1823.
† The author of "Menander's Mirror" in the *Times Lit. Sup.* of Jan. 22nd, 1944, p. 39.

crisy, the answer was long ago indicated by La Rochefoucauld in the remark that hypocrisy was the homage paid by vice to virtue. Hypocrisy indeed is playing one's part upon the stage without genuine feeling and consequently playing it ill; but the part has none the less to be played, or else the very memory of the piece will presently disappear.

Byron was an angel, though an angel fallen, and of that he is witness against himself. Confronted by the grace and tenderness of some of his lines, none can doubt that he had been given an angel's part to play; whilst his sharp asides reveal a soul jarred and disgusted by men's wretched travesty of the drama that is theirs to make or mar. Shelley, on the other hand, was precisely an 'ineffectual 'angel. He renders his part in diction of great beauty, but it was a part that he had written for himself without any regard for the rest of the play. As Aubrey de Vere* justly observed, all the 'wild' ideas of revolutionary writers had been put forward with more power by him than by any man. He mused as habitually as the most religious man on some great deliverance for the human race; but in his scheme the Deliverer was to be, not a God-man but a Man-god, not a compassionate Redeemer descending to earth, but a Titan fighting his way upwards and hurling mountains against a heavenly citadel. Such an angel was, dramatically speaking, ineffectual. Wholly incapable of the mystic's 'prayer of quiet', Shelley ranted even while he was touching the lyre of Orpheus and drawing from it exquisite sounds. I could even imagine Rabelais matching them to one of those iridescent icicles which, as the reader will recall, Pantagruel picked up on the confines of the Frozen Sea and tossed to Panurge to be melted in his hands. Again and again, whilst one watched the Drama proceeding on the world's stage, that comparison seemed to hold good; and from Allegra's exquisitely bound copy of Shelley's poems I could have picked countless pearls unstrung that the ingenuous poet had let drop before the acquisitive Panurges of our time. One ought, perhaps, to keep that enchanting volume more shamefacedly locked-up than Archdeacon Grantley kept his Rabelais; for, as I think, Shelley's Poems possess far more dangerous charms and witcheries than any within the compass of the Curé de Meudon. I had read in it with Allegra beside that very Ligurian Sea where there had fallen upon Maurois's "Ariel" the last sea-change; and no place, perhaps, was better calculated to clothe the Poet's elfin soul with the vestment of an angel of light.

* See W. Ward's "Life of Aubrey de Vere", pp. 333–8.

Of the siren-singers upon the Ligurian strand it was, however, Byron, not Shelley, who had understood the drama of the Fall of Man; and to that singular great sinner, not to the faithless husband of the luckless Harriet, I found myself turning as the scenic development seemed to reach a final climax. He stood, for the mind's eye, statuesque against the outline of the Seven Hills, and then stepped forward with cloak thrown back and arm extended. I did not think Fortune could have sent a more unexceptionable cicerone. The modern Kingdom of Italy had not blurred his grace of thought, nor the modern monument to Victor Emmanuel blotted out his larger vision. The last man to be accounted a clerical, Byron, where his judgment confirmed a catholic view, seemed beyond suspicion of prejudice. His eye, casting as it passed on a glance at the Coliseum and at Hadrian's 'Mole', swept across the Eternal City, and rested on St. Peter's. Then with a great air, worthy of the subject and the scene, he pointed to 'the vast and wondrous Dome . . . Christ's mighty shrine above His martyr's tomb . . . worthiest of God, the holy and the true' among all 'temples old and altars new'. He did this, as I say, in the grand manner, and then declaimed the lines that men once knew so well with so much feeling as to make them all his own:

> Enter: its grandeur overwhelms thee not;
> And why? it is not lessen'd—but thy mind,
> Expanded by the Genius of the spot,
> Has grown colossal, and can only find
> A fit abode wherein appear enshrined
> Thy hopes of immortality—and thou
> Shalt one day, if found worthy, so defined
> See thy God face to face, as thou dost now
> His Holy of Holies; nor be blasted by his brow. *

He would make me feel, as he intended, like one climbing some Alpine height whose very grace conceals its giant stature; and then again like one upon some rolling ocean which must be studied piecemeal in its creeks and bays to grasp its magnitude. It is no fault in what you see, he would say, if the fullness of its glory escapes you:—

> . . . Our outward sense
> Is but of gradual grasp —and as it is
> That what we have of feeling most intense
> Outstrips our faint expression; even so this
> Outshining and o'erwhelming edifice

---

* "Childe Harold's Pilgrimage", IV, stanza 155.

Fools our fond gaze, and greatest of the great
Defies at first our Nature's littleness,
Till, growing with its growth, we thus dilate
Our spirits to the size of that they contemplate.

Then pause, and be enlighten'd; there is more
In such a survey than the sating gaze
Of wonder pleased, or awe which would adore
The worship of the place, or the mere praise
Of Art and its great Masters, who could raise
What former time, nor skill, nor thought could plan;
The fountain of Sublimity displays
Its depth, and thence may draw the mind of Man
Its golden sands, and learn what great Conceptions can. *

The Church of which Byron had written in such terms had been conceived in the hour when the spirit of the Renaissance touched the domed summit of its classic grace and, simultaneously, the spirit of the Reformation struck with all its strength at the rock-hewn foundations of the Apostolic See. Yet the outer courts of this temple were filled with the praise of sage and hero and seemed as if they might well have served for an entrance to Dante's 'noble castle' and the spot, lofty and luminous, whither he withdrew to participate in the mild, majestic talk of pagan poets and conversed for a while with Homer and Horace, Ovid and Lucan and that Virgil in whom above them all his soul delighted. But, within, the Church was all glorious with the strength and beauty pertaining to the citadel of the City of God and seemed armed, to the utmost power of sacrifice, for the defence of the faith once delivered to those two saints whose bodies lay buried beneath its Altar.

So might a Catholic think; but let a Protestant likewise have his say. "It is the dome", remarks J. A. Symonds, "that makes St. Peter's what it is—the adequate symbol of the Church in an age that had abandoned mediaevalism and produced a new type of civility (*sic*) for the modern nations. . . . This mighty temple is the shrine of Catholicity, no longer cosmopolitan by right of spiritual empire, but secularised and limited to Latin races. At the same time it represents the spirit of a period when the Popes still led the world as intellectual chiefs. Raised by proud and secular pontiffs in the heyday of renascent humanism it seems to wait the time when the high priests of a religion no longer hostile to science . . . will chaunt their hymns beneath its spacious dome!" †

* "Childe Harold", IV, stanzas 155-9.
† J. A. Symonds, "Renaissance in Italy—The Fine Arts", Chap. II.

As so often with hostile writers, the essential fact stands out clearly enough despite contentious adjectives and controversial asides. Upon the dome—'the vast and wondrous dome'—the Papacy had struck the note of a new era and sent it pealing through Christendom like an alarm-bell summoning men to defend the City of God. The Church was ready still to confound the world, but neither with the whispered chanting of the Mass in the catacombs, nor, as in the Middle Age, with the soaring hymn of the Angelus from tower and steeple, but with a theology elucidated and reinforced by the renascent witness of the Humanities.

"You must understand, Mary," a friend of mine once heard an American say to his wife, as they watched a Corpus Christi or other procession in the Piazza outside St. Peter's, "that these are people for whom science does not exist." He spoke for himself and for Symonds too. But there are some, very well-qualified to form an opinion, like the late Friedrich von Hügel, who have passed a different judgment on the assimilation of knowledge by Catholic minds. "Sometimes I ask myself," von Hügel wrote to a niece, "the wisest, widest, deepest men I have known—are they not all Roman Catholics? Yes, they are."* If that were so—and Pasteur, another excellent judge, would not have denied it—then St. Peter's had fulfilled its destiny and brought even physics, which sometimes so rashly claims all knowledge for its province, under the same spacious dome as the knowledge of God and man.

Allegra's season, as I have explained, was pre-eminently Christmas; and I could imagine with what delight she would have beheld a pageant so rich in Renaissance feeling as that, but lately mentioned, wherein the pagan gods, hearing at last that the true God is near, come creeping up on Christmas Eve to the Capitol to worship and adore in the Church of the Ara Coeli. I can imagine, too, how complete would have been her satisfaction if, by the waving of some magician's wand, that little party of Bohemians, which, as set forth in "Trilby" with all George du Maurier's marvellous sleight of hand, had on a Christmas Eve set out from the Quartier Latin to attend Midnight Mass at the Madeleine, had been seized by the hair (after the manner of angels in the days of Daniel), raised from Paris and set down in Rome, so that a delegation of artists—Taffy, the Laird, and Little Billee, or whomsoever else you will—might join themselves to the picturesque procession of pagan Gods moving towards Christian altars. For that, too, would have been in the style of the Renaissance,

* F. von Hügel, "Letters to a Niece", p. xxxvi.

which seemed designed to act as a kind of liaison-officer between the Pagan and Christian worlds and to bring all fallen Nature sweetly under the banner of grace. I have stated long since that this was Allegra's book no less than my own, and I say it again, as this book draws to its close, because I have at no point felt more sure of her influence and sympathy than in what I have just said. She was spiritually a child of the Renaissance, and unconsciously, and so much the more strikingly for that, her whole being suggested that the long episode of the Reformation, culminating as it did in the Revolution, had been an inartistic, not to say hideous, error. One could read it just as easily, I thought, in the depth of her radiant eyes as on the page of history which treats of the latter end of the arrogant German soul, paganised, not purified, by thinking along Protestant lines. Her natural poise of mind had enabled her to skip three centuries of European disintegration and avoid the mud that both sides have slung and by which both have been spattered. If anything had been needed to show me that Europe had not run true to that slow change and motion which, to recall Pater's simile already quoted, seems as if it had slept for a hundred years, Allegra's instinctive bent, not towards Catholicism as such, but towards the civilisation that Catholicism had created, would have shown it me. And, if Leonardo is rightly indicated as the Hamlet of the age and country to which in heart and mind she belonged, then it will be seen that the place that he had in her picture of life was in perfect line with what has just been said.

It was not given to me, however, to be in Rome with Allegra for any Christmas; and I have no better title to search my memories of the Eternal City by the light of lamp or candle, borrowed from the Holy Crib, than by the sunlight of June, playing upon the roses, red and golden, of Corpus Christi. Our stay there fell in spring time. On the Palatine—in the palaces of the Caesars—the judas-trees were bright with blossom; and on the Vatican—above the tomb of the Apostles—the stage was set for the Easter Mass at St. Peter's. It happened thus, then, that we saw the Christian drama at its greatest, as one might say, on its greatest day, and saw, therewith, everyman's short journey through time swept into the mystic orbit of the world's desire and the world's design. Perhaps, without that experience, no one will perfectly perceive Christ in His statesman's place in human history; so essential does a perfect conjunction of time and place and liturgy appear to be to this vision of Christendom.

Of liturgy, no less than of time and place! St. Theresa—and she was writing whilst St. Peter's was building—has a striking passage, deploring, as only a true artist in the mysticism of human life would be moved to do, the travesty of the Mass that had been made by the Reformers. The Latin Races, it must be remembered, were contributing much to the new configuration of Christianity; and among the Latin races none more than the Spanish. Whilst Vittoria had formulated the international ethic of colonial enterprise desiderated by the discovery of Columbus, and Lope de Vega and Calderon (both of them, like Vittoria, priests) were anticipating, by plays which introduced picaresque and plebeian elements, the coming style in drama, St. John of the Cross and St. Theresa were mapping out with rare precision the milestones of the mystic way. It is commonly said that St. Ignatius Loyola provided the Papacy with its prætorian guard by founding the Order of Jesus just as Rome was thrown on the defensive by the rise of Protestantism; and doubtless this statement has its measure of truth. But it is St. Theresa who, in the same century and country, touches the heart of the matter when she instructs her discalced Carmelites that "the soldiers of Christ . . . are the contemplatives and those engaged in prayer",* and warns them that the enemies whom contemplatives fear are, not open enemies, but 'the traitors, the devils who transform themselves into angels of light and come disguised'. The mutilation of the Mass by the Protestants was consequently to the last degree offensive to her as a mystic—a thing, in her own words, 'ugly, abominable and disgraceful'. And this view, here so violently expressed by the outraged artist, is in a mild manner endorsed by an eminent Anglican writer on mysticism—Evelyn Underhill†—who deliberately selects the Roman Missal as best qualified to show the mystic life of man moving into relation with the Eucharist and so losing itself in the Corpus Christi mysticum—the mystical body of Christ. The restrained, artistic merit of what is thus liturgically achieved lies, if one critic is right, in a certain urbanity which enables us "to express our inner life in all its fulness and depth without divulging our secrets". "The liturgy", he continues, "here accomplishes on the spiritual plane what has been done on the temporal by the dignified forms of social intercourse, the outcome of the tradition created and handed down by sensitive people. This makes communal life possible for the individual, and yet insures him against unauthorised

* "Way of Perfection", c. XL.   † "The Mystic Way", p. 338.

interference with his inner self; he can be cordial without sacrificing his spiritual independence; he is in communication with his neighbour without on that account being swallowed up and lost among the crowd. In the same way the liturgy preserves freedom of spiritual movement for the soul by means of a wonderful union of spontaneity and the finest erudition. It extols *urbanitas* as the best antidote to barbarism, which triumphs when spontaneity and culture alike are no more."*

'Urbanitas'—the urbanity of the City of God—that is perhaps the impression par excellence which the movement of the Renaissance as it reaches, religiously speaking, its artistic apex in St. Peter's, has the power to convey. Though the earth be never so unquiet, though the nations rage and the people imagine a vain thing, here, in its Roman citadel, Urbanity in its finest form pursues its way untroubled up the great nave of the church until it finds its consummation of grace in the sacrifice of the Altar. Like some high emotion dramatically handled with perfect taste, it seems to make the whole world kin. The individual soul, entering with the multitude the House of God and at first staggered by its own littleness and lowness, grows aware of the majestic courtesy of the place, is reassured by the triumphant 'Gloria in excelsis' of the choir, and then carried forward on a great cloud of witness towards the affirmations of the Creed.

At the Easter Mass the witnesses to the Resurrection who come forward are the Apostles whose bodies lie beneath St. Peter's Church —St. Paul directly by means of his letter to the Corinthians, St. Peter indirectly through the Gospel of St. Mark, where his testimony is generally recognised to have guided the hand of the Evangelist. For this reason among others that august anniversary may claim to display in Rome to the fullest degree the grace of the grand manner. Not dimmed nor dwarfed by the surpassing scenery of Michelangelo's design, there can be perceived between the lines of the liturgy the outline of the church of the catacombs, where perhaps Mark's brief factual gospel held priority of place among the matter-of-fact inhabitants of the metropolis. And still, through all the layers of the years, do the simplicity and strength of the Roman use and usage dominate the resplendent grandeur of the Renaissance Church; and still in the artless words of the Easter sequence can be seen with what childlike humility, even in its greatest hours, the voice of prayer recalls and renews its youth.

* R. Guardini, "Spirit of the Liturgy", p. 22.

To assist at an Easter Mass, such as I witnessed with Allegra in Rome almost exactly (as I write) twenty years ago, was, as I have already indicated, to invite an interpretation of human history far more searching and satisfying than all the rest. If God continued, according to Pascal's formula, to conceal Himself from prying eyes, St. Peter's bade fair to betray the secret of His policy. The pressure of historic circumstance was in fact such that the significance of the Thing done at Calvary could with difficulty, as it seemed to me, be concealed from any eye trained to assess political events and consequences. Christ had been lifted up at Jerusalem; but, if the matter had stopped there, one might well wonder whether He could in any convincing sense be said to have drawn all men unto Him. It was Christian Rome which had fully understood that the Eucharist was no mere feast of remembrance but a continuation of Calvary with both a major and minor Elevation of the Host implicit in its significance. Here lay drama more moving than any that the mind of man had yet come on—drama so touching that, as is well known, St. Louis was moved to salute it as an act done for love of him once long ago by One he had never seen. So passionate, indeed, was the pathos of the scene that, when the French Revolution started to substitute its own hollow reading of the riddle of the universe, some of its advocates thought it worth while to imagine 'A Last Supper of the Girondins', which seems to have had almost as little substance in fact as distinction in detail.

Here as elsewhere it would have been well for the world if the spirit of finesse had been more active. The Mass can be said, as it has been said, an infinite number of times, but the event of Calvary quite obviously cannot be repeated. Talleyrand's Voltairean advice to the enterprising revolutionary who proposed to invent a new religion and inquired how best to begin, is here in point. The Bishop, formerly of Autun, blandly recommended that Sieyès (if Sieyès it was) should get himself crucified and rise again the third day, and thus incidentally said the last word upon all subsequent projects of new religions. There will be no successor to Christianity, if only because Love can no farther go. It is as in physics with light, than which, we are told, nothing can be swifter. The Great Lover has come, has been raised to the Cross and will be sacramentally in agony until the end of the world. No man can steal the genius of that drama from Him, nor substitute another in its place.

The reader will, doubtless, appreciate that a spectacle so moving in conception, so magnificent in form, and so mysterious in character as the Mass at its greatest, is calculated to transform any estimate of drama and design. I began to see more clearly still the implications of the divided stage in the Looking-Glass world. All profound representations or reflections of life rested upon the postulate of some conflict proceeding between powers of good and evil; and unless the identification of these was obvious and incontestable, a play, however thrilling its episodes or stirring its language and action, drifted down gradually from drama to melodrama. The effect of the two storeys on the Looking-Glass Stage was to make this distinction painfully apparent. On the upper storey, where the classical tradition of the Humanities, steadied and sweetened by the Mass, retained its hold, both the plot and performance of the piece responded to the demands of human judgment on its loftiest plane. Heart and mind, in other words, were at one, the former deeply moved, the latter fully persuaded, so that the spectator felt his whole nature rising on even pinions of sympathy and thought. But on the lower storey it was otherwise. There the performance, for all its wealth of sensations and slogans, left one like a man struggling in a tangle of trees and wondering how in the world he would ever get a sight of the wood.

Thus, if the argument of the play in the upper storey might sometimes be styled cryptic or even apocalyptic, the argument in the lower grew so increasingly confused as to seem wanting altogether. I shall perhaps be able to make this impression rather clearer if I give a specific illustration. It happened, a little before I left the theatre, that there was being given on the upper stage the War of Gog and Magog as recorded by St. John the Divine, or at least something so like it as to make the identification almost inevitable. This particular conflict had in vision synchronised, as the student doubtless recalls, with the close of the Millennium. Satan, loosed from confinement, had started afresh to deceive the nations, raked the four corners of the globe for his victims and swept the inhabitants of the earth, like so much flying sea-sand, into multitudinous battle. His principal agents in this enterprise were Gog and Magog, gigantic figures looking their grim and ghastly part to perfection. A spectator must have been dull in the wits not to see that he had here to deal with 'evil things'. The struggle was indeed on so prodigious a scale that one might have taken, or mistaken, the resistance offered to these ruffians for an effort on the part of some power making for righteousness to reach that river of life upon the banks of which there was alleged to stand a tree with healing in its leaves for the wounds of the nations. One might even have dreamed that the Kingdom of God had joined final issue with the Prince of this World or, which is the same thing, that Love was locked in its last conflict with Force and Violence. For sooner or later it must come to that, if the apocalyptic design of the Drama, as discovered in the statesmanship of Christ, was to reveal the large lines of its action and the radiant humanity of its meaning.

One had, however, only to study the pantomime proceeding on the lower storey to see that any inferences of this kind were premature and delusive. One might see from a thousand trivial details that the same plot was in process of execution on this stage as on the stage above, yet the general effect was one of such unintelligible confusion that the word pantomime alone seemed appropriate. What were apparently human beings, though wearing the masks of animals, were here engaged in internecine conflict. In the forefront of the vast stage Vultures, Bears, Frogs and Lions and many other kind of creatures had produced a spectacle of carnage beyond description; whilst in the background the rider on the white horse to whom I have already referred, moved industriously to and fro, his satellites, on their variously-coloured mounts, black, bay and pallid, attending. The scene of destruction was so ghastly, the ferocity of the combatants so uncompromising, the instruments of death so dreadful that I could not but fancy that the nemesis of knowledge had come at last and that I was listening to the death-knell of civilisation tolling from those very towers and steeples whose bells had been accustomed to ring out the chimes of Christmas.

Everywhere, as one could see, men's hearts were failing them from fear of what might be coming on the earth. But, beyond that, I must confess, I could not make very much of the business. At first, it is true, I supposed I had solved the enigma of this seeming madness; for I saw that the predatory Vultures and Bears had got together and that the brave Lions, whose teeth had been mostly drawn and their claws closely clipped by their imbecile keepers, were opposing them with the aid of the croaking Frogs, who had obviously but little stomach for the fight. But when the Lions, after roaring defiance at the Bears, suddenly turned round and made common cause with them, I no longer knew whether I was standing on my head or my heels, so complete was my astonishment. A large body of Eagles shortly afterwards gave aquiline assistance to this ursine and leonine alliance; and I felt assured that in due course the Bears would get the better of the Vultures. But how that was going to bring in any reign of righteousness the action of the play gave no indication; nor did the earlier conduct of the Bears appear to justify any but adverse anticipations. I was constrained, therefore, to watch the subsequent proceedings in much the same way as I imagine men of former times used to look on at cock-fights and bull-fights; and, though I saw almost incredible feats of daring and courage performed on every side, I could not see that the ultimate triumph was calculated to produce any result at all proportionate to the sacrifice or suffering involved.

Many of the audience, however, appeared to think very differently from myself and to find the show a good one. I remember in this connection being especially delighted and amused by an old clergyman who kept clapping his hands most vigorously whenever the Bears scored a success. It seemed that he had identified their proceedings with the imitation of Christ and their victory with the advent of the Kingdom of God; and, if old clergymen were always as clever as they should be, I should give him credit for having understood what was going forward. As it was, however, though I am not insinuating that this worthy man was guilty of such a trahison des clercs as has been charged against some members of his profession, I must admit that I entertained a dreadful suspicion that he had made even less sense of the piece than I had done myself—and for the excellent reason that there was in fact little sense to be made. All the real drama, tested by the presence of clear-cut motives, was to be found in the upper storey; and the rest was but melodrama, pantomime, opera bouffe, or what you will, with sensation and song and jest to camouflage its mental chaos and mortal pain. The claque, claque, claque of the old clergyman haunted me long after I had quitted the Looking-Glass world, and drove me to alternating emotions of laughter and tears. He at all events entertained no exaggerated expectations in respect of the power to overcome the world of the faith that he professed.

"This world", Horace Walpole had written to Lady Ossory some few years before the French Revolution broke out, "is a comedy to those that think, a tragedy to those that feel." It was doubtless, when he wrote, fast coming to that. The lack of any comprehensive design in the theatre of life made for that curious disintegration of

Being which shows so plainly in Mr. Churchill's misapprehension of Pascal's famous observation distinguishing, yet without seeking to disunite, the heart's reasons from those of the mind. Independent departments of emotion and thought are now familiar and enable total war to be waged without undue inconvenience or serious compunction. The formula is simple. By the use of the appropriate drug a sense of dual personality is produced in the human soul: the Sermon on the Mount, including the blessing on the peace-makers, is put temporarily into cold-storage; prayers for peace are offered up simultaneously with demands for unconditional surrender; and the most ruthless means or measures are justified by the prospect or promise of a speedier end. Nothing could have been more significant than the silence of the Lords Spiritual when one of their number, bolder than the rest, sought to put a drag on the devastation. They were plainly too bewildered to speak, though the occasion was precisely one that called for their moral judgment.

It had not been always precisely thus. Mr. Bryant has lately quoted from a letter of William Pitt addressed in the summer of 1797 to his Foreign Secretary, George Grenville, who entertained views temperamentally more in line with those now in fashion. "I feel it my duty", Pitt had written, "as an English Minister and a Christian to use every effort to stop so bloody and wasting a war."* He had to deal with the French Directory, all its members at its inception regicides, some of them, like Barras, revolutionary rascals, and others, like Carnot, revolutionary fanatics. But that had made no difference to Pitt's conception of his duty 'as an English Minister and a Christian'. The Revolution had not yet divided the human soul into close compartments, mental and moral, though, as Pitt's language shows, these could be distinguished. And the little episode is interesting because there have been few men in English politics who have made so great a name for patriotism as the younger Pitt, or perhaps, since he seemed a Whig in his time, but in aftertimes a Tory, who present so fair a model of what a patriotic minister must wish to be. What a world of difference lay between Pitt's so sensitive language and such a high-sounding phrase as 'unconditional surrender'! And what a contrast lies between the restraint with which Pitt's disciples closed the last phase of the Napoleonic drama and the repression with which we have every reason to anticipate that our own grand melodrama is going to conclude. How prudent Wellington and

* Quoted by A. Bryant, "Age of Endurance", p. 208.

Castlereagh had been not to demand the impossible of France in 1815. And per contra how inconsiderate Mr. Churchill had been to demand from Germany just that which he of all men who can be named would have been the last to concede, had some chance or mischance given him birth on the other side of the Rhine. Trifles light as the wording of a phrase, subtle distinctions such as that latent in Pitt's famous dictum that England should save herself by her *exertions* but Europe by her *example*, sufficed to show the difference between Drama with its grand design and melodrama with its shortness of thought.

Such reflections would keep coming out of the mirrors and into my mind as I watched the play drawing, for myself, to its appointed end; and I do not pretend that I found them particularly agreeable. Was it possible by any chance that Marlborough, whom Thackeray charges so severely in "Esmond" with keeping the war of his time in being beyond the need, was repeating himself in his descendant? Who dares yet pretend to say with any assurance? We should none of us see the end of all these things—we upon whom all the ends of the world had come.

Anyhow it seemed time to be going; for already I fancied the reflections were beginning to fade from the mirrors. I found my way out of the Looking-Glass world as best I might, and tumbled or stumbled into Wonderland in the effort. At least I feel almost sure it was Wonderland, for I caught a glimpse, as I passed, of Old Father William. He was of course standing on his head, and from this point of vantage promising, as I gathered from an onlooker, the moon to the million. But that after all was what he was there to do. There's no fool, the observant say, like an old fool; yet one should not, for that, make fun of 'old hopefuls'. They make up magnificently, like Father Christmas, and if in due time we find them out, we must not be more critical than becomes the children that we are. The better worlds of the politician are only the wonderland of Father William; and everyone is free to go and make-believe there as much as he likes and as long as he can. It is perhaps more doubtful whether we have any title to impose our fond imaginations upon others. When one is a child one thinks as a child, but there comes a time for putting away childish things, and among them, the pranks of Old Hopefuls in drear-nighted Decembers. Grand Opera would most likely be prejudiced, if one were to maintain the Christmas pantomime, with clown and columbine to match, beyond

Candlemas, and, should that date or its equivalent presently arrive, there might be something to be said for a tableau of our Lady's Court with, inset, some version of the Passion Play. After thirty years and more the beauty of the boys' faces that I saw at Ober-Ammergau remains with me. Their owners had been rehearsing from early childhood in the streets and lanes of the village in the hope of being someday called upon to take the part of the Christus; with the result that the beauty of this imitation had worked its way into their flesh. Yet they were Germans, presumably long since called away by their melodramatic politicians for other work!

Chapter XVIII

FIRELIGHT

SKYLIGHT at the house-top! Starlight studding the floor of heaven! Twilight, as one wandered through the dark night of sense! Light diffracted from broken mirrors! Light reflected as one entered the Looking-Glass world! Then, in the theatre of time recovered—le temps retrouvé—searchlight, limelight, spotlight, what you will! And now, at last, firelight!

It had always been a good companion—one of the very best. Far better, so far as I was myself concerned, than tobacco; and, if one had company, then again an excellent mixer. Raleigh was, doubtless, a great man, but not, as the saying is, 'a patch' upon Shelley's friend Prometheus—assuming the truth, that is, of the revolutionary myth which gives to the latter the credit of bringing fire to mankind. Not of course that such assumptions were very safe to make; reformers and revolutionaries being quite as much addicted to fables as other folks—from the great Foxe of the Protestant martyrology to the great Thiers of the Napoleonic Legend. Let such things be, however; for firelight does not tempt to savage controversy or cause the fire of the tongue to kindle. I think that even Landor, who fought with most people, had found that out, and that the strange line which introduces his last word on life is best explained as a proud man's admission of it:—

> I strove with none, for none was worth my strife.
> Nature I loved and, next to Nature, art:
> I warm'd both hands before the fire of life;
> It sinks, and I am ready to depart.

Discussion there must be, if life were to be at all interesting; but the only argument worth while at the fireside is one's own life's argument, elucidated, passed through purgatorial fire, and encircled by some soft gem-like flame of memory's making.

Fireside evenings in the Chinese Room, with Allegra sitting by the hearth, would thus return to mind and make one wonder whether one could ever meet the firelight again on such even terms and keep piling on the logs whilst the logs themselves piled up one's thoughts. Perhaps in some Bleak House, where, though the prevailing wind

346

blew from the east, one might hope to find a habitation, if no home, and company, if not of flesh and blood! Perhaps there, in the fire-light, authors, 'growing rash', would step down from the book-cases, even though Glendower's magic power to summon spirits from the vasty deep was wanting to me. Perhaps, if only the locality were sufficiently haunted! A bleak house in Bath, of which city not only Landor, but Dickens were somewhile citizens, might well hold the secret how to cast a spell upon Lawrence Boythorn and fetch him back from the grave to devise imaginary conversations about human things. Only there would be abundance of fuel needed to warm such cold hands as his, and, as I write, all the vestal fires of the Humanities look like failing all Europe over and the very torch-lights of learning like flickering out for lack of some oil of gladness.

The England I had known seemed to look back at me from dying embers—that old, fair, free, independent England which had gone her own way in the world and taught her children to go theirs. I was glad to have known the great age of Victoria; for I had never doubted its greatness, whatever opinion the young might please to hold of it. Take it for all in all, it stood higher in my belief than the romantic age of Elizabeth or the Augustan age of Anne. Saving only Shake-speare, it had produced as great men as the one and written as grace-ful English as the other. Its public life was not much amiss, freer anyhow than politics had been under the last of the Tudors and purer, too, than they had been under the last of the Stuarts. If Lecky were any judge, England had in fact possessed between 1832 and 1867 as good a constitution as it has ever enjoyed. The Victorians had known how to produce interesting côteries in the fathers of the Oxford Movement, in the Pre-Raphaelite brotherhood, in the Cambridge Apostles, in the 'Souls'—and good conversation of different kinds to match them. They had managed to correct the morals of the Regency, calm the unrest of the European Revolution, raise the moral credit of the rich and the financial credit of the poor, and (the Crimean and Boer Wars being omitted and perhaps regretted) give England a period of peace without a peer in English history.

The period had shown indeed one marked foible or folly, but in a time of such rare success and prosperity, a pardonable one. It had grown to think of moral progress as the automatic effect of many inventions, and had hardly dreamed that a time might come when wise men would speak of the discovery of the internal combustion engine as Seth may be supposed to have spoken of his father's consumption of the apple of knowledge. Not everyone, it is true, had shared this pleasing illusion. Three or four at least of the outstanding men of that time had been at some pains to voice their doubts and disbeliefs. Ruskin had seen how poorly the artistic and evangelical inspiration of the period compared with that of the Middle Age. Carlyle, though himself bewitched by the Germans, had mocked in his rough way at the Manchester School and the cheery irresponsibles who took their pleasure in 'shooting Niagara'. But the two constructive geniuses of the period—those two remarkable men who, according to one legend, played together as children in a London Square—saw that the self-satisfaction of the reign required to be transcended quite as much as it required to be exposed. Disraeli was never more dexterous than in undermining the prestige of the Liberal school of thought and anticipating the criticism of it by the Christian Socialists. The astute allusions in "Sybil" to the economic, as well as the romantic aspect of the society that in pre-Reformation days had gathered about the institution of the Abbey; the depreciation of the Whig aristocracy as a 'Venetian oligarchy'; the subtle remark of Sidonia that "man is born to obey and to adore"—all in their way made for the creation of an England which would venerate the Throne, trust a populus that included the plebs, accept for its motto 'imperium et libertas', seek to hold India by the jewelled magic of an Imperial Crown and the Dominions by the simple word of freedom translated into temperate discussion and working compromise. It was in line with this appreciation of his compatriots as an island-people, in some respects as peculiar and isolated as the Jews themselves, that Disraeli had emphasised the value of independence in the conduct of foreign policy. "The abstention of England", as he put it, "from any unnecessary interference in the affairs of Europe is the consequence, not of her decline of power, but of her increased strength." Upon the merit of this independence, if upon nothing else, the leaders of both political Parties were in his time agreed, Clarendon and Gladstone no less than he himself and Salisbury. And the memorable phrase so often associated with the last-named—splendid isolation—merely summed up their common faith that, as Clarendon phrased it, "England should keep entire in her own hands the means of estimating her own obligations upon the various states of facts as they arose". Holding thus, by virtue of her strength, the balance of power in her hands, and casting her weight into either scale as the course of events might dictate, the British Government had secured a rare dignity and independence and been able to serve the interests of peace in Europe almost as effectively as to act as trustee for the safety and welfare of its own people—its foremost and, perhaps, its only authentic obligation.

If Englishmen wanted to do more than this, if they desired to enter the inner life of Europe, then, were their own independence of political action to be preserved, it would have to be at a much deeper level than was afforded by Continental understandings, alliances or entanglements. It would have, in a word, to be on the plane of that Christian civilisation in which the foundations of Christendom had been laid. Newman's peculiar genius became clear here. Without any interest in politics as such, his mind had been gradually drawn by the study of the humanities and history, as well as by the development of his own inner life, towards those Continental ties which had been once so tightened and knotted by the mission of Augustine. In that first Canterbury, rather than in any late Lambeth style, England had it in her power to make, if she chose, a direct contribution to the peace of Christendom—a contribution of mind and spirit worthy of herself, worthy of the inspiration of her great cathedrals and of such abbeys as Disraeli had celebrated in "Sybil" under the imaginary name of Marney—abbeys, to use his language, "as vast and as magnificent and as beautiful as your Belvoirs and your Chatsworths, your Wentworths and your Stowes . . . thirty or forty in (a) county, the proprietors of which were never absent."*
"These holy men", Disraeli had made his spokesman continue, ". . . built and planted, as they did everything else, for posterity: their churches were cathedrals; their schools colleges; their halls and libraries the muniment rooms of kingdoms; their woods and waters, their farms and gardens were laid out and disposed on a scale and in a spirit that are now extinct; they made the country beautiful and the people proud of their country."

Thus, their minds converging upon the same sublime idea by different approaches, Disraeli had glanced for a moment at the catholic foundation of Christian Society which Newman spent a lifetime in tracing out and seeking to restore. The statesman had been of course far too astute in later days to recommend to his Protestant countrymen the thesis which the churchman was at so

* Disraeli, "Sybil", Chap. 4.

great pains fully to develop; and Tory Democracy, so far as Disraeli was concerned, concluded in a 'Patriot King' and 'Faery Queen', not in the cosmopolitan creation of the Catholic Church. The 'Young England' of his imaginative youth had made him a dreamer of dreams; but the staid England of his politic old age had looked at the Oxford Movement, not liked it any too well, and left its waters to run high and then, in due season, its channel to turn dry. The whole episode was well worth studying in connection with what Montaigne had said of the English mind and its want of real integrity. That strange instrument of thought would never believe, as a Scottish philosopher has maintained, that no-one ever tried to break logic, but logic in the end broke him. Always it slipped away, at the crisis of the argument, with a strong profession of doubt in logical processes.

It was, however, upon the merits of our English defects that the mind tended to dwell in the dying firelight. The tolerance that attends the dislike of hard thinking had surely gone some way to the making of the easy England one had grown up into, and known, and cared for so well. How much one had owed to it—and to that part of it especially which had charmed the Squire of Hughenden! How companionable had been the now doomed and dying squirearchy! How well they had fitted into those smiling corners of England where one had passed so many happy hours! How modestly, despite all the talk of their arrogance, had they mostly gone about their business! I had seen much of them in their leisure hours; and the long September days, when in their company I had followed the wild or wily partridge over roots and stubble, had in reminiscence charms and humours hardly less keen than those which Dickens worked into the sporting days of Wardle cum Pickwick. Lovely memories of watching, as one walked, the purple hills of Purbeck across the blue lagoon of Poole blended with recollections of village cricket and local contests in field or park against good men long since gone to ground. That small corner of the Hardy country had taught me in its quiet way the truth about that larger country which Disraeli had visualised and sought to perpetuate.

The kindly England of the old English squirearchy had perished at the hands of two men, generously equipped to illustrate all that was best in it; and there had been few greater ironies amongst all the ironies of our time. It was Grey's diplomacy which, by reversing Salisbury's policy of independence and by extending Lansdowne's Anglo-French entente until it became in effect a military understanding, had made Britain, without her really realising it, a pledged piece on the European chess-board, instead of a Power free to take action on the actual issue, or to abstain. It was Lord Halifax's diplomacy which, by reversing Pitt's time-honoured decision not to intervene in Polish affairs, where, without the aid of one of the adjoining Empires, no intervention could succeed, had saddled the country, unconsulted and uncomprehending, with a guarantee which must cost her her honour or imperil her life. The England of Disraeli had been lost to us amid such misconceptions of British policy; and I doubted whether any man had the power any more to restore its essentials, counsel he never so wisely. Only the historian, it may be, as he passes his eye over the events of this time and takes their measure from their results, would notice curiously that, had Lord Halifax been willing in 1939 to allow Russia to do to the Baltic Republics and Poland and Finland what, still a member of the British Government, he seemed to be consenting to in 1944, the World War might never have occurred or, if it had occurred, might have spared us something of our now lost inheritance. But justice, if, as Pascal says, it is not the same on both sides of the Pyrenees, so neither does it appear to be the same at the two ends of a lustrum.

M. Maritain in an interesting critique of Pascal's political ideas has charged him with 'a kind of Christian cynicism'.* A philosopher rather than a historian, M. Maritain has perhaps overlooked the fact that by Pascal's time the Great Society had begun to disintegrate under the influence of the Reformation. Already the 'Great Design' of Henri Quatre for a United States of Europe, or perhaps more truly for a hegemony of France, was seeking to substitute itself for 'Our Lady's Regency'. Under Pascal's very eyes l'Éminence Rouge, with the aid of l'Éminence Grise—Richelieu with the aid of Père Joseph—was promoting the religious divisions of Germany. It seems idle in the circumstances for M. Maritain to oppose St. Catherine of Sienna's remark that "the great force of conservation is holy justice" to Pascal's lucid diagnosis of the world as it is. St. Catherine belonged to an age when men were still agreed in principle, if seldom in practice, that justice lay in the imitation of Jesus Christ and in communion with the historic Church of His foundation. By Pascal's time the Nations had taken the

* "Redeeming the Time", p. 32.

definition of justice into their own hands; and he looked at the world as it was, is and is likely to continue for any period that we can measure. "Other foundation can no man lay", the Apostle had observed, "than that which is laid."* In default, however, of any solid foundation for international justice, one had to make do with shifting custom. Everyone feels the force of that he has been accustomed to; and probably M. Maritain himself, if he weighed the title of France to Alsace, had felt that the fact that she held it from 1648 onwards counted for more than the fact that she secured it in very dubious circumstances. Custom, whatever its faults, is at least less complicated than any other conception of justice in a world grown utterly impatient of abstract standards of cosmopolitan right and wrong.

The relation between this disintegration of the bare idea of justice and the intransigence of modern warfare hardly seemed to be perceived by modern politicians. Not even the incontestable failure of the Peace of 1919 and of the League of Nations, which was both its child and its guardian, had taught them that a consensus of minds or at least a compromise of opinions must precede any durable settlement. They continued to think in terms of frontiers fixed by the force of the victors in the flush of victory but binding none the less on all concerned in it. As if every imposed or dictated peace, no matter who made it, did not lay a train of hatred which, like those underground movements we have encouraged in enemy-occupied countries, might one day explode, and perhaps when least desired! As if the vengeance which old offenders may have deserved would ever seem justice to a younger generation that held itself innocent! As if a nation would ever agree that it deserved to be beaten, to be held down, to live in leading-strings, to learn what its masters think proper to teach it! The long tale of human history showed only too often that a nation could cherish its griefs and its grievances from one generation to another. The repeated Scriptural injunction to leave vengeance to God was, after all, a dictate of common sense.

In fact, as Pascal had seen, the human mind, confused by its hatreds and its sentiments, had become far too fallible to recognise where in any particular case justice really lay. No statesman had ever expressed more succinctly than he what all our politicians are ever busy hiding—the hard truth that, whilst justice is subject to dispute, force is obvious and incontestable. "Thus", as he had contended,

* 1 Cor. III, 11.

"one could not put force into the hands of justice, because force contradicts justice and affirms itself to be just. And so, not being able to make what is just strong, what is strong has been taken for just."*
It was a ruthless piece of diagnosis; but no one with eyes to see that Great Britain was even now condoning on one side of the Vistula what she condemned on the other, could conveniently find fault with it.

The intellectual confusion of nations might indeed be suspected of nearing its climax when the same type of politician who, a few years ago, promised collective security with the aid of small nations and egregiously failed to provide it, came forward with a new plan for a world to be made safe and free through an association of Four Great Powers; two of them Anglo-Saxon and standing for as much Christianity as "my William" may like taught in his schools, which is little enough; the third professedly Anti-God and lying to-day, according to an authority singularly well-equipped to form a judgment, 'at the mercy of the sadistic mind'†; the fourth rooted and grounded in the positivism of Confucius or the pessimism of the Buddha. One might really suppose that some Minister of State or Member of Parliament had wandered out in his leisure hours into Smith Square, and, perceiving the famous church constructed (so they say) on a plan of Queen Anne's designing, which involved no greater effort on the part of Her Majesty than the turning of a table upside-down, had seized upon this singular architectural device as a new model for cosmopolitan security. A table indeed the Four Powers might provide, and perhaps even a round table, but nevertheless a table with its legs in the air, and those legs of very varied length and strength. What morals, weighty or even light, we should be able to rest upon it they may reasonably wonder who reflect that, not so many years ago, Mr. Churchill was commending Signor Mussolini as an antidote to the poison of Bolshevism.‡ Never surely had politicians and publicists been so hard pressed for the plan of a better world.

* "Pensées", 298.

† Julia de Beausobre, "Creative Suffering", p. 38. Mme. de Beausobre, the author of that singularly charitable account of life and suffering in Russia under the Bolshevik Régime, "The Woman Who Could Not Die", argues, in the pamphlet quoted from, that the Russian attitude towards suffering (as illustrated in Dostoyevsky's novels) has resulted in sadist and masochist national complexes which she analyses with a subtlety that only a Russian perhaps could pretend to. I must refer any reader, critical of what I have written, to this little book of Mme. de Beausobre's for my justification.

‡ Speech to the Italian and Foreign Press, Jan. 20th, 1927.

And never perhaps could Pascal's irony have played upon their shallow minds with more amusing results.

The accelerated progress of many inventions had been bringing the nations of the world nearer to one another by leaps and bounds: yet at no time would they appear to have distrusted one another more or hated one another so much. Everywhere the apple of knowledge was multiplying the curse of Cain. There had been a remedy—the remedy of which the relics of Our Lady's Regency were reminiscent —but the Nations of Europe had taken their own course and, having rejected religious unity as the basis of communion, had lapsed from point to point until their intransigence in warfare had become the measure of their incapacity for concord. The apostles of progress continued, indeed, to cry "Peace! Peace!" But none followed. For they did not understand the things that belonged to their peace any better than the Jews some nineteen centuries ago and more.

Minds more mystical even than Pascal's had penetrated to the core of the human situation in the Middle Age. Thomas à Kempis had observed how desperate was the injury man did to his nature by not becoming a follower of Jesus Christ. And St. Bonaventure had demonstrated how terrible was the human situation unless the true Light of the World stood in its place at the centre of thought and on the hill-top of the Eternal City. In his estimate of man's wretched case Pascal had in fact represented the end of a great tradition of political thought. "On its way from St. Augustine to Pascal", Gilson has remarked, "the Christian theme of man's misery without God runs through St. Bonaventure's philosophy."* And St. Bonaventure's philosophy was the intellectual expression of the Franciscan soul as exemplified in its founder. Once, but only once, in our time had that gracious tradition made itself felt in international affairs. It is on record that Pius XI, when he had to consider the size of the proposed Vatican City, asked himself what St. Francis would have deemed necessary for the purpose in view and, having thus ascertained what was the least possible, demanded no more. No lesser Government, no larger State, so far as I knew, had shown the smallest sign of imitating that singular example. Rather, they had asked for all they could hope to get and, when they had got it, like Oliver but without Oliver's excuse, had begun asking or grasping for more. Of such a world Pascal's theory remained the correct diagnosis.

Better things might, doubtless, have been expected of the heritage

* Gilson, "The Philosophy of St. Bonaventure", p. 385.

of the last century than this bitter antagonism of nationalities and nations. Nowhere for instance was there to be found a more charming picture of the world that our wars have swept away than in Stefan Zweig's description of old Vienna. A bourgeois and a Jew, he had no interest in adulating the Ancien Régime in its last refuge from the Revolution; yet no man had written more sympathetically, even though not uncritically, of the capital of the Habsburg Empire. A few phrases from his elaborate tribute are more eloquent than any paraphrase of mine. "The genius of Vienna—a specifically musical one," he had said, "was always that it harmonised all the national and lingual contrasts. Its culture was a synthesis of all western cultures. Whoever lived there and worked there felt himself free of all confinement and prejudice. Nowhere was it easier to be a European."* It was the downfall of this city at peace with itself, of this culture fitted to form a model to all Europe, of this metropolis integrating many peoples and races and tongues on the foundation of fine art, that the 'progressives' of our time, in virtue of their dogma of nationality, had desired to see: and they saw it and were—some of them within my knowledge—sad.

The domination of all Eastern Europe by Russia—the probable, outstanding result (together with the loss by Britain of the supremacy of the seas) of the present War—might not satisfy the little nationality-states of Eastern Europe any better than the substitution of King Stork for King Log satisfied the croaking frogs. Time would show; but the shadow on Time's sundial would not creep back. It had been left to General Smuts to suggest to the British Public that in Russia, with her vast resources of men and minerals and territory, the world must envisage a Power, powerful beyond any former conception in all the attributes of force; a Power which, if and when Germany and Japan were completely disarmed, would, within her huge sphere, be able to give her slightest wish the force of law.

"Unable to fortify justice," so Pascal's diagnosis had run on, "men had justified force, so that the just and the strong might hold together and that there might be peace, the sovereign good."† All this profound insight of Pascal's, like the profound irony of the Gospels, was thus turned towards a supreme end, a sovereign good. He saw that the justice that came out of force could never, with the minds of men perverted as they were, prove more than a name, to cover the

* Zweig, "The World of Yesterday", c. 1.   † "Pensées", 299.

working of human wills and human desires. Peace on the other hand offered men the occasion of recommending Christianity and with Christianity the justice of God. He who, like St. Louis, was willing to give his foe of his charity and out of his good-will more than in his eyes that foe had any right to claim, had evidently made such a move towards a change of heart in himself, and in his adversary, as no force and fighting would ever produce. Men, as the history of Christianity showed, are at long last impressed, not by the rude methods of warfare which they themselves practise, but by the generosities they have never conceived, the chivalries they have never practised, the nobilities they have never known. At long last! Patience, as Pitt had said, was the greatest gift of statesmanship. It was to be observed in its highest manifestation in the statesmanship of Christ.

It was not equally to be observed in all His professed followers. With them the plain obligation upon every man who takes benefit from the state to defend it in the faithful spirit of the pagan centurion, appeared to be frequently confused with the fond fancy that the conversion of the world to Christianity could be effected by forceful methods. Violence might thus advance without observation from strength to strength. Catholics of all men perhaps had the most obvious duty to see that this did not occur. For they had a kingdom organic, visible, and in all its implications suzerain. They alone amongst men could hope to derive such strength from union as to be able to insist that international disputes should be settled without the appalling sacrifice to Moloch of millions of young men, which is all that secular politicians and self-constituted peace-makers appear to have the sense or power to recommend. Though in England a negligible body, so far as politics were concerned, and more eager, perhaps, to show themselves patriots than prove themselves Christians, Catholics, in such countries as Germany and Italy, possessed the strength of numbers. One battalion of martyrs there would give any government furiously to think; whilst the passive resistance of thirty millions would force the most tyrannical to its knees. So long, however, as Catholic, or any other form of Christianity, was identified with good citizenship as defined by a servile state, so long, for lack of martyrs, would soldiers be made of men who might else have learnt to demonstrate the virtues of patience, forbearance and lovingkindness in their dealings with mankind. The 'corona martyrum' had yet to seem a nobler prize than the 'corona militum'.

Allegra was not attracted by politics nor, as she has told me, did she think that political women did the best by their sex. But I liked to remember that the first long conversation I had with her turned upon the then Lord Lansdowne's much-abused letter, advising negotiation in the last war. We know now, despite some high journalistic assurances to the contrary at the time, that Lansdowne had consulted the Foreign Office and that the Permanent Under-Secretary had told him the letter would do good. And I felt glad to recollect that Allegra's delicate judgment had been in line with that of two men whom I place high among those I have greatly admired in life—George Prothero and Arthur Elliot*—in thinking that her great-uncle's courageous action had been right. The crowd, however, carried the day and had in due course reason to lament the consequences. Wilhelm II was a bit of a bully, but Herr Hitler was a bully complete in all his parts. A bad neighbour is a bad neighbour; but he knows little of this world who fancies that, by driving a bad neighbour out, he can make sure of getting a better, and knows less still of another who supposes that a house swept and garnished is immune from being possessed anew, and by devils more malignant and numerous than before.

*   *   *   *   *   *

The fire was burning low upon the hearth; the firelight was flickering to an end; the shadows in the room were deepening. It was time for bed. Might one hope to go there not fretfully, with one's tale so nearly told? One had looked back; but, even if we could, which of us would go back into the years that are gone? There is no passage more striking in the delicate French idyll which once lay on so many tables in the London and Paris of its time—Mme. Craven's "Récit d'une Soeur"—than that where Alexandrine de la Ferronays reviews her lost happiness, under the influence of a superb sunset in July, only to tell her sister-in-law that all that pleases us on earth is shadow. ". . . La vérité de tout cela est au ciel. Et aimer, aimer, après tout, n'est-ce-pas sur terre, ce qu'il y a de plus doux? Je te demande s'il n'est pas facile de concevoir qu'aimer l'amour même doit être la perfection de cette douceur. ... . Je ne me serais jamais consolée, si je n'avais pas appris que cette amour-là existe pour Dieu, et celui-là dure toujours."†

I turned to look for a book to take up to bed. Allegra's "Shelley", as I saw the scene, was lying on the table and, when I took it up, the

---

* Editors, respectively, in their time, of the Quarterly and Edinburgh Reviews.
† "Recit d'une Sœur", II, pp. 392–3.

book opened at lines to which an old man seemed to have more right than their young author:

> O world! O life! O time!
> On whose last steps I climb,
>   Trembling at that where I had stood before;
> When will return the glory of your prime?
>   No more—Oh, never more!
>
> Out of the day and night
> A joy has taken flight;
>   Fresh spring, and summer, and winter hoar
> Move my faint heart with grief, but with delight
>   No more—Oh, never more!

The words made a lovely music; and their grace of retrospect, unlike Shelley's magic prospects, lacked nothing in truth. Yet it was not quite what I wanted to read myself into my last sleep with. I put it back, and glanced at the shelf where the few books of Allegra's that the fall of the House had left me stood ranged, and picked out that volume of Pater's "Marius" which I had read with her in Rome —the one with the chapter in it describing the Christmas Mass in the catacombs adjacent to the villa of the Caecilii, upon one of whose tomb-stones the Mass was actually celebrated. There were words in that description which gave me pause:—"In the old pagan worship", I read, "there had been little to call the understanding into play. Here, on the other hand, the utterance, the eloquence, the music of worship conveyed, as Marius readily understood, a fact or series of facts for intellectual reception." Yes! such reception had had very much its place in the criticism of life, very much its part in the appraisement of life's shadows and symbols. Yet still the book was not precisely what was wanted for this last good-night. I took out another from the case—a little book, delicately bound in fine red leather, à Kempis's "Imitation of Christ". Allegra, though it had been hers, had not, I think, especially cared for it. Suggesting as she did, both in her approach to life and to death, the mystic's so-called 'way of affirmation', she may instinctively have felt that à Kempis followed too exclusively for her taste the adjacent 'way of rejection'. Sibi unitus et simplificatus! The goal was indeed the same, whatever path one took, but it was by the transfiguration, not the renunciation of all things that Allegra had rendered her road so transparent. Diaphanous herself, she had, as I saw, deserved to be matched by something which I can only call opalescence, in another; and, had that happened, the foregoing studies of manhood under bodily, mental, or spiritual preoccupation might, as I thought, have merged in one of some more integrated personality radiating different hues beneath transforming light. But Emily Brontë has expressed the image of such fulness of being among the lines which bear the name of "The Philosopher's Conclusion"; and, before such poetry as hers, prose must flee away:—

> I saw a Spirit standing, Man,
> Where thou dost stand—an hour ago;
> And round his feet three rivers ran
> Of equal depth and equal flow—
>
> A golden stream, and one like blood,
> And one like sapphire, seemed to be,
> But where they joined their triple flood
> It tumbled in an inky sea.
>
> The Spirit bent his dazzling gaze
> Down on that Ocean's gloomy night,
> Then—kindling all with sudden blaze,
> The glad deep sparkled wide and bright—
> White as the sun; far, far more fair
> Than the divided sources were!

Sibi unitus et simplificatus! The perfect integration of man's being! Body, mind, and spirit brought to a unity by the vision of diaphanous grace and flooding the inky sea of our mortal confusion with immortal beauty—that was a mysticism within the reach of many to whom self or circumstance denied a sterner application of the old monk's ideal. My hand turned over a few more pages of the little red book; and then the tranquil voice seemed to begin again, but afterwards fell silent as if there were nothing further to be uttered. "If", it said, "thou dost lean more on thine own reason or industry than on the power of Jesus Christ, which brings thee into subjection, seldom and slowly wilt thou become enlightened: for God wills us to be perfectly subject unto Himself and to be lifted above all reason by the fire of love."*

Then at length, the book still in my hand, I turned to go to bed, and, as I climbed the stair, from landing to landing of that bleak house, I knew, so to say, in all the marrow of my bones, by all the faculties of my mind, with all the energy of my spirit, that I should hear no other word of life, no later summing-up of the human situation more

* "Imit. Chr.", I, 14.

searching than that which had just met my eye. It was, if you will, no more than a platitude, but a platitude despised and rejected by the most part of men, whatever they might pretend to themselves or others. Yet, for all that, since from its earliest enunciation it had stood the racket of close upon two thousand years and satisfied so many fine and finished minds, a platitude well proved! One might feel in fact as confident that mankind would meet with no criticism of life so coherent and convincing as that they would continue to hold it cheap or pass it by. And one might suspect that it was the consummating tragedy of a world, so subtly incongruous in thought as to be supremely comic in effect, that men would not play their part in the divine comedy of the universe.

*　　*　　*　　*　　*　　*

I started to write this book in the confident expectation that the House which gave it its name and fashion would survive for at least a generation to serve as Allegra's memorial. I thought that perhaps the charm of the structure in conjunction with the grace she gave to its adornment might serve to make good the deficiencies of its last chronicle and chronicler. Dis aliter visum! To the gods, if not to God, it has seemed best otherwise. I can only trust, then, that this attempt to appreciate, to amplify, to illustrate Allegra's approach to life, and show her being and becoming in association with another soul which she moved, as we are told that love moves all things high and lowly, may not altogether fail of its purpose for lack of the express image of its original idea.